Beethoven

Piano Sonatas
Op. 2 – Op. 28

Their Creation, Origins and Reception History
Incorporating
Contextual Accounts of Beethoven and His Contemporaries

BEETHOVEN

As depicted by the life mask taken by Franz Klein in 1812

(derived from a copy in the author's possession)

BEETHOVEN

PIANO SONATAS
OP. 2–OP. 28

THEIR
CREATION ORIGINS
AND
RECEPTION HISTORY

Incorporating contextual accounts of
Beethoven and his contemporaries

Terence M. Russell

Jelly Bean Books

Published by
Jelly Bean Books
136 Newport Road
Cardiff
CF24 1DJ

ISBN: 978-1-915439-09-3

www.candyjarbooks.co.uk

CONTENTS

AUTHOR'S
NOTE

I have cherished the idea of making a study of the life and work of Beethoven for many years. This statement requires a few words of personal reflection. I first encountered Beethoven in my early piano lessons — Minuet in G major, WoO 10, No. 2. At the same time I became acquainted with his piano pupil Carl Czerny — *Book One, Piano Studies.* My heart sank when I discovered the rear cover advertised a further *99* books in the same series — scales, arpeggios studies for the left hand, studies for the right hand — all the way to his Op. 824! By coincidence, my *Czerny Book One* was edited by Alec Rowley — who had the same surname as my music teacher. In my childish innocence, I often wondered why *he himself* never appeared to give me a lesson!

In my teenage years I found myself drawn ever closer to Beethoven's music in the manner that ferromagnetic materials are ineluctably held captive in the sway of a magnetic field. The impulse to which I yielded is well described in words the conductor Bruno Walter gave in one of his rare public addresses: 'It is my belief that young people at that age are more easily impressed by what is heroic and grandiose; that they more easily understand works of art in which passionate feelings are violently uttered in raised accents, and that the lighter sounds of cheerfulness are less impressive to them.' I do indeed recall the stirring effect made on me on first hearing the Overture *Egmont*, the unfolding drama of the Fifth Symphony and the declamatory opening chords of the *Emperor* Piano Concerto.

I resolved to read everything I could about Beethoven, starting with Marion Scott's pioneering English-language study of the composer in the *Master Musicians series*. My father took out a subscription for me for *The Gramophone* magazine, enabling me to read reviews of the new 'LP' recordings – none of which though I could afford! The LP was then – 1950s – beginning to supplant the 78 rpm shellac records, stacks of which could be purchased for as little as six pence each in 'old' money. At this same time I had the privilege of hearing Beethoven's music performed by the *Hallé Orchestra* under the baton of Sir John Barbirolli, and experienced the *Carl Rosa Opera Company* perform the composer's only opera *Fidelio*; I borrowed the piano-reduction score from the City Library to become better acquainted with this moving work – only to find the score's fists full of notes were well beyond my capabilities. Nonetheless, since then *Fidelio's* every note has been woven into my DNA. I also recall the period when the *London Promenade Concerts* were designated 'Friday night is Beethoven night'.

Through these influences I resolved to visit Vienna to see where Beethoven had lived and worked. But how? The support for such travel was beyond the means of my family. Fortunately in my final year at school (1959) an opportunity presented itself. I saw a poster that stated *WUS — World University Service* — required volunteers to work in the Austrian town of Linz to help relocate refugees who were living there in improvised wooden shacks — displaced and dispossessed victims of the Second World War. To those participating all expenses would be paid together with free accommodation — in one of the crumbling wooden shacks! From Linz, I planned to make my way to Vienna.

I applied to *WUS* and, despite being a mere school-leaver, I was accepted. The *WUS* authorities doubtless reasoned the building-trade skills I had acquired during my secondary education in the building department of a technical school would be useful. This proved to be the case. At the refugee camp I dug trenches and was allowed to assist as a bricklayer. All about me were wide-eyed children eager to help but mostly getting in the way. I recall one afternoon when a reporter from *The Observer* newspaper paid a visit to our construction site to gather material for an article he was writing on European post-war recovery — he generously admired my trenches and brickwork!

Of lasting significance was another visit, this time from a Belgian priest. He took a group of us to the nearby *Mauthausen* Concentration Camp, recently opened as a silent and solemn memorial to those who had perished there. It was a deeply moving experience. Years later I learned of the views of the ardent Beethovenian Sir Michael Tippet. After the horrors of the *Holocaust*, he posed the question for mankind: 'What price Beethoven now?' He posited: 'Could we any longer find solace in Beethoven's setting of Schiller's *Ode to Joy* and its utopian vision — "Be embraced you Millions"?'

My refugee contribution duly came to end and Vienna beckoned. On arrival there I found scenes reminiscent of *The Third Man* and *Harry Lime*. I recall, for example, encountering cobblestones piled high in the streets waiting to be replaced after having been disturbed by the heavy armoured vehicles that had so recently passed over them. But Vienna was welcoming. I visited the houses where Beethoven had lived and worked and paused outside others associated with him that were identified by a commemorative plaque and the Austrian flag. A particularly memorable occasion was attending a recital in the great salon within the palace of Beethoven's noble patron Prince Lobkowitz – the very one where the *Eroica* Symphony had been premiered. Ultimately, my steps led me to the composer's first resting place in the *Währinger Ortsfriedhof.* I paid silent homage to the great man and, as I did so, discovered nearby the resting place of Franz Schubert to whom Beethoven was an endless source of admiration and inspiration.

I felt a youthful impulse to discover yet more about Beethoven and his music. But absorption in musicology would have to take second place. My chosen career beckoned in the guise of architecture – 'the mother of the arts' and 'the handmaid of society'. There was room though for Beethoven's music and from that time on it has been my constant companion through attendance at recitals, in concerts and music-making in the home. And at home a reproduction of Franz Kline's 1812 study of the composer has greeted me each day for more than half a century.

On my retirement from a career in architectural practice, research and university teaching, the opportunity finally presented itself for me to devote time to researching Beethoven musicology. Having attained my eightieth year also emboldened me to make progress with my good intentions!

With these autobiographical remarks outlined I will say a few remarks about my working method – see also the comments made in *Editorial Principles.*

As a member of staff of The University of Edinburgh, I had the good fortune to have access to the *Reid Music Library*, formed from a nucleus of books bequeathed by General John Reid and augmented over the years by such custodians as Sir Donald Francis Tovey, sometime *Reid Professor of Music* and renowned Beethoven scholar. Over a period of three years, I made a survey of the many works in the Reid collection. I consulted each item in turn making records on paper slips — many hundreds — that I deemed to be relevant for my researches. I confined my searches to book-publications, as reflected in my accompanying bibliography. All of this was quite some years ago, the cut-off date for my researches being 2007. Beyond this date I have not surveyed any further works. I am mindful though that Beethoven musicology and related publication continue to be a major field of endeavour in the manner of the proverbial 'ever rolling stream'.

In the intervening years since completing my archival researches, personal tribulations associated with family illness and bereavement slowed my progress in giving expression to my projected intentions. Latterly, however, with renewed energy, and more time at my disposal, I have been able to make progress. My studies take the form of a set of monographs. These trace the creation origins and reception history of each of Beethoven's piano sonatas and string quartets. The resulting texts also incorporate contextual accounts of Beethoven and his contemporaries. Also included in my musicological surveys are two related Beethoven anthologies. The set of monographs in question, identified by short title, are:

Beethoven: An anthology of selected writings.
Beethoven: The piano sonatas: An anthology of selected writings.

V

The Piano Sonatas:
Op. 2—Op. 28
Op. 31—Op. 81A
Op. 90—Op. 111

The String Quartets:
Op. 18, Nos. 1—6
Op. 59, Nos. 1—3 (Razumovsky); Op. 74 (The Harp);
  Op. 95 (Quartetto Serioso)
Op. 127, Op. 132 and Op. 130 (Galitzin)
Op. 131, Op. 135; Grosse Fuge, Op. 133 and Op. 134
  (Fugue transcription)

I provide further information about these studies in the introduction to each individual monograph. Suffice it for me to state here the basic premise upon which my work is founded. I believe it is rewarding, concerning the life of a great artist, to find connections between who he *was* and what he *did*, in Martin Cooper's words 'between his personality, as expressed on the one hand in human relationships, and on the other in artistic creation'. (*Beethoven, The Last Decade*) That is not to say I consider it essential to the enjoyment of Beethoven's music to know this or that fact about it. His music can be enjoyed, as millions do, with — in Robert Simpson's apt phrase —'an innocent ear', for what it is and how it reaches out to us in purely musical terms without any prejudging of its merits based upon extra-musicological facts.

I must make a further point. I am mindful that a scholar who ventures into a field of study that is not rightly his may be regarded with some suspicion. In this regard I can but ask the reader to place his or her trust in me in the following way. I have attempted to bring to my work the care which publishers and their desk editors have required of me in my book writings relating to architecture — listed elsewhere.

As inferred, it is now more than sixty years since I paid homage to Beethoven in Vienna's *Währinger Ortsfriedhof* and my warmth of feeling towards the composer and his music have grown with the passing of the years. My studies are not intended to be propaedeutic — that would be pretentious. However, if in sharing with others what I have to say contributes to their knowledge and understanding of the composer, and thereby increases their own feelings towards him and his works, my own pleasure in bringing my work to completion will be all the more enhanced.

It is perhaps fitting that my studies should appear in Beethoven's 250th Anniversary Year — I must confess more by chance than design!

When Beethoven arrived in Vienna, he was unknown. He was armed though with a note of encouragement from his youthful friend and benefactor Count Ferdinand Waldstein. It contained the often-quoted words: 'Receive Mozart's spirit from Haydn's hands.' Some forty years later Beethoven passed away in the House of the black-robed Spaniards at 200 *Alservorstädter*, the *Glacis* where he had lived since the autumn of 1825. Soldiers had to be called to secure the doors to the inner courtyard of the house from the pressure of onlookers. His body was blessed in the *Alservorsttädt Parish Church*, schools were closed and perhaps as many as 10,000 people formed a funeral procession — an honour ordinarily reserved for monarchs. The *Marcia Funebre* from the composer's Op. 26 Piano Sonata was performed at the funeral ceremony. Franz Grillparzer read the funeral oration. Franz Schubert, who, as remarked in life so admired Beethoven, was one of the pallbearers. The composer's mortal remains were lowered into a simple vault. Beethoven now belonged to history.

Dr Terence M. Russell
Edinburgh 2020

INTRODUCTION

The subjects of this study are the creation origins and reception history of Beethoven's piano sonatas. It is one of three that broadly correspond with the generally accepted periods into which the compositions of the composer's maturity are held to conform and which have been described as 'imitative', 'heroic' and 'introspective'. In our first study, the piano sonatas Opp. 2 – 28 are considered; in the second, the piano sonatas Opp. 31 – 81a; and in the third, the piano sonatas Opp. 90 – 111. Conformably with these studies are two companion works *Beethoven: An Anthology of Selected Writings* and *Beethoven:* and *The Piano Sonatas: An Anthology of Selected Writings.* The former of these provides the reader with texts and quotations that position Beethoven as a figure in the history of culture and humankind. The latter is a more focused study that brings together over-arching views concerning the piano sonatas as expressed by composers, musicologists and performing artists. The reader, with a particular interest in Beethoven's keyboard music, will find the survey-writings contained in the *Sonatas Anthology* will also serve as an introduction to our three sets of piano-sonata studies.

Beethoven was one of the foremost virtuoso pianists of his day. His piano pupil Ferdinand Ries considered his powers of invention, when improvising at the keyboard, 'to be matchless with regard to the wealth of ideas which poured forth, the moods to which he surrendered and the challenges he imposed upon himself'. It is not surprising, therefore, that throughout his life Beethoven turned to the piano sonata as a vehicle for exhibiting pianistic display and the expression of intense musical feeling. Only in his closing years did he leave off from writing piano sonatas in favour of the medium of the string quartet.

The collection of writings presented here, derive from the piano-sonata compositions of Beethoven's so-called first period. They take the form of extended essays that may serve the reader as a source of reference — in the manner of programme notes to a recital. Accordingly, the remarks relating to each piano sonata are 'free standing' and can be read independently. That said they are also interlinked by the events unfolding in the composer's life. An attempt has been made, therefore, to interrelate the individual piano-sonata essays so that they may be read as a continuous narrative — in typical book fashion. A summary outline of this narrative is provided in the Index for each individual piano sonata. Thereby, the reader is provided not only with a guide to the contents discussed in each sonata-text but also has an over-arching time-line of the principal events bearing on Beethoven's life and work.

By way of an introduction to the individual essays, the following is a summary-outline of the compositions included in this part of our survey.

Beethoven, the emerging piano-writing virtuoso, made his debut in the genre of the piano sonata with the three compositions that constitute his Op. 2. We set aside here discussion of the three youthful works from his days in Bonn – the so-called *Kurfürstensonaten* (WoO 47) – composed in 1782 and 1783. Beethoven's Opus 2 Sonatas owe a debt to the models of Haydn and Mozart, and the developing piano schools of the Italian Muzio Clementi and the Bohemian Jan Dussek; he absorbed their angular style, energy and pianistic structures and made them his own. The three Sonatas Opus 2 made their appearance in 1795, and in Marion Scott's words are: 'The earliest peaks in that magnificent series of thirty-two sonatas which run parallel to Beethoven's symphonies like a mountain chain in music and is not less glorious, though on a different scale.'

With the publication of the Piano Sonata Op. 7, Beethoven expanded the form to yet new and greater dimensions. It is longer than the *Appassionata* Sonata and would not be exceeded in scale until the creation of the *Hammerklavier* Sonata more than twenty years later. Op.7 has been described as being no less than 'Beethoven's first masterpiece'. It exemplifies the composer's quest to extend the formal boundaries of compositions in this medium. Writing in the June 1806 issue of the *Zeitung für die elegante Welt*, the reviewer remarked: 'This sonata is considered to be amongst the most splendid by this original composer. It forms a great and noble totality. A heroic fire constitutes the dominant feature of its character and is also demanded of the performer.'

The Op. 10 Piano Sonatas constitute a trilogy. Throughout his life Beethoven chose to work intermittently on two or three related compositions. He appears to have enjoyed, thereby, exploring different contrasts in mood and style between works that were gestating together in his imagination. Consider, for example, the singular characteristics that distinguish the Fifth and Sixth Symphonies which, nevertheless, share a common creative time-period. In William Kinderman's estimation: 'The Sonatas [Opus 10, Nos. 1–3] are admirably contrasted in character, particularly in their first movements: the terse, dramatic idiom of the C minor Sonata sets into relief the relaxed, mischievous spirit of the F minor, whereas the dynamic brilliance of the third Sonata, D major, expands the formal design from within.' A review of the Op. 10 Piano Sonatas appeared in the *Allgemeine musikalische Zeitung* of 9 October 1799. This was based on the first edition of the works that had been published in September 1798. The reviewer recognised Beethoven for being 'a man of genius', with 'originality', 'possessing an abundance of ideas' and who 'goes entirely his own way'.

The formal title of Beethoven's Piano Sonata in C minor, Op. 13 is *Grand Sonata Pathétique.* It is one of the few compositions to bear an authentic title sanctioned by the composer. The title admirably embodies the spirit of the piece of which Donald Tovey remarks 'nothing so powerful and so full of tragic passion had hitherto been dreamt of in pianoforte music'. The sonata has subsequently found a permanent place in the pianist's repertoire and indeed in popular culture. Ferdinand Ries relates how Beethoven played the *rondo* 'with a very special expressiveness'.

Beethoven followed the Sonata *Pathétique* with two further sonatas that comprise his Op. 14. In scale and style these works are mutually compatible and are occasionally performed in recital as a pair. Both sonatas are less dramatic than their famous predecessor. Their character is more genial and less spectacular; perhaps for this reason they have sometimes been overlooked or have been unjustly dismissed as lesser works. The modest scale and restrained tonal sonorities of the Op. 14 Piano Sonatas see Beethoven returning to the lighter concept of the genre that he had already explored in the Piano Sonatas Nos. 1 and 2. As such, they are well suited to the more intimate style of performance typical of a domestic-scale, chamber-music environment.

Beethoven's Piano Sonata in B-flat major, Op.22 is the composer's eleventh piano sonata in the series bearing an opus number and made its appearance more-or-less contemporaneously with several other of his major compositions. These include: Pianoforte Concerto in C (Op. 15); Quintet for Piano and Wind (Op. 16); Sonata for Pianoforte and Horn (Op. 17); Six String Quartets (Op. 18); Pianoforte Concerto in B flat (Op. 19); Septet (Op. 20); and the Symphony No. 1 (Op. 21). This body of work is testimony to Beethoven's creative development and growing experience in composition. Op. 22 is a large-scale work with a performing time of about 25 minutes; perhaps for this reason Beethoven gave it the sub-title *Grande Sonate*. He was particularly pleased with this creation and regarded it as being 'really something' — or words to that effect.

In the context of Beethoven's creative development, the Piano Sonata in A-flat major, Op. 26 may be considered alongside his two contemporary piano sonatas that form the composer's Op. 27. All three works derive from around the year 1800. With the Piano Sonata Op. 26, Beethoven returned to a four-movement structure. In the two Piano Sonatas, Op. 27, Eric Blom considers these 'show the composer emancipating himself from the classical sonata pattern and doing it as drastically as possible'. This is most evident in the first movements in which Beethoven substitutes music that is cast in a more free form than was typical of the period. Perhaps with this in mind, he gave both works the sub-title *Sonata quasi una fantasia*. In selecting this expression it is as though Beethoven were preparing the listener for his unorthodox procedures — rather as Franz Schubert was to do twenty years later in designating the expression *Wanderer Fantasie* for what would be his most virtuosic and technically challenging piece for the keyboard.

The opening bars of Beethoven's Piano Sonata Op 27, No.2 *The Moonlight* have been compared, in their familiarity, with the opening words Shakespeare gives to Hamlet in his celebrated Soliloquy. Just as Shakespeare's words *To be or not to be* are memorable and instantly recognisable, so too are the opening bars of Beethoven's *Moonlight* Piano Sonata, even to those who know little about classical music and nothing at all about Beethoven — such has become the world-wide popularity of the opening of this particular sonata. In 1802, a review of Beethoven's Op. 26 was published in Issue No. 4 of the *Allgemeine musikalische Zeitung* together with the two Piano Sonatas Op. 27. Although the three works were published separately the reviewer comments upon them collectively: 'These are the three piano compositions with which Herr v[an]. B[eethoven] recently enriched a selected few cultivated musicians and accomplished pianists. I say enriched, because they are truly an enrichment and belong among those few works of art of the present day that will scarcely ever grow old; certainly number three [the *Moonlight*] can never grow old.'

Beethoven's Piano Sonata Op. 28, *The Pastoral*, has been described as 'the cheerful, happy, much less known neighbour of the C-sharp minor Sonata'. Although composed in 1801, in close proximity to the C-sharp minor Sonata, it nevertheless differs fundamentally from that work. This illustrates Beethoven's capacity, and preference, to work simultaneously on compositions of a strikingly different character. In the words of William Newman: '[It] is typical of Beethoven's tendency to alternate a passionate and driving work with a calm and restful one.' In the Op. 28, Barry Cooper finds Beethoven benefiting from turning to a work of a more 'relaxed' and 'less experimental' kind. He notes Beethoven's 'complete contrast of style' in the Op. 28 with its 'lengthy, relaxed, totally unheroic, and pastoral ... mood'. In the Piano Sonata Op. 28, Maynard Solomon sees Beethoven withdrawing 'to a relative traditionalism' from which he 'will gain strength for a new creative urge'. We trace the next stage of the composer's development in the second series of our piano sonata studies.

TMR

EDITORIAL
PRINCIPLES

By its very nature a study of this kind draws extensively on the work of others. Every effort has been made to acknowledge this in the text by indicating words quoted or adapted with single quotation marks. Wherever possible, for the sake of consistency, I have retained the orthography of quoted texts making only occasional silent changes of spelling and capitalization. Deleted words are identified by means of three ellipsis points ... and interpolations are encompassed within square brackets [ ]. Quoted words, phrases and longer cited passages of text remain the intellectual property of their copyright holders.

I address the reader in the second person notwithstanding that the work is my own. It follows that I must bear the responsibility for any errors of misunderstanding or misinterpretation for which I ask the reader's forbearance. A collaboration I must acknowledge is the help I received from the librarians of the Reid Music Library at the University of Edinburgh. Over the three-year period it took me to compile my reference sources, they served me with unfailing courtesy, often supplying me with twenty or more books at a time. In converting my manuscript into book format, I wish to thank my editorial coordinator, William Rees, for his support and painstaking care. I would also like to thank Shaun Russell for his work designing the cover for each of the nine volumes.

My admiration for Beethoven provided the initial impulse to commence this undertaking and has sustained me over the several years it has taken to bring my enterprise to completion. That said, I am no Beethoven idolater. I am mindful of the danger that awaits one who ventures to chronicle the work of a great artist. I believe it was Sigmund Freud who suggested that biographers may become so disposed to their subject, and their emotional involvement with their hero, that their work becomes an exercise in idealisation. In response to such a charge let me say. First, I am no biographer. I do however make occasional reference to Beethoven's personal life and his relationships with his contemporaries. Second, I acknowledge Beethoven has his detractors. Accordingly, I have not shrunk from allowing dissentient voices, critical of Beethoven and his work, to be heard. These, however, are few and are silenced amidst the adulation that awaits the reader in support of the endeavours of one of humanity's great creators and one who courageously showed the way in overcoming personal adversity.

TMR

BEETHOVEN'S
FINANCIAL
TRANSACTIONS

B eethoven's negotiations with his music publishers make many references to his compositions. Today they are recognised for what they are — enduring works of art — but referred to in his business correspondence they appear almost as though they were mere everyday commodities — for which he required an appropriate remuneration. Beethoven resented the time he had to devote to the business-side of his affairs. He believed an agency should exist, for fellow artists such as himself, from which a reasonable sum could be paid for the work (composition) submitted, leaving more time for creative enterprises. In the event Beethoven, like Mozart before him, had to deal with publishers largely on his own. Beethoven, though, did benefit in his business dealings from the help he received from his younger brother Kasper Karl (Caspar Carl). From

1800, Carl worked as a clerk in Vienna's Department of Finance in which capacity he found time to correspond with publishers to offer his brother's works for sale and — importantly — to secure the best prices he could. In April 1802 Beethoven wrote to the Leipzig publishers Breitkopf & Härtel: '[You] can rely entirely on my brother who, in general, attends to my affairs.' Whilst Carl promoted Beethoven's interests with determination, he appears to have lacked tact and made enemies. For example, Beethoven's piano pupil Ferdinand Ries — who for a while also helped the composer with his business negotiations — is on record as describing Carl as being 'the biggest skinflint in the world'. The currencies most referred to in Beethoven's correspondence are as follows:

silver gulden and florin: these were interchangeable and had a value of about two English/British shillings

ducat: 4 1/2 gulden/florins: valued at about nine shillings

louis d'or: This gold coin was adopted during the Napoleonic wars and the French occupation of Vienna and Austria more widely. It had a value of about two ducats or approximately twenty shillings or one-pound sterling.

Beethoven was never poor — in the romantic sense of 'an artist starving in a garret'. On arriving in Vienna in 1792, he was fortunate to receive financial support from his patron Prince Karl Lichnowsky who conferred on him an annuity of 600 florins that he maintained for several years. Between the months of February and July of 1796, Beethoven undertook a concert tour taking in Prague, Dresden, Leipzig and Berlin. He was well received and wrote to his other younger brother Nikolaus Johann: 'My art is winning me friends and what more do I want? ... I shall make a good deal of money.' Later on, in 1809, Napoleon Bonaparte's youngest brother Jérôme Bonaparte offered Beethoven an appointment at his Court with the promise of an income of 4,000 florins. Alarmed at the prospect of losing Beethoven — now the most celebrated composer in Europe — three of Vienna's most notable citizens, namely, the Archduke Rudolph (Beethoven's only composition pupil), Prince Kinsky and Prince Lobkowitz settled on the composer the same sum of 4,000 florins. Inflation, however, brought about by the Napoleonic wars, soon eroded its value; personal misfortune to Lobkowitz and Kinsky also took its toll.

Beethoven undoubtedly had to work hard to secure a reasonable standard of living. Notwithstanding, despite his occasional straitened circumstances, he contributed gener-ously to the needs of others. For example, he allowed his works to be performed free of charge at charitable concerts; in 1815 his philanthropy earned for him the honour of Bürgerrecht — 'freedom of the City'.

Beethoven earned a great deal of money when his music was performed, to considerable acclaim, at several concerts held in association with the Congress of Vienna (1814-15). He did not though benefit from it personally; he invested it on behalf of his nephew Karl. It is one of the misfortunes of Beethoven's life that in money-matters he was culpably improvident. This is poignantly evident in a letter he wrote on 18 March 1827 to the Philharmonic Society of London just one week before his death; the Society had made him a gift of £100. He sent the Society 'his most heartfelt thanks for their particular sympathy and support'.

TMR

Each creative work becomes a part of the universe, just like a flower, or human being. Consequently, a sonata sounds different to each gifted interpreter. This is the real mission of our particular talents.

Arthur Rubinstein, *My young years*, 1983

PIANO SONATAS
OP. 2, NOS. 1-3

'[All] are agreed that [the Opus 2 Sonatas] are the
first of Beethoven's solo compositions which have
intrinsic value. Earlier work is of interest in
displaying his course of development, but these
[works] show something of his essence. Immatu-
rity is past, and the whole force of his personality
is now at work. The artist is now in command of
his own tremendous flow of ideas and is able to
give them form and shape ... The threefold Op.
2, however, was but the first step in Beethoven's
steady progress towards a sonata form of monumental greatness ... Colour and physiognomy are
indicated by key: mournful passion in the F
minor, sunny gaiety in the A major, and joyful
brilliance in the C major Sonata.'

Paul Bekker, *Beethoven*, 1925, pp. 97–8.

'The three Sonatas [Opus 2] made their appearance in 1795, the earliest peaks in that magnificent series of thirty-two sonatas which runs parallel to Beethoven's symphonies like a mountain chain in music and is not less glorious, though on a different scale.'

Marion M. Scott, *Beethoven*, 1940, p. 132.

'Beethoven began his piano [sonata] publications with the three Sonatas Op. 2 dedicated to Haydn; works full of inexhaustible inspirations, of ravishing freshness of youth.'

Oskar Bie, A history of the pianoforte and pianoforte players, 1966, p. 169.

'Despite the vastness of the journey Beethoven was to undertake in the next thirty years these early sonatas [Opus 2] are, in their own way, masterpieces.'

Denis Matthews, *Keyboard Music*, 1972, p. 171.

'Haydn used to term Beethoven ... "Grand Mogul" and would ask: "What's our Grand Mogul up to?" Haydn may have been amused by his erstwhile pupil's delusions of grandeur but he was certainly very much aware of his artistic stature as revealed even in these early products of his muse.'

H. C. Robbins Landon, *Haydn: The Years of the Creation:*

1796–1800, 1977, p. 69.

'As the first of the thirty-two sonatas with opus
numbers, the three Sonatas Op. 2 – respectively,
impassioned, gay, and brilliant – make a remarkably fine start.'

William S. Newman, *The Sonata in the Classic Era*, 1983,
p. 511

'The F minor Sonata ... shows a terse dramatic
concentration, whereas the second Sonata ... is
more expansive and radiant in character, and the
C major Sonata is brilliant and virtuosic with
cadenzas in the outer movement.'

William Kinderman, The Piano Sonatas in: The Cambridge
Companion to Beethoven, Glenn Stanley, editor, 2000, p.
112.

'The first three pianoforte sonatas, Op. 2, show
the different elements in Beethoven's early styles
as clearly as possible.'

Donald F. Tovey, *Ludwig van Beethoven* in: *The Classics
of Music*, Michael Tilmouth, editor, 2001,
    p. 334.

The Piano Sonatas Op. 2, Nos. 1–3 derive from the
period 1793–4 when Beethoven was receiving formal
instruction in counterpoint from Johann Albrechtsberger.
His principal teacher, Joseph Haydn, was then planning his

second London Tour. Haydn had been introduced to the little known but brilliantly gifted young composer Ludwig van Beethoven in Bonn – when coming home from his first London tour. He had planned to take Beethoven with him to London on his return there for the summer season, but the political situation in Europe conspired against this. Instead, Haydn agreed to give Beethoven lessons in Vienna. It later transpired the arrangement suited neither of them; Beethoven became dissatisfied with Haydn's instruction and his own unorthodox ways were uncongenial to the more prosaic Haydn.[i]

Beethoven worked intensively on the sonatas in 1794, developing a fuller command of his contrapuntal technique as he did so.[ii] The sonatas were completed in Vienna in the summer of 1795. Although composed at the time when, as remarked, he was receiving musical instruction, Beethoven's Op. 2 Sonatas are not apprentice pieces, evolved in response to formal musical pedagogy, but are singularly imaginative creations that speak with a new and original voice.[iii] They reveal 'a pronounced personal style in melody and phrase structure'[iv] and illustrate Beethoven's growing compositional ability, developing psychological self-confidence and his 'all-embracing qualities'.[v] In these sonatas Beethoven also demonstrates his ability to 'imbue an apparently simple, even trivial, figure with intense significance'. Also apparent is his craft in 'developing such figures into long paragraphs' combined with his unfailing sense of 'key relations' so that 'seemingly disparate ideas unfold and link up with logic and dramatic purpose'.[vi] Moreover, his extensive use of the minor-mode and bold modulations are 'individual traits ... that set his work apart from that of his precursors'.[vii] They establish no less than 'a new world of feeling';[viii] they are 'works full of inexhaustible inspirations, of ravishing fresh-ness of youth'.[ix] In the Op. 2, Nos. 1–3 Piano Sonatas, we

4

find early evidence of what Romain Rolland has described as 'characteristics of the two great currents of Beethoven's genius; the direct expression of the personal soul and the constructive intelligence'.[i]

Whilst Beethoven's Opus 2 Sonatas owe a debt to the models of Haydn and Mozart, the developing piano schools of the Italian Muzio Clementi and the Bohemian Jan Dussek also influenced them considerably.[ii] By way of further illustration, we learn from Beethoven's close associate and biographer Anton Schindler, that the composer's relatively modest musical library contained almost all of Clementi's sonatas for which: 'He had the greatest admiration ... considering them the most beautiful, the most pianistic of works.'[iii] The youthful Beethoven, and emerging piano-writing virtuoso, absorbed their angular style, energy and pianistic structures – and made them his own.[iii] In this context, musicologist Alexander Ringer comments: 'Comparative studies [of the manner in which Beethoven assimilated ideas drawn from the work of other musicians] in no way endanger Beethoven's historical or artistic stature: they add to a growing body of evidence that his justly celebrated originality derived not so much from any particular novelty of invention as from a matchless power of integration and sublimation of the widest variety of musical practices.'[xiv]

Beethoven's style and exploration of remote key-relationships, even in these sonatas, is distinctive: '[His] textures are richer and more complex; modulations are more frequent and daring; motivic development is more intensive; contrasts are sharper and more dramatic; and emotions, whether of exuberance, tenderness or anguish, are much more strongly characterized.'[xv] It was these qualities in Beethoven's music that prompted Clementi, a few years later in the role of music publisher, to seek Beethoven out in Vienna. He records: 'By a little management ... I have at last made a complete conquest of that haughty beauty, Beethoven.' The result of this 'conquest' was Clementi's agreement to publish three quartets, a symphony, an overture and, in Clementi's words, 'a concerto for violin which is very beautiful'.[xvi] He remained a faithful admirer of Beethoven and continued to purchase all the English editions of his compositions including the last majestic Piano Sonata Op. 111.[xvii]

Between 1793–5, Beethoven had composed the Piano Trios Op. 1 dedicated to Prince Karl Lichnowsky (see later). Themes from a discarded Trio in E flat of this period were regarded sufficiently highly by Beethoven as to be used subsequently by him in the Piano Sonata in F minor, Op. 2.[xviii] Earlier still, he had composed three quartets for piano and strings (WoO 36) that are modelled on sonatas by Mozart. Perhaps for this reason he held them back from publication but later drew on melodic ideas from them for the Piano Sonatas Op. 2, Nos. 2 and 3. Ideas from these discarded works were also later used in the Sonata *Pathétique*.[xix] Before Beethoven, the piano sonata had consisted typically of three movements characterised as 'fast — slow — fast'. The prevailing Italian model offered the alternative two-movement structure with typical tempi of 'fast' followed by 'faster'. In his early piano sonatas, Beethoven alternated between a three-movement structure and an expanded four-movement form.[xx] Each of the Piano Sonatas Op. 2 expands the conventional three-movement design to four movements 'with a Minuet and Trio in penultimate position'.[xxi]

Our reference above to Beethoven making use of discarded themes, provides us with a suitable prompt to comment briefly here on aspects of the composer's working methods. From his earliest days he was given to jotting down ideas for potential compositions on any available piece of manuscript paper — what he self-disparagingly referred to as his 'bad habit'.

About two hundred loose sheets of sketches date back to Beethoven's days in Bonn, from about 1790 or even earlier. These have subsequently been assembled into two large gatherings, the larger of which is now preserved in the British Library and is known as the 'Kafka Sketchbook' (more correctly 'miscellany') — taking its name from its one-time owner Johann Nepomuk Kafaka. Beethoven later systematised his sketching procedure by binding together bundles of pocket-sized sheets that he could take with him on his much-loved strolls in the country; later still he made use of ready-bound sketchbooks.[xii] These provided him with the means of not only sketching more systematically but also more extensively, particularly as his compositions grew in scale and complexity posing related challenges in solving large-scale problems of musical continuity and construction. Today the sketchbooks that have survived have, like the Kafka Sketchbook, acquired the names of their various owners — to which we make occasional reference in our subsequent commentaries.[xiii] Suffice it here to state the following general remarks.

Beethoven would set down ideas for a new piece, starting on a fresh page, frequently noting ideas for different movements alongside each other. As his powers of invention took hold, he would insert further thoughts cramming them into any available space or even going back to make use of pages previously left blank. As a consequence, sketches for different compositions co-exist side-by-side, many to be discarded but others to be fully worked into the compositions we know and cherish today. In his lecture 'Questions about music' Roger Sessions, in his role as Charles Eliot Norton Professor, remarked: 'Beethoven could have made a great deal out of any one of the earlier versions [of his sketches] ... Obviously it would have been a different piece, and since that piece is not in existence, we can never know what it would have been like.'[xxiv]

Gustav Nottebohm, a pioneer in the study and decipherment of Beethoven's sketchbooks, has this to say: '[In] spite of this unsystematic procedure it is evident that as a rule Beethoven was clear about his objectives from the start; he remained true to his original conceptions, and once an idea was grasped, he carried it through to the end ... We may seek [in the sketchbooks] the artist himself, in the unity of his whole character and spirit, and in the harmony of his inner powers.'[xxv] In his scholarly commentary to Beethoven's sketchbooks, Alan Tyson suggests they may have 'performed a special function for him in maintaining his morale as well as in facilitating his creative processes'. They did indeed become indispensible to him and at times, when his working method came up in conversation, he was given to quoting from Schiller's *Joan of Arc*: ' Without my banner I dare not come.'[xxvi]

Beethoven was twenty-five at the time when his first piano sonatas, bearing an opus number, were published and their power and originality were apparent to the audiences who first heard them. One reviewer was prompted to comment: 'We have a number of beautiful sonatas by [Beethoven], amongst which the last ones [Op. 2] particularly distinguish themselves.'[xxvii] This same reviewer admired 'the unusual velocity of [Beethoven's] playing' and found him 'astounding in the way he masters the most formidable difficulties with the greatest of ease'.[xxviii] A measure of Beethoven's pre-eminence, amongst even the most accomplished pianists of the day, is conveyed in an anecdote told to the father of Carl Czerny by the keyboard virtuoso, and would-be rival of Beethoven, Joseph Gelinek. Inspired by Gelinek's account of Beethoven's playing, Czerny's father was motivated to seek out Beethoven and persuade him to give lessons to his then ten-year old son Carl. He thereby initiated a pupil-teacher relationship that would permanently enrich Beethoven musicology, to which we make occasional reference in our later commentaries to other of the composer's piano sonatas. The piano would remain Beethoven's chosen instrument throughout his life, until the last few years when he turned his attention to the medium of the string quartet. A sample of 140 of the composer's more important opus numbers, reveals more than forty were written for solo piano, almost thirty chamber works with piano accompaniment and many lesser pieces not designated an opus number.[xix]

Concerning Gelinek, his prowess at improvisation had impressed even Mozart and, later in his career, Carl Maria von Weber was so taken by Gelinek's playing that he wrote an epigram in celebration of his powers.[xx] On being invited to take part in a pianistic contest with Beethoven, Gelinek rashly boasted: 'We are going to thrash him soundly! I'll work him over!' A few days later, quite dejected, he bemoaned: 'That young man is possessed of the devil. Never have I heard such playing! He will play me and all of us to death! And how he improvised!' Beethoven had apparently improvised on a theme of Gelinek's choosing and then performed compositions of his own (unspecified) that Gelinek regarded as 'wonderful and grandiose to the highest degree'. He adds how Beethoven achieved effects 'such as we have never even dreamed of'.[xxi xxii xxiii xxiv] Gelinek appears to have swallowed his pride since he went on to create a piano arrangement of Beethoven's First Symphony and later composed a set of variations on the *Allegretto* of the Seventh Symphony.[xxv] .

The celebrated English pianist and composer Johann Baptist Cramer heard Beethoven play sometime in 1798.

Notwithstanding that he was generally regarded as being Beethoven's equal, in technical perfection, he is reported as being 'completely entranced' by Beethoven's powers of extemporization. The musicologist and harpsichordist Tilman Skowroneck has made a survey of the thirty-three published accounts of Beethoven performing at the keyboard. These bear testimony to him being: 'one of the foremost players' of his day; receiving 'universal applause' on eight occasions; earning praise for his 'mastery of technical difficulties, brilliancy, or ease of performance'; and prompting favourable remarks relating to his capacity for 'fast sight-reading from complicated manuscripts'.[xxvi] Franz Gerhard Wegeler was a close friend of Beethoven in their days together in Bonn, and he recalls how Beethoven's playing was at this time judged to be 'rude and hard' but a formative influence appears to have come about when Beethoven heard Johann Franz Sterkel perform. He was regarded as one of the finest pianists (more correctly, exponents on the fortepiano) in the whole of Germany whose playing was 'refined and elevated to the utmost ... graceful and pleasing'. On Beethoven hearing him play, Wegeler remarks: '[He] stood with attention ... for this grace and delicacy, if not power of execution, were a new revelation to him.'[xxvii] Later, Beethoven reciprocated Cramer's good feelings towards him by admiring Cramer's own pianistic touch and 'the quietness, smoothness, the pliability of the movements of his hands and fingers, the exceptional clearness and correctness of his style, [that he considered] rendered his performances unique'.[xxviii] As musicologist Alexander Ringer has observed: 'Beethoven, far from rejecting convention, never ceased to make careful selective use of a broadly based repertory of generalized ides representing a great variety of stylistic strains.'[xxix][xl]

In the 1790's Haydn was the preeminent musical figure

in Vienna and, indeed, throughout Europe. Beethoven was still evolving his reputation, projecting his image as an accomplished pianist in the salons of his patrons and, to the more distant musical public, through the medium of his compositions. In the context of the former, performing in the salons, as we have just seen with reference to his encounter with Gelinek, Beethoven had to hold his own. In this regard he was merely following a tradition. By way of illustration, some ten years previously (1783) we find Mozart writing to his father describing his own musical contest, at the Imperial Court, with the famed exponent of the fortepiano Muzio Clementi. Both participants had to play sonatas and then to develop improvisations on themes from them. In his autobiography, Karl (Carl) Dittersdorf judged Clementi's playing to be 'art or artifice alone', whereas he considered Mozart's playing combined 'art with *taste*' [Dittersdorf's emphasis].[xli] In his *Recollections*, Carl Czerny writes of Beethoven's own powers of improvisation: 'The rapidity with which [Beethoven] examined, and the excellent manner in which he played even manuscript and full score compositions, were astonishing. In this respect no one approached him.'[xlii]

Tia de Nora remarks, in her study of the politics of music in Vienna at the period in question, musical patronage and social hierarchy were mutually interlocked. It was in the salons of the aristocracy that Beethoven first gave expression to his more radical departures from musical orthodoxy through the medium of his pianoforte improvisations. These departures progressively found their way into his published works and, thereby, could be appreciated by the wider musically inclined members of the public. The awareness, and growing appreciation, of Beethoven's originality was also disseminated to wider audiences through the medium of such journals as the *Allgemeine musikalische Zeitung*.[xliii]

Notwithstanding his pre-eminence in the genre of keyboard improvisation, Beethoven's path to recognition would not be an easy one. As Carl Dahlhaus has remarked, at the turn of the new century (1800) the piano-variation form was not held in high regard by a certain class of music critics who, in Dahlhaus's words, 'took the artistic character of music seriously'. By their reckoning, 'elaborating figuration of a greater or lesser degree of virtuosity ... encouraged banality'.* Beethoven would progressively dispel any such notions with his six principal sets of piano variations, namely: Variations (6) on an original theme in F major, Op. 34, composed in 1802 and published in 1803; Variations (15) with Fugue on a theme from *Prometheus*, in E flat major, composed in 1802 and published in 1803; Variations (32) on an original theme in C minor, WoO 80, composed in 1806 and published in 1807; and the crowning glory of his achievement in this form, Variations (33) on a waltz of Diabelli in C major, Op. 120, composed between 1819—23 and published in 1823.

With regard to the period under consideration, the piano contest fulfilled a social role. It enabled the aspiring artist to establish his standing, with respect to his would-be rivals, and to impress potential patrons. Piano contests also served as forums in which rival musical styles, both compositional and pianistic, could be compared. In this regard Beethoven was doubly fortunate. He would soon have the support of a patron and, central to our discussion of his writing for the keyboard, he lived at a time when the pianoforte was undergoing a transformation that would have a direct bearing on the scale and ambition of his compositions. As Luciano Berio observes, in his discussion of the endeavours of the creative artist seeking to give form to his aspirations and transformations, 'the history of music, like any other history, chooses the right instruments and people at the right time'.*

In England, an entry in the *Encyclopaedia Britannica* for 1797 claimed the fortepiano to be nothing less than 'a national instrument'.[xli]

During the period 1800–30, the piano – more correctly the pianoforte – underwent transformations little short of a metamorphosis; no other instrument in Western culture experienced comparable changes. Evidence of this is found in such innovations as the extension of the keyboard, heavier and thicker strings, stronger frame, firmer action and the development of the sustaining pedal. These contributed to the instrument's range, tone colour, dynamics and sustaining ability, changes, which were to influence Beethoven's style of writing for the keyboard so markedly. Carl Czerny attributed the increase in the performer's virtuosity to these innovations, yielding, in his words, 'to greater fullness of the accompaniment and of the chords, brilliant passages, great fluency, the frequent and striking use of the pedal, arbitrary passing notes and singular harmonies'.[xlii]

The compass of the keyboard extended in Beethoven's lifetime broadly as follows – we cite instruments owned personally by the composer: Anton Walter (1785), Viennese maker, five octaves and two notes, from the third F below middle C to the third G above; Sébastien Érard (1803), French maker, extended the top range a fourth higher to C; John Broadwood (1817), English maker, six octaves from the third C below middle C to the third C above; and Conrad Graf (1825), Viennese maker, extended a further fourth higher to F. Beethoven had access to several other instruments, not least those on which he performed in the salons of members of the aristocracy. The pianoforte authority Derek Melville has identified instruments of the period in question that have, or may have, a close association with each of Beethoven's individual piano sonatas.[xliii]

Notwithstanding the challenges posed by Beethoven's

new sonatas, there is evidence they quickly found their way into Vienna's musically discerning salons. In the case, for example, of the gifted pianist Baroness Dorothea von Ertmann, by the time she was seventeen, in 1798, she already had most of Beethoven's published piano music in her extensive library — including the Piano Sonatas Op. 2.ᵈⁱˣ It has been conjectured she was probably among the first to play all of Beethoven's piano sonatas. Beethoven later conferred immortality on Dorothea by dedicating to her his Piano Sonata Op. 101.ᴵ Writing of the Piano Sonatas Op. 2, some 30 years after their publication, Beethoven's old friend Franz Wegeler could still recall how 'they created such a sensation throughout the [musical] world'.ᴵ

At the time when Haydn was returning to Vienna from England (August 1795), Beethoven played his three new sonatas at one of Lichnowsky's Friday morning concerts. The Prince, already an admirer of Beethoven, would soon become one of his staunchest supporters and patrons. He was a competent pianist himself, a former pupil of Mozart, and 'a real connoisseur' with 'a great talent for music' and possessed of judgement that was 'profound and correct'.ᴵⁱ It is reasonable to assume the Prince would possess the finest instruments of the day and make these accessible to Beethoven.ᴵⁱⁱ Beethoven had by this time been resident in Vienna for almost three years and was well established in Vienna's musical society. In this context, worthy of remark is that it has been suggested his acceptance into the salons of the Austro-Hungarian aristocracy may, in part, have been due to the fact that its members may have considered *van*, in his name, to be the equivalent of *von* in theirs — a mark of distinction and nobility; in other words Beethoven, unorthodox in demeanour and unkempt in appearance, was nonetheless regarded as being 'one of theirs'.ᴵᵛ

Beethoven had arrived in Vienna in November 1792 to

find the city still sorrowing from the death of Mozart – he had died there in straitened circumstances in December 1791. Beethoven had been sent on his way to Vienna with a note of encouragement (29 October 1792) from his friend and benefactor Count Ferdinand Waldstein bearing the often-quoted words: 'Receive Mozart's spirit from Haydn's hands.' lv lvi lvii

In addition to his parting words to Beethoven, Waldstein made him a gift of a small, portable pianoforte by the German builder Tufenbruch. Although this would soon be rendered inadequate for the composer's ever-demanding needs, he retained the instrument all his life – probably as a gesture of appreciation to his old friend. lviii Beethoven's diary entries show that for some time following his arrival in Vienna, he hired various instruments that cost him about half his monthly house rent. lix He is thought to have eventually received the gift of fortepiano by the Hungarian builder Sebastyén Vogel from Princess Lichnowsky, the wife of his future patron Prince Karl Lichnowsky. lx

We have said the piano was Beethoven's chosen instrument and the means by which he established his reputation in Vienna. Moreover, he took a keen interest in its development suggesting on occasions to manufacturers how it might be improved. Before proceeding further with our discussion of the Op. 2 Piano Sonatas, therefore, we will remark on the instruments with which Beethoven himself was familiar. But first a few words concerning nomenclature. References to Beethoven's 'early period' instruments often refer to, and interchange, such terms as flügel, clavecin, klavier (clavier), clavichord and fortepiano. As we shall discover, in our later commentaries, contemporary publishers' announcements to the composer's piano sonatas, from Op. 2 through to Op. 27, cite the option to the performer of them being suitable for either the clavecin or pianoforte. Subsequently, as

Beethoven's pianistic style and expression developed, his compositions are offered as being suitable for the pianoforte only — reference to the clavecin being dropped. Later still, when Beethoven was giving expression to his preference for German-language designations, he adopted the term *Hammerklavier* in one or another of the early copies of his last five sonatas — Op. 111 being the exception. In our remarks, we shall mostly use the term 'piano' and refer to Beethoven as a 'pianist'.[lxi]

The frame and primary components of the fortepiano of Beethoven's day were constructed entirely from wood. The outer casing, of instruments destined for wealthy clients, might incorporate such decorative features as gilded ormolus, inlay work and even painted scenes. The sounding board was thin and flexible. As a consequence of the lightweight timber frame, there was a limit to the string-tension that could be imposed with the strings themselves being made from narrow-gauge wire. The leather-covered hammers were correspondingly small. On the positive side, the keys were narrower than those on a modern-day instrument, permitting the span of an octave to be achieved by relatively small hands. Beethoven himself was a slight figure being only about 155 cms. (five feet, one inch) tall. He could just span a ninth. Carl Czerny describes Beethoven's hands as being 'covered with hair and the fingers very broad, especially at the tips'. Another description suggests his fingers 'looked as though they had been chopped off short and were nearly all the same length'.[lxii] (Representations of Beethoven in art and sculpture as a muscular, tousled-haired colossus may fulfil a romantic ideal but are misleading.)

The action of a typical Viennese fortepiano was light and conducive to the execution of rapid passagework with a resulting clear and precise tone. Because of the light construction, instruments were not overstrung (the bass strings did not cross over the middle range). The action of a typical Viennese piano has been described as 'light and shallow, [its] speech is extremely rapid ... dampening is extremely precise made possible by the use of leather-covered wedges ... the clear precision allows for utmost clarity and possibly more rapid tempi ... a more neutral tone-colour, but with distinctive timbres in the bass, middle and treble registers'. Virtuosi could exploit these features of the Viennese instruments, particularly in their rendering of the so-called *Alberti-bass* figuration, typical of fortepiano music of the period, in which recurrent passages in the lower register of the keyboard are required to oscillate in rhythmic fashion. The instruments of contemporary English makers, notably based in London, possessed a somewhat heavier action with a corresponding fullness of tone.[liii] Perhaps the most significant difference between the pianoforte of Beethoven's time and the modern-day instrument was the limited range of its keyboard. Beethoven was initially restricted to five octaves, then six (about 1809 — the period of composition of the *Emperor* Piano Concerto) and later still to six-and-half octaves — in time to influence the composition of the composer's late piano sonatas. The standard seven-and-a-half keyboard, typical of today's pianos, was never available to Beethoven. However, as already remarked, he was fortunate to live — more precisely to be composing — at the period when the pianoforte was undergoing a transformation more profound than that of any other Western musical instrument. Instrument frames became stronger, the action was firmer, heavier strings were used and foot pedals superseded the old-fashioned knee-action devices. These developments enriched the instruments' range, tone colour, dynamics and sustaining powers.

No instrument on which Beethoven is known to have

played, dating from his early years in Bonn, has been identified. That he was familiar with the fortepiano, as distinct from its precursor the harpsichord, can however be conjectured from the surviving part of his early Concerto in E-flat major (WoO4) that designates it as being 'pour le Clavecin ou Forte-Piano'. Beethoven is known to have had a high regard of the instruments of the brothers Schantz that he described as being 'good and durable'. Schantz's fortepianos were the chosen instrument of Joseph Haydn who paid the considerable sum of more than thirty golden ducats for one. Johann Schantz founded a workshop in Vienna in 1787 with his older brother Wenzel. The Schantz fortepiano was lightly constructed and incorporated features typical of Viennese fortepianos of the period. These included two knee levers: the left one for raising the dampers — thereby increasing sonority; and the right one for bringing into action the 'moderator' — a strip of cloth interposed between the hammers and the strings in order to mute the sound.[liv] It is on such a fortepiano as this that the young Beethoven was compelled to practice for hours on end until, as he was to recollect later in life, 'the blood boiled beneath his finger nails'.[lv] We have a tantalising impression of what the youthful composer may have looked like from the silhouette created of him in 1786 by Joseph Neesen. At this time the sixteen-year old Beethoven was organist at the Court of the Archbishop of Cologne. He is depicted wearing a wig, trimmed neckerchief and probably a tailcoat. The original is now lost but a lithograph survives and was used as the frontispiece to Ferdinand Ries's and Franz Gerhard Wegeler's pioneering (1838) study of Beethoven *Biographische Notizen über Ludwig van Beethoven* ('Beethoven Remembered').[lvi]

Beethoven would almost certainly have been familiar with the instruments of the famous pianoforte manufacturer from Augsberg, Anton Joseph Stein.[lvii] When his daughter

Nanette married Johann Andreas Streicher, the two became significant pioneers in the development of the fortepiano and, moreover, established a salon that became the centre of Vienna's musical life. Beethoven greatly appreciated the qualities of Streichers' pianos and for some time preferred them to those of other manufacturers. Their names will recur in our later remarks.[lviii]

It is possible Beethoven may have been familiar with Mozart's Walter fortepiano. This was the instrument Mozart acquired a few years after it was made in 1782 and upon which he performed in Vienna's concert rooms and at his 'academy' (benefit) concerts. Beethoven met Mozart on the occasion of his first visit to Vienna in April 1787, and may have received some lessons — he was then seventeen years of age. From this it can reasonably be assumed he acquired some familiarity with Walter's new, state-of-the-art instrument.[lix] On Mozart's death, in 1792, his surviving widow Constanza could not fined a buyer for this, now most revered of keyboard instruments, and it duly passed into the possession of her oldest son Carl who donated it in 1856 to the predecessor of the Salzburg *Mozarteum Foundation* who today have it on display in Mozart's former Salzburg residence.[lx]

In April 1796 — just after the composition of the Op. 2 Piano Sonatas — when Beethoven was settled in Vienna, it is recorded he performed on a Walter fortepiano at the house of the actor Willibrand Joseph Müller 'to the enchantment of the listeners'.[lxi] We are told Beethoven's style of playing was very restrained 'with his hands so very still; wonderful as his execution was, there was no tossing of them to and fro, up and down; they seemed to glide over the keys, the fingers alone doing the work'.[lxii] Czerny's own recollections of Beethoven's playing support Müller's account: 'His bearing was masterfully quiet, noble and beautiful without the slightest grimace, only bent forward low as his deafness grew upon him.'[lxiii]

We have remarked Beethoven performed at this period at Prince Lichnowsky's morning concerts. It is from about this time that he began to take a particular interest in the mechanics and functioning-mechanism of the fortepiano. He had a particular regard for Walter's instruments and was even prepared to purchase one when other makers were prepared to let him have one of theirs' on advantageous terms.[lxiv] Haydn, who was on personal terms with Walter, was well acquainted with his fortepianos although he did regard them as being somewhat expensive. An example, surviving from the period, is preserved today in the *Kunsthistorisches Museum* Vienna.[lxv] Walter's instruments were sturdy — Mozart's for example was made from seasoned walnut. Their compass was five octaves, from the third F below middle C to the third F above. Walter's instruments adopted the so-called *Prellmechanik* action that had been perfected in 1781 by the innovative instrument maker Johann Stein. With this, each hammer was mounted on top of the keys and thereby struck the strings directly. The consequence was a keyboard very responsive to the player's touch.[lxvi] Of particular interest to Beethoven, in his search for ever-more expressive feeling in his keyboard music, was the shifting-pedal device that Walter incorporated in his instruments. This was located just below the keyboard and was operated by the knee enabling the so-called *una corda* facility to be obtained. With this, the key action was shifted to the right so that the hammers would strike one of the two, or two of the three strings only. As we shall see in our later discussions, Beethoven began to insert *una corda* markings into his pianoforte music from about 1806.

From the foregoing it is evident that what we will call 'the keyboard sound-world' into which Beethoven delivered his Opus 2 Sonatas was a rapidly changing one. It was also one from which he would directly benefit and to which he would contribute immeasurably. It is an aspect of Beethoven's art to which we will return shortly and which will feature from time to time in our later discussions. For the present we will resume our comments regarding the composer's first piano sonatas of his maturity.

Beethoven considered his new sonatas sufficiently illustrative of his artistic ideals for them to be worthy of publication bearing opus numbers. With their publication he 'makes one of the strongest statements about his own personality in relation to his great predecessors [Haydn and Mozart]'. They had composed sets of piano works as collections, in which each composition makes an individual contribution to the whole. 'At no time, however, did they group together three works more different from each other and so remote from what had preceded them. Each work is unique in its shape and material.'[lxxvii] Moreover, with four movements at his disposal, Beethoven begins to replace the classical minuet with the more dynamic and boisterous scherzo — as in the case of the second and third sonatas. He thereby commenced a compositional procedure to which he was to return in many later works.[lxxviii]

The Opus 2 Piano Sonatas were announced on 9 March 1796 in the *Wiener Zeitung*) ('Vienna Journal') and were published by Beethoven's first publisher Artaria. The sonatas were dedicated to Joseph Haydn — the only professional composer ever to receive such a dedication from Beethoven with the exception of Antonio Salieri. This was despite the tension that had earlier existed between master and pupil. Beethoven had resented Haydn's suggestion that he should hold back publication of the third of his Piano Trios Op. 1 — the one he cherished the most.[lxxix] Also, Haydn had wished to have the Title Page of Beethoven's first works inscribed 'Pupil of Haydn' but Beethoven resisted. He acknowledged he had received instruction from Haydn but asserted 'he had never learned anything from him'.[lxxx] In later years he would renounce these headstrong views and even speak of his mentor with respect and affection. There was the occasion, for example, when the composer and publisher Anton Diabelli called on Beethoven to present him with a lithograph of Haydn's rather modest birthplace — in the village of Rohrau in Lower Austria. It gave Beethoven much pleasure prompting him to remark: 'Just see the little house, and such a great man was born in it.'[lxxxi]

Haydn must have been impressed by the assurance of his gifted pupil's mastery, even if he found his compositions 'here and there too subversive in method and violent in expression for his taste'.[lxxxii] We should also recall how Haydn, in his capacity as Kapellmeister to Prince Nicholas Esterhazy, had commended Beethoven warmly to the Elector of Bonn — Maximilian Franz. In a letter to the Elector, sent from Vienna in November 1793, Haydn requested financial support for Beethoven and praised several of his compositions — including a set of piano variations. He says, prophetically: 'On the basis of these pieces, expert and amateur alike cannot but admit that Beethoven will in time become one of the greatest musical artists in Europe, and I shall be proud to call myself his teacher.'[lxxxiii] The Elector's reply was withering. He declined financial support, doubted Beethoven's progress in composition and suggested he return to Bonn before incurring further debts.[lxxxiv] Beethoven's response was to stay in Vienna forever.

In the Opus 2 Sonatas Beethoven was already beginning 'the process of formal expansion' that would lead to works of 'unprecedented ambition' and 'rhetorical weight'.[lxxxv] He was clearly intent upon making a big impact and to 'take Vienna by storm'.[lxxxvi] The Piano Sonatas Op. 2 are conceived on a relatively large scale and, as previously intimated, expand the more typical three and four movement piano-sonata structures of Haydn and Mozart; the final one in the series, for example, has a performing time of more than 25 minutes. All three sonatas have four movements — a format usually reserved at this period for the string quartet and symphony.

We have remarked how closely Beethoven followed the technical development of the pianoforte, of his familiarity from his Bonn days with the five-octave keyboard typical of the period, and of the emerging extension of the compass of the instrument accompanied by such other features as an increase in sonority and capacity for more expressive tone colour. These changing circumstances had significant compositional implications for Beethoven. Most significantly, at the period in question, he was frequently constrained by the upper limits of the available keyboard, 'rewriting the transposition of parallel passages so as to keep within the prescribed limits'. As keyboards expanded, especially in the treble, he was able to venture into the pianistic realms that would be further explored by such younger composers as Schubert and Weber.[lxxxvii] These considerations also raise present-day related issues concerning the 'authentic' interpretation of his piano music.[lxxxviii] For the moment, we can observe Edwin Fischer's discerning remark: 'There are still many passages where transfer to the now customary higher register may mean sacrificing beauties which arose from Beethoven having made a virtue of necessity.'[lxxxix] The importance of the piano to Beethoven as an aid to composition is also worthy of mention. Czerny writes in his reminiscences: 'Beethoven was accustomed to composing everything with the aid of the piano, and would try out a given passage countless times.'[xc] Progressive deafness impelled him to torment his instruments severely in his efforts to capture their sound and would eventually isolate him from the keyboard altogether. These are circumstances we reserve for later discussion. For the present we will comment briefly on the composer's concert tour of 1796 and his growing enthusiasm for the Streicher pianoforte.

Between the months of February and July of 1796, Beethoven undertook a concert tour taking in Prague, Dresden, Leipzig and Berlin. He was well received and earned 'considerably money' from the nobility in whose salons he performed. In Berlin, Beethoven met the distinguished pianist Freidrich Himmel and performed for Friedrich Wilhelm II, King of Prussia. In Dresden, he played accompaniments for one and a half hours to the delight of the Elector of Saxony who afterwards presented the composer with a gold snuffbox. His improvisations at the keyboard thrilled and enchanted his audiences, who found them 'rich in fantasy' with 'striking changes from adagio to allegro' — hallmarks of Beethoven's piano playing that would soon find a place in his piano-sonata writing. Later in the year (23 November) he gave a concert in Pressburg (Bratislava) to considerable acclaim. We discuss the musical implications of these events in our later commentaries. For now we confine ourselves to the pianoforte on which Beethoven had performed and the relationship he had with its makers.

The instrument in question was a Streicher — considered by some to be the equal of, and possibly even superior to, the Walter pianoforte to which we have referred. The Streicher manufacturer was a partnership between Nanette Stein and Johann Streicher who had moved to Vienna in 1794, shortly after which they became acquainted with Beethoven. As a child Nanette had been hailed as a prodigy and once performed for Mozart. However, more relevant to our narrative, as the daughter of Johann Stein — the celebrated builder of organs and pianofortes — she had learned the business of pianoforte manufacture and its technical intricacies and thereby — which is remarkable for the period in question — was 'the guiding spirit of the firm'. Her husband Johann, who was also an accomplished pianist, looked after the firm's business affairs. It is with him that Beethoven transacted a spirited correspondence at various times throughout his life on the subject of the pianoforte and how it might be improved. In the composer's declining years Nanette was of great assistance to Beethoven with regard to the management of his household affairs — concerning which he was almost pathologically incapable. The Streichers became important figures in Vienna's musical society. Their salon, in which their finest instruments were on display, became a venue for the great and the good in Vienna's musical society; distinguished guests, for example, included Beethoven's only composition pupil, and accomplished pianist, the Archduke Rudolph — youngest son of the Emperor Leopold II. Busts of celebrated composers adorned the room including that of Beethoven, commissioned by the Streichers from the sculptor Franz Klein.[xiv] Indeed, such was the social standing of the Streichers' salon that it became a sort of 'testing ground [and] whoever wanted to give a public concert was obliged to perform first in the Streichers' salon before an invited audience'.[xv] On one occasion Nanette and Johann themselves performed, giving a rendering of Carl Czerny's two-piano arrangement of Beethoven's *Pastoral Symphony,* prompting some members of the audience to cast their gaze admiringly at Klein's rendering of Beethoven's countenance.[xvi]

Beethoven wrote to Andreas Streicher from Pressburg on 23 November enthusing: 'I received ... your fortepiano, which is really an excellent instrument ... Anyone else would try to keep it for himself.' However, he could not refrain from pointing out to Streicher what he considered to be its limitations. 'It robs me of the freedom to produce my own tone.' But he adds, good-naturedly, 'This must not deter you from making all your fortepianos in the same way.' The reason for his reservations is revealing: '[No] doubt there are few people who cherish such whims as mine' — by which he really means make such demands of the instrument.[xvii] A few weeks later he wrote once more to Streicher complaining that the pianoforte is 'the least studied of all instruments' and goes on to say that it is like 'merely listening to a harp'. He looks forward to the time 'when the harp and the pianoforte will be treated as two entirely different instruments'.[xviii]

A Streicher fortepiano from this period cost about 66 ducats (about thirty pounds sterling) whereas a Walter fortepiano could be had for 50 ducats (about twenty-three pounds sterling). Moreover, although the Streichers were innovative pianoforte builders, their predilection was in favour of the lighter-sounding instrument.[xix] This is evident from a pamphlet they published sometime around 1801 titled, Notes on the 'Playing, Tuning and Maintenance of the Fortepiano'. This was issued on the sale of each of their instruments to ensure its proper care and maintenance. From it can be inferred the accepted fortepiano sound of the period. Streicher (it was probably Andreas who wrote the pamphlet) advocates the then current Viennese ideal of 'light playing and pearly passage work' in which flowing sequences of notes could be compared to 'matched pearls'. A restrained pianistic approach to playing is advocated with no 'pounding' and 'torturing the instrument'. Streicher had no time for the showy performer: 'By moving his body, arms and hands he seems to want to show how difficult the labour undertaken by him is.' He gives the following advice: 'All musical instruments, even the human voice, have their own range of expression, which cannot be transgressed without making a bad impression on the listener, or provoking reproaches from the connoisseur [Streicher's emphasis].'. As Tia de Nora remarks, on the basis of her study of Beethoven's compositional procedures in the context of Streicher's system of piano aesthetics, Streicher's precepts militated against Beethoven's 'tendency towards the strenuous and the dramatic, as opposed to the conventionally lighter and cleaner style'. Equally, we can appreciate how champions of such a style of playing, as the Streichers' were advocating, would find favour with a Viennese audience seated of an evening in their salon. In our later commentaries we will encounter just such keyboard executants, and would-be pianistic rivals of Beethoven, in the guise of Daniel Steibelt and Joseph Wölfl.

The Streichers would in due course improve their fortepianos in response to the growing demand for a sturdier instrument and one with a greater compass. Such developments were due in no small part to Beethoven's encouragement and the new style of pianoforte sound he was promoting in such works as his Piano Sonatas Op. 2. On his tour of Vienna in 1809, the German composer and music critic Johann Reichardt became acquainted with Beethoven's piano muisc and recalled: 'Streicher has been persuaded away from the compliant ... musical characteristics of other Viennese instruments. On Beethoven's insistence he has given his instruments more resistance and elasticity. A forceful performer thus has a greater basic and continuous control over the instrument ... he has given his instrument a greater and more diverse character.'. Later still (about 1816) Nanette Streicher patented an even more fully developed fortepiano with a compass of six and a half octaves and a *una corda* action foot pedal to allow the performer to depress a chord or to achieve a swell or diminuendo.⁴⁸ It was probably this instrument that, as his hearing deteriorated, Beethoven requested the Streichers to adapt so that he could capture more of its sound. It is believed they attached a form of acoustic hood above the keyboard so as to reflect back more of the sound.⁴⁹ Beethoven's need for such a facility is poignantly revealed in a letter from the period in question when he wrote to Nanette Streicher referring to the benefits of his ear trumpet. This had been adapted for him by its inventor Johann Maelzel.⁵⁰

An anecdote links the Streichers and the Op. 2 Piano Sonatas with a gifted young maiden by the name of Fräulein Elisabeth von Kissow. At an early age she showed pronounced musical talent, prompting her father to send her to Vienna to receive instruction from Andreas Streicher and his wife Nanette. Streicher laid before von Kissow Beethoven's recently published piano sonatas observing how 'the ladies did not care to play them because they were too unintelligible'. Undeterred, the girl not only mastered them — and other works of Beethoven — but also was invited to perform at the private musical entertainments in the homes of Counts Lichnowsky and Razumovsky. Beethoven, who had heard Kissow play, wrote to Andreas Streicher in the following terms: 'I congratulate you on being so fortunate as to be able to display through such a talent your own understanding of music; and, moreover, I am delighted that this dear little girl, who is so talented, has *you* for her teacher [Beethoven's emphasis].' He then takes up his favourite topic: 'There is no doubt that so far as the manner of playing it is concerned, the pianoforte is still the least studied and developed of all instruments; often one thinks that one is merely listening to a harp.'⁵¹

Beethoven so prized Elisabeth von Kissow's talent that for the next few years he sent her a copy of his newest pieces, usually accompanied with a typical Beethovenian jocular note.[xvii] Later in life Elisabeth, as Frau von Bernhard, recalled her musical impressions of the time when she received her instruction from the composer: 'I still remember clearly both Haydn and Salieri sitting on a sofa on one side of the small music-room, both carefully dressed in the old-fashioned way with perruque [periwig], shoes and silk hose, whereas even here Beethoven would come dressed in the informal fashion of the other side of the Rhine, almost ill-dressed.'[xviii] During his early years in Vienna, there is evidence Beethoven did make attempts to overcome his social and sartorial deficiencies. Entries from an account book of his personal income reveal he acquired black silk stockings, boots, and incurred expenses for a wig maker and a dancing master — although, with regard to the latter, his piano pupil Ferdinand Ries recalls: 'He could never learn to dance in time, and his clumsy movements lacked all charm.'[xix]

Speaking of Beethoven's first acknowledged piano sonatas, Glenn Gould says: 'The Beethoven Op. 2's ... have great dramatic flair, but they also have an incredibly pure, quartet-like concept of voice-leading which you never find in later sonatas, except perhaps for isolated moments like the first movement of Op. 101 or the second movement of Op. 109.'[xx] Writing of Beethoven's youthful individuality and range in the Op. 2 Piano Sonatas, Charles Rosen remarks: 'Each work is strikingly different in character and form. Pathos is succeeded by sociability and brilliance. Formal patterns, typical of Mozart, are followed by techniques learned from Haydn. The sonority incorporates textures from concerto, symphony and chamber music.'[xxi]

The wording of the announcement of the three sonatas in the *Wiener Zeitung* was based, in part, upon the Title Page of the new works that states: *'Trois Sonates pour le Clavecin ou Piano Forte, composées et dédiées à Mr. Joseph*

Haydn, Docteur en Musique par Louis van Beethoven. Op. 2. Vienne chez Artaria et Co.' Haydn's honorary degree in music had been conferred upon him by the University of Oxford in 1791. Haydn now had an international reputation and was regarded as one of Vienna's musical treasures. He was both a great and popular composer, contributing to numerous charity concerts, 'foreshadowing the sort of reputation that Beethoven's success continued and expanded'.[cii] It is open to question though whether the venerable Haydn ever fully appreciated his erstwhile pupil. Although he himself had been such a great innovator in the 1760s and 1770s, he now found Beethoven 'moving too fast into realms in which he felt unfamiliar'. Evidence for him thinking this is found in Giuseppe Carpani's biography of Haydn, the second edition of which was published in 1812. Carpani recounts how Haydn was once asked by one of his friends, sometime in 1805, 'what he thought of the young composer?' 'The old man replied with all sincerity: "His first works pleased me considerably, but I must admit that I don' t understand the later ones".'[ciii]

Beethoven's publishers recommended his new piano sonatas in the following terms: 'As the previous work of the same composer [the three Trios Op. 1], were received by the public with so much favour, the same result is expected from the present work. The more so, as it offers, besides its value as a Composition, also the opportunity of judging with what effect Herr van Beethoven treats the instrument, not only with regard to strength, but also delicacy.'[civ cv cvi]

---

[i] Beethoven's early relationship with Haydn, in the context of his visits to London, is outlined in *Musical Visitors to Britain*, David Gordon, 2005, pp. 93–4.

[ii] Barry Cooper, 2000, p. 52.

[iii] A sheet of manuscript paper survives from this period (authorities date it from between 1792–6) that reveals the extent to which Beethoven's musical studies co-existed alongside his more personal creativity. It reveals no fewer than 18 compositional drafts. See: Beethoven House, Digital Archives, Library Document No. NE 105. Digital Archive Library Document BH 81,

from this time, is also of interest. It illustrates the youthful Beethoven's study of a four-part canon by the theorist Johann Kirnberger.

[iv] Anton Schindler, 1860, English edition: Donald MacArdle, editor, 1966, p. 110.

[v] Denis Matthews, 1985, p. 78.

[vi] Denis Matthews, 1972, p. 171.

[vii] Donald J. Grout and Claude V. Palisca, editors, 1988, p. 629.

[viii] Wilfrid H. Mellers, 1957, p. 56.

[ix] Oskar Bie, 1966, p. 169.

[x] Romain Rolland, 1937, p. 118.

[xi] Clementi's 'bravura playing' and 'brilliant figurations' placed him at the forefront of the pianists of his day. Contemporaries admired his 'brilliant feats of technical proficiency' and 'pearliness of touch' in rapid passages. In the same year of Beethoven's death (1827) a retirement banquet was held in Clementi's honour to celebrate his achievements as 'the father of pianoforte playing'. See: Leon Plantinga, 1977, pp. 292–3.

[xii] Anton Schindler, 1860, English edition: Donald MacArdle, editor, 1966, p. 379.

[xiii] See, for example: Harold Truscott, *The piano music*, in: Denis Arnold and Nigel Fortune, editors, 1973, pp. 68–88.

[xiv] Alexander A. Ringer, *Beethoven and the London pianoforte school* in: Paul Henry Lang, 1971 pp. 255–6. Ringer remarks that Vienna, like the British capital, offered music — 'the favourite art of the middle classes'. In his discussion of Beethoven's London contemporaries, he cites the following outstanding musician-pianists of such divers backgrounds as: the Italian-born Clementi (for his 'melodic rhythmic eccentricities'); the Bohemian Dussek (for his 'anticipations of romantic keyboard idioms'); the German Cramer (for his 'glittering passagework'); and the Irishman Field (for his 'sentimental elegance' — and one may add his anticipations of Chopin).

[xv] Barry Cooper, 2000, p.58.

[xvi] Thayer-Forbes, 1967, pp. 417–8.

[xvii] Several of Clementi's English editions appeared earlier than their German counterparts, e.g., Opp. 73, 77, 81a and 119. See text and note 23, in: Paul Badura-Skoda, editor, 1970, p. 8.

[xviii] Thayer-Forbes, 1967, p. 123.

[xix] Maynard Solomon, 1977, pp. 46–7.

[xx] Leon Plantinga discusses Beethoven's first piano sonatas in the context of the early stylistic growth of the piano sonata. See: Leon Plantinga, 1984, p. 29 *et seq.*

[xxi] William Kinderman, *The piano sonatas* in: *The Cambridge companion to Beethoven*, Glenn Stanley, editor, 2000, p. 113.

[xxii] The artist Donna Dralle has created an imaginary study in pencil and watercolour titled *Beethoven stitching a notebook.* See: http//www.graphixnow.com/fine_art/images/fine_art_pgs/lvbsew.jpg

[xxiii] See: Joseph Kerman, *Beethoven's early sketches* in: Paul Henry Lang, editor, 1971, pp. 13–36. Kerman, quoting Dr. Hans Schmidt of the Beethoven Archive, Bonn, suggests nearly 400 sketch sources of various kinds have to date been identified, consisting variously of single sheets, bifolia (double sheets), bound sketchbooks and miscellaneous gatherings. Of his predisposition to set his thoughts down in draft form, Kerman concludes: 'Beethoven seems to have experienced a compulsion to get things down on paper — not only musical monographs, but also drafts of all kinds — he had a veritable

commitment to the graphic act.' For a facsimile illustration of a typical two-page bifolium, of the kind Beethoven carried around with him, see: Beethoven House, Digital Archives, Library Document, Sammlung H. C. Bodmer, HCB BSK 16/24.

xxiv Edward T. Cone, editor, *Roger Sessions on music: collected essays*, 1979, p. 45.

xxv Gustav Nottebohm, 1979, pp. 4–7.

xxvi Alan Tyson, *Sketches and autographs*, in: Denis Arnold, and Nigel Fortune, editors. *The Beethoven companion*, 1973, pp. 443– 58.

xxvii Thayer-Forbes, 1967, p. 125. The review was published under the title *Virtuosi and Dilettante from Vienna* (1796). It is reproduced in full in: Wayne M. Senner (et. al.), 1999, pp. 7–8.

xxviii H. C. Robbins Landon, 1992, p. 57. The text is derived from the *Jahrbuch der Tonkunst für Wien und Prag,* 1796.

xxix With acknowledgment to Derek Melville, *Beethoven's pianos* in: Denis Arnold and Nigel Fortune, editors, 1973, p. 48.

xxx For a brief account of Joseph Gelinek and his relationship with Beethoven see: Peter Clive, 2001, pp. 124–5.

xxxi From the recollections of Carl Czerny, see: Paul Badura-Skoda, editor, 1970, p. 4. Czerny conveyed his father's recollections of Gelineck to Beethoven's early biographer Otto Jahn.

xxxii Johann Schenk provides further testimony to Beethoven's powers of improvisation. He gave instruction to Beethoven in counterpoint (1793) and was immensely impressed by his pupil's technical virtuosity: 'My ear was continually charmed by the beauty of the many varied motives which he wove with wonderful clarity and loveliness into each other, and I surrendered my heart to the impressions made upon it.' Johann Schenk, in: O. G. Sonneck, 1927, pp. 14–5.

xxxiii For an account of Gelineck's meeting with Beethoven, see: Thayer-Forbes, 1967, p. 139.

xxxiv Until Beethoven's hearing deteriorated, his powers of improvisation were generally regarded as being without equal. However, one evening in 1804 Beethoven took part in a pianistic contest with Georg Joseph Vogler in which he may not have emerged the victor. Vogler was a theorist, organist, pianist and composer and improvised on a theme given by Beethoven who in turn improvised on a theme of Vogler's. A guest at the event later recorded in his diary that although he was greatly impressed by Beethoven's improvisation, it had not aroused in him 'the enthusiasm inspired by Vogler's learned playing'. Doubtless Beethoven's flights of fancy and departures from pianistic convention had proved too much for some. See: Beethoven House, Digital Archives, Library Document, B 937 and Peter Clive, 2001, pp. 381–2.

xxxv For a summary account of Gelineck's life and musical achievements, see: Peter Clive, 2001, pp. 124–5.

xxxvi Tilman Skowroneck, *The keyboard instruments of the young Beethoven*, in: Scott G. Burnham and Michael P. Steinberg, editors, 2000, pp. 33–79. Skowroneck has derived his observations from two primary sources, namely, Thayer Forbes, pp. 105–257 and H. C. Robbins Landon, 1994, pp. 33–79.

xxxvii Wegeler's account is recalled in Thayer-Forbes, 1967, p. 103.

xxxviii As quoted by Derek Melville in *Beethoven's pianos* in: Denis Arnold and Nigel Fortune, editors, 1973, p. 48.

xxxix Alexander A. Ringer, *Beethoven and the London pianoforte school* in: Paul Henry Lang, editor, 1971, p. 254.

[xl] For a modern-day interpretation of how Beethoven may have appeared, when absorbed in one of his improvisations, see the illustration by the artist-sculptor Donna Dralle reproduced in the website text, *The unheard Beethoven* to the *Allegretto* in B minor, WoO 61.

[xli] As quoted by Tia De Nora, 1997, pp. 150–1.

[xlii] As recollected by Carl Czerny in: Ludwig Nohl, 1880, p. 47.

[xliii] As quoted by Tia De Nora, 1997, pp. 150–1.

[xliv] Carl Dahlhaus, 1991, p. 156.

[xlv] David Osmond-Smith, editor and translator, *Luciano Berio: Two interviews with Rossana Dalmonte and Bálint András Varga*, 1985, p. 50.

[xlvi] As quoted by Alexander Ringer in: Paul Henry Lang, editor, 1971, p. 241.

[xlvii] Leonard G. Ratner, 1992, p. 31

[xlviii] Derek Melville identifies the following instruments that he considers have a direct connection, or association, with various Beethoven piano sonatas: John Broadwood, Conrad Graf, Sébastien Érard, Georg Haschka, Matthäus Heilmann, Robert E, Smith, Johann Andreas Stein, Matthäus Andreas Stein, Robert Stodart, William Stodart, and Nannette Streicher. See: Derek Melville, *Beethoven's Pianos*, in: Denis Arnold and Nigel Fortune, editors, 1973, p. 47.

[xlix] Theodore Albrecht, 1996, Vol. 1, Letter No. 78, pp. 131–2.

[l] For concise information concerning Dorothea von Ertmann and Beethoven see: Peter Clive, 2001, pp. 102–4 and Paul Nettl, 1975, p. 49. For a miniature portrait of Dorothea von Ertmann, see: H. C. Robbins Landon, 1970, p. 104, plate 72.

[li] Franz Wegeler, 1838, English edition: 1988, p. 113. For engraved portraits of Wegeler, with brief biographical details, see: Beethoven House Bonn, Digital Archives, and Library Document W 162.

[lii] These are the views of Beethoven's pupil Carl Czerny who was well acquainted with the Lichnowsky family. See, for example: Paul Badura-Skoda, editor, 1970, p. 8.

[liii] For a wider discussion of the instruments available to Beethoven see: Tilman Skowroneck, *The keyboard instruments of the young Beethoven*, in: Scott G. Burnham, and Michael P. Steinberg, editors, 2000, p. 153. Skowroneck comments: '... Beethoven became used to the best fortepianos of his time (the Stein instrument in Bonn) and after 1791 he used the various types common in Vienna ... and that he was well aware of their different characteristics, choosing Walter for himself, but not rejecting the Stein/Streicher model.' (pp. 177–8).

[liv] H. C. Robbins Landon, 1992, p. 79.

[lv] Theodore Albrecht, 1996, Vol. 1, Letter No. 13g.

[lvi] Tia de Nora asserts: 'The concept of Mozart's "spirit" provided a conceptual mantle under which the greatness of a subsequent composer could be lodged.' Tia de Nora, 1997, p. 158.

[lvii] For a reproduction of Beethoven's Album, open at the pages showing Waldstein's text together with his silhouette, see: Hans Conrad Fischer, and Erich Kock, 1972, p. 107.

[lviii] This observation, and the remarks that immediately follow relating to Beethoven and the fortepiano, owe a debt to Ernest Closson, *History of the Piano*, 1947. The reader interested in this aspect of Beethoven musicology will find of value, as the present writer has, Sandra Hyslop's text, *Beethoven's pianos*, on *Facebook*, 2012.

lix Thayer-Forbes, 1967, p. 135.

lx A fortepiano made by Vogel is today housed in The National Museum of America that is inscribed 'Louis van Beethoven/S. A. Vogel'. See: website *Vogel Grand Pianos*.

lxi For a fuller contextual account of the terminology used to describe the keyboard instruments of Beethoven's time, see: Tilman Skowroneck, *The keyboard instruments of the young Beethoven* in: Scott G. Burnham, and Michael P. Steinberg, editors, 2000, pp. 153–4 and William S. Newman, 1963, p. 510.

lxii As recollected by Carl Czerny and Beethoven's youthful friend Frau von Gleichenstein in: Ludwig Nohl, 1880, p. 41 and footnote 1.

lxiii For a general survey of the piano and its precursors, see: Robert Palmieri, editor, *Encyclopaedia of the piano*, 1996. For a detailed discussion of the instruments of Beethoven's time, see: Derek Melville, *Beethoven's Pianos* in: Denis Arnold, and Nigel Fortune, editors, pp. 41–68, 1973.

lxiv Derived from the Cover and Sleeve Notes to the recording: *Beethoven in Context* by Ella Sevskaya, (no date), Quil 303.

lxv A fortepiano of the kind described is preserved in its original condition at the *Accademia Bartolomeo Cristofori* in Florence. A reproduction of a 1795 Schantz fortepiano is on display in the Schloss Kremsegg Museum at Kremsmünster, Austria.

lxvi See: Beethoven House, Digital Archives, Library Document Sammlung Wegeler, W 171. Neesen's silhouette was once considered to be the earliest known surviving likeness of Beethoven until 1952 when an anonymous portrait of the composer came to light. It is thought to portray him as a boy aged thirteen. See: Beethoven House 'Beethoven Gallery'.

lxvii The role of Stein in the development of the fortepiano is discussed by Derek Melville, *Beethoven's Pianos* in: Denis Arnold and Nigel Fortune, editors, 1973, p. 57. For an illustration of a pianoforte by Johann Andreas Stein of 1796, see: Plate 22 in Ernest Closson's *History of the piano*, 1947.

lxviii For a portrait of Nannette Streicher, together with a brief history of her connection with Beethoven, see: Beethoven House, Digital Archives, Library Document B 155/b.

lxix Tilman Skowroneck, *The keyboard instruments of the young Beethoven*, in: Scott G. Burnham and Michael P. Steinberg, editors, p. 153. Skowroneck suggests Beethoven's compositional experience of the fortepiano can be traced back to the surviving part of the early concerto in E flat, WoO4 that bears the title '*Un Concert/pour le Clavecin ou Forte-Piano Composé par/Loius van Beethoven*'.

lxx See website article, with accompanying illustration, *Mozart's Original Instruments*.

lxxi *Ibid*, See also H. C. Robbins Landon, 1970, p. 51.

lxxii As cited by Müller and quoted in, Thayer-Forbes, p. 337.

lxxiii *Ibid*, p. 368.

lxxiv See: Beethoven's letter of November 1802 to his friend Nikolaus Zmeskall in which he discusses his relationships with Vienna's piano manufacturers, in Emily Anderson, 1961, Vol. 1, Letter No. 66, pp. 82–3.

lxxv For a discussion of the Walter fortepiano and an illustration of the example preserved in Vienna's *Kunsthistorisches Museum*, see: Ernest Closson, *History of the piano*, translated by Delano Ames and edited by Robin Golding, 1947, plate 26 and related text.

lxxvi For a detailed description of the *Prellmechanik* action, with illustrations, see: Wikipedia article *Johann Andreas Stein*.

lxxvii Philip Downs, 1992, pp. 580–2.

lxxviii The evolution of this aspect of Beethoven's development is remarked upon in *A History of Western Music*, Donald J. Grout and Claude V. Palisca, editors, 1988, p. 629.

lxxix Maynard Solomon, 1977, p. 67.

lxxx Franz Wegeler, 1838, English edition, 1988, p. 75.

lxxxi Gerhard von Breuning, 1874, English edition, 1992, pp. 98–9. Diabelli made the gift of the lithograph of Haydn's birthplace when Beethoven was in his last illness. Gerhard von Breuning was a frequent visitor to Beethoven at this time and helped to have the lithograph framed.

lxxxii Eric Blom, 1938, p. 5.

lxxxiii Thayer-Forbes, 1967, p. 144 and Theodore Albrecht, 1996, Vol. 1, Letter No. 16. For a commentary on this extended and eloquent letter, with remarks concerning the compositions mentioned therein, see also: H. C. Robbins Landon, 1959, pp. 141–2.

lxxxiv Theodore Albrecht, 1996, Vol. 1, Letter No. 17.

lxxxv Maynard Solomon, 1977, p. 194.

lxxxvi Barry Cooper, 2000, p. 52.

lxxxvii *Instruments, Temperaments, and Tempos* in: Leon Plantinga, 1999, p. 293.

lxxxviii The implications for interpreting Beethoven's early sonatas, in the context of different keyboards and sonorities, is discussed in *Historical problems in Beethoven performance* in: *Beethoven performers and critics*, Robert Winter, editor, 1977, pp. 41–51.

lxxxix *Beethoven's instruments* in: Edwin Fischer, 1959, p. 83.

xc From the recollections of Carl Czerny, see: Paul Badura-Skoda, editor, 1970, p. 13. Czerny also states (p. 6) that his own performance of Beethoven's works did not always go down well. He comments 'the pianoforte had not yet begun to have the splendid effect it does now'.

xci For a documentary study of Beethoven's Concert Tour, see: H. C. Robbins Landon, pp. 53–4.

xcii Hans Conrad Fischer and Erich Kock, 1972, p. 12. These authors quote Carl Czerny who assigned Beethoven's improvisations to a number of categories. Czerny lists: a type of variation based on the structure of the first movement or the final rondo of a sonata movement; free variations; what he describes as 'a mixed type' such as is found in his solo Fantasia Op. 77; and a style of improvisation like that written out in his Choral Fantasy Op. 80.

xciii See *The Years 1796 and 1797* in Thayer–Forbes, 1967, pp. 180–218.

xciv This is the bust that is frequently reproduced as a frontispiece in works celebrating Beethoven's life and work. It was derived from a facial likeness of the composer taken by Klein, a professor of sculpture, in 1812. The likeness was later adapted by the sculptor Kaspar Zumbusch for his monumental seated sculpture of Beethoven that now adorns Vienna's *Beethovenplatz.*

xcv For an illustration of Streichers' pianoforte showroom see: Hans Conrad Fischer and Erich Kock, 1972, p. 23.

xcvi Peter Clive, 2001, pp. 357–9.

xcvii Emily Anderson, 1961, Vol. 1, Letter No. 17, pp. 24–5. For a facsimile reproduction of this letter see: Beethoven House, Digital Archives, Library Document NE 94.

xcviii *Ibid* 1961, Vol. 1, Letter No. 18, pp. 25–6.

xcix The Streicher fortepiano of this period was of relatively lightweight construction

———

with a five-octave range of F – F. For an illustration of such a fortepiano from 1814, see: Edwin Marshall Good, 1982, p. 78 and fig. 3.2.

ⁱ As quoted by Tilman Skowroneck, *The keyboard instruments of the young Beethoven*, in: Scott G. Burnham, and Michael P. Steinberg, editors, 2000, pp. 167–8.

ⁱⁱ Tia de Nora, 1997, p. 175.

ⁱⁱⁱ Cited in: Hans Conrad Fischer and Erich Kock, 1972, p. 13. See also: Edwin Marshall Good, 1982, p. 71 and Tia de Nora, 1970, p. 179.

^{iv} A copy of Nanette Streicher's fortepiano of 1816 is preserved in the Yale Collection of Musical Instruments. See Website: *Ludwig van Beethoven, Beethoven's Pianos.*

^v No details of this adaptation appear to have survived. A tantalising inference may be drawn from a letter Beethoven wrote to Nanette Streicher on 26 August 1817 when he remarks: 'I have long desired to make its [the piano in question?] acquaintance. See Emily Anderson, 1961, Vol. 2, Letter No. 844, pp. 726–7.

^{vi} Emily Anderson, 1961, Vol. 2, Letter No. 844, p. 726. For an illustration of the various ear trumpets Beethoven used, see: Derek Melville, 1973, Plate 8. Images of these poignant contrivances can also be viewed by accessing the Beethoven House Digital Archive.

^{vii} Emily Anderson, 1961, Vol. 1, Letter No. 18, pp. 25–6. For a facsimile reproduction of this letter, see: Beethoven House, Digital Archives, Library Document NE 95.

^{viii} The reminiscences of Fräulein von Kissow, as Frau von Bernhard, are told in: Oscar Sonneck, 1927 pp. 19–20.

^{ix} As recounted in *Vienna and its Musical Life* in: *Haydn. The Years of the Creation*, H. C. Robbins Landon, 1977, p. 25.

^x Hans Conrad Fischer, and Erich Kock, 1972, pp. 29–30.

^{xi} Glenn Gould in conversation with the film maker Bruno Monsaingeon. See: Tim Page, 1987, pp. 36–7.

^{xii} Charles Rosen, 2002, p. 123.

^{xiii} Tia De Nora, 1967, p. 99.

^{xiv} As told in, *Haydn. The Years of the Creation,* H. C. Robbins Landon, 1977, p. 507. It should be added that Carpani himself was not an ardent admirer of Beethoven. He appreciated his instrumental music but, for example, detested *Fidelio.* See: Peter Clive, 2001, pp. 66–7.

^{xv} Derived from the Augener Edition No. 8030 of *Beethoven's Piano Sonatas* (undated).

^{xvi} For a facsimile image of the Title Page to the Artaria Edition see the Beethoven House Website: Beethoven House Bonn, Digital Archives, Library Document HCB C Op. 2.

^{xvii} For an impression of the famous publishing house of Artaria & Co., as it appeared in the late eighteenth century, see: Leon Plantinga, 1999, Plate 3.

PIANO SONATA
IN F MINOR,
OP. 2, NO. 1

'The *Sturm und Drang* manner of Op. 1, No. 3
[Piano Trio in C] is continued and refined in the
great F minor Sonata with which the set [of the
Piano Sonatas Op. 2] opens.'

H. C. Robbins Landon, *Haydn in England, 1791–1795*,
1976, p. 67.

Edwin Fischer is one of an earlier generation of perform-
er-musicologists who refer to the Piano Sonata Op. 2,
No. 1 as the 'little *Appassionata*' on the grounds that it shares
the same key of F minor – the only two of Beethoven's
piano sonatas in this key. He adds how 'the last movements,
with their uninterrupted figuration and excitement, resemble
each other'. It has even been suggested that the sharing of
themes, the use of musical structures and the tempestuous

rhythmical driving in the two sonatas are 'the same idea in different guises'. The sonata has been described as 'homage to Mozart, transported into a new and more violent affective world' and whose moods and feelings are 'psychologically developed as a subjective whole'. Denis Matthews describes the work as 'a terse drama played out in epigrams'. Beethoven embraces the four-movement design used only twice before by Haydn in his early works.

The opening theme of the first movement has similarities with the opening of the first movement of Mozart's celebrated Symphony No. 40 in G minor but the parallel is coincidental and their sound-worlds are completely different. Beethoven's theme is, in effect, a form of the so-called *Mannheim rocket* — an arpeggiated rising figure. To recall Mozart one more, he had used a leaping figure in his earlier Symphony No. 25, also in the key of G minor. For his melodic inspiration Beethoven returned to the third of his piano quartets written in Bonn when he was fifteen. Romain Rolland regarded this movement as being 'pure Haydn music' with 'only the glimmer of the future Beethoven [coming] in with that lovely little tune in the Coda'. Twenty years later he added: 'While he is still employing the accepted words and phrases, his rough, brusque, biting accent imposes his own signature on the borrowed modes of speech.' The music has been described as 'entirely characteristic of Beethoven in its driven quality and succinct expression'.

Sketches for the first movement of the Piano Sonata Op. 2, No. 1 survive in a manuscript now held in the Glinka Museum in Moscow. It consists of a single oblong sheet with the name 'Beethoven' pencilled in the upper corner of the recto page. In the words of Boris Schwarz, who has studied the manuscript: 'The Moscow sketch shows the movement at [an] advanced stage, revealing the creative process with unusual clarity.' The notation includes ideas for the movement's exposition, development and recapitulation, executed in careful manuscript notation that is quite uncharacteristic of the composer's later sketches. Schwarz assigns the manuscript to the year 1793.[xiii] Carl Czerny – who received instruction from Beethoven and knew his piano sonatas well – found the character of the first movement to be 'fervent and impassioned, energetic and varied'.[xiv] By the seventh bar we find Beethoven using the dynamic expression mark *ff*. It is almost as though he were issuing a challenge to Haydn, who, in all his sixty-two piano sonatas only ever used this designation twice.[xv] Robbins Landon detects the same atmosphere of 'intellectual density' here that he considers pervades the composer's previously mentioned Piano Trio in C, Op. 1, No. 3. He believes Haydn would have been impressed by the technical level of the piano part: '[The] semiquaver octaves in triplets in Op. 2, No. 1 set a new standard in piano technique, and there are other passages equally startling to the amateur.'[xvi] Alfred Brendel likens the work to a 'skeleton', but one of huge interest because 'it demonstrates how the motivic concentration is organized'. Everything, he argues, 'derives from the first theme' and is subjected to what he describes as 'the technique of foreshortening'.[xvii] By this means, Beethoven builds up the 'driving force' of the music by progressively shortening the musical structures and phrases into ever-smaller units thereby 'to create long spans of tension'.[xviii] [xix]

The second movement of Op. 2, No. 1 uses material, re-worked and enhanced, from the adagio of the youthful Piano Quartet No. 3 in C major WoO 36 (1785). Its prevailing mood has been likened subjectively to a child's prayer that 'comforts if it does not find a hearing' and where there can be found 'perfect peace' and 'clear sunshine'.[xx] Rolland remarks on the music as being 'pure reverie' and

of 'an enchanted world that lies before us'.ˣˣⁱ Many writers
have been moved to use such words and imagery to express
the varied emotions awakened by Beethoven's slow movements. They have been likened to tone poems that 'stand
on a pinnacle by themselves, unsurpassed and unap-
proached by any other works of their kind'.ˣˣⁱⁱ The inner-
workings of this magic are analysed by, amongst others,
Alfred Brendelˣˣⁱⁱⁱ and Donald Tovey.ˣˣⁱᵛ In the third movement Beethoven is content to exploit the conventional
minuet form but nonetheless provides music that exploits
syncopations, dramatic pauses and his trademark sharp
dynamic contrasts. To quote Rolland once more, he cites
influences of Mozart 'but the sensibility is simpler, less
ornate, nearer to nature; the spirit of the young composer
lacks some of the nuances of the [mature] Mozart'.ˣˣᵛ

The *Prestissimo* finale 'is a work of youthful violence
with its many indications of fortissimo and its brilliant
arpeggios'.ˣˣᵛⁱ It contains the first of Beethoven's 'stormy
finales'.ˣˣᵛⁱⁱ The energy of this movement, and the transition
from the second to the third part of it, 'exhibit the true
Beethoven'.ˣˣᵛⁱⁱⁱ He may, however, have been confined by the
upper limits of the available keyboards of the day, 'rewriting
the transpositions of parallel passages so as to keep within
the prescribed limits'. Later in his career he would be
'liberated from those limits' and be able to explore the very
high sounds familiar to us in the music of composers of his
younger generation like Schubert and Weber.ˣˣⁱˣ In his
analysis of this sonata, Egerton Lowe reminds the reader
how Beethoven told his friend Charles Neate that he never
wrote anything without having a picture in mind. For Lowe,
this picture 'begins with the first note of the sonata, and is
not finished until the last note is heard'.ˣˣˣⁱ

[i] Edwin Fischer, 1959, p. 19.

[ii] Stewart Gordon, 1996, p. 147.

[iii] Charles Rosen, 2002, p. 123.

[iv] Ernst von Elterlein, 1898, p. 37.

[v] Denis Matthews, 1972, p. 166.

[vi] Philip Radcliffe, *Piano music* in: *The age of Beethoven, The new Oxford history of music*, Vol. VIII, Gerald Abraham, editor, 1988, pp. 335–8.

[vii] Harold Truscott, *The piano music* [of Beethoven] in: Denis Arnold, editor, 1973, p. 76.

[viii] Discussed by David Dubal in conversation with Alfred Brendel in: David Dubal, 1985, pp. 99–100.

[ix] Discussed by Denis Matthews in the context of C.P.E. Bach in: Denis Matthews, 1967, p. 13.

[x] Romain Rolland, 1917, p. 133.

[xi] Romain Rolland, 1937, p. 121.

[xii] Martin Geck, 2003, p. 69.

[xiii] Boris Schwarz, *A Little-known Beethoven sketch in Moscow* in: Paul Henry, New York, W. W. Norton 1971, pp. 39–40. Schwarz's article includes a facsimile reproduction of the manuscript sketches in question at p. 41, Plate 1. These indicate the care taken by the composer to record his thoughts in a controlled and legible manner.

[xiv] Carl Czerny in: Paul Badura-Skoda, editor, 1970, p. 23.

[xv] As cited by Derek Melville, *Beethoven's pianos* in: Denis Arnold and Nigel Fortune, editors, 1973, pp. 41–68. Melville reminds us that Beethoven never used *fff* in his piano markings. He used *pp* and *ppp* in his last sonatas.

[xvi] H. C. Robbins Landon, 1976, p. 67 as quoted by Tia de Nora, 1976, p. 129.

[xvii] Alfred Brendel, 2002, pp. 110–11.

[xviii] Alfred Brendel, 2001, pp. 46–7 and p. 69.

[xix] Alfred Brendel's views concerning 'foreshortening' and melodic 'fragmentation' are discussed by William Kinderman in: *The path to mastery, Beethoven*, 1997, p. 31 and *The piano sonatas* in: *The Cambridge companion to Beethoven*, Glenn Stanley, editor, 2000, p. 112.

[xx] Ernst von Elterlein, 1898, p. 38.

[xxi] Romain Rolland, 1937, p. 124.

[xxii] Egerton Lowe, 1929, p. 3.

[xxiii] Alfred Brendel, 2001, pp. 58–65.

[xxiv] Harold Craxton and Donald Francis Tovey, *Beethoven: sonatas for pianoforte*. London: The Associated Board, [1931], *Piano Sonata No. 1*, 1931.

[xxv] Romain Rolland, 1937, p. 124.

[xxvi] Charles Rosen, 2002, p. 124. Rosen also draws attention to Beethoven's insistent use of the minor mode as a pre-figuration of the sonatas of Chopin, Schumann and Liszt.

[xxvii] Maynard Solomon, 1977, p. 102.

[xxviii] Ernst von Elterlein, 1898, p. 40.

[xxix] Leon Plantinga, 1999, p. 293.

[xxx] C. Egerton Lowe, 1929, p. 6. A performance of the Piano Sonata in F minor, Op. 2, No. 1, has been recorded by David Leigh on a fortepiano of 1786 by the London maker Robert Stodart. Source, LME label 2313.

PIANO SONATA
IN A MAJOR,
OP. 2, NO.2

'The second sonata is flawless in execution and
entirely beyond the range of Haydn and Mozart
in harmonic language, except in the Finale.'

Donald Francis Tovey, *Ludwig van Beethoven* in: *The
Classics of Music*, Michael Tilmouth, editor, 2001, pp.
317–22.

T he Piano Sonata Op. 2, No. 2 has a more extended
time-scale than that of Op. 2, No.1 being about a third
longer. With this sonata, Romain Rolland considered
Beethoven had made distinct advances in both 'form and
design of construction'. It is also conceived more independently from that of its contemporaries but still owes something
to them such as, for example, Clementi's Piano Sonata Op.
10, No. 3, published in 1783. Carl Czerny described
Beethoven's composition as being 'spirited and vivacious,

energetic and resolute'.[iii] Edwin Fischer found in Piano Sonata No. 2 'the air of a bright spring day' combined with 'exuberance and cheerfulness' showing Beethoven 'was capable of happiness as well as sorrow'. He also has interesting things to say about repeats in Beethoven's piano sonatas. He argues these derive from dance suites — where repeats were played several times over to suit the dancers. In the early sonatas he suggests they may occasionally be omitted unless they fulfil an emotional need and are psychologically necessary. Concerning interpretation, Fischer's own teacher took the view — with a hint of levity — 'If it went all right [first time] ... thank God, and go on'![iv]

The time-scale in this work is 'luxurious' — it compares with Beethoven's longer sonatas — and its harmonic progress is consequently 'leisurely'. Humour is present, sometimes 'playful' and occasionally 'ferocious' being interwoven with 'challenging outbursts of virtuosity'.[v] Beethoven's humour is also 'subversive'. Wilfrid Mellers cites Beethoven's 'extreme modulations' that he considers to be 'startling if not anarchic'; he draws a parallel between Beethoven's pianism and his 'flouting of social etiquette'.[vi]

In 1798, Beethoven performed the *Adagio* and *Rondo* from his Op. 2 Piano Sonata at a concert in which he also played his new Piano Concerto in C major. The pianist-composer Johann Tomaschek was present and later recalled how Beethoven's playing stirred him strangely 'to the depths of his soul' to such an extent that he left off from playing the piano for several days.[vii] Whilst Tomaschek admired Beethoven's 'powerful and brilliant playing' he found fault though in his 'daring leaps' adding: 'Not infrequently the unsuspecting listener is jolted violently out of his state of joyful transports.'[viii] [ix] Regarding performance, and contemporary attitudes towards authenticity, we should bear in mind the three sonatas that comprise Beethoven's Op. 2, were composed at a time when the harpsichord was by no means an antiquarian curiosity. In his essay on Beethoven's sonatas — written on the occasion of the composer's death-centenary — the music critic and scholar John Fuller-Maitland commented: 'Almost the whole of the three can be transferred to the harpsichord without loss of effect, the second, in A, actually gains something of brilliance from the sparkling quality of the plucked strings.'[i]

The opening of the A major Sonata was considered by Donald Tovey to be one of the most powerful passages in Beethoven's early works. He remarks on its series of 'startling modulations' and 'Beethovenish energy' and invites the listener to become acquainted with Haydn's String Quartet in A major Op. 20, No. 6 where, 'he will find in much the same part of the movement a delightful discursive passage'.[ii] Beethoven's recourse to 'sharp accents' and 'broad extensions of chords by means of octaves' are typical of his more adventurous piano writing and, as Oskar Bie comments, 'remained to the end a characteristic of the author'.[iii] Beethoven's modulations must have astonished his contemporaries in part through their inherent newness but, primarily, 'in the speed and intensity with which they move'.[iv] Anton Schindler, Beethoven's amanuensis during his later years, relates how Beethoven was interested in the writings of the contemporary mystical poet and musician Christian Schubart. He characterised the musical keys with feelings and ascribed to them a certain 'psyche.'[v] This serves to remind us how carefully Beethoven thought about 'key coloration' as a factor in musical expression. The musicologist Leon Plantinga remarks similarly on the capacity of 'exotic keys' and 'remote modulations' to evoke 'surprise and wonder'. He cites the first movement of the Sonata Op. 2, No. 2 as an early example in nineteenth-century music of the capacity of Beethoven's pianism to achieve such 'shock value'.[vi]

The nineteenth-century musicologist Ernst von Elterlein regarded the whole first movement of the Piano Sonata Op. 2, No. 2 as being 'cast in one mould' and to be 'full of fresh and uniformly harmonious expression of feeling'. He considered the original genius of Beethoven to appear in this movement with the first dawnings of Beethoven's later humour.[xvii] Barry Cooper comments on the movement's opening sustained chords with their 'pizzicato-like bass [that] would have been possible only on the relatively new fortepianos of the time'.[xviii] Concerning restraint in the use of repeats, alluded to previously, Tovey is quite clear here: 'In public performance this highly dramatic movement is more impressive without repeats at all.'[xix] Charles Rosen, discussing the challenges of playing the broken octave arpeggios that occur in bars 84—90, suggests the performer appearing to 'having to struggle even slightly with the passage gives it psychologically greater force with the public'.[xx]

The opening of the slow movement uses material from the youthful Piano Quartet No. 3 (WoO 36).[xxi] It is marked *Largo Appassionata* that is unusual in Beethoven's sonatas. The deeply expressive scoring here makes use of four voices and their pizzicato-like moving bass has been found 'suggestive of string-quartet writing'[xxii] and to be possessed with 'orchestral colouring'.[xxiii] Czerny discerned a religious character in the movement and urged the adoption of a strict *legato* in the chords to achieve 'a choral-like swelling of the harmony'.[xxiv] William Kinderman also refers to the choral-like main theme having 'a noble, hymn-like character'.[xxv] In his autobiography, Vaughan Williams remarks how he studied the slow movement of Beethoven's Piano Sonata Op. 2, No. 2 to further his own compositional development. He comments: 'It has so many points of subtle structure and development which only a close bar-by-bar analysis reveals.'[xxvi] Like Tovey before him, he commended this method of study to his own pupils.[xvii]

The third movement is playful in character and is marked *scherzo*. This is Beethoven's earliest use of this term in a piano sonata. He was not, however, the first to use the expression. It has been traced, for example, in the work of Haydn, notably, the String Quartets Op. 33 of 1782.[xviii] Beethoven used the designation *scherzo* sparingly in his keyboard writing but it would be prophetic of his use of the scherzo-form in many of his later orchestral works. This was apparently one of Beethoven's favourite movements and some have found in it traces of Russian and Slavonic melodies.[xix]

The final *Rondo Grazioso* 'has grace that owes much to Mozart'.[xx] This observation calls to mind Brendel's remark: 'Because Beethoven is deemed *heroic* and *mankind embracing* it is easy to forget that he could, in a very personal way, be graceful and even elegant.'[xxi] Fischer reminds the performer that the lightness and grace required here should be evoked by the player's attitude. He remarks how 'we listen with our eyes as well as our ears, and the artist must not convey the slightest hint of difficulty or exertion'.[xxii] This requires, not least, accuracy and clarity in scale-playing as discussed by Egerton Lowe who learned this from the titan of the keyboard, and respected pedagogue, Theodor Leschetitzky — himself a pupil of Czerny.[xxiii] The closing *grazioso* movement of the A major Piano Sonata has been described as 'the first great rondo finale in Beethoven's sonatas' and a worthy precursor of the graceful movements that bring Beethoven's Piano Sonatas Opp. 7, 22 and 90 to a close.[xxiv] As we have seen, from our opening quotation, Donald Francis Tovey esteemed Beethoven's Piano Sonata Op. 2, No. 2 highly and concluded: 'If the later work of Beethoven were unknown there would be very little evidence this sonata was by a young man.'[xxv]

[i] Romain Rolland, 1917, p. 135.

[ii] Harold Truscott, *The piano music* in: Denis Arnold and Nigel Fortune, editors, 1973, p. 76.

[iii] From the recollections of Carl Czerny, see: Paul Badura-Skoda, editor, 1970, p. 24.

[iv] Edwin Fischer, 1959, pp. 22 –3.

[v] Denis Matthews, 1972, p. 171.

[vi] Wilfrid Mellers, 1957, pp. 56–7.

[vii] Thayer-Forbes, 1967, p. 207.

[viii] H. C. Robbins Landon, 1992, p. 81.

[ix] Tomaschek's impressions of Beethoven improvising are also recounted in O. G. Sonneck, 1927, p. 22. He considered Beethoven's 'frequent daring deviations from one motive to another' disturbed the music's 'organic connection' and 'sprang from a too exuberant conception'.

[x] John A. Fuller-Maitland, *Notes to the Beethoven sonatas* contributed to the *Special Issue* of the *Musical Times*, Vol. VIII, No. 2, 1927, pp. 218–23. This edition was published in book form.

[xi] George Dyson takes a somewhat contrary view stating: 'The sonatas of Beethoven have a personal and detailed eloquence quite outside the view of the harpsichord.' George Dyson, 1932, p. 84.

[xii] Donald Tovey, *Beethoven*, 1944, pp. 41–2 and p. 88. See also Tovey's article *Ludwig van Beethoven* in: *The classics of music*, Michael Tilmouth, editor, 2001, p. 335.

[xiii] Oskar Bie, 1966, p. 169.

[xiv] Philip Radcliffe, *Piano music* in: *The age of Beethoven, The new Oxford history of music*, Gerald Abraham, editor, 1988, Vol. VIII, pp. 338–9.

[xv] Anton Schindler, 1860, English edition: Donald MacArdle, 1966, pp. 366–7.

[xvi] *Instruments, temperaments, and tempos* in: Leon Plantinga, 1999, p. 297.

[xvii] Ernst von Elterlein, 1898, p. 41.

[xviii] Barry Cooper, 1991, p. 240.

[xix] Donald Tovey, *Piano Sonata No. 2*, 1931.

[xx] Charles Rosen, 2002, p. 125.

[xxi] Barry Cooper, 1991, p. 244.

[xxii] Stewart Gordon, 1996, p. 150.

[xxiii] Philip Radcliffe, *Piano music* in: *The age of Beethoven, The new Oxford history of music*, Gerald Abraham, editor, 1988, Vol. VIII, pp. 338–9.

[xxiv] From the recollections of Carl Czerny see: Paul Badura-Skoda, editor, 1970, p. 25.

[xxv] William Kinderman, *The Piano Sonatas* in: Glenn Stanley, editor, 2000, p. 114.

[xxvi] Vaughan Williams, 1953, p. 155.

[xxvii] Gustav Holtz also held Beethoven's piano sonatas in high regard. In his correspondence with Vaughan Williams he admits to not knowing enough about Beethoven's sonatas and suggests to 'VW' the possible benefit of 'analysing a Beethoven sonata then writing one in the same form'. See Ralph Vaughan Williams, 1959, p. 17 and p. 23.

[xxviii] Stewart Gordon, 1996, p. 151.

[xxix] Ernst von Elterlein, 1898, p. 42.

[xxx] Romain Rolland, 1917, p. 136.

xxi Alfred Brendel, 2002, p. 112.

xxii Edwin Fischer, 1959, p. 22–3.

xxiii C. Egerton Lowe, 1929, p. 13.

xxiv William Kinderman, *The piano sonatas* in: Glenn Stanley, editor, 2000, p.114.
See also: Liner Notes to *Beethoven: The complete sonatas,* Philips, 1996.

xxv Donald Francis Tovey, *Ludwig van Beethoven* in: *The classics of music,*
Michael Tilmouth, editor, 2001, pp. 317–22. A performance of the Piano
Sonata in A major, Op. 2, No. 2 has been recorded by Jörg Demus on a
fortepiano of 1808 by the London maker William Stodart. Source:
Harmonia Mundi HMS 30 673.

PIANO SONATA
IN C MAJOR,
OP. 2, NO. 3

'The brilliant C major Sonata Op. 2, No. 3, is
studded by cadenzas in the outer movements,
including a triple trill in the finale — features more
associated with the display genre of the concerto.'

William Kinderman, *Springboard to Later Achievements*,
Liner notes accompanying *Beethoven, The Complete
Sonatas*, Alfred Brendel, 1996, Phillips 446 909-2, p. 45

The last of Beethoven's Op. 2 piano sonatas is considered to be the finest and most technically challenging
for the performer with its 'flights of arpeggios and sixths and
its C major brilliance'. The key of C held a special appeal
for Beethoven and it is interesting to note that his only fully
written-out fugue for the keyboard is in this key. It was

probably a counterpoint apprentice-piece created for his teacher Johann Albrechtsberger. The piano writing in this sonata is 'overtly brilliant' and 'stakes a claim to the grand public style' in a manner 'intended to impress listener and performer'. In this work 'the young Beethoven [takes] delight in his own unusual pianistic skill'. Beethoven's pupil Carl Czerny, a pianist of remarkable technical accomplishments, considered the Op. 2, No 3 Piano Sonata to contain 'much that claims the most brilliant playing and bravura from the pianist'. Eugene d'Albert thought Beethoven's accomplished piano writing elevated the sonata to that of 'a virtuoso piece'. Not surprisingly, the C major Sonata 'is beloved of virtuoso pianists for its outward glitter'. For these reasons it can suffer at their hands, the temptation being to dash off its arpeggios and broken octaves with an effect 'like the rattling of the dishes at a royal banquet'! Beethoven was already a 'full musical personality' by the time he composed his Op. 2 Piano Sonatas and Alfred Brendel reminds us how Beethoven's music in this work is 'symphonic' in scope and 'rather new'. Brendel considers Beethoven pushes the orchestral boundaries even further than had Haydn in his last Piano Sonata in E flat. He concludes: 'With all its pianistic brilliance, this is a very orchestral piece ... It is full of marvellous musical ideas, full of freshness and confidence!'.

The thematic material of the first movement, with its four-part texture, is a further reworking of the composer's youthful Piano Quartet No. 3 (WoO 36) composed in Bonn when he was fifteen. The composer's youthfulness is, however, soon set aside. Donald Tovey considered Beethoven's piano writing here embodies one of his most 'epoch-making discoveries', namely, 'the art of organizing a long series of apparently free modulations by means of a systematic progression in the bass'. The movement's 'florid cadenzas' have features in common with Clementi's Piano Sonata Op. 36, and the *sforzandi*, 'so characteristic of Beethoven' make an appearance. Also noteworthy here are the number and variety of the movement's sections. For one pianist-teacher, these invoke courtly images of a past romantic era. The first subject is heroic in character. The passage following is stormy, perhaps evocative of a voyage to a distant court. The second subject is plaintive, calling to mind a princess watching alone from her tower. She shows delight at her hero's safe arrival but is soon left alone with her thoughts. In the final exposition these are expressed in joyous pleasure. Another commentator finds in the movement 'youthful freshness and vigour' suggestive of 'a bright active life'. Romain Rolland, alluding to French decorative imagery, characterises the first movement as being something akin to 'an Empire style, square of trunk and shoulders, of a pompous strength, now and then a little tedious, but noble, sound, virile, scorning the insipid and the trifling'.

The movement is extended in scope. It 'abounds in the turns and trills characteristic of the time' and should be taken at a tempo 'fast enough to give the utmost brilliance to the semiquaver passages' and 'must be performed with fire and energy'. Beethoven discards the strict sonata form for a structure more akin to a free-form fantasia. A low E is required in the left-hand octaves at the end of the *Codetta* that was outside the compass (F–F) of the five-octave pianoforte available to Beethoven at the period of the sonata's composition. By the 1820s, the keyboard was sufficiently extended to make the low E possible. In the piano sonatas to Opus 31, Beethoven appears to have confined his ambitions to five octaves notwithstanding that instruments, from as early as 1803, were being built having a compass of six octaves. In later life Beethoven contemplated publishing a complete edition of his works that would incorporate revisions of his early compositions. He did not, however, live to see his wishes fulfilled.

The first movement terminates with an arpeggio-filled cadenza prompting Tovey to remind the performer that 'cadenzas, of all forms of music, ought to sound as if they were extemporised'.[xxi] Beethoven deploys such an abundance of motives — 'intoxicating runs', 'brilliant octave passages', 'striking discords' and 'high-spirited trills' — we can almost imagine him improvising. 'Beethoven exhausts the resources of virtuosity.'[xxii]

The second movement opens with one of Beethoven's dignified slow themes. It is pervasive and 'a sense of inward happiness breathes through its tones'.[xxiii] Perhaps there is a suggestion even of 'religious solemnity'[xxiv] with a 'dream-like veil' cast over the music's 'delicate lyricism'.[xxv] In this Adagio, Czerny considered Beethoven displayed the romantic direction by which he later created 'a species of composition which carried instrumental music to such a pitch of refinement that it resembled even poetry and painting'. In such works he adds 'we no longer hear the mere expression of feeling, we see fine pictures — we *hear* the narration of circumstances'.[xxvi] Denis Matthews is in no doubt the mood prevailing here is indeed 'romantic'.[xxvii] For Rolland, it is 'pure reverie' and 'the first flowering of the young man's tenderness'.[xxviii]

For some interpreters of this work, pictures and imagery abound in the third movement. 'What frolicsome joy ... children playing in the meadows ... dancing, playing hide and seek [and] running hither and thither'.[xxix] The scherzo is 'one of Beethoven's gems of comic music' having a 'jocular character'. Its trails of staccato notes are 'almost evocative of laughter'.[xxx] For good measure Beethoven teases both the performer and listener with opposing moods; in the major, 'light, humorous music' is pitted against 'mock bluster' in the minor.[xxi] Perhaps the writing here is also 'autobiograph-ical' insofar as it may provide clues as to how Beethoven's pianism distinguished him from his rivals. Czerny, for example, comments on his teacher's 'unique facility in negotiating quick leaps without disturbing the flow of the music or its beat'.[xxii]

The *Allegro assai* finale is a showcase for virtuosity. It is full of sparkling life, 'a little Bacchanalia, the product of bold, youthful petulance, an episode in a period of *Sturm und Drang*'.[xxiii] It requires a dazzling technique with rapid parallel chords — sixths that expand into octaves — upward runs and trills and strings of staccato chords.[xxiv] Beethoven unites 'improvisation' with 'hard thinking' in a display of temperament 'of so explosive a kind that it sets the soul in an uproar'.[xxv] Additionally, it manifests the influence of the concerto form with which Beethoven was also concerned at this time.[xxvi] The finale is thoroughly Beethovenish with a coda 'full of pauses, key-surprises, and false starts'.[xxvii] In the closing cadenza it is evident that Beethoven was intent 'to show off his performance style to the greatest advantage'.[xxviii]

Bernard Shaw reviewed a performance of the C major Piano Sonata at a London concert in 1877. He remarked: 'It is a relief to hear some of the earliest works of the master in these days, when players so seldom condescend to go behind Op. 10 or Op. 13.'[xxix] Sergei Prokofiev was asked to orchestrate a Beethoven piano sonata for string quartet when he was studying composition under Rimsky-Korsakov at the St. Petersburg Conservatory — he was fifteen at the time. He initially chose the Piano Sonata in C major but abandoned the attempt in favour of orchestrating some of Schubert's four-hand marches.[xl] When Claudio Arrau was questioned about his early acquaintance with Beethoven, whilst still only a child, he replied: 'I felt completely at ease in his music from the very beginning and I knew that Beethoven would be a major force in my musical world.' The first sonata he studied was Beethoven's Op. 2, No. 3.[ii] Tovey held Beethoven's Piano Sonata in C Major in high regard. He considered if Beethoven's early works had been mostly in the style of Opus 2, No. 3, and had he died before producing anything more characteristic, then: '[It] would have been possible to argue that here was an ambitious composer who evidently aspired to be greater than either Mozart or Haydn.'[iii]

[i] Denis Matthews, 1972, p. 171.

[ii] John Cockshoot, 1959, pp. 28–37. The manuscript of the fugue in C is in the British Museum (British Library).

[iii] Stewart Gordon, 1996, p. 152 and Marion Scott, 1940, p. 134.

[iv] Charles Rosen, 2002, p. 128.

[v] Edwin Fischer, 1959, p. 25.

[vi] From the recollections of Carl Czerny, see: Paul Badura-Skoda, editor, 1970, p. 26.

[vii] Romain Rolland, 1917, p. 136.

[viii] Dennis Matthews, 1967, p. 15.

[ix] Alfred Brendel in conversation with David Dubal, 1985, p. 100. For an extended analysis of the construction of Beethoven's Piano Sonata in C major, see: Carl Dahlhaus, 1991, pp. 159–64.

[x] See, in particular, bars 25–45, as discussed by Donald Tovey, 1944, p. 34. The youthful origins of this sonata are also considered by William Kinderman, *The piano sonatas* in: *The Cambridge companion to Beethoven,* Glenn Stanley, editor, 2000, p. 114.

[xi] Donald Tovey *Ludwig van Beethoven* in: *The classics of music,* Michael Tilmouth, editor, 2001, pp. 317–22.

[xii] Philip Radcliffe, *Piano music* in: *The age of Beethoven, The new Oxford history of music, Vol. VIII,* Gerald Abraham, editor, 1988, pp. 338–9.

[xiii] C. Egerton Lowe, 1929, p. 14.

[xiv] Ernst von Elterlein, 1898, pp. 43–4.

[xv] Romain Rolland, 1937, p. 121.

[xvi] Romain Rolland, 1917, p. 137.

[xvii] Harold Craxton and Donald Francis Tovey, *Beethoven: sonatas for pianoforte.* London: The Associated Board, [1931], *Piano Sonata, No. 3.*

[xviii] From the recollections of Carl Czerny, see: Paul Badura-Skoda, editor, 1970, p. 26.

[xix] Ernst von Elterlein, 1898, p. 44.

[xx] Donald MacArdle, 1966, p. 110 and p. 193.

[xxi] Donald Tovey, 1931, *Piano Sonata No. 3.*

[xxii] Paul Bekker, 1925, p. 96.

[xxiii] Ernst von Elterlein, 1898, p. 44.

[xxiv] Paul Bekker, 1925, p. 97.

[xxv] William Kinderman, *The piano sonatas* in: *The Cambridge companion to*

    Beethoven, Glenn Stanley, editor, 2000, p. 114

xxvi From the recollections of Carl Czerny, see: Paul Badura-Skoda, editor, 1970, p. 27.

xxvii Denis Matthews, 1972, p.171.

xxviii Romain Rolland, 1937, p. 140. In the Op. 2, No. 3 Piano Sonata, Rolland is not, however, prepared to confer upon Beethoven his full status. He describes his compositional procedures as being more suggestive of the carpenter than the architect. But, he adds: '[We] soon see him take up the pencil in his turn and make draughts of his own ... enlarging the forms with a joyous ease, as in the Sonata in E flat major, Op. 7.'

xxix C. Egerton Lowe, 1929, p. 18.

xxx William Kinderman, 1996, Liner Notes to *Beethoven: The complete sonatas,* Philips 446 909 2. See also: William Kinderman, *The piano sonatas* in: *The Cambridge companion to Beethoven,* Glenn Stanley, editor, 2000, p. 115.

xxxi William Kinderman, 1997, p. 214.

xxxii Cited in: Konrad Wolff, 1990, p. 157.

xxxiii Ernst von Elterlein, 1898, pp. 45–6.

xxxiv William Kinderman, *The piano sonatas* in: Glenn Stanley, editor, 2000, p. 115 and Marion Scott, 1940, p. 134.

xxxv Paul Becker, 1925, p. 97.

xxxvi Barry Cooper, 1991, p. 240.

xxxvii Dennis Matthews, 1985, p. 16,

xxxviii Charles Rosen, 2002, p. 130.

xxxix Bernard Shaw in: Dan Laurence, editor, *Shaw's music: the complete musical criticism in three volumes,* 1981, Vol. 1, p. 87.

xl Sergey Prokofiev, 1979, p. 104.

xli Claudio Arrau in conversation with David Dubal, 1985, p. 25.

xlii Donald Tovey, 1944, p. 89.A performance of the Op. 2, No. 3 Piano Sonata in C major has been recorded by Malcolm Binns on a fortepiano from the period 1770–5 by the German maker Mattäus Hellmann. Source: L'Oiseau-Lyre D 182 D3.

PIANO SONATA
IN E-FLAT MAJOR,
OP. 7

'This sonata is considered by the reviewer to be
amongst the most splendid by this original composer. It forms a great and noble totality. A heroic
fire constitutes the dominant feature of its character and is also demanded of the performer.'

Zeitung für die elegante Welt, 14 June 1806.

With the publication of the Piano Sonata Op. 7,
Beethoven expanded the form to yet new and greater
dimensions. It is longer than the *Appassionata* Sonata and
would not be exceeded in scale until the creation of the
Hammerklavier Sonata more than twenty years later. Op.
7 exemplifies Beethoven's quest to extend the formal
boundaries of compositions in this medium. This quest was

a life-long pre-occupation as Donald Tovey observes in the concluding remarks to his essay on the E-flat Sonata: 'Throughout his life, Beethoven was dealing with forms that had just become capable of vast new developments.'[iv] It seems curious today that a composition of such originality should have once fallen into neglect. This appears to have been the case since the contributor to the death-centenary issue of *The London Musical Times* felt disposed to write: 'It has always puzzled me why the flowing Sonata in E-flat, Op. 7, like Op. 22 in B flat, is so very seldom to be heard in public. Both are examples of the old form in its perfection and represent so well the ground plan of the design afterwards altered by Beethoven and others.'[v] [vi]

The sonata was probably completed in early 1797.[vii] The only reliable evidence for the date of composition is an announcement of its publication by the publishing house Ataria in the *Wiener Zeitung* (Vienna Journal) of 7 October 1797.[viii] The Title Page of the sonata proclaims the following, styled in the French language as was a typical procedure of the period: *Grande Sonate pour le Clavecin ou Piano Forte, composée et dédiée à Mademoiselle la Comtesse Babette de Keglevics, par Louis van Beethoven, Oeuvre 7. Vienne chez Artaria et Co.*[ix]

There are a number of points of interest here. Beethoven himself appears to have been aware of the significance of the scale of his new creation by sanctioning the use of the expression *Grande Sonate* on the Title Page and by assigning the work a single opus number, instead of including it within a collective opus number, which, as we have seen, he allocated to his first three sonatas.[x] Moreover, the engraving to the first edition utilises capital letters in a bold font.[xi] Of no-less interest is the dedicatee Babette de Keglevics. She was one of the most distinguished amateur pianists of her day. In fact she must have been formidably gifted since she was just seventeen when Beethoven dedicated his new sonata to her. She died aged just thirty three but not before Beethoven had bestowed upon her the further dedications to his Ten Variations in B flat, on the duet *La stessa, la stessissima,* from Salieri's Opera *Falstaff* (WoO 73, 1799), The First Piano Concerto (1801) and the celebrated Six Variations Op. 34 (1803). In 1801 Babette, whose full name was Anna Luisa Barbara Keglevics [Keglevich] von Buzin, married Prince Odescalchi. He was an imperial chamberlain at one of whose musical soirées Beethoven's popular Septet Op. 20 was performed. Count von Keglevics, Babette's nephew, has left a charming anecdote. At the time he was writing his new sonata, Beethoven lived near to his youthful pupil's Vienna apartments — the precise details of Beethoven's residence are not known. It was apparently her master's habit to give her lessons attired in his morning gown, complete with slippers and a tasselled night-cap! This may, however, be an exaggerated family story. Of related interest is a reminiscence of Carl Czerny — who himself started to have lessons with Beethoven a few years after Babette. Czerny records Beethoven had considerable affection for Babette and may possibly have been in love with her. Czerny even suggests that the sobriquet *Appassionata* should have been conferred on the Piano Sonata Op. 7 and not upon the celebrated Piano Sonata Op. 57. Whatever the circumstances, he informs us how Beethoven's Op. 7 was composed 'in a very impassioned mood'.

Beethoven was certainly susceptible to women, of all stations in life, as they frequently were to him. Such was the extent of his emotional attachment that, in Beethoven's day, the Piano Sonata Op. 7 was nicknamed *Die Verliebte* which has been variously translated as *The Enamoured, The Maiden in Love* and *The Lovelorn Maiden*. At least one modern-day commentator has found musical corroboration for the nickname of the sonata in its 'energy and grace', its 'moonlight-like triplets' and its 'caressing themes' — 'soft as the arms of the loved one'![vii]

Beethoven's growing standing in Viennese society may be briefly mentioned here. On 10 February 1797, the *Society for the Protection of Widows and Orphans of Musicians* placed Beethoven on its mailing list to receive free tickets for all its forthcoming concerts — an honour that had been similarly bestowed upon Joseph Haydn. This was in recognition of Beethoven's previous service to the Society. He had appeared at its Easter concerts on 29 and 30 March 1795 playing his Piano Concerto in B flat Op. 19, on the former, and improvising at the piano at the latter.[viii] We have previously remarked (see Op. 2, Nos. 1–3) that Beethoven had given recitals on his extended concert tour, taking in Prague, Dresden and Leipzig; he was now 'winning his spurs' at home.[ix] His piano sonatas were becoming known, notwithstanding that they were found to be technically demanding. It is worthy of recalling once more that when the piano-maker, and friend of Beethoven, Andreas Streicher gave one of his own piano-pupils one of the Piano Sonatas Op. 2 to study, he felt obliged to comment: 'These are new pieces which the ladies [do] not want to play, finding them too difficult.'[x]

The Piano Sonata Op. 7 has been described as no less than 'Beethoven's first masterpiece'.[xi] It invokes the sound-worlds of Dussek and Clementi but with 'an even greater polythematic breadth' and 'opportunities for virtuoso outbursts'.[xii] Clementi's Piano Sonatas Op. 2, No. 2 and Op. 12, No. 4 have been cited as major sources of influence.[xiii] [xiv] Notwithstanding that Beethoven may have taken inspiration from such precursors, his own work looks to the future with a 'complexity of thought ... variety and originality of ideas ...

and ingenuity of their interrelationships' that reach levels 'well-nigh unfathomable'.[xx] Beethoven's contemporaries recognised these qualities in the music. Anton Schindler, Beethoven's amanuensis, found in the Sonata Op. 7, albeit somewhat prosaically, 'a continuation of Beethoven's personal style in melody and phrase structure'.[xxi] Czerny is more fulsome, recognising the work's 'vehement style' and even suggesting it 'must be played in a similar manner'.[xxii] The Artaria edition of the sonata of 1797 has been mentioned. Two further editions appeared in 1805, one from the *Bureau de Musique* in Leipzig and the other from J. Andre in Offenbach.

There is perhaps only one cloud that cast its shadow over this radiant picture of Beethoven's newly burgeoning genius. On 29 May 1797 he had cause to write to Franz Gerhard Wegeler — his old Bonn friend who was then a physician and who later became Professor of Medicine at the University of Bonn. Beethoven informs Wegeler: '*I am well and I may say that my health is steadily improving*' (Beethoven's italics).[xxiii] This cryptic statement is considered by some to be a reference to a serious abdominal illness that may have been associated with the composer's progressive loss of hearing and, thereby, would determine no less than the future direction of his life and art.[xxix] The circumstance is doubly poignant for the following reason. At about the time Beethoven was starting work on his Piano Sonata Op. 7, his former teacher Johann Albrechtsberger had written him a birthday greeting saying: 'I wish you all the best on your *Name Day* tomorrow. God give you health and happiness.'[xx]

Turning now to the construction of the sonata, the first movement is marked *Allegro molto e con brio* and portends 'unusual outbursts of vigour and passion'.[xxi] The group of motifs that form the first subject have been described as 'rhetorical chords'. These serve to secure the attention of the listener, in the same manner that composers such as Haydn did to open their symphonies – mindful how audiences of the day took time to settle down and listen to the music.[xxii] Czerny encourages the performer to play this movement 'with fire and energy' so that it may produce 'the effect of a very brilliant piece'.[xxiii] The extensive use of repeated notes gives the music 'a momentum of its own as well as a unifying feeling'.[xxiv]

Commentators agree that Beethoven's writing in the first movement confronts the performer with considerable technical challenges including 'long skips, legato octaves, very fast broken octaves [and] scales that must be almost as rapid as a glissando'.[xxv] [xxvi] Even Tovey, not one easily intimidated by pianistic technical challenges, refers here to the movement's 'passages of outstanding difficulty'.[xxvii] Alfred Brendel considers the first movement to be 'technically one of the most demanding pieces Beethoven ever wrote' and suggests this is the reason why it is treated with caution, and a slow tempo, in the concert hall.[xxviii] Discussing the craftsmanship that Beethoven expended on this movement, Egerton Lowe urges the performer should take care to observe the composer's expression marks. In so doing, he invokes an observation of Sir George Grove: 'There is hardly a bar in his [Beethoven's] music of which it may be said with confidence that it has been rewritten a dozen times.'[xxix]

Dika Newlin recalls Arnold Schoenberg teaching composition at the University of California in the late 1930s – she was in his class. A student asked Schoenberg to comment on 'that devilish little elaboration [not specified] in the first movement [of the Sonata Op. 7]'. Newlin tells us: 'Peeking coyly from behind one of his beatific smiles, Schoenberg replied: "One should not explain this. This one must feel".'[xl] In another of Newlin's classes, Schoenberg analysed several Beethoven piano-sonata first movements. Newlin raised Beethoven's methods of 'condensed repetition' which merely prompted Schoenberg to remark — once again with more humour than musicological insight: "When you say condensed, I always think of steam!" The expression he required was of course 'reduction'.[xli]

Worthy of mention here is that Rimsky-Korsakov used to require his students to orchestrate Beethoven sonatas for chamber orchestra — often selecting the first movement of a particular work. Sergey Prokofiev, one of Rimsky's former students, recalls how such classes could last for four hours.[xlii] In the years 1902–3, Igor Stravinsky also experienced such lessons in orchestration with Rimsky-Korsakov. He was required to set passages of Beethoven sonatas and Schubert quartets, which were then criticised and corrected. Prokofiev clearly appreciated these classes that he describes as being 'unforgettable'.[xliii]

Earlier commentators have found the joy of love in the first movement of the Piano Sonata Op. 7.[xliv] Others of this generation perceive the first movement as being a 'tone-picture rich in colour and character' conveying even 'the impression of going into a garden, gorgeous with a profusion of the finest and brightest flowers'. At the same time 'this many-coloured play of sounds is full of soul ... the reverent player and hearer will easily understand everything and the rare beauties of the music will speedily reveal themselves'.[xlv]

Silence pervades the second movement. The silence here is variously measured, dramatic and eloquent prompting one 'to think forward to the *Introduzione* of the *Waldstein*'.[xlvi] The movement is marked *Largo, con gran espressione* that Charles Rosen considers combines 'the opposing and almost contradictory technique of a hymn with an operatic accompanied recitative'. He further believes the slow choral-like passages to have been a source of inspiration for the central section of Schubert's affecting Sonata in B flat major.[xlvii] Rosen's esteem of this movement is embodied in the words of others; the 'deep seriousness' that reigns throughout the movement is imbued with 'eloquent pauses'.[xlviii] [xlix] Commenting on this music, the nineteenth-century lion of the keyboard Anton Rubinstein was moved to remark: 'A musician is known by his basses. In the Sonata Op. 7, the bass of the *Largo* alone is, in my opinion, worth twice as much as (many) a whole sonata.'[l]

Discussing the tension induced by the movement's passages of slow broken rhythms, Tovey comments: 'Beethoven is evidently working at high emotional pressure.'[li] Elsewhere he invokes a dictum of Plunket Greene — in his day a renowned interpreter of Schubert *Lied* — remarking: '[The] first rule of song-singing applies throughout this wonderful and most solemn movement — *Sing through your rests.*' (Tovey's italics) Later in his essay Tovey has words of encouragement for the performer not able to stretch a tenth — as required here in certain passages: 'Swing up to the tenth as quickly as possible, you need not hurry ... habit produces confidence.' He then adds, tantalisingly: 'At least four of the greatest pianists now living cannot *strike* tenths.' Who could he have had in mind — writing as he was in the early 1930s?[lii] Lowe, who describes the slow movement as 'this wonderful tone poem', also mentions technical consid-erations. To assist the performer shape his interpretation of the music he cites remarks of Czerny — taken from his *Pianoforte School*: 'There occurs in every line [of music] some notes or passages where a small and often impercep-tible relaxation or acceleration of the movement is necessary to embellish and increase the interest; to introduce these occasional deviations is the great art of a good player.'[liii]

The serenity that permeates the *Largo* has drawn from commentators and musicians down the years much evoca-

tive word-imagery. Romain Rolland found in the *Largo* 'religious calm' ... 'rich colouring' ... 'the tones of the flutes and other woodwind instruments' and even, in parts, 'the song of birds'.[iv] Writing twenty years later, Rolland was no less moved by the music but described it in somewhat more restrained terms: '[With] its great, serious, firmly drawn melody — frank and healthy, without a touch of society, insipidity or equivocal sentiment about it; of all the Beethoven meditations this is the one that, while not concealing anything of itself, is accessible to everyone.'[v] Edwin Fischer, however, expresses doubts on this occasion as to whether poetic imagery is helpful as a means of conveying personal musical feelings to others. He cites Hans Pfitzner's remark that 'the description of a piece of music is like the painting of a dinner'! Despite his reservations, Fischer then concedes how the mood of the slow movement suggests to him 'the picture of a summer landscape with gigantic cumulus clouds from which later on raindrops fall [notably the staccato semiquavers in the left hand — bar 25]'.[vi]
[vii] To conclude these preliminary remarks we recall Ernst von Elterlein who, writing at the close of the nineteenth century, states: 'A sacred and exalted tone pervades these strains which give insight into the depths of the soul. Stronger and stronger becomes the pressure ... it is as if fate were knocking at the door ... the soul [is] reminded of the pain of living ... What a powerful and dramatic passage.'[viii]

Sketches exist for the third movement, *Allegro e Minore*, in the so-called Kafka Sketchbook. From his days in Bonn Beethoven adopted the habit of recording his musical thoughts on oblong sheets of paper, folded about the middle to yield pages measuring about eight by five inches (twenty by thirteen centimetres). A collection of these sheets then formed the basis of a pocket sketchbook that could serve the composer on his country walks, enabling him to jot down tentative ideas as they entered his head, or, as Alan Tyson puts it, 'the honey that the bee had gathered in the meadows'.[lix] When back home Beethoven would then transfer ideas, recorded in pencil, onto ruled sheets of manuscript paper that formed the basis for his desk sketchbooks — to which we make further reference in our commentaries to later works.[lx] The Kafka Sketchbook consists of a collection of some 124 leaves of miscellaneous shape and paper type; its name derives from its original owner, Johann Kafka, who later sold it to the British Museum (British Library) in 1875.[lxi]

Sketches for the sonata consists of various compositional drafts that are found amongst notions for bagatelles and it is conjectured that ideas for the third movement were originally intended for such a piece, before being incorporated into the sonata.[lxii] In this movement Beethoven adopts the Italian expression *mancando*. This is one of the few Italian expressions used by Beethoven and may be taken as signifying 'a very decided *fading away* in time and tone'.[lxiii] The movement functions as a minuet and trio and Tovey considered the *Minore* to include some of the most challenging passages in the sonata.[lxiv] An atmosphere of 'brooding silence' has been detected here with perhaps even an anticipation of Schumann and Brahms.[lxv] This atmosphere has also been perceived as 'an exercise in tone colour, with melody hidden in an arpeggiated motion of triplets'.[lxvi] Reflecting on Beethoven's earliest sonatas, Harold Truscott remarks how their *Menuetto* movements contain passages that are 'quiet, gentle [and] reflective' but perhaps no more so than here in the Trio to Op. 7.[lxvii]

In the 1806 review of the Piano Sonata Op. 7 mentioned above, the composition's 'overpowering passion' is considered to be matched equally by its 'tender complaisance'. Modern-day assessments have evoked similar expressions of feeling, especially relating to the *Rondo, Poco allegretto e grazioso* of the fourth movement. Here the music has been variously described as 'most songful',[lviii] imbued with 'great charm',[lix] 'tender and overflowing'[lx] and 'most delicately sensuous ... the crowning lyrical climax to the work'.[lxi] There is Mozartian feeling also, 'Mozart at his best'[lxii] and Mozart 'extended'.[lxiii] Rolland found a particular kind of enchantment in the music in which for him 'the sentiment is like a child that runs to you and stands between your knees'.[lxiv]

There are a few passages in the *Rondo* where Beethoven was confined by the limitations of the keyboard of his day; for example, in the treble repeat at bar 89 the high G was not available. In considering such passages as this, Tovey reminds us: 'It is by no means certain that Beethoven would have made the passages exactly parallel whatever the compass on the instrument.'[lxv] Less equivocal is the eternal truth enunciated by Czerny in his encouragement to the performer to master the technical and emotional challenges posed by Beethoven's Piano Sonata Op. 7: 'Practice is the great magician, who not only makes apparent impossibilities performable, but easy. Industry and practice are the creators of all that is great, good and beautiful on the earth.'[lxvi]

---

[i] This is the first recognised published review of the Piano Sonata Op. 7. The text and translation are derived from Wayne M. Senner, et al, 1999, p. 141.

[ii] This observation has been made by several commentators, see for example: Charles Rosen, 2002, p. 130.

[iii] Matthew Rye, BBC Website Radio 3: *Beethoven Experience*, 3 June 2005.

[iv] Donald Tovey, 1944, p. 86.

[v] John A. Fuller-Maitland, *Notes to the Beethoven sonatas* contributed to the Special Issue of *The Musical Times*, Vol. VIII, No. 2, 1927, pp. 218–223.

[vi] The Piano Sonata Op. 7 is still not a favourite on the concert platform even today. Alfred Brendel suggests the reasons may be 'the piece's relatively quiet and lyrical ending, the length of the slow movement — which demands considerable audience attention, and, not least, the technical challenges posed by the first movement.' See: Alfred Brendel in conversation with David Dubal, 1985, p. 101.

[vii] Barry Cooper, 1991, p. 70.

[viii] Thayer-Forbes, 1967, p.198. Artaria moved to Vienna in 1770 where his

company became one of the largest publishing houses, bringing out works by Haydn and Mozart as well as Beethoven. For a portrait of Carlo Artaria see Beethoven House, Digital Archives Library Document B 1234.

[ix] Derived from the Augener Edition No. 8030 of *Beethoven's Piano Sonatas* (undated).

[x] The greater dimensions of the Piano Sonata Opus 7 are noted by Eric Blom, 1938, p. 25.

[xi] For a facsimile image of the Title Page to the Artaria Edition see: the Beethoven House Website: Beethoven-House Bonn, Digital Archives, Library Document C7/12.

[xii] The dedications to Babette de Keglevics are placed in the wider context of her family relationships in: Peter Clive, 2001, p. 250.

[xiii] The story has its origins in a letter written by Count von Keglevics: Thayer-Forbes, 1967, p. 198.

[xiv] *Ibid*, 1967, p. 292.

[xv] The anecdote is recalled in: William Newman, 1963, p. 512 and Paul Badura-Skoda, editor, 1970, p.12.

[xvi] This remark, in the context of Piano Sonata Op. 7, is considered by Denis Matthews, 1967, p. 17.

[xvii] Marion Scott, 1940, p. 135.

[xviii] Theodore Albrecht, 1996, Vol. 1, Letter No. 24, p. 46.

[xix] This is a direct reference to the importance of the Piano Sonata Op. 7 as considered by Romain Rolland, 1917, p. 139.

[xx] As recounted in: Martin Geck, 2003, p. 20.

[xxi] This is the view of Walter Riezler as recollected by Maynard Solomon, 1977, p. 104.

[xxii] Giorgio Pestelli, 1984, p. 232.

[xxiii] Denis Matthews, 1985, p. 80.

[xxiv] Alexander A. Ringer discusses the influence of Clementi's piano sonatas in: *Beethoven and the London pianoforte school.* In support of his claims he provides extensive comparative musical quotations. See: Paul Henry Lang, 1971, p. 244 *et seq.*

[xxv] Barry Cooper, 1991, p. 71. Cooper rates the Piano Sonata Op. 7 highly and devotes considerable space to it.

[xxvi] Anton Schindler, 1860, English edition: Donald MacArdle,1966, pp. 110–11.

[xxvii] From the recollections of Carl Czerny, see: Paul Badura-Skoda, editor, 1970, p. 28.

[xxviii] Emily Anderson, 1961, Vol. 1, Letter No. 27, p. 30.

[xxix] Grove makes brief reference to such an illness (p. 78). According to some reports the illness may have been typhus (Cooper, *Beethoven*, 2000, p. 72.) Beethoven's many illnesses are considered in detail by François Mai in: *Diagnosing genius*, 2007.

[xxx] Theodore Albrecht, 1996, Vol. 1, Letter No. 21, p. 41.

[xxxi] Dennis Matthews, 1967, p. 17

[xxxii] Eric Blom, 1938, p. 26.

[xxxiii] From the recollections of Carl Czerny, see: Paul Badura-Skoda, editor, 1970, p. 28.

[xxxiv] Matthew Rye, BBC Website Radio 3: *Beethoven experience*, 3 June 2005.

[xxxv] Charles Rosen, 2002, pp. 130–31.

[xxxvi] Similar remarks are made by Edwin Fischer (1959, p.34) who offers the

performer guidance as to the interpretation of the first movement.

xxxvii Harold Craxton and Donald Francis Tovey, *Beethoven: Sonatas for pianoforte*, London: The Associated Board, [1931], *Piano Sonata No. 4* p. 87.

xxxviii Alfred Brendel in conversation with David Dubal, in: David Dubal, 1985, p. 101.

xxxix C. Egerton Lowe, 1929, p. 22.

xl Dika Newlin, 1980, pp. 142–3.

xli *Ibid*, 1980, p. 255.

xlii Sergey Prokofiev, 1979, p. 121.

xliii Igor Stravinsky, 1975, p. 21 and Robert Craft, 2002, p. 39.

xliv See, for example, the views of Romain Rolland, 1917, p. 139.

xlv Ernst von Elterlein, 1898, pp. 47–8.

xlvi Denis Matthews, 1967, p. 17 and 1985, p. 80.

xlvii Charles Rosen, 2002, p. 132.

xlviii Philip Radcliffe, *Piano music* in: *The age of Beethoven, The new Oxford history of music, Vol. VIII*, Gerald Abraham, editor, 1988, p. 339 and p. 629.

xlix Friedrich Blume, 1972, p. 40.

l Derived from one of Rubinstein's historical lectures and quoted in Henry E. Krehbiel, 1971, p. 171.

li Donald Tovey, 1944, p. 92.

lii These, and related remarks, are to be found in Donald Francis Tovey, 1931, p. 86.

liii C. Egerton Lowe, 1929, pp. 22–3.

liv Romain Rolland, 1917, p. 139.

lv Romain Rolland, 1937, pp. 125–6.

lvi Edwin Fischer, 1959, p. 34.

lvii Sir Hubert Parry in his *Beethoven* also raises the question of the inadequacy of words to convey feelings in music. He writes: 'The power of Music to express subtle gradations of feeling is so much greater than language, that in most cases the attempt to describe the meaning of the former by the latter is almost hopeless. It can often give no more than the baldest suggestion of the outline, and leaves all the more characteristic elements of the music and its internal working untouched.' See: Sir C. Hubert Parry, *Beethoven* in: David Ewen, editor, 1968, p. 120.

lviii Ernst von Elterlein, 1898, pp. 47–9.

lix Alan Tyson, 1963, see: 'Commentaries to Beethoven's sketches'.

lx For a modern-day interpretation of how Beethoven may have appeared, when working at his desk, see the illustration by the artist-sculptor Donna Dralle reproduced in the website, *The unheard Beethoven* to the text, *The creatures of Prometheus*.

lxi As remarked in the text, the Kafka Sketchbook is named after Johann Kafka who sold it to the British Museum (British Library) in 1875. It consists of various compositional drafts. See: Douglas Johnson, 1985, pp. 511–23.

lxii Thayer-Forbes, 1967, pp. 198–9.

lxiii C. Egerton Lowe, 1929, p. 24.

lxiv Harold Craxton and Donald Francis Tovey, *Beethoven: Sonatas for pianoforte*, London: The Associated Board, [1931], *Piano Sonata No. 4*, p. 87.

lxv Romain Rolland, 1917, p. 140.

[lvi] Charles Rosen, 2002, p. 133.

[lvii] Harold Truscott, *The piano music* in: Denis Arnold, editor, 1973, p. 80.

[lviii] Matthew Rye, BBC Website Radio 3: *Beethoven experience*, 3 June 2005.

[lix] Edwin Fischer, 1959, p. 35.

[lx] Denis Matthews, 1967, p. 17.

[lxi] William Kinderman, Liner notes to *Beethoven: The complete sonatas*, Alfred Brendel, 1996, Philips 446 909 2.

[lxii] Romain Rolland, 1917, p. 140.

[lxiii] Charles Rosen, 2002, p. 133.

[lxiv] Romain Rolland, 1937, p. 131.

[lxv] Harold Craxton and Donald Francis Tovey, *Beethoven: Sonatas for pianoforte*, London: The Associated Board, [1931], *Piano Sonata No. 4*, p. 87.

[lxvi] Carl Czerny cited in: C. Egerton Lowe, 1929, p. 26. A performance of the Piano Sonata in E-flat major, Op. 7 has been recorded by Malcolm Binns on a fortepiano of 1794 by the London maker John Broadwood. Source: L'Oiseau-Lyre, D 182 D3.

PIANO SONATAS
OP. 10, NOS. 1–3

'The Sonatas [Opus 10, Nos. 1–3] are admirably
contrasted in character, particularly in their first
movements: the terse, dramatic idiom of the C
minor Sonata sets into relief the relaxed, mischievous spirit of the F minor, whereas the dynamic
brilliance of the third Sonata, D major, expands
the formal design from within.'

William Kinderman, *The Path to Mastery* in, *Beethoven*,
1997, p. 37.

'Now begins the glorious series of sonatas.' So com-
mences Alexander Wheelock Thayer in his account
of the origins of the Piano Sonatas Op. 10, Nos. 1–3.
Thayer is not, however, referring exclusively to the Op. 10
set of sonatas but also to the *Pathétique*, *Waldstein* and the
Appassionata that were all published within ten years of the

appearance of the Op. 10s. These great works form part of our later account. For the present, we concern ourselves with the Piano Sonatas in C minor, F major and D major that comprise the three compositions Beethoven designated as his Opus 10.

The Op. 10 Piano Sonatas constitute a trilogy. Throughout his life Beethoven chose to work intermittently on two or three related-compositions. He appears to have enjoyed, thereby, exploring different contrasts in mood and style between works that were gestating together in his imagination; consider, for example, the singular characteristics that distinguish the Fifth and Sixth Symphonies which, nevertheless, share a common creative time-period. In the case of the three Piano Sonatas Op. 10, they form a triptych, 'thoroughly contrasted in character yet integrated by subtle interrelationships'. In his discussion of the order and sequence of Beethoven's early compositions, Anton Schindler remarks how this was sometimes 'to create an effect of increasing tension from one to the next'. Other opposing idioms are evident in the Op. 10 Sonatas; for instance, they abound in 'sudden contrasts' and 'whimsical, unpredictable humour'.

In the first two sonatas of the Op. 10 set, Beethoven explores a shorter and less-imposing sonata concept. Both works are about half the length of their commanding predecessor, the Piano Sonata Op. 7, and both are confined to a three-movement format. Beethoven reduces their structure by eschewing 'lengthy codas', 'extended developments' and such other 'internal devices'. His innovation was also typical of a type of three-movement sonata that was beginning to appear without minuets or scherzos, being concise and 'polarised into thematic areas that provided as much contrast as possible'. The first sonata of the set was also expressive of a genre of C minor piano-music that, in

71

Beethoven's hands, would emerge resplendent in the form of the Sonata *Pathétique*.

Beethoven's 'pronounced style in melody and phrase structure', already apparent in the Op. 2 Piano Sonatas — notably the F minor Sonata and the *Adagio* of the C major Sonata — is even more distinctive in 'the movements with unifying characteristics' in the C minor and the D major Sonatas of Op. 10. Several hallmarks of Beethoven's *piano oratory* are also found in these early sonatas such as *rhetorical pause* and *caesura*. By means of these devices, Beethoven introduces sudden breaks and points of rhythmic division and the implied lengthening of written notes without expressly designated rests. In short, '[All] the characteristic graduations of the naïve, the sentimental, the serious, the gay and the passionate are to be found in these sonatas.' It has been suggested, moreover, that the trilogy of sonatas published as Op. 10 'displays an artistic scope and original-ity' that Beethoven achieved only years later in other musical genres. Common features of the Op. 10 Piano Sonatas are their 'sudden contrasts and unexpected turns', 'whimsical, unpredictable humour' and 'rhetorical contrasts' that often 'juxtapose a forceful expression invested with rhythmic tension and dissonance, on the one hand, with the emer-gence of a plaintive or lyrical voice on the other'. The musical influences of Clementi and Dussek occur in these sonatas. From them he absorbed a sense of 'atmosphere' and 'structure', probably unconscious of any particular origin, to an extent that 'they had become part of him'— but Beethoven manipulates these 'with a much more assured hand'. Writing of the manner in which Beethoven assimi-lated ideas drawn from the work of other musicians, Alexander Ringer asserts this in no way endangers Beethoven's historical or artistic stature, but rather adds to a growing body of evidence that 'his justly celebrated originality derived not so much from any particular novelty of invention as from a matchless power of integration and sublimation of the widest variety of musical practices'. Oskar Bie, in his study of the history of the pianoforte, considers that down to the Op. 10 Piano Sonatas 'we stand on the classical ground of the sonata' but in the Op. 10s 'appear the first important irregularities'. He cites the 'definite design' found in the first and second sonatas and, in the third, 'that wonderful D minor movement, with its utter abandonment to melancholy'.

Several of Beethoven's original sketches for the Opus 10 Piano Sonatas have been preserved in the so-called Fischhof Miscellany — a collation of single manuscript leaves representing Beethoven's compositional drafts for the period 1790–9. From about July–August 1798, Beethoven adopted his habit of recording musical thoughts in sketch-books — now valued for providing insights into the workings of his creative mind. It may be that the challenge of writing the six string quartets Op.18, prompted him to work more systematically in pre-assembled sketchbooks than on loose leaves and bifolia — large folded-sheets. Beethoven may have begun work on the three Piano Sonatas Op.10 as early as 1795 or 1796. The sketches reveal the composer's predisposition to work on several pieces simultaneously and, as remarked, to juxtapose different styles and genres of composition. We may make a further generalisation here. In his composing methods Beethoven frequently resorted to two somewhat contrasting procedures that have been described as 'sculptural' and 'architectural'. In the former, he may be seen as searching for the shape of a theme or phrase, often rejecting one idea after another — chipping away as it were — until the final form has been resolved to his satisfaction. In the case of the latter, he more resembles the architect, content initially to sketch out broad ideas for

73

a movement — laying out the ground plan — that could be enriched and completed at a later date.[xvi]

Following the conventions of the period, in July 1798 the Vienna music publisher Joseph Eder opened a list of subscribers for Beethoven's new sonatas in the *Wiener Zeitung* (Vienna Journal).[xvii] This was the protocol whereby the subscriber, or dedicatee, paid a negotiated sum that conferred rights of possession over the music for a stipulated period — typically a year.[xviii] In the case of the Piano Sonatas Op. 10, they were announced as being published on 26 September 1798. The Title Page reads: '*Trois Sonates par le Clavecin ou Piano Forte, composeès et dédiées à Madame la Comtesse de Browne, nee de Vietinghoff, par Louis van Beethoven, Oeuvre 10, à Vienne, Chez Joseph Eder sur le Graben.*'[xix] Worthy of remark is that the compositions were considered as being suitable for the clavecin, or harpsichord. This was, however, rapidly becoming an anachronism, given the powerful sonorities Beethoven was now imparting to his works for the keyboard. The outmoded term would in fact persist, even with the publication of the Sonata *Pathétique*, but thereafter publishers began to adopt the expression *pianoforte* on the title pages of Beethoven's new works for the keyboard.[xx]

A few remarks should be made here concerning the dedicatee Countess Anna Margarete von Browne and her husband Count Johann Georg von Browne-Camus. The Count was employed in the Russian Imperial Service by Empress Catherine II. He is described as being a man 'full of excellent talents and beautiful qualities of heart' but whose immense wealth disposed him, in later life, to recklessness and culpable improvidence.[xxi] The family showed much consideration to Beethoven in his early years in Vienna. Beethoven responded by dedicating a number of compositions to Margarete, in addition to the Piano Sonatas Op. 10.

These include the Twelve Variations in A major on the then popular *Danse Russe* from the Ballet *Das Waldmädchen*. Such dedications were important, even to the independent-minded Beethoven. They were made, most typically, to persons of high standing from whom he had received, or had hopes of receiving, some favour or pecuniary benefit. The circumstance calls to mind Samuel Johnson's somewhat withering definition of a patron: 'Commonly a wretch who supports with insolence, and is paid with flattery'! This could not be said, however, of Count Browne. In the case of the dedication to his wife, he presented Beethoven with the gift of a riding horse! It was not long though before the composer, absorbed in his work, forgot all about the animal — until the day arrived when he received a large bill for its fodder and maintenance!

Before concluding our introductory remarks concerning the Piano Sonata Op. 10, brief mention should be made here concerning Beethoven's mental outlook in 1798. This is revealed in a short note he wrote to his close friend Nikolaus Zmeskall, at the period when the sonatas were being published. Zmeskall was a civil servant employed in the Hungarian Court chancellery and rendered many small services to Beethoven — for which he was inevitably rewarded with friendly, wounding-barbs and badinage — such as being called 'Baron Muck-Driver'! In his note, Beethoven states: 'Power is the moral principle of those who excel others, and it is also mine.'[xii] This is typical of the aphoristic and cryptic utterances that abound in Beethoven's letters and notes. By means of such expressions and personal communings, he appears to have strengthened his resolve and self-belief, especially in times of illness or adversity. On this occasion, concerning his remark to Zmeskall, it is possible Beethoven was emboldening himself and setting his mind to the creation of 'one of his noblest and most original works' — the *Eroica* Symphony.[xxiii] [xxiv]

A review of the Op. 10 Piano Sonatas appeared in the *Allgemeine musikalische Zeitung* of 9 October 1799. This was based on the first edition of the works that had been published, as remarked, in September 1798. The reviewer, whose name is not stated, recognised Herr Beethoven for being 'a man of genius', with 'originality', 'possessing an abundance of ideas' and who 'goes entirely his own way'. For the critic in question though, it appears Beethoven went a little too far. The composer is censured on the grounds his gift 'too often causes him to pile up ideas without restraint and to arrange them by means of a bizarre order'. He does, however, conclude with a compliment — albeit a somewhat backhanded one: 'There are undoubtedly few artists to whom one must exclaim: save up your treasures and be thrifty with them.'[xxv] [xxvi] [xxvii]

[i] Thayer-Forbes, 1967, p. 213.

[ii] Barry Cooper, 2000, p. 74.

[iii] Anton Schindler, 1860, English edition: Donald MacArdle, 1966, p. 67.

[iv] William Kinderman, 1997, p. 37.

[v] Stewart Gordon, 1996, p. 156.

[vi] Giorgio Pestelli, 1984, p. 232.

[vii] Anton Schindler, 1860, English edition: Donald MacArdle, 1966, pp. 110–11 and pp. 417–18.

[viii] William Kinderman, *A trilogy of contrasts*, Liner Notes to *Beethoven: The complete sonatas*, 1996, Philips 446 909-2.

[ix] Harold Truscott, *The piano music* [of Beethoven] in: Denis Arnold, editor, 1973, pp. 74– and p. 93.

[x] Alexander A. Ringer, *Beethoven and the London pianoforte school* in: Paul Henry Lang, editor, 1971, pp. 255–6.

[xi] Oskar Bie, 1966, p. 175.

[xii] Barry Cooper, 1991, p. 15.

[xiii] Douglas Johnson, 1985, p. 77. For a discussion of Beethoven's sketches for the Op. 10 Piano Sonatas, see: *Style determinants*, Paul Mies, 1929.

[xiv] Barry Cooper, 2000, p. 73.

[xv] Thayer-Forbes, 1967, p. 213.

[xvi] The division of Beethoven's working procedures into two distinct categories, as evident from the surviving sketchbooks, was first remarked upon by the Viennese musicologist Gustav Nottebohm. For brief related contextual information, combined with musical illustrations, see: Denis Matthews, 1967, p. 39.

[xvii] Peter Clive, 2001, pp. 98–9 and Thayer-Forbes, 1967, p. 213.

xviii Barry Cooper, 2000, p. 72.

xix A facsimile representation of the Title Page can be viewed on the Beethoven House Website, Digital Archives, H. C. Bodmer Collection, Library Document HCB Op. 10. The wording is also stated on older editions of Beethoven's sonatas, e.g. Augener Edition, London, No. 8030, undated.

xx For a brief consideration of this see: Denis Matthews, 1985, p. 80.

xxi Thayer-Forbes, 1967, p. 212.

xxii Emily Anderson, 1961, Vol. 1, Letter No. 30, p. 32. Beethoven would occasionally summon Zmeskall to do his bidding by sending him a note set in the guise of a humorous, and inventive, musical canon. See, for example, the sketch-leaf preserved in the Beethoven House Collection, Digital Archives, Library Document HCB BSK 14/62, Hess 276.

xxiii Thayer-Forbes, 1967, p. 203.

xxiv The ambassador of the French Republic for the Austrian Court, in the spring of 1798, was Jean Bernadotte — General Bernadotte. Anton Schindler remarks that it was from him that Beethoven conceived the idea for the *Sinfonia Eroica*; see: Schindler-MacArdle, 1966, pp. 115–6.

xxv Wayne M. Senner, 1999, Vol. 1, pp. 142–44. See also: Thayer-Forbes pp. 278–9 and Anton Schindler pp. 77-8.

xxvi For a discussion of the importance of the newly-emerging music criticism in the early issues of the *Allgemeine musikalische Zeitung*, in relation to the wider contemporary understanding of Beethoven's compositions, see: *Transforming Beethoven criticism in the AMZ* in, *Beethoven and the construction of genius*, Tia De Nora, 1997, pp. 179–185.

xxvii A review of the composer's Violin Sonatas Op. 12, composed between 1797–8 also appeared in a contemporary issue of the *Allgemeine musikalische Zeitung*. The newness in Beethoven's style was clearly disturbing to the reviewer. He first likens himself to being invited to stroll through an inviting wood with a friend but instead finds 'only hostile entanglements' and finally emerges as if from a thicket 'exhausted and disheartened'. The reviewer acknowledges Beethoven goes his own way then can't resist adding, 'but what an eccentric, tortuous way it is! Intellect, intellect and more intellect, but without nature, without song!' Cited in: Martin Geck, 2003, p. 26.

PIANO SONATA
IN C MINOR,
OP. 10, NO. 1

'Op. 10, No. 1 marks the first appearance in the
piano sonatas of Beethoven's celebrated "C
minor mood", the tempestuous character
reflected in pieces like the *Sonata Pathétique* and
the Fifth Symphony.'

William Kinderman, Liner notes to *Beethoven: The Complete Sonatas*, Alfred Brendel, 1996, p. 45 (Philips 226
909-2).

C minor is the key that for Beethoven is so often
associated with music of a 'tempestuous and strife-
ridden character'. As implied in our opening quotation, it
is the key of the *Pathétique* Sonata and of the profoundly
contemplative Piano Sonata Op. 111 with which Beethoven

bade farewell to the genre. It is also Beethoven's 'heroic key', as in the Funeral March to the *Eroica* Symphony, the Overture *Coriolan* and, pre-eminently, the Fifth Symphony.[ii] The origins of Beethoven's C minor piano-world can be found in the piano sonatas of Clementi and Dussek.[iii] The composer who most comes to mind however, as a source of influence, is Mozart, notably in his Piano Sonata in C minor, K 457. This was published in 1785, was known to Beethoven and was much admired by him. Although Beethoven's C minor Piano Sonata 'was a considerable advance in personal expression'[iv] he 'could not yet match Mozart on his own ground'.[v] Beethoven's C minor is more 'rough hewn' than Mozart's. Beethoven's star, in 1798, was in the ascendant but had still to reach its apogee.

This is the first of Beethoven's piano sonatas to have only three movements. A fourth movement was planned but Beethoven abandoned the enterprise. He later used the material on which he had been working for two other compositions, namely, the Bagatelles WoO 52 and WoO 53.[vi] Before considering the sonata in detail, we can enjoy an anecdote concerning the piece that comes from the modern era. The musician Boris Lossky studied piano with Dmitry Shostakovich and recalls him playing Beethoven's C minor Piano Sonata for an examination, sometime in the spring of 1918. He describes Shostakovich as looking 'fragile ... somewhat like a small sparrow' and 'blank faced'. Of his playing though Lossky writes: 'I can still hear the music in my head as he played it. Through his reflective and intro-spective performance he showed a remarkable quality of concentration.'[vii] Shostakovich was then just twelve years old.

Sketches for the first movement of the C minor Piano Sonata, Op. 10 are found with sketches for a soprano air for Ignaz Umlauf's comic opera *Die schöne Schusterin* (WoO 91) and variations for three wind instruments.[viii] This is typical

79

of Beethoven who frequently worked on a number of compositions at the same time. The epithet 'passionate' has been bestowed on this movement, with 'its far-flung opening gestures', 'breathless pauses' and 'its melodic suspensions ... suggestive of suppressed agitation'.ⁱˣ Perhaps it was with such considerations as these in mind that disposed Carl Czerny to write for the would-be performer: 'In a quick and fiery time. An earnest spirit must sway the feelings. The character of the whole [to be] decided and manly.'ˣ The opening sonorities 'dug up from the bass register' have been likened figuratively to 'a rock built out of harmonies, from which untapped sources of energy ... spring forth'.ˣⁱ Contrasts and silences assume significance here. 'Pauses are no less important than the notes: the rapport of sound with silence imparts tension ... Beethoven distils these contrasts with the utmost concentration.'ˣⁱⁱ There are contrasts also between 'strength and gentleness' and between 'passion and tenderness', examples of Beethoven's *rhetorical principles* to which reference was made in our introductory remarks.ˣⁱⁱⁱ The 'concentrated expression' found in this movement, is not merely an 'effusion of a youthful, emotional *Sturm und Drang*'. The Beethoven who emerges here is 'as much a clear-sighted rationalist as a romantic visionary'.ˣⁱᵛ

In our commentary to the Piano Sonata, Op. 2, No. 1, we remarked that Romain Rolland detected Beethoven employing, in his musical language, 'the accepted works and phrases' but was also introducing his own 'brusque, biting accents' and was imposing his own 'signature on ... borrowed modes of speech'. In his consideration of the Piano Sonata, Op. 10, No. 1, he finds 'a heroic turn of mind declares itself'. In his view: 'The design is sometimes heavy; the line no longer has the feline inflexions that were characteristic of Mozart and his imitators; both [Op. 2, No. 1 and Op. 10, No. 1] are drawn with a sure hand; they are the shortest possible route from one idea to another, and a route laid out broadly — the great roads of the spirit.'ₓᵥ

Alexander Ringer has made a close study of the parallels that may be found between Beethoven's early piano sonatas and those of his Czech contemporary Jan Ladislav Dussek. He was renowned for his technical prowess and in public performance exploited his handsome features by sitting at the keyboard with his profile to the audience — the first artist so to do and thereby earning for himself the epithet *le beau visage*! Contemporary engravings of Dussek portray a young man with wavy hair and handsome features. Ringer has shown that in his Op. 10, No. 1 Piano Sonata, Beethoven appears to quote directly from the opening movement of Dussek's Piano Sonata Op. 39, No. 3 — both were published at about the same time. We remark in our later commentaries that other sonatas of Beethoven also appear to owe a debt to Dussek's pioneering keyboard style.ₓᵥⁱ In this context, also worthy of mention, is Dussek's contribution to what may be termed the London pianoforte school. Dussek was on friendly terms with the London pianoforte maker John Broadwood and it was in part a response to the innovative nature of Dussek's piano music that Broadwood was encouraged to develop the range and strength of the fortepiano beyond that of the instruments then available. Beethoven himself was the direct beneficiary of these developments when, towards the end of his life, he received one of Broadwood's new instruments as a gift.

The slow movement of the Op. 10, No. 1 Piano Sonata, 'too beautiful to need superlatives',ₓᵥⁱⁱ is an extended sonata-form structure — it occupies half the length of the entire piece. This intense Adagio is arguably 'the most finely proportioned and balanced movement in Beethoven's piano sonatas so far', with 'a part-model in the *Mesto* from Clementi's Sonata in E flat'.ₓᵥⁱⁱⁱ It makes use of traditional ornamentation that resembles the work of Beethoven's contemporary, Nepomuk Hummel.[xix] Carl Czerny was an admirer of Hummel's writing for the piano and his pianism, concerning which he writes: 'If Beethoven's playing was distinguished by immense power, characteristic expression, unparalleled bravura and fluency, Hummel's was a model of the utmost purity, cleanness, elegance and tenderness; and has the combined characteristics of Mozart's style with the judicious principles of the Clementi school, his execution always excited admiration.'[xx]

Discussing the first movement of the Piano Sonata, Op. 10, No. 1, Alfred Brendel enthuses: '[This] is one of those serene adagios that only Beethoven could write. From very early on one recognises Beethoven as the master of the adagio.'[xxi] In Rolland's estimation, 'a melodic stream makes its way along unhurriedly opening out at the end into a placid estuary ... with its great, serious, firmly drawn melody — frank and healthy, without a touch of society, insipidity or equivocal sentiment about it'. He concludes: 'Of all the Beethoven meditations this is the one that, while not concealing anything of itself, is accessible to everyone.'[xxii]

To assist the performer capture the mood of this Adagio, Edwin Fischer suggests 'take a deep breath from bar 24 onwards' so as not to hurry the semidemiquavers and, thereby, 'to feel as one the whole passage leading to the recapitulation'.[xxiii] Also with performance in mind, Czerny writes: 'With the most intense feeling which can be produced on the instrument by a beautiful touch and strict *legato*.'[xxiv] This guidance is echoed by Donald Tovey who encourages the artist to cultivate 'a rich singing-tone ranging from a Chopinesque lightness', in the rapid semidemiquavers, 'to an Italian *bel canto* in the long notes'.[xxv]

The Finale is marked *prestissimo* throughout the entire movement this being one of only two such occasions

Beethoven gave this indication in a piano sonata — the other being in the second movement of the Piano Sonata Op. 109. The layout of the movement is concise to the extent of being 'violently compressed'[xxvi] and possessed of 'energy and intensity that foreshadow the first movement of the Fifth Symphony'.[xxvii] As remarked, Beethoven originally planned this movement on a larger scale[xxviii] but finally decided to cast the music into a three-movement 'breathless series of events'[xxix] instilled with 'the spirit of the scherzo'.[xxx] Nineteenth-century commentators found the influence of Mozart in this movement, whilst recognising 'the true spirit of Beethoven pervades the whole'.[xxxi] More recent musicology recognises Beethoven's debt to Clementi, but Clementi 'so pushed out of sight that almost all that remains on the surface is the intense rapidity of [Beethoven's] music'.[xxxii]

Amidst the compression and 'angularity',[xxxiii] Beethoven's irrepressible sense of humour is never far away, occasionally erupting and inducing the composer to insert *wrong* notes to which attention is drawn by being marked 'fortissimo'.[xxxiv] The humour though is not so much fun as high spirits and is enshrined in music that demands a consummate pianistic technique. As Czerny encourages: 'The humorous perform-ance can only be attained by the masterly subjugation of all mechanical difficulties'[xxxv] — words of wisdom from the first pianist to commit to memory all of Beethoven's piano sona-tas. The *prestissimo* finally dissolves, in William Kinder-man's memorable phrase, 'into a silence of pregnant irony'.[xxxvi]

---

i   William Kinderman, 1997, p. 37 and a *Trilogy of contrasts*, Liner Notes to: *Beethoven: The complete sonatas*, 1996, Philips 446 909-2.

ii Maynard Solomon, 1977, p. 103.

iii See: Harold Truscott *The piano music* [of Beethoven] in: Denis Arnold and Nigel Fortune, editors, 1973, pp. 68–88.

iv Eric Blom, 1938, p. 33.

v   Dennis Matthews, 1967, p. 18.

vi Thayer-Forbes, 1967, p. 213.

vii Lossky's reminiscences are recollected in: Elizabeth Wilson, 1994, pp. 13–5.

viii Thayer-Forbes, 1967, p. 213.

ix Eric Blom, 1938, p. 33.

x From the recollections of Carl Czerny see: Paul Badura-Skoda, editor, 1970, p. 30.

xi Giorgio Pestelli, 1984, p. 232.

xii William Kinderman, 1997, p. 38 and Liner notes to: *Beethoven: The complete sonatas*, 1996, Philips 446 909-2. For a more extended discussion of the mood and construction of this movement, see also, Kinderman, 1997, pp. 37–9.

xiii Anton Schindler, 1860, English edition: Donald MacArdle, 1966, pp. 417–18. Schindler makes (controversial) suggestions for playing the first movement of Op. 10, No. 1 by advocating the insertion of additional rests – to achieve greater 'rhetorical' effect. See: Alfred Brendel, 2001, p. 22.

xiv William Kinderman, 1997, p. 38 and Liner notes to: *Beethoven: The complete sonatas*, 1996, Philips 446 909-2.

xv Romain Rolland, 1937, p. 121.

xvi Alexander A. Ringer, *Beethoven and the London pianoforte school* in: Paul Henry Lang, editor, 1971, p. 249.

xvii C. Egerton Lowe, 1929, p. 28.

xviii Harold Truscott *The piano music* [of Beethoven] in: Denis Arnold and Nigel Fortune, editors, 1973, p. 93.

xix Charles Rosen, 2002, p. 136.

xx Carl Czerny as recalled in: Ludwig Nohl, 1880, p. 44.

xxi Alfred Brendel in conversation with David Dubal, in: David Dubal, 1985, p. 101.

xxii Romain Rolland, 1937, p. 126.

xxiii Edwin Fischer, 1959, p.37.

xxiv From the recollections of Carl Czerny see: Paul Badura-Skoda, editor, 1970, p. 30.

xxv Harold Craxton and Donald Francis Tovey, *Beethoven: Sonatas for pianoforte*, [1931], *Piano Sonata in C minor, Op. 10, No. 1*, 1931, p. 114.

xxvi Donald Tovey, 1944, p. 91.

xxvii Barry Cooper, 2000, p. 73.

xxviii Thayer-Forbes, 1967, p. 213.

xxix Denis Matthews, 1967, p. 18.

xxx Romain Rolland, 1917, p. 141.

xxxi Ernst von Elterlein, 1898, pp. 51.

xxxii Harold Truscott *The piano music* [of Beethoven] in: Denis Arnold and Nigel Fortune, editors, 1973, p. 96.

xxxiii This is the expression used by Charles Rosen, 2002, p. 136.

xxxiv William Kinderman, *A trilogy of contrasts*, Liner Notes to *Beethoven: The complete sonatas*, 1996, Philips 446 909-2.

xxxv From the recollections of Carl Czerny see: Paul Badura-Skoda, editor, 1970, p. 30.

xxxvi William Kinderman, 1997, pp. 39.A performance of the Piano Sonata in C minor, Op. 10, No. 1 has been recorded by Malcolm Binns on a fortepiano of 1794 by the London maker John Broadwood. Source L'Oiseau-Lyre: D 182 D3.

PIANO SONATA
IN F MAJOR,
OP. 10, NO. 2

'There's a good definition of this sonata by
Adolph Bernhard Marx, who said the first movement is the present, the second is the future, and
the third is the past, as far as styles go.'

Alfred Brendel in conversation with David Dubal, in David
Dubal, *The World of the Concert Pianist*, 1985, p. 101.

The Piano Sonata in F major abounds in 'high spirits'
and confronts both performer and listener with
'Beethoven the humourist'. Here we have 'humour in
plenty' amounting even to 'a complete comedy' of Beethovenian frolicsome-invention. Perhaps when composing this
music Beethoven had in mind his old teacher Haydn who
was himself possessed, musically speaking, of a mischievous
sense of humour. It may be that Beethoven was simply

taking as his point of departure 'the comic strain already present in the finale of Op. 10, No. 1'. The humour in this sonata shows itself in 'abrupt statements' that 'twist and turn', very much as was Beethoven's humour prone to do in the form of the puns that abound in the letters to his close — and long-suffering — friends. The cheerful character of this sonata may account for its 'somewhat loose texture', perhaps suggesting even how Beethoven may have sounded when improvising, taking up one idea after another and going on to invent a new section. Alfred Brendel considers Beethoven's humour 'continues the tradition of Haydn', and adds: 'I would sorely miss the humour in a Beethoven performance.' William Kinderman is equally sympathetic to Beethoven's humour here and likens his 'meandering' piano writing to 'a coyish good-natured capacity for just getting lost'.

Artur Schnabel was one of the first pianists in modern times to play the entire cycle of Beethoven sonatas in the concert hall, and offers discerning observations regarding their interpretation in his edition of the sonatas. Commenting upon the Op. 10, No. 1, he encourages the performer 'to render song-like passages without recurring to the pedal'. Based on his study of the original autographs, he also has things to say about Beethoven's expression marks, implying they should be treated with caution. He states: 'Binding arcs, accents and manners of touch in [Beethoven's] autographs were often indicated ... with confusing flightiness and carelessness — especially in the early works.' Of interest is that Schnabel's contemporary Bella Bartok, in his youth as a concert pianist, performed the F major Sonata frequently in his broadcasts over Budapest Radio between 1922 and 1928.

An anecdote links this piano sonata with a former pillar of the British musical establishment, Sir Hubert Parry. In his undergraduate days, at the University of Oxford, he was co-founder of *The Music Club* and it was at this period Beethoven's pianos sonatas 'cast a powerful spell' upon him. His Diary for 27 December 1866 records: 'Practised all morning — Beethoven mostly.'[xiii] The work he studied intently was the Piano Sonata in F, Op. 10, No. 2. In later life, Parry succeeded Sir Charles Grove as Director of the Royal College of Music. In that capacity he contributed an extended essay on Beethoven that includes an evaluation of his works, including the piano sonatas.[xiv]

The first movement Allegro is 'in the comic mode' and from the outset 'it proclaims its witty eccentricity'.[xv] Carl Czerny designates the movement as 'gay and lively' and 'bustling and merry'.[xvi] To Romain Rolland the spirit of the music suggested 'a soldier on horseback, relaxing his fever and bathing in freedom'. He asks: 'Who ever showed us fresher streams than the composer of the first allegro of the F major Sonata, Op. 10, No. 2?'[xvii] The opening figure 'sparkles with life'[xviii]; perhaps this is the reason why the piece is something of a favourite amongst the more able young pianists. The movement was a favourite of Beethoven, who revelled in 'the unexpected', 'the incongruous' and even 'the grotesque'.[xix] Beethoven takes delight here in adopting one of his favourite compositional ploys, namely, of leading the music into the 'wrong key' before 'establishing the true identity of the music'.[xx] Perhaps distant echoes of Haydn can be heard in passages that are variously 'jocose', 'cheerful', 'merry' and 'roguish'.[xxi] The *fortissimo* marking, however, is pure 'early Beethoven'.[xxii] Commenting on Beethoven's capacity to develop ideas from simple material, as evident in this movement, one commentator has likened his ability to that of a French chef 'who can make an excellent soup from a couple of old bones'![xxiii] The parallel is not flattering but it would have appealed to Beethoven. We recall how, when invited to elaborate a waltz theme of Anton Diabelli, he initially dismissed Diabelli's subject matter as 'a cobbler's patch' before eventually creating from it arguably the greatest ever set of piano variations.

The *Allegretto* is a minuet and replaces the slow movement.[xxiv] Once more the wit and good humour are suggestive of Haydn but are combined with emotional depths. The wit and humour implicit in the music once got the better of Enrique Granados during a master class session he was leading at the academy where he was then a professor of piano. A young woman was performing the Allegretto movement at his request but was taking the passage at an inappropriately fast tempo. Instead of restraining her, Granados indulged his sense of humour by encouraging her saying 'Faster! ... Faster!' The perplexed student duly obliged by increasing the rapidity of her playing. At the close of the movement, Granados congratulated his protégé with the exclamation: 'Very good. Now we can dance!'[xxv]

More seriously, can we perhaps imagine the young Schubert admiring the textures and construction here and working similarities into the Scherzo of his Piano Sonata in B flat?[xxvi] Oskar Bie appears to think so: 'The sportive Beethoven lies in the lap of nature ... in the hurrying ghost-like Scherzo with its Schubertian-like romantic middle-movement.'[xxvii] 'Melodic breadth' is a feature of Beethoven's later style and it is evident in this music.[xxviii] Donald Tovey's enthusiasm prompted him to assert: 'Beethoven's early lyric pathos is at its height in this quiet movement.'[xxix] 'Gravity' and 'seriousness of character' stand in complimentary relation to the 'comic-burlesque' that comes later in the finale.[xxx] Romain Rolland characterises the musical feeling created by Beethoven as being 'mysterious and somewhat eerie'.[xxxi]

These sentiments were anticipated in the nineteenth

century by the musicologist Ernst von Elterlein. He writes: 'The whole is so imaginative, so ethereal, and has such a magical effect, that it awakens in me a feeling like that of Goethe's words in *Faust*: "Cloud and trailing mist o'er head/Are now illuminated/Air in leaves, and wind in reed/And all is dissipated".'xxii

In the final *Presto* the influence of Haydn is once more evident, in particular, relating to the animated finales of his string quartets. The style is 'fugal' with 'contrapuntal display' and has been described as 'the ancestor of the Mendelssohn *scherzo*'.xxiii The atmosphere is pervaded by 'wit', 'musical laughter' and 'humour' but of a refined kind that, in Jean Paul Richter's teasing phrase, 'inverts the sublime'.xxiv To convey the music's 'buoyant energy'xxv, Czerny emboldens the performer to bring out the main theme clearly each time it occurs and thereby achieve the 'brilliant effect' Beethoven requires.xxvi Tovey, a performer of considerable pianistic accomplishments, observes — somewhat dispassionately — how the first two movements 'make no demands on an advanced technique' but then concedes, 'Beethoven gives us a finale as difficult as many later things four times as large'.xxvii

In establishing the fugato character in the music, Beethoven may have looked back for inspiration to the Two-Part Invention in F, of J. S. Bach.xxviii His source may equally have been more commonplace in the form of the sounds of an outdoor rustic wind-band. Is Beethoven perhaps treating us to a 'bucolic revelry' complete with a bassoon 'setting off the fugato and collecting all the players together over a drone-bass'?xxix The key here is after-all that of F major, Beethoven's 'relaxed open-air key', and the same key as the *Pastoral Symphony* — his most life-affirming work bearing on the joys of the open-air.

i Stewart Gordon, 1996, p. 156.

ii Harold Truscott, *The piano music* in: Denis Arnold and Nigel Fortune, editors, 1973, p. 96.

iii Ernst von Elterlein, 1898, p. 50.

iv This is the opinion of Alfred Brendel who additionally remarks: 'It is humorous in the outer movements, and continues the tradition of Haydn in this respect.' Alfred Brendel in conversation with David Dubal, in: David Dubal, 1985, p. 101.

v William Kinderman, 1997, p. 38.

vi Eric Blom, 1938, p. 39.

vii Edwin Fischer, 1959, p. 38.

viii Alfred Brendel in conversation with David Dubal, in: David Dubal, 1985, p. 101.

ix William Kinderman, 1997, p. 40.

x For more deeply considered philosophical insights into Alfred Brendel's views on the role of humour in music, relating to the Piano Sonata Op. 10, No. 2, see: *The sublime in reverse* in: Alfred Brendel, 2001, pp. 108–9.

xi Artur Schnabel, Preface to *Klaviersonate Nr. 6, F Dur Op. 10, Nr. 2*, Verlag Edition, No. 128 (undated).

xii Malcolm Gillies, editor, 1993, p. 68.

xiii Jeremy Dibble, 1992, pp. 50–1.

xiv C. Hubert H. Parry, *Beethoven* in: David Ewen, 1968, pp. 105–131.

xv Charles Rosen, 2002, p. 137.

xvi Carl Czerny, *On the proper performance of all Beethoven's works for the piano* in: Badura-Skoda, editor, 1970, p. 31.

xvii Romain Rolland, 1937, p. 122.

xviii C. Egerton Lowe, 1929, p. 31.

xix William Kinderman, *A trilogy of contrasts*, Liner Notes to *Beethoven: The complete sonatas*, 1996, Philips 446 909-2.

xx Stewart Gordon, 1996, p. 156.

xxi Ernst von Elterlein, 1898, p. 52.

xxii Harold Craxton and Donald Francis Tovey, *Beethoven: Sonatas for pianoforte*, [1931], *Piano Sonata in F Major, Op. 10, No. 2.*

xxiii C. Egerton Lowe, 1929, p. 32.

xxiv Charles Rosen, 2002, p. 137.

xxv As recalled in: Walter Aaron Clark, 2006, p. 71.

xxvi Denis Matthews, 1967, p. 18.

xxvii Oskar Bie, 1966, p. 174.

xxviii Paul Mies, 1929, pp. 107–8.

xxix Harold Craxton and Donald Francis Tovey, *Beethoven: Sonatas for pianoforte,* [1931], *Piano Sonata in F Major, Op. 10, No. 2.*

xxx William Kinderman, *A trilogy of contrasts*, Liner Notes to *Beethoven: The Complete Sonatas* (Philips 446 909-2) 1996.

xxxi Romain Rolland, 1917, p. 143.

xxxii Bayard Taylor, *Faust* (*The Golden Wedding of Oberon and Titania*), Ward Lock & Co., c. 1870, p. 142.

xxxiii Charles Rosen, 2002, p. 138.

xxxiv Cited by William Kinderman in, *A trilogy of contrasts*, Liner Notes to *Beethoven: The complete sonatas*, 1996, Philips 446 909-2. See also:

William Kinderman, 1997, p. 40.

xxxv Stewart Gordon, 1996, p. 156.

xxxvi From the recollections of Carl Czerny, see: Paul Badura-Skoda, editor, 1970, p. 31.

xxxvii Harold Craxton and Donald Francis Tovey, *Beethoven: Sonatas for pianoforte,* [1931], *Piano Sonata in F Major, Op. 10, No. 2.*

xxxviii Edwin Fischer, 1959, p. 39.

xxxix Denis Matthews, 1967, p. 18. A performance of the Op. 10, No. 2 Piano Sonata in F major has been recorded by Malcolm Binns on a reproduction fortepiano modelled on that of Mozart's Anton Walker pianoforte of 1780. Source Nonesuch: N—78008.

PIANO SONATA
IN D MAJOR,
OP. 10, NO. 3

'This sonata is one of the greatest works of
[Beethoven's] first period, if not, indeed, the
greatest of them all.'

Romain Rolland, *Beethoven and Handel*, 1917, p. 143.

'The D major Sonata ... is a superb work ... The
individuality of style is absolute and unchallenged,
the structure of all the movements is flawless.'

Marion Scott, *Beethoven*, 1940, p. 135.

'In the D major Sonata, Op. 10, No. 3,
Beethoven's power appears with an intensity
which must have come more as a shock than as
a revelation to his contemporaries. It is doubtful

whether any part of it except the exquisite minuet can have been acceptable to orthodox musicians in 1798.'

Donald Tovey, *Beethoven*, 1944, p. 92.

'This is the greatest of the three sonatas [Op. 10], its four movements forming a wonderful unity. The happy distribution of interest among contents, formal beauty and pianistic brilliance has made it a great favourite in the concert hall.'

Edwin Fischer, *Beethoven's Pianoforte Sonatas*, 1959, p. 39.

'I've always considered there to be five or six sonatas that are especially perfect and rounded. Amongst the early sonatas I would mention the D major Sonata Op. 10, No. 3 with its astonishing overall impact.'

Alfred Brendel, *The Veil of Order*, 2002, p. 111.

Beethoven was in his twenty-eighth year when the Piano Sonata Op. 10, No. 3 was published. By now he was 'supported, encouraged and esteemed by [Vienna's] aristocracy in a way that has hardly ever been the lot of a young artist'. For the final sonata of the Op. 10 trilogy, Beethoven returned to a four-movement structure. In so doing he was 'underscoring many of the compositional procedures he had pioneered in the Piano Sonatas Op. 2 and Op. 7'. The work is expansive, being almost twice the length of its predecessor the Piano Sonata in F. By universal acclaim the Piano Sonata in D major is a composition of the highest worth, praised for its 'formal beauty', 'wonderful unity' and the scope it provides for 'pianistic brilliance'. The individuality of its style is considered 'absolute and unchallenged', and the structure of its movements 'flawless'. This sonata 'blends character and maturity of expression' in a manner that makes it 'the most lastingly interesting of the earlier piano sonatas'. The work as a whole is possessed of 'heroism', 'tragedy' and 'triumph' — the very hallmarks of Beethoven's indomitable spirit.

In this composition, we find Beethoven once more pressing against the boundaries of the physical limitations of the keyboard of his day. Anton Schindler reminds us that Beethoven's piano music, up to the Piano Sonatas Op. 31 (1803), was confined to the limited compass of five octaves. One consequence of this was Beethoven did not have available the third A above middle C and had similar limitations in the lower register. With particular regard to the D major Piano Sonata, he had to forsake the high F sharp that is required in some bravura arpeggios and broken octave passages — now supplied in modern editions. As remarked, in relation to Beethoven's earlier sonatas, the range of the piano was progressively undergoing transformation and with it a new style of musical expression — but not everyone viewed this as progress. Rossini, no less, writing to his distinguished friend Leopoldo Cicognara — art historian and critic — lamented the innovation. He expostulates: 'Ever since the five notes were added to the harpsichord, I have maintained that a dire revolution was brewing in our art.' Rossini considered things had started to go wrong when Haydn introduced 'strange chords, artificial passages, and daring novelties into his compositions' but, he adds in mitigation, 'at least he still preserved a sublimity and traditional beauty which would excuse such things'. As for

Beethoven? Rossini thought his new compositions were 'lacking in unity and natural flow and [were] full of arbitrary oddities'. He considered Beethoven had 'corrupted taste in instrumental music completely'._{viii} We should exonerate Rossini though by also mentioning that some years later (1822) after writing this letter, he was introduced to Beethoven in person and was deeply moved by the experience. We narrate elsewhere how Richard Wagner sought out Rossini in Paris to learn all about this encounter._{ix}

Brief mention can be made here concerning the London music season in the mid-nineteenth century. In 1855, Sir Charles Hallé gave a series of piano recitals for *The Musical Union*. We remember Hallé today as a celebrated conductor, but he was also a fine pianist who performed all of Beethoven's piano sonatas — on the very day he died he had been practising one! It so chanced that Louis Spohr was in London in 1855 and heard Hallé perform the D major Piano Sonata Op. 10. After the concert, Spohr made some flattering remarks about Hallé's performance and proclaimed the D major to be 'a fine sonata', adding, 'not antiquated'. The latter remark left Hallé somewhat perplexed. Was Spohr perhaps trying to say that he regarded the Piano Sonata Op. 10, No. 3 as modern sounding? At about this same period, George Bernard Shaw, in his capacity as a London music critic, also heard Hallé perform Beethoven's Sonata Op. 10, No. 3 at a recital in the City. He considered Hallé's artistry as being self-effacing, remarking — with characteristic wit: 'Sir Charles is not a sensational player ... The secret is that he gives you as little as possible of Hallé and as much as possible of Beethoven.'_x We encounter Shaw once more as music critic, this time writing for *The Hornet* on 29 August 1877. He had heard a remarkable rendering of the *Largo* of the D major Piano Sonata in an orchestration by one W. Hepworth. Shaw was an accomplished amateur pianist – he enjoyed playing piano-reductions of Beethoven symphonies with his sister – and his review is discerning: 'The arrangement is for the most part successful, but although their melancholy tones are in keeping with the work, we think the four horns are too constantly employed.' He also considered the *arpeggios*, 'so effective in the original', to be 'completely overpowered by the wood and heavier stringed instruments'.[xi][xii]

The splendours of the D major Piano Sonata are evident in the rhythmic urgency of the opening bars of the first movement. Whilst some of the 'keyboard patterns' here can be traced to the influence of Muzio Clementi, 'the architectural certainty and economy are Beethoven's own from start to finish'.[xiii] Another influence on Beethoven appears to have been Dussek's Piano Sonata Op. 35, No. 2. Alexander Ringer, in his comparative study of the sonatas of Dussek and Beethoven, comments on the extent to which Dussek influenced the composer, 'not only rhythmically, harmonically, and dynamically, but also structurally'. He concludes: 'At that relatively early stage in his career, it would seem, Beethoven was ready to go to great lengths to enhance his growing reputation as a sparkling young virtuoso, even if this meant copying the mannerisms of established colleagues.'[xiv]

Carl Czerny describes the first movement as 'quick and fiery' and thought it enshrined the very spirit of the sonata that he regarded as 'grand and significant' with 'the character of the whole ... decided and vigorous' and worthy of 'brilliant performance'.[xv] 'What storm and dash there is in the first movement!' The restless 'rushing and hurrying' is repeated and intensified until 'there is scarcely a moment to rest'. Moreover, the atmosphere is 'pervaded by youthful vigour and heroism'. Can we perhaps see, albeit yet dimly, 'the creator of the *Eroica* Symphony'?[xvi]

The 'hallmark of Beethoven's forceful early style' is

evident in the *Presto*, and throughout the movement 'the 'internal dynamism ... strains the formal framework of the Classical sonata and expands it from within'.[xvii] The writing illustrates remarkably Beethoven's 'partiality for rhythmic themes' and for his use of 'simple scale progressions'.[xviii] 'Most of the first movement derives directly from its first four notes: rarely has so much been made of so little.'[xix] The four-note motif acts as 'a powerful unifying device'. It appears throughout the movement 'sometimes inverted', 'going up instead of down' and 'sometimes used imitatively'.[xx] The movement is 'a wonderful evolution from the first four-note figure'[xxi] with the *Presto* marking, 'unusual in a first movement', imparting 'new vitality' to what are 'standard accompanying patterns'.[xxii] Beethoven's sketches survive and reveal how the composer, 'by means of latent and sub-conscious work', made the four-note motif 'assume very complicated associations'.[xxiii] This aspect of Beethoven's workmanship prompted Romain Rolland to enthuse: '[How] he laboured to purge his thought of vagueness, to eliminate everything superfluous, to seek and find always the most concise and most striking expression.'[xxiv] Carl Dahlhaus provides a detailed analysis of the construction of this movement, together with insights into its underlying aesthetic[xxv], and Alfred Brendel has explored the text's 'form and psychology'[xxvi].

Eugenie Schumann has left an account of piano lessons with her gifted mother Clara. Alongside the study of Czerny's *School of Velocity*, Beethoven 'formed the nucleus of every lesson'. Eugenie studied one Beethoven sonata after another 'with great thoroughness'. Her mother did not let the smallest inexactitude pass. She considered what had been written was sacred, remarking: 'Do you think Beethoven would have taken the trouble to write all this notation ... if he had meant it to be otherwise?' At one lesson the first movement of the D major Sonata Op. 10, No. 3 was studied — doubtless to the required level of exactitude.[xxvii] [xxviii] Nearer to our own time, the American musician Dika Newlin recalls Arnold Schoenberg teaching composition at the University of California in the autumn of 1939. She was in his composition class and Schoenberg — known affectionately as 'Uncle Arnold' — selected the *Presto* from Beethoven's Op. 10, No 3 Sonata for study. He considered it to be a worthy model relating to the elaboration of sonata form and the structural functions of harmony.[xxix]

The slow movement is 'one of the great tragic utterances in early Beethoven' in which 'struggle' and 'resignation' intertwine within sonata form to yield the effect of 'light dispelling darkness'.[xx] Moreover, these qualities are played out over an extended time-scale; the movement occupies nearly half the playing-time of the entire sonata. 'Passion and tenderness' permeate the music from its 'opening five-bar phrase to its beautiful closing with those amazing tonic pedal chords'.[xxi] Donald Tovey is unequivocal: 'The slow movement is not only Beethoven's first essay in tragedy, but is by far the most tragic piece of music that had ever been written up to that time.'[xxii] Beethoven designates the movement *Largo e mesto* in response to which Denis Matthews suggests *mesto* is to be taken as 'sad or gloomy' and, thereby, invokes 'overwhelming pathos and sustained tension'. Matthews considers there may have been extra-musical influences at work in Beethoven's mind at the time of the sonata's composition. Was he perhaps reflecting upon the death of his mother, to whom he was so attached, or was his spirit burdened by the thought of encroaching deafness — 'manly sorrow borne with fortitude'?[xxiii] [xxiv] Writing almost half a century earlier, Rolland expressed similar thoughts: '[It] is in the monumental *Largo e mesto* ... that the full grandeur of Beethoven's soul is for the first time revealed

... From the opening chords ... the soul of the listener yields to the hand of the master ... It is the chorus of an antique tragedy ... The personal pain here becomes the good of all; and by its very plenitude the elegy of a man expands to the epic of a race or of an epoch.'[xxxv] More objectively, was Beethoven simply responding, albeit with great emotion, to the dictates of his creative muse? Consider, for example, how Beethoven was so moved by Mozart's Piano Concerto in D minor, K 466, as to compose fully written-out cadenzas for it and to play the work at the benefit concert for Mozart's widow, held in the Vienna Court Theatre on 31 March 1795.[xxxvi]

Beethoven's sustained sombre mood in the slow movement has been likened to a 'poem of melancholy' and reminds the listener how Beethoven 'could move a whole audience to tears when he extemporised'.[xxxvii] The music is said to have been conceived under the influence of Beethoven having read the passage describing Klärchen's death in Goethe's *Egmont* – to which he returned in 1810. It has also been suggested Beethoven's **Largo e mesto** makes 'a striking affinity' with the despairing final bars of the slow movement of Schubert's Quartet **Death and the Maiden.**[xxxviii] William Kinderman considers this sombre movement 'exemplifies the young Beethoven's impressive command of tragic compression in music'. He invokes Schiller's dictum that 'the depiction of suffering *as such* is not the purpose of art', rather, 'what must be conveyed is resistance to the inevitability of pain or despair'.[xxxix] In his estimation of Beethoven's achievement, Egerton Lowe prefaces his remarks with a quotation from Spinoza: 'Whatever is, is in God, and without God nothing can be; or conceived.' He further cites the tribute paid by Carl Reinecke, a nineteenth-century interpreter of the work: 'One must forever stop with awe before it.'[xl] These noble utterances are consistent with

Beethoven's own manner of invoking elevated aphoristic sayings; he was, for example, acquainted with the writings of Homer, Plutarch, Goethe, Schiller, Dante and Shakespeare. He kept written-out texts from them on his writing desk by way of strengthening his personal resolve.

Anton Schindler recalls telling Beethoven one day what a great impression his pupil Carl Czerny had made on an audience and went on to ask Beethoven about the mood prevailing in the D major Piano Sonata Op. 10. Beethoven was usually reticent to discuss such matters; he once laconically replied to such a question, 'I have written the notes, it is for you to discover the meaning.'[xli] Regarding the slow movement of the Piano Sonata Op. 10, he favoured Schindler with a more considered response. He acknowledged it conveyed 'the spiritual condition of a person consumed by melancholy' and implied that Czerny's audience 'had felt the nuances of light and shadow'.[xlii] Concerning interpretation, Charles Rosen remarks: 'The extraordinary pathos of the *Largo e mesto* presents a temptation to play too slowly.' He attributes this to the much-increased sonority of modern-day instruments compared with the weaker sustaining power of Beethoven's keyboard.[xliii] Czerny has advice here for the performer, he states: 'To perform music of this nature, it is not enough to put oneself in the appropriate frame of mind. The fingers and hands themselves must affect the keyboard with a different, a heavier weight than is necessary for happy or tender compositions, in order to bring out the more resonant tone of each note and to give life to the slow pace of the serious Adagio movement.'[xliv]

The Minuet of the third movement begins under the impact of the foregoing 'elegy', prompting Edwin Fischer to encourage the performer 'to give a sense of release' to the music 'like the gentle chords of the storm in the *Pastoral*

Symphony'.[xl] Tovey refers here to the 'deep poetry of this movement'.[xli] Lyricism triumphs in the *menuetto*. Making use of simple motifs, Beethoven brings about 'transformations of significance by touch and phrasing [that] were indispensable to his sense of composition'. Matthews suggests the lyrical feeling that prevails may owe a debt to the '*compassionate* second subject' in Mozart's D minor Concerto which, as remarked above, Beethoven greatly admired.[xlvii]

Humour, perhaps revealing the influence of Haydn,[xlviii] permeates the final movement and 'makes great play with a three-note fragment'.[xlix] Czerny regards Beethoven's humour here as 'serene and capricious'.[l] He also recalls how Beethoven could take 'a few insignificant notes' and use the material 'for the construction of a whole improvised work similar to the finale of the Piano Sonata in D major Op. 10, No, 3'. With the improvisation over, Czerny remarks, 'Beethoven would break out into hearty satisfied laughter'.[li] Some of Beethoven's ideas for this music have been preserved in the Kafka Sketchbook (see Piano Sonata Op. 7).[lii] Beethoven's 'few insignificant notes' co-exist with sketches for a cadenza to the C major Piano Concerto that he performed in Prague in 1798 — further evidence of how he worked on several compositions at the same time.[liii] Regarding this working method, Konrad Wolff pays Beethoven the following compliment: 'It is precisely because Beethoven understood the importance of the thematic substance for his oeuvre, and was aware that the individualization of a new work takes time and effort, that he was constantly making sketches.' This is the view of many who have studied Beethoven's surviving sketches, noting how they served to shape the final form of a motif or melodic phrase. As Wolff concludes, 'hence the miracles of the opening measures of the first movement of ... the Finale of the D major Piano Sonata Op. 10, No. 3'.[iv] Others who have studied Beethoven's scores are in agreement: 'The more one studies and analyses this magnificent work, the more intimately acquainted will one become with Beethoven's unique method of working-out ideas.'[v] In this context, Edwin Fischer should be allowed the last word: 'We leave this work with a sense of having met a personality who is still young but who has already experienced the main elements of human feeling, tasted ecstasy as well as deepest grief, the blessings of consolation and the exuberance of an eternally creative nature.'[vi]

[i] Carl Czerny reflecting on the progress of his teacher. From the recollections of Carl Czerny, see: Paul Badura-Skoda, editor, 1970, p. 8.

[ii] Stewart Gordon, 1966, p. 157.

[iii] Edwin Fischer, 1959, p.39.

[iv] Marion Scott, 1940, p. 135.

[v] Eric Blom, 1938, p. 33

[vi] Adapted from Harold Truscott *The piano music*, in: Denis Arnold and Nigel Fortune, editors, 1973, p. 96.

[vii] Anton Schindler, 1860, English edition: Donald MacArdle, 1966, p. 402 and p. 406.

[viii] Rossini to Cicognara, 12 February 1817. See: Sam Morgenstern, editor, 1956, pp. 103–4.

[ix] Wagner's meeting with Rossini, and Rossini's impressions of Beethoven, are recalled in: *Richard Wagner's visit to Rossini* (Paris 1860), Edmond Michotte, 1860.

[x] Michael Kennedy, 1960, p. 72. Kennedy also tells the same anecdote in *The autobiography of Charles Hallé*, 1972, p. 10. Shaw's own text, together with numerous of his other concert reviews, is published in: *London music in 1888-89*, Bernard Shaw, 1937, pp. 41–2.

[xi] George Bernard Shaw in: *Shaw's Music*, Dan. H. Laurence, 1999, Vol. 1, p. 183.

[xii] The orchestral quality of Beethoven's writing is also noted by Stewart Gordon, 1996, p. 157.

[xiii] Denis Mathews, 1967, p. 19.

[xiv] Alexander A. Ringer, *Beethoven and the London pianoforte school* in: Paul Henry Lang, 1971, pp. 247–8.

[xv] From the recollections of Carl Czerny, see: Paul Badura-Skoda, editor, 1970, pp. 31–2.

[xvi] Ernst Von Elterlein, 1898, p. 55.

[xvii] William Kinderman, 1997, p. 41.

[xviii] C. Egerton Lowe, 1929, p. 35.

[xix] Charles Rosen, 2002, p. 138. In the construction of the first movement, Rosen

> pays tribute to Beethoven's grasp of music theory — a reminder Beethoven had thoroughly studied the *Well Tempered Clavier* of J. S. Bach in his youth.

xx Stewart Gordon, 1966, p. 157.

xxi Romain Rolland, 1917, p. 143.

xxii Denis Matthews, 1985, p. 81.

xxiii Paul Mies, 1929, pp. 116–7.

xxiv Romain Rolland, 1937, p. 141.

xxv Carl Dahlhaus, 1991, pp. 145–8.

xxvi Alfred Brendel, 2001, pp.49–51.

xxvii Marie Busch, 1927, pp. 91–7.

xxviii Clara Schuman also censured Anton Rubinstein for performing as many as four Beethoven sonatas at a single recital on the grounds: 'One sonata of Beethoven's needs one's whole soul.' See: Berthold Litzman, editor,1913, Vol. II., p. 422. In our own time, Artur Schnabel once played five sonatas in one evening. See: Artur Schnabel, 1961, pp. 122–3.

xxix Dika Newlin, 1980, pp. 100–1.

xxx Adapted from: William Kinderman, 1997, p. 42 and William Kinderman *Beethoven* in: *Nineteenth-century piano music* in: Larry R. Todd, editor, 2004, pp. 56-7.

xxxi Romain Rolland, 1917, p. 143.

xxxii Donald Tovey, 1944, p. 92. Tovey also remarks upon the 'tragic' slow movement of the String Quartet Op. 18, No. 1 as a further example of Beethoven's 'progress in rivalling Mozart in such designs'.

xxxiii Denis Matthews, 1967, p. 19 and 1985, p. 81.

xxxiv Ernst von Elterlein, 1898, p. 55.

xxxv Romain Rolland, 1937, pp. 126–7.

xxxvi Thayer-Forbes, 1967, p. 478.

xxxvii Marion M. Scott, 1940, p. 135.

xxxviii Edwin Fischer, 1959, p. 40, derived from C. Egerton Lowe, 1898, p. 37. Lowe himself was influenced by the writing of the pianist and composer Carl Reinecke.

xxxix William Kinderman, *The piano sonatas* in: *The Cambridge companion to Beethoven*, Glenn Stanley, editor, 2000, pp. 115–7.

xl C. Egerton Lowe, 1929, p. 37.

xli *Ibid*, p. 37.

xlii Anton Schindler, 1860, English edition: Donald MacArdle, 1966, p. 421.

xliii Charles Rosen, 2002, p. 139.

xliv Carl Czerny cited by Anton Schindler, 1860, English edition: Donald MacArdle, 1966, p. 421.

xlv Edwin Fischer, 1959, p. 41.

xlvi Harold Craxton and Donald Francis Tovey, *Beethoven: Sonatas for pianoforte*, [1931], *Piano Sonata in D major*, 1931, p. 147.

xlvii Dennis Matthews, 1967, p. 20.

xlviii Donald Tovey, 1944, p. 192.

xlix Dennis Matthews, 1985, p. 81.

l From the recollections of Carl Czerny, see: Paul Badura-Skoda, editor, 1970, p. 32.

[l] Czerny as recalled in: H. C. Robbins Landon, 1992, pp. 181–2.
[li] The Kafka Sketchbook is named after Johann Kafka who sold it to the British Museum (British Library) in 1875. It consists of various compositional drafts. See: Douglas Johnson, 1985, pp. 511–23.
[lii] Thayer-Forbes, 1967, p. 213.
[liv] Konrad Wolff, 1990, p. 114.
[lv] C. Egerton Lowe, 1929, p. 40.
[lvi] Edwin Fischer, 1959, p. 41. A performance of the Piano Sonata in D major, Op. 10, No. 3 has been recorded by Jörg Demus on a fortepiano of 1802 by John Broadwood. Source Musical Heritage Society OR 317.

PIANO SONATA IN C MINOR, OP. 13

GRAND SONATA PATHÉTIQUE

'This well-written sonata is not unjustly called *pathetic*, for it really does have a definitely passionate character.'

Allgemeine musikalische Zeitung, 19 February 1800.

'This glorious work is so well known and deservedly popular that it serves better than any other for the fullest possible analysis of what is known as sonata form, as well as simple rondo and rondo-sonata forms.'

C. Egerton Lowe, *Beethoven's Pianoforte Sonatas*, 1929, p. 41.

'[It] certainly deserves its title; for dramatic pathos
... gushes from it to the heart's content ... [The]
dramatic — theatrical — elements in the *Pathétique* are undeniable.'

Romain Rolland, *Beethoven The Creator*, 1937, p. 141.

'[This] is the first piece of music to be composed
for ten fingers and a lock of hair. Physical gyra-
tions of the limbs, tossings of the head, are
unavoidable if one is to play the piece as though
one believed in it.'

Wilfrid Mellers, *The Sonata Principle*, 1957, p. 58.

'[In] Op. 13, Beethoven continued a great Viennese tradition in which both Haydn (Symphony
No. 52) and Mozart (Piano Concerto in C minor,
K. 491) had excelled: the *Sturm und Drang* of C
minor, a key which obviously awoke in their
hearts the strongest emotions of power, grandeur
and tragedy.'

H. C. Robbins Landon, *Haydn: the Years of the Creation:
1796–1800*, 1977, pp. 499–500.

'It is the most dynamically propulsive of
Beethoven's piano sonatas thus far ... and the first
whose movements are clearly linked through the
use of related thematic material and conscious
reminiscences.'

Maynard Solomon, *Beethoven*, 1977, p. 105.

'The sonata fully deserves its acclaim. It surpasses any of [Beethoven's] previous compositions, in strength of character, depth of emotion, level of originality, range of sonorities ... anticipating in many ways his style of the next decade.'

Barry Cooper, *Beethoven*, 2000, p. 82.

'The power of the musical language is stronger, the range of keys is wider, and the keyboard writing is almost orchestral in colour, making greatly increased claims for the piano.'

Martin Geck, *Beethoven*, 2003 pp. 69–70.

The formal title of Beethoven's Piano Sonata in C minor, Op. 13 is 'Grand Sonata *Pathétique*'. It is one of the few compositions to bear an authentic title sanctioned by the composer. Beethoven's publisher, as a way of stimulating the musical public's interest, probably conferred the title on the work — to which, it would seem, Beethoven raised no objection. Whatever the precise origins, the title admirably embodies the spirit of the piece of which Donald Tovey remarks, 'nothing so powerful and so full of tragic passion had hitherto been dreamt of in pianoforte music'. The German historian Oskar Bie, discussing Beethoven's emerging pianistic language, considered 'the mighty Sonata in C minor' to be 'the first of his great tragic outbreaks'. With regard to the composer's 'revelling in the gloomy' he observes: 'Upon the heavy, slow introductory passage follows the stormy first movement, whose themes are, first, a tempest of rage, secondly, an utter despair, and the *Grave* intrudes its monitory remembrances in the midst.',

The sonata has subsequently found a permanent place in the pianist's repertoire and popular culture. Its popularity may, in part, derive from the manner in which we respond to certain kinds of music; as Harold Truscott remarks, 'tragic or sombre music always has more adherents than cheerful or humorous music'. In support of Truscott's contention, consider, for example, the universal popularity of Schubert's String Quartet *Death and the Maiden.* The title of the *Pathétique* (*moving* or *full of pathos*) has been taken to imply sorrow and rage and the expression of passionate emotions. It personifies the nineteenth-century romantic idea of 'a contest between an unhappy man and fate'. This interpretation is close in spirit to Romain Rolland's imagery. He invites us to think in theatrical terms: 'The piano-tenor ascends the stage and engages with the prima donna in a give-and-take dialogue of swelling melodrama in the style of *Il Travatore*; and both of them indulge in noble gestures and high-flown phrases ornamented after the manner of operatic vocalises.' Marion Scott sees tragedy in the *Pathétique* as the young feel it, 'with the glamour of urgency, even exaltation, of a *Romeo and Juliet'.* Her remarks serve to remind us Beethoven was still a young man at the time he wrote the sonata whose own inner-emotions were in a state of turmoil with the realisation of his worsening deafness — and with it his progressive social isolation and failure to find a partner in life. These considerations make us mindful of Ernst Toch's moving words: 'The *Pathétique* and *Appassionata* Sonatas are prayers of thanks, as by one who has experienced the deity.' Moreover, Beethoven was also reaching out to a new kind of pianism in which the piano would increasingly become 'a dynamic rather than a melodic instrument'; with the *Pathétique* he 'cracks sonata form with a passion that is almost melodrama'.

The sonata was published in 1799. The Title Page proclaims: '*Grande Sonata Pathétique pour le Clavecin ou Piano Forte, composée et dédiée à Son Altesse Monseigneur le Prince de Lichnowsky, par Louis van Beethoven. Oeuvre 13.*' Joseph Elder published the work in Vienna with a further edition appearing by Hoffmeister who announced it on 18 December of the same year. The dedication to Prince Lichnowsky is further evidence of Beethoven's indebtedness at this time to his patron and benefactor. Worthy of mention also is the solicitude shown to Beethoven by Lichnowsky's wife Princess Maria. It is said she took such care of Beethoven that 'he often wondered why she did not cover him with a glass case for fear of his being touched or breathed on by some unworthy mortal'. As in the case of the Piano Sonata Op. 7, Beethoven once more published a sonata separately, rather than as a group of three, with the assignment of a single opus number; this, with the designation 'Grand', provides some indication of the significance the work held for him in his progress as a composer of piano sonatas. Beethoven was always eager to see his work in print and was all too frequently vexed to discover errors and misrepresentations in his intended notation. Anton Schindler relates: 'Among the older Viennese publishing establishments were some that were all too often guilty of careless work, despite all the composer's efforts.' Citing the first and second movements of the Sonata *Pathétique* he continues, 'a great number of the execution marks were omitted that are truly necessary not merely for colouring but for accurate performance'.

No substantial sketches for the *Pathétique* have survived. Drafts for a sonata movement in C minor however exist from 1798 and contain ideas that were later incorporated into the *Pathétique* Sonata; these indicate Beethoven's early thoughts for a 'slow chordal introduction characterized by dramatic rests'.[xvi] Sketch fragments are found in the so-called Landsberg No. 7 Sketchbook, formerly owned by the collector Ludwig Landsberg and later purchased by the Berlin Royal Library.[xvii] [xviii] Musical influences on Beethoven can be traced to Mozart's Sonata in C minor, K. 457 and his later *Fantasia* K, 475. However, whereas Mozart is 'fiery but classically disciplined'[xix] in the *Pathétique* Beethoven 'pursues his C minor daemon to greater lengths'.[xx] Schindler considered all the significant features of Beethoven's pianistic articulation are to be found in the early piano sonatas, up to and including Op. 13. He states: 'All the characteristic gradations of the naïve, the sentimental, the gay, and the passionate are expressed in these sonatas.'[xxi] Of the *Pathétique* he enthuses: 'What the *Pathétique* was in the hands of Beethoven ... was something that one had to have heard, and heard again, in order to be quite certain that it was the same already well-known work.'[xxii] Ferdinand Ries, Beethoven's pupil, also remarks on Beethoven's interpretation of his own compositions: 'In playing he would hold the tempo back in his *crescendo* with *ritardando*, which made a very beautiful and highly striking effect.' Ries also remarks how Beethoven rarely allowed his notation to be embellished with additional notes or ornaments. *The Pathétique* was apparently such an exception; Ries was allowed to add 'a few notes' to the *Rondo* — but he does not tell us what they were![xxiii]

We should briefly consider here Beethoven the pianist in relation to other contemporary masters of the keyboard. These were Beethoven's potential rivals in the salons but from whom, as a composer, he was prepared to learn and whose ideas he was at times prepared to adapt into his own compositions.

In September 1799, the year of publication of the *Pathétique* Sonata, the celebrated pianist Johann Cramer arrived in Vienna. He remained there through the following winter and according to contemporary newspaper accounts 'earned general and deserved applause for his playing'. He also developed a cordial relationship with Beethoven, to the benefit of his pianism. Writing of this, Thayer remarks upon the advantages to Beethoven of him enjoying the company of a pianist 'whose noblest characteristics were the same as Mozart's'.^{xxiv} Beethoven esteemed Cramer's *Piano Studies*, published a few years later, and considered the study of them to be ideal preparation for the performance of his own sonatas.

Earlier in the year (March) Beethoven had occasion to engage in friendly rivalry with a pianist of recognised formidable powers. He was the Austrian-born Joseph Johann Baptist Wölfl (Woelfl). He was more than six feet tall and, significantly, nature had conferred upon him enormous hands.^{xxv} As a consequence he could span ten notes — and more — just as easily as others could span an octave, making it possible for him to perform continuous double-stopped passages 'as quick as lightening' and 'to overcome difficulties that for other pianists would be impossible'.^{xxvi} Thayer writes of Wölfl: 'It was no longer the case that Beethoven was without a rival as pianoforte virtuoso. He had a competitor fully worthy of his powers.'^{xxvii} Wölfl appears to have divided Vienna's musical circles equally for and against him. Although he is described as being trained in Mozart's school of piano playing, character-ised by a clear, precise tone, his powers of virtuosity appear at times to have dominated his playing, prompting a reviewer of the *Allgemeine musikalische Zeitung* to record: 'Herr W's works ... have exaggerated difficulties for those who perform them, and are approached with a certain amount of circumspection.'^{xxviii} Beethoven's encounter with Wölfl took place in the home of Baron Raymond von Wetzlar, an accomplished musician who had himself been on familiar terms with Mozart. The composer Jan Tomaschek was present and has left an account of the meeting between the two virtuosi that was later recalled by Beethoven's close friend Ignaz von Seyfried: 'Each brought forward the latest product of his mind. Now one ... and the other gave free reign to his glowing fancy; sometimes they would seat themselves at two pianofortes and improvise alternately on themes they gave each other.' Tomaschek concluded: 'It would have been difficult, perhaps impossible, to award the palm of victory to either one of the gladiators in respect of technical skill.' It appears that Wölfl was the more popular for those present who preferred the more showy style of performance. However, it was Beethoven who won the day for the connoisseurs able to respond to what Tomaschek describes as, playing that was 'brilliant and powerful [if] not infrequently jolted the unsuspecting listener violently out of his state of joyful transports'.[xxii]

Writing of the contest between the two, the reviewer in the *Allgemeine musikalische Zeitung* reported: '[Beethoven] shows himself to the greatest advantage in improvisations, and here, indeed, it is most extraordinary with what lightness and yet firmness in the succession of ideas Beethoven not only varies a theme given to him on the spur of the moment by figuration ... but really develops it. Since the death of Mozart, who in this respect is for me still the *non plus ultra*, I have never enjoyed this kind of pleasure in the degree in which it is provided by Beethoven.'[xxx]

Our final reference to one of Beethoven's contemporary 'lions of the keyboard' relates to his meeting the following year with the German-born pianist and composer Daniel Steibelt; what ensued amounted to a pianistic confrontation. Steibelt was born in Berlin and toured as an accomplished pianist. It was in this capacity when he arrived in Vienna on a concert tour from Paris. His prowess at the keyboard had earned for him, with the public at large, the reputation for being a formidable virtuoso — although professional musicians were inclined to dismiss him for being something of a showy charlatan. Beethoven and Steibelt met at the house of Count Moritz Fries for a pre-arranged pianistic *contest.* Fries was a wealthy banker, a patron of the arts and a founder member of the famed *Gesellschaft der Musikfreunde.* For his later generosity to Beethoven, he was rewarded with the dedication of his Seventh Symphony. On the evening in question, Steibelt performed a carefully prepared *improvisation,* having provocatively chosen a theme used by Beethoven in his then recently published Trio in B flat major, Op. 11. Ries, although not present himself, relates how this 'outraged Beethoven's admirers as well as Beethoven himself'. It was then Beethoven's turn to improvise. He went to the piano, turned upside down the copy of Steibelt's music — a quintet of his own composition — and 'hammered out a theme from the first few bars with one finger' and 'improvised in such a manner that Steibelt left the room before Beethoven had finished'. He shunned Beethoven's company ever after.[xxxi]

Such anecdotes as the foregoing illustrate the pressures to which Beethoven was subject in order to maintain his position as a virtuoso in Vienna's salons and to continue to win the admiration and support of his patrons. However, it is Beethoven the composer to which we now redirect our attention.

At the same period Beethoven was demonstrating his pianistic prowess, his fame as a composer was also becoming known more widely. His piano sonatas, sets of piano variations and other instrumental works were being published in Vienna and he had achieved wider recognition when on his concert tour in Prague, Dresden and Berlin.

On this occasion he had written to his younger brother Nikolaus Johann in the following terms: 'My art is winning me friends and renown, and ... this time I shall make a good deal of money.'.xxii In the summer of 1799, Beethoven wrote to his close friend Karl Amenda in terms of similar self-confidence. He tells Amenda he had been invited to visit Poland where, he jests, 'I can amuse myself quite well ... and there is plenty of money to be made there too!'xxiii Amenda was a clergyman and violinist; he was sufficiently accomplished to perform with Beethoven and to be tutor to the children of Prince Lobkowitz – one of Beethoven's patrons. The visit to Poland, like so many of Beethoven's planned excursions to other countries, never took place. However, in late 1799, Amenda wrote an affectionate letter to Beethoven typical of the kind he received from close friends who were well aware of his developing fame and emerging genius: 'You are responsible not only to yourself ... but indeed to the general progress of your art.'xxiv

In 1800, the recently established journal *Allgemeine musikalische Zeitung* published a review ostensibly in celebration of Joseph Haydn to whom it accorded 'the first place' with regard to his symphonies and quartets, 'wherein no one has yet surpassed him'. Beethoven, a still relatively unknown composer, is not, however, overlooked; the reviewer comments how he may even usurp the venerable master 'if he calms his wild imaginings'!xxv In the *AmZ* review of the *Pathétique* Sonata of 19 February 1800, the reviewer elaborates his remarks concerning the Piano Sonata Op. 13 and concludes: 'It must be a pleasant feeling for the Viennese music public ... to have so many excellent artists. [Herr] van Beethoven unquestionably belongs to them.'xxvi Schindler, ever eager to promote Beethoven's reputation, commends the review, and the reviewer, with his own observations: 'The review ... contains the first hint ... that

114

the critic has penetrated some of the intrinsic poetry rather than stopping at the technical aspects of the work.' He then adds his own plaudits: 'The admirable sonata is well named *Pathétique*, for it is indeed deeply emotional in nature.'[xxxvii]

The popularity and fame of the *Pathétique* soon spread. Czerny, who had just become a pupil of Beethoven, attributed the success of the sonata to it being 'easier to study, than the former ones, and has therefore been highly esteemed'.[xxxviii] In its review of the composition of 6 August 1807, the music journal *Zeitung für die elegante Welt* enthused: 'Friends of alluring and imposing melodies will admire this sonata no less than connoisseurs of harmonic art.'[xxxix] Evidence for this is borne out in the reminiscences of the composer and writer on music Johann Friedrich Reichardt. He visited Vienna in the autumn of 1808 and remained there until the spring of the following year. His reflections on Vienna's musical life include an account of a performance of the C-sharp minor Piano Sonata by Baroness Dorothea von Ertmann (see Piano Sonatas Op. 2, Nos. 1–3).[xl] He enthuses how her interpretation exhibited 'a degree of power and expression that delighted us all ... It is impossible to imagine anything more perfect on the most perfect of instruments'. Reichardt is referring here to a Streicher piano that he considered to be 'filled with the sprit of an entire orchestra'. He recalls how Beethoven had encouraged the instrument maker Streicher to modify his instruments so as to give them greater sonority: 'Streicher has, by Beethoven's advice and desire, abandoned the soft, yielding, and rebounding touch of the other Viennese instruments, and substituted greater firmness and elasticity, so that the *virtuoso* [Reichardt's italics] who plays with power and feeling has the instrument more under his control in sustaining and resting on sounds, and for all the more delicate marks of expression.'[xli]

Schindler, reflecting on the period 1809–13, noted that piano music was in great demand and how music dealers reported: 'The Sonata *Pathétique* sells more copies than any other piece.' Beethoven was not impressed. Schindler recalls how he regretted he had ever added the designation *Pathétique* to the Op. 13 Sonata: 'The whole world', he complained, 'seizes upon a single sonata because it has a name that the pianist can exploit.'_{xlii} Czerny also recollects how Beethoven, later in life, expressed similar feelings concerning the *Moonlight* Sonata. He tells how the composer complained people were always talking about the C-sharp minor Sonata, prompting him to assert: 'Really, I have written better things. The F-sharp minor Sonata [*Appassionata* Op. 57] is something again!'_{xliii}

In the nineteenth century the popularity of the *Pathétique* was firmly established. In 1804, the music publisher Hans Nägeli published a volume of contemporary compositions under the title *Répertoire des clavecinistes* that included a reprint of the *Sonate Pathétique.*_{xliv} Felix Mendelssohn conveys the emotional impression the C minor Sonata made upon audiences in the nineteenth century in a letter to his teacher Carl Zelter. He was asked to play the piano at a musical soirée and chose to perform the *Pathétique.* At its conclusion he could not help but notice the impression the music had made – doubtless augmented by his own remarkable artistry. He informs Zelter: 'When I had finished ... the ladies were weeping [and] the gentlemen hotly discussing the importance of the work.' Mendelssohn was not allowed to depart before providing the details of a number of Beethoven sonatas that several of the female pianists present wanted to learn._{xlv}

When on a concert tour in Grätz, in May 1846, Franz Liszt was a guest of Felix Lichnowsky, grandson of Prince Lichnowsky – the original dedicatee of the Piano Sonata

Op. 13. Liszt improvised on a theme from the *Pathétique* and received a typically enthusiastic report in the local newspaper: 'Liszt's ... incomparable rendering made the deepest impression on all present.' Proposing a toast at a subsequent banquet, Liszt concluded with some words of Beethoven: 'There is nothing higher than to draw nearer to the Godhead than other men, and to pour out its divine rays over the human race.'[xlvi] In his later years, Schindler lived to see the *Pathétique* increase in popularity beyond even Beethoven's imaginings. For example, in 1860, the year of publication of his biography of Beethoven, the music publisher Julius André had begun to expand his business by issuing piano-duet arrangements of Beethoven's piano sonatas. This made the pieces more accessible to a wider public of amateurs by sharing the difficulties of performance between four hands. But Schindler was contemptuous: 'This is one of the most deplorable and most bizarre phenomena this commercialised epoch has seen in the music-publishing business.'[xlvii]

Sir George Grove, of music-dictionary fame, cherished the *Pathétique*. Writing to a friend he remarks: '[Isn't] Beethoven inexhaustible ... That sonata [Op. 13] is one of my magic things ... so noble, so peculiar, so *new*.'[xlviii] Also, at this period, Beethoven was being celebrated in the three-dimensional arts, in ever-dramatic terms. The French sculptor Antoine Bourdelle, for example, created an impression of Beethoven that he titled *La Pathétique* or *Beethoven à la Croix*. Bourdelle's imagery reveals how strongly Beethoven epitomised the concept of the 'suffering and struggling genius' for many artists of the late nineteenth century.[xlix]

The Sonata *Pathétique* was composed seven years after the death of Mozart, and in that time the range and sonority of keyboard instruments had increased considerably. The prevailing fortepianos, however, still lacked the sonority and capacity for dynamic gradations that became possible with the instruments of Beethoven's maturity. Gerhard von Breuning, the son of one of Beethoven's closest friends, owned a fortepiano by Joseph Brodman, one of the leading makers of the day. Beethoven would have been familiar with such instruments; Brodman's were renowned for the resilience of their soundboard and the capacity of their strings for sustaining the increased tension being demanded of them, not only by Beethoven but by other of his contemporaries such as Muzio Clementi and J. B. Cramer. Breuning still owned his Brodman at the time he wrote his biographical notes about the composer (1874) and was disposed to remark: 'When one looks at the Brodman grand piano ... considered one of the best makes at that time, with its tiny tone and mere five and a half octaves, one finds it hard to conceive how it could have been adequate for Beethoven's tempestuous improvisations.' Wanda Landowska, the celebrated harpsichordist, has the following to say of Beethoven's accommodation to the limited pianoforte of his day: 'In his first sonatas, and even in the *Pathétique*, the compass is only five octaves.... [Beethoven] preferred to do with the instrument he had at his disposal and condensed his inspiration into the space of five octaves, sometimes doubling back a phrase, which is not without a particular charm.'

Beethoven's Piano Sonata in C minor, Op. 13 has been associated with some remarkable examples of youthful genius. Czerny was but ten years old when the violinist and mandolin player Jean-Baptist Krumpholz took him to see Beethoven; Jean-Baptist was the brother of the accomplished harp virtuoso, Wenzel Krumpholz whose claim to fame was the introduction of pedals to the harp. Czerny affirms that Jean-Baptist Krumpholz was among the first to recognise Beethoven's genius and inspired others with his own enthusiasm. It was through his good offices that Czerny's father was allowed to visit the composer with a view to securing lessons for his gifted son — it being known Beethoven had little interest in child prodigies. Czerny, who could already play almost all the piano works of Mozart, recalls 'what joy and terror I greeted the day on which I was to meet the admired master'. He found the composer's room presented a most disorderly appearance; papers and articles of clothing were scattered about everywhere. 'The walls were bare and hardly a chair was to be seen save the wobbly one at the Walter fortepiano.'[ii] Czerny is referring to the fortepiano Beethoven owned, at this time, made by the celebrated Viennese maker Anton Walter (see Piano Sonatas Op. 2, Nos. 1–3).[iii] Czerny discerned Beethoven wearing a morning coat of some long grey material and trousers to match — he thought he looked like Robinson Crusoe! He also noticed the composer had cotton wool protruding from his ears 'steeped in a yellowish liquid' — indicative of one of Beethoven's many attempts to find relief for his loss of hearing. At Beethoven's request to play, Czerny responded with a rendering of Mozart's great C major Piano Concerto, K. 503; Beethoven, after some initial hesitation, supplied the orchestral melody with his left hand. Czerny continues: 'The satisfaction he expressed gave me the courage to play his Sonata *Pathétique* which had just appeared.' At the conclusion of the piece, Beethoven turned to Czerny's father and said: 'The boy has talent. I will teach him myself and accept him as my pupil.'[iv]

Ignaz Moscheles was a mere seven years old when he determined to study the *Pathétique* Sonata! He was then resident in his hometown of Prague, and did not have the means to purchase the music. Undeterred, he recalls: 'Although but seven years old, I actually ventured upon copying Beethoven's Sonata *Pathétique.* Imagine if you can how I played it; imagine also the Beethoven fever to which I fell in those days.'[iv] However, when the young Moscheles sought the opinion of his teacher Friedrich Dionys Weber, he was cautioned away from such 'hair brained' compositions and was 'warned against playing or studying eccentric productions ... before [he] had developed a style based on more respectable models.'[lvi]

Ferdinand Ries began piano lessons with Beethoven in 1801 and continued with him for a few years until he was recalled to Bonn for military service. His recollections provide an insight into Beethoven the teacher: 'Beethoven takes more trouble with me than I could have believed. Each week I receive three lessons, usually from 10 o'clock to 2.30. I can almost play his Sonata *Pathétique*, which might give you pleasure, because the precision that he demands is hard to imagine.'[lvii] Ries continued to have a close relationship with Beethoven. A few years after starting his lessons with the composer, he made his public debut playing Beethoven's Third Piano Concerto adding a cadenza of his own. Years later he acted as the composer's overseas agent and did much to promote his new works with the London publishers and the then recently formed Philharmonic Society. Finally, in the context of youthful performer's of the *Pathétique*, mention may be made of Beethoven's nephew Karl. In 1820, when Karl was age fourteen, Beethoven placed his musical studies in the hands of Joseph Czerny — no relation of Carl Czerny. (It should be mentioned in passing that, after years of legal wrangling, Beethoven had been made Karl's co-guardian.) In one of Beethoven's surviving Conversation Books — which the composer then required in everyday discourse — Czerny recollects: '[Karl] played for me today a sonata by Mozart and the *Sonate Pathétique*, so now I know his ability.'[lviii] Karl went on to become a competent pianist.

The first movement of the sonata is marked *Grave* and opens with a slow introduction. Edwin Fischer likens the movement to 'an excerpt from the piano arrangement of a symphonic work'.[lx] Glen Gould also considers the *Pathétique* to be 'symphonically inclined' and draws a parallel with the imposing *Grave* and the slow introductions Beethoven employs in his First, Second, Fourth and Seventh Symphonies.[lx] Alfred Brendel likens the atmosphere of the *Pathétique* to passages found in Gluck's operatic music — particularly at the beginning.[lxi] This was the first time Beethoven had opened a piano sonata with a slow introduction and, thereby, as Barry Cooper affirms, 'a new path is forged'; the *Grave* is not only a 'prologue' it 'introduces a new dimension of expression' into the music.[lxii] Tovey regarded Beethoven's opening as: 'A magnificent piece of Homeric fighting.'[lxiii] Truscott is no less enthusiastic, describing Beethoven's introduction as 'splendidly new'.[lxiv] [lxv] A feature of this newness is: 'Sonata form is no longer an obligatory norm, but the point of departure for individual design.'[lxvi] Silence is also used in a new way: 'No composer before Beethoven had exploited silence in this way.'[lxvii] Schindler gives a detailed account of the Opus 13 Piano Sonata. Although he was primarily a violinist, he enjoyed Beethoven's company and claims he studied the piano sonatas with the composer. Of the celebrated opening chords he writes: '[They] should be struck firmly, then allowed to die away almost completely.'[lxviii]

The *AmZ* review, cited above, perceptively describes Beethoven's Piano Sonata Op. 13 as having 'a definitely passionate character' and being 'noble and melancholy'.[lxix] The reviewer was probably Johann Rochlitz, a founder contributor to the *Allgemeine musikalische Zeitung* (1798) and a fervent admirer of Beethoven — although some of his later reviews earned Beethoven's occasional irony and critical displeasure.[lxx] 'Pathos' and 'earnest passion' permeate the mood of the first movement augmented by 'strong determination'.[lxxi] Although only a young man, Beethoven here exemplifies an 'impressive command of tragic expression' and an 'attitude of resistance' — 'even defiance is evident'.[lxxii] His music has 'concentrated power' and is 'loaded with dark pathos'. Invoking the views of the Beethoven scholar Harry Goldsmidt — that certain musical phrases can be read as verbal texts — Martin Geck proposes: 'Beethoven's composition is partly rhetorical, as if the piano were a human voice.'[lxxiii]

By 1799, the key of C minor was assuming particular significance for Beethoven. It was also the key chosen by other composers wanting to suggest the 'pathetic' in music and this tonality already had strong associations with several of Beethoven's earlier compositions. For example, in his youthful Bonn days it was the key of his first published work, the *Dressler* Variations and the important *Joseph Cantata*. Later came the powerful String Trio Op. 9, No. 3 and the previously discussed Piano Sonata Op. 10, No.1.[lxxiv] Beethoven's use of C minor also foreshadowed things to come in the form of the First Symphony, the Third Piano Concerto, the Violin Sonata Op. 30, No. 2 and, of course, the Fifth Symphony.[lxxv] In the sonata's closing *Allegro*, some consider the agitated feeling that is present may be a recollection by Beethoven of similar ideas he used in his youthful *Electoral* Sonata WoO 47, No. 2.[lxxvi] Czerny describes the music here as 'extremely impetuous ... a brilliant character, in the symphony style'.[lxxvii] Was Schubert perhaps recalling, and then absorbing, the mood of Beethoven's *Pathétique* Sonata when he set about composing his own great, and troubled, Piano Sonata in C minor, D. 958?[lxxviii]

The second movement is one of Beethoven's most well known and much-loved slow movements and, in Fischer's words, 'one of Beethoven's most glorious inspirations'.[lxix] Some commentators praise this movement in terms bordering on the pious and reverential: Romain Roland refers to the 'wonderful serenity' that prevails and which 'breaths a religious calm';[lxx] Ernst von Elterlein suggests 'a profound peace takes possession of the master's soul' and is given expression in 'the sustained singing theme'.[lxxi] Beethoven does indeed designate the slow movement *Adagio cantabile* – 'in a singing style' – that is both 'consoling' and exploits the piano's 'singing quality'.[lxxii] In her estimation of the music, Marion Scott invokes the imagery of a 'southern love scene', proposing: '[What] could be more softly flowing than Beethoven's slow movement with its almost unbelievably melodic loveliness and velvety tone?'[lxxiii] Philip Radcliffe suggests the composition of the slow movement of the Piano Sonata Op. 13, 'must have sunk deeply into Beethoven's conscience' and then re-emerged, in variant form, in such near-contemporary works as the String Quartet in G major Op. 18, No.2, the Septet Op. 20 and, more distantly in expanded form, in the slow movement of the Ninth Symphony.[lxxiv] Truscott acknowledges the beauty of Beethoven's *Adagio* and also draws attention to the probable influence on him of Jan Dussek whose own Piano Sonata Op. 35, No. 3 had been published just two years before Beethoven's. Truscott believes Dussek supplied Beethoven with 'the rhythmic shape of his main theme', that, interestingly, is given the performer's direction *patetico*.[lxxv]

Two anecdotes concerning the *Adagio* of the Sonata *Pathétique* are of particular interest. The first concerns Arnold Schoenberg at the period when he was teaching 'Form and Analysis' at the University of California. The musician and writer Dika Newlin was in his class in the summer of 1939. She recalls the second movement of Op. 13 formed the basis of his instruction — which was apparently transacted with Schoenberg's typical humour — despite his failing health.[lxxxvi] Mrs. Richard Powell, better known by her maiden name of Dorabella Mary Penny, met Edward Elgar in the summer of 1904 and discussed the encrypted 'meaning' of his *Nimrod* Variation. (Dorabella was herself the subject of the tenth *Nimrod* Variation — the *Allegro Intermezzo*.) Elgar's reply is tantalising. He mentioned Beethoven as a source of influence: 'Yes, can't you hear it at the beginning? Only a hint, not a quotation.' Dorabella concludes: 'That night my mind was full of all that I had heard, and of the *Nimrod* Variation. The serenity of the Beethoven air (*Adagio*, Sonata in C minor, Op. 13) riding triumphant over sordid worries.'[lxxxvii]

The mood of the *Rondo* finale is less intense and serious than the previous two movements. In the opinion of Charles Rosen, not until the *Waldstein* Sonata does Beethoven 'find a way to endow a rondo with significant grandeur' although he acknowledges some of the drama of the first movement is captured in the coda of the finale.[lxxxviii] Interestingly, Anton Rubinstein, the great nineteenth-century champion of Beethoven, who regularly played four or five sonatas at a typical recital, suggested the Op. 13 might be more appropriately titled the *Dramatic*, given the 'action' and 'dramatic life' that characterises the work as a whole.[lxxxix] Von Elterlein also remarks on the energy of the finale, describing it as being 'full of power for fresh exertions and renewed activity'.[xc] The last movement may have been originally conceived for more then one instrument, possibly for the combination of piano and violin; in this context sketches for the last movement also occur with ideas for the String Trio Op. 9, dating from 1798.[xci] Ries tells how Beethoven played this particular rondo 'with a very special expressiveness'. He also remarks how Beethoven's playing could at times be 'most capricious' — doubtless he had little time to practise his compositions. Notwithstanding, Ries adds that he usually kept a very steady rhythm 'and only occasionally, indeed, very rarely, speeded up the tempo somewhat'. Reflecting more generally, Ries considered Beethoven's powers of invention at improvisation to be matchless with regard to the wealth of ideas which poured forth, the moods to which he surrendered and the challenges he imposed upon himself: 'His improvising was ... the most extraordinary thing one could ever hear, especially when he was in a good humour or irritated.' He concludes: 'All the artists I ever heard improvise did not come anywhere near the heights reached by Beethoven in this discipline.'[xxii] A correspondent in the *AmZ* of 22 April 1799 also remarks how Beethoven excelled in improvisation, bringing forth a 'most extraordinary ... succession of ideas, varied on the spur of the movement and enriched with figuration'.[xxiii]

Claudio Arrau, reflecting on his youth, states that he learned the Piano Sonata Op. 13 when young but that it was not until he was seventeen before he really understood it. He refers to a moment of revelation that gave him the interpretive insight he had been missing: 'Suddenly, it occurred to me that the last movement is full of anxiety, a tremendous anxiety infuses it.' From that moment, Arrau developed his own way of playing the movement.[xxiv] Czerny's view is close to Arrau's; he describes the mood of the conclusion as 'fiery'.[xxv] Wilfrid Mellers reminds us that when considering the prevailing mood of the *Pathétique* Sonata, we should be mindful how Beethoven's deafness would soon cut him off from the world physically as well as spiritually and he would become 'a law until himself to find salvation'. Reflecting more generally on the composer's future creative life, Mellers' adds: 'The more ferocious are the blows of fate, the more energetically must Beethoven's will subdue them. His art becomes the imposition of order upon chaos. The Mozartian equilibrium between the artist and his world has gone.'[xvi] Having invoked these somewhat troubled thoughts, it is perhaps fitting to conclude with two accounts that bear testimony to the manner in which Beethoven's *Pathétique* Sonata has given solace to humanity in ways, and under circumstances, beyond the composer's wildest imagining. Arthur Rubinstein recalls his time in Paris during the Great War. He visited a hospital where soldiers were being treated. He recounts how his eyes caught sight of an upright piano in the corner of the room. It was abominably out of tune and two or three keys were mute but he sat down and began to play: 'I played the Sonata *Pathétique* of Beethoven; I had never played it like that before. It was not how it sounded it was how I felt. I was ready to cry, and so was everyone present.'[xvii] The gifted Jewish violinist Alma Rosé was interred in Birkenau Concentration Camp where she eventually perished. For a time she was allowed to create a small chamber orchestra. Her friend and fellow inmate Anita Lasker-Wallfisch survived to recall a performance of the Sonata *Pathétique* arranged for three violins and cello. Her account is deeply moving. She recalls: 'How can I describe that evening ... It was a link with the outside, with beauty, with culture – a complete escape into an imaginary and unattainable world ... We lifted ourselves above the inferno of Birkenau into a sphere where we could not be touched by the degradation of concentration camp existence.'[xviii]

---

[i] The text and translation are derived from: Wayne M. Senner (*et al*), 1999, p. 148.

[ii] The only other piano sonata to which Beethoven sanctioned a title was his Op. 80a, *Les Adieux*.

[iii] The title of the sonata and its compositional origins are discussed by Barry Cooper, 2000, p. 83 and Stewart Gordon, 1996, p. 158.

ᶦᵛ Harold Craxton and Donald Francis Tovey, *Beethoven: Sonatas for pianoforte, Piano Sonata in C minor, Op. 13*, [1931], p. 63.

ᵛ Oskar Bie, 1966, p. 169.

ᵛᶦ Harold Truscott, *The piano music* [of Beethoven] in: Denis Arnold, editor, 1973, p. 99

ᵛᶦᶦ William Newman, 1963, p. 514.

ᵛᶦᶦᶦ Romain Rolland, 1937, p. 141. Later in his writings, Rolland apologized to the reader for perhaps being too hard on a work he considered had become rather too famous and had, thereby, 'falsified the public judgement of Beethoven'.

ᶦˣ Marion Scott, 1940, p. 136.

ˣ Ernst Toch cited by Diane Jezic, 1989, p. 135.

ˣᶦ Wilfrid Mellers, 1957, pp. 57—8.

ˣᶦᶦ For a facsimile reproduction of the Title Page see: Beethoven House, Digital Archives, Library Document No. Elder, 128.

ˣᶦᶦᶦ There is uncertainty concerning the precise sequence of the Elder and Hoffmeister Editions. See: Barry Cooper, 2000, p. 83 and Peter Clive, 2001, p. 99. Credit for the first publication probably goes to Hoffmeister.

ˣᶦᵛ The quotation is derived from the historical notes to the Augener Edition No. 8030 of the Piano Sonata Op. 13. See also: Peter Clive, 2001, pp. 205—6.

ˣᵛ Anton Schindler, 1860, English edition: Donald MacArdle, 1966, p. 69.

ˣᵛᶦ Barry Cooper, 1990, pp. 67—8.

ˣᵛᶦᶦ The Landsberg Sketchbook is discussed by Douglas Johnson (*et al*) 1985, pp. 103—6.

ˣᵛᶦᶦᶦ For further commentary on the surviving sketches of the Piano Sonata Op. 13, see: Barry Cooper, 2000, p. 82 and Paul Mies, 1929, p. 32 and p. 182.

ˣᶦˣ Wilfrid Mellers, 1957, p. 58.

ˣˣ Denis Matthews, 1972, pp. 172—3.

ˣˣᶦ Anton Schindler, 1860, English edition: Donald MacArdle, 1966, p. 417.

ˣˣᶦᶦ Anton Schindler cited in H. C. Robbins Landon, *Beethoven*, 1970, p. 61.

ˣˣᶦᶦᶦ Ferdinand Ries recalled in Thayer-Forbes, 1967, p. 367.

ˣˣᶦᵛ *Ibid*, p. 211.

ˣˣᵛ In this regard Wölfl was not unlike Sergei Rachmaninoff who stood six feet five tall and could span almost an octave and a half.

ˣˣᵛᶦ Hans Conrad Fischer and Erich Kock, 1972, p. 12.

ˣˣᵛᶦᶦ Thayer-Forbes, 1967, p. 204.

ˣˣᵛᶦᶦᶦ Quoted by Tia de Nora, 1997, pp. 149—50. The story of Beethoven's encounter with Wölfl is also described in: H. C. Robbins Landon, 1976—80, p. 592.

ˣˣᶦˣ Tomaschek's recollections, as recalled by Ignaz von Seyfried, are preserved in: Ludwig Nohl, 1880, pp. 35—7. For other accounts of the encounter between Wölfl and Beethoven see also: Thayer-Forbes, 1967, pp. 205—7 and Tia de Nora, 1997, pp. 152—4.

ˣˣˣ Thayer-Forbes, 1967, p. 205.

ˣˣˣᶦ Ferdinand Ries in: Franz Wegeler, 1838, English edition, 1988, p. 71. For a more extended account of Beethoven's pianistic confrontation with Steibelt, see: Thayer-Forbes, 1967, p. 257.

ˣˣˣᶦᶦ Letter of 19 February 1796. See Emily Anderson, 1961, Vol. 1 Letter No. 16, p. 22.

ˣˣˣᶦᶦᶦ Emily Anderson, 1961, Vol. 1 Letter No. 32, p. 34. The letter is preserved in facsimile as: Beethoven House Digital Archives Library Document HCB

BBr 139.

xxxiv Theodore Albrecht, 1996, Vol. 1, Letter No. 31, p. 56.

xxxv The *AmZ* review is cited in: H. C. Robbins Landon, *Haydn: The years of the Creation*, p. 1977, p. 590.

xxxvi Wayne M. Senner (*et al*), 1999, p. 147.

xxxvii Anton Schindler, 1860, English edition: Donald MacArdle, 1966, pp. 78–9.

xxxviii From the recollections of Carl Czerny, see: Paul Badura-Skoda, editor, 1970, p. 33.

xxxix Wayne M. Senner (*et al*), 1999, p. 148.

xl Reichardt's recollections of musical life in Vienna were published in Amsterdam in two volumes (1809–10) under the title *Vertraute Briefe geschbrieben auf einer Reise nach Wien.*

xli From the recollections of Johann Friedrich Reichardt in: Ludwig Nohl, 1888, pp. 72–3.

xlii Anton Schindler, 1860, English edition: Donald MacArdle, 1966, p. 162.

xliii From the recollections of Carl Czerny, see: Paul Badura-Skoda, editor, 1970, p. 7.

xliv Peter Clive, 2001, p. 243.

xlv,45 From a letter of Felix Mendelssohn to Carl Zelter 22 June 1830 cited in: *The view of posterity*, Elsie and Denis Arnold in: Denis Arnold and Nigel Fortune, editors, 1973, pp. 499–500.

xlvi Adrian Williams, 1990, p. 227.

xlvii Anton Schindler, 1860, English edition: Donald MacArdle, 1966, pp. 443–4. Schindler here overlooks the piano arrangements made of Beethoven's compositions in his own lifetime, including some sanctioned by him.

xlviii Letter to a friend dated 24 May 1891 in: Charles L. Graves, 1903, p. 368.

xlix For a representation of Bourdelle's sculpture, with accompanying text, see: Beethoven House, Digital Archives Library Document B 1972.

l Gerhard von Breuning, 1874, English edition 1992, p. 38.

li Wanda Landowska, 1926, p. 48.

lii This description is consistent with Johann Schlosser's observation: 'Beethoven's way of working did not fit the conventions of a regulated household.' Johann Aloys Schlosser, 1827, edited by Barry Cooper, 1996, p. 77.

liii The instruments of Anton Walter were considered to be among the finest of their day. Mozart purchased one that is preserved in his birthplace at Salzburg. See our text: Piano Sonatas Op. 2, Nos. 1–3.

liv The reminiscences of Carl Czerny are told in: Oscar Sonneck, 1927 pp. 25–7. Czerny adds that Beethoven's first lessons concentrated on practice of the all the scales and the adoption of a good hand position, the latter being, as Czerny remarks, 'Something at the time still unknown to most players'. His audition with Beethoven must have been doubly challenging since a number of distinguished musicians were also present, including Mozart's pupil Franz Süssmayr.

lv As told in William Newman, 1963, p. 513. For a similar account, see also: Thayer-Forbes, 1967, p. 242.

lvi Weber had arrived in Vienna in 1806 and soon became part of an 'anti-Beethoven clique'. See: Tia De Nora, 1997, Table 12 and p. 159.

lvii Taken from a letter of Moscheles to the music publisher Nikolaus Simrock. See: Theodore Albrecht, 1996, Vol. 1, Letter No. 58, p. 100.

lviii Peter Clive, 2001, p. 82.

lix Edwin Fischer, 1959, p. 46.

lx Glen Gould cited in: Tim Page, 1987, p. 51.

lxi Alfred Brendel in conversation with David Dubal see: David Dubal, 1985, p. 102.

lxii Barry Cooper, 1991, pp. 240–1.

lxiii Donald Tovey, *Piano Sonata C minor, Op. 13*, 1931, revised by Barry Cooper, 1998, p. 63.

lxiv Harold Truscott, *The piano music*, in: Denis Arnold and Nigel Fortune, editors, 1973, p. 99.

lxv Similarities of dramatic feeling have also been found in Verdi's Opera *Macbeth*, in particular Lady Macbeth's first *scena*. See: Harold Craxton and Donald Francis Tovey, *Beethoven: Sonatas for pianoforte, Piano Sonata in C minor, Op. 13*, [1931], p. 273.

lxvi Martin Geck, 2003, p. 70.

lxvii Wilfrid Mellers, 1957, p. 58.

lxviii Anton Schindler, 1860, English edition: Donald MacArdle, 1966, p, 446, n. 319 and pp. 497–501.

lxix Wayne M. Senner (*et al*), 1999, p. 147.

lxx Rochlitz is suggested as the reviewer by William Newman, 1963, p. 513. For brief biographical details of Rochlitz, together with a portrait, see: Beethoven House Digital Archives Library Document B 1326.

lxxi Ernst von Elterlein, 1898, pp. 58–9.

lxxii William Kinderman, *The piano sonatas* [of Beethoven], in: *The Cambridge companion to Beethoven*, Glenn Staley, editor, 2000, p. 117.

lxxiii Martin Geck, 2003, p. 70.

lxxiv Adapted, in part, from Barry Cooper, 2000, pp. 83–4.

lxxv Beethoven's use of C minor, in the context of his growing development of the piano sonata, is mentioned by Maynard Solomon, 1977, p. 103.

lxxvi This is the view of Barry Cooper, 2001, p. 84 and Maynard Solomon, 1997, p. 46.

lxxvii From the recollections of Carl Czerny, see: Paul Badura-Skoda editor, 1970, p. 33.

lxxviii See: Alfred Brendel, 2002, p. 124.

lxxix Edwin Fischer, 1959, p. 47.

lxxx Romain Rolland, 1917, pp. 134.

lxxxi Ernst von Elterlein, 1898, pp. 59–60.

lxxxii Denis Matthews, 1985, p. 81.

lxxxiii Marion Scott, 1940, p. 136.

lxxxiv Philip Radcliffe, Piano music in: *The age of Beethoven*, The new Oxford history of music, Vol. VIII, Gerald Abraham, editor, 1988, p. 340.

lxxxv Harold Truscott, *The Piano music* [of Beethoven] in: Denis Arnold, 1973, editor, p. 99. Similar views are expressed by Eric Blom, 1938, p. 57.

lxxxvi Dika Newlin, 1980, p. 70.

lxxxvii Mrs. Richard Powell, 1994, pp. 131–2.

lxxxviii Charles Rosen, 2002, p. 144.

lxxxix Edward Krehbiel, 1971, p. 165.

xc Ernst von Elterlein, 1898, pp. 60–1. Elterlein also considers the formal construction of the final movement to be suggestive of Mozart.

xci Thayer-Forbes, 1967, p. 214 and p. 514.

xcii Ferdinand Ries in: Franz Wegeler, 1838, English edition, 1988, p. 87–8.

xciii Cited in Thayer-Forbes, 1967, p. 215.

xciv Claudio Arrau in conversation with David Dubal, see: David Dubal, 1985, p. 25.

xcv From the recollections of Carl Czerny, see: Paul Badura-Skoda editor, 1970, p. 33.

xcvi Wilfrid Mellers, 1967, p. 61.

xcvii Arthur Rubinstein, 1973, p. 437.

xcviii As movingly recounted in: Richard Newman, 2000, pp. 261–2. A performance of the Piano Sonata in C minor, Op. 13 has been recorded by Malcolm Binns on a fortepiano of 1802 by Matthäus Stein, source: L'Oiseau-Lyre: D 183 D3. The work has also been recorded on a fortepiano of 1800 by Johann Schantz by Ella Sevskaya, source: *Beethoven in Context*, Quil 303. Sevskaya makes the following observations: 'The *Pathétique* sounds more intimate if less full of pathos, with the subtle sound of this piano than on a modern grand.' Sevskaya is referring to her performance on the Johann Schantz instrument of 1800. She adds: 'The *Rondo* takes on a light character, and if it is possible to do justice to the description, "not stormy but with the expression of a lament" which Czerny claims is how Beethoven envisaged this movement.' Source: Sleeve notes to her recording *Beethoven in Context*, Quil 303.

PIANO SONATAS
OP. 14, NOS. 1—2

'For me ... these sonatas are among the sweetest and most sympathetic children of Beethoven's heart.'

Edwin Fischer, *Beethoven's Pianoforte Sonatas: A Guide for Students and Amateurs*, 1959, p. 48.

'I love both sonatas from Op. 14. They are most sensitive works in pastel colours, and the second contains a great deal of fun.'

Alfred Brendel in: *The World of the Concert Pianist*, David Dubal, 1985, p.103.

Beethoven followed the Sonata *Pathétique* with two further sonatas that comprise his Op. 14. In scale and style these works are mutually compatible and are occasionally performed in recital as a pair. Both sonatas are less dramatic than their famous predecessor. Their character is more genial and less spectacular; perhaps for this reason they have sometimes been overlooked or have been 'unjustly dismissed as minor works'. Extensive sketches exist for No. 1 and place the main period of its composition from mid-1798 through to the autumn of 1799. Less is known of the creation origins of No. 2. In committing so many of his preliminary thoughts in the form of sketches, Beethoven was following a working procedure he had already established years previously when still a youth in Bonn. As Donald Tovey remarks: 'No artist has left more authoritative documentary evidence as to the steps of his [creative] development than Beethoven.' His sketches and compositional drafts cover the so-called 'three-periods' of his career, and give insights into the origins of many of his most important works; throughout, the same level of rigorous self-criticism, integrity and tireless search for 'perfection' is evident.

Tovey further remarks, 'if we regard his sketches as a diary, their significance becomes inestimable'.

Publication of the Op 14 Piano Sonatas was announced in the *Vienna Journal* on 21 December 1799 as: '*Deux Sonates pour le Piano Forte, composée et dédiées à Madame la Baronne de Braun, par Louis van Beethoven. Oeuvre 14. Vienne chez T. Mollo et Comp.*' Tranquillo Mollo had established his publishing business just one year before the publication of Beethoven's Op. 14 Piano Sonatas. He brought out several other works of the composer including the First Piano Concerto and the ground-breaking String Quartets Op. 18. The dedicatee Baroness Josephine Braun was an accomplished pianist and wife of Baron Peter Braun, a civil servant, industrialist and theatre manager. He occupied a powerful position in Vienna's cultural and musical life through his control over the Royal and Imperial Theatres (Kärntnertor-Theater and Burgtheater) and his ownership of the Theater an der Wien — where the ill-fated premier of the first version of Beethoven's opera *Leonora* (*Fidelio*) took place. Although Braun was an excellent pianist himself, his enemies alleged he was indifferent to the arts — a possible consequence of the enmity held against him arising from his single-minded control over the planning of his theatre programmes. Even Beethoven, whose relationship with Braun was at times turbulent, had to be circumspect. The inference is that by bestowing the dedication of the Op. 14 Piano Sonatas on Baroness Josephine, Beethoven would thereby secure favour for a future theatre-concert of his own — primarily to premier his First Symphony that he was then completing.

The modest scale and restrained tonal sonorities of the Op. 14 Piano Sonatas see Beethoven returning to the lighter concept of the genre that he had already explored in Piano Sonatas Nos. 1 and 2 of his Op. 10 set. As such they are well suited to the more intimate style of performance typical of a domestic-scale, chamber-music environment. In assisting our understanding of the character of these sonatas, Edwin Fischer remarks how we are too ready to label Beethoven as *heroic*. We overlook that there can be gentle heroes. Fischer encourages: 'Let us not forget Beethoven's gentle side.' In the same spirit, Paul Bekker reminds us how we mistakenly consider Beethoven as 'a purely tragic figure' whose music is self-revelatory of inner conflict; this, he protests, 'is a one-sided estimate which does less than justice to the great composer's delight in life and the joys thereof'. Also relevant to an understanding of the spirit of the Op. 14 Piano Sonatas is the fact that, having just completed the stormy and tempestuous Piano Sonata

Pathétique, it is understandable the composer would wish to turn his mind to works of a contrasting mood. As Denis Matthews observes: 'Many composers have turned from a powerfully dramatic work to a more relaxed one.'[xiv]

Concerning the mood prevailing in the two Piano Sonatas Op. 14, Anton Schindler gives an account of a conversation with Beethoven that he states took place sometime in 1823. He describes how he raised the question with the composer of the 'inner meaning' of his piano sonatas — a subject upon which the composer is known to have been particularly reticent. Concerning the Op. 14 Sonatas, he alleges Beethoven said they embodied a form of dialogue between two principles whose meaning was inherent within the music and which required no interpretive words to be written above the score.[xv]

In our desire for a better understanding of Beethoven, we want to believe in the veracity of such remarks as the forgoing. On this occasion, however, it has to be conceded some commentators have reservations the conversation ever took place, or, if it did, that Schindler may have elaborated the account to suit his own ends.[xvi] Konrad Wolff though gives Schindler the benefit of the doubt. He discusses Schindler's interpretation at some length and considers his views may have some 'inner truth'. He cites the manner in which, from the start, 'right hand and left hand are brought into rhythmic and melodic opposition' — 'pleading' and 'resisting'.[xvii] William Newman also remarks on the 'person-ified conflict', thought by some to be inherent within the Op. 14 Piano Sonatas. He then observes, in more everyday terms, how much they differ from their dramatic predeces-sor the Sonata *Pathétique*: '[They] are relatively quiet and intimate, distinguished by their charm, wit, and craftsmanship.'[xviii]

Carl Czerny heard Beethoven perform the two Piano

Sonatas Op. 14 and studied them himself shortly after he had started taking lessons with the composer – sometime between 1801–02. His legacy of these studies is preserved, regrettably all too succinctly, in his later writings on the interpretation of Beethoven's works for the piano. Czerny's performance-indications deviate somewhat from the *Urtext* (original edition) but Paul Badura-Skoda, in his editorial commentary to Czerny, regards them as being 'noteworthy' and, in part, 'very beautiful'. He singles out Czerny's crescendo and diminuendo 'wedges' and conjectures they 'could well go back to Czerny's own study with Beethoven'.[xix]

[i] For example, Svyatoslav Richter performed the two Piano Sonatas Op. 14 as a pair at one of his London recitals in 1963. 'His intimate manner suited them, for they resist any attempt at the grand manner.' As recalled by Denis Matthews, 1967, p. 22.

[ii] Philip Radcliffe, *Piano music* in: *The age of Beethoven, The new Oxford history of music, Vol. VIII,* Gerald Abraham, editor, 1988, pp. 340.

[iii] Barry Cooper, 2000, p. 245. Earlier commentators have suggested Beethoven was working on the Op. 14 Piano Sonatas as early as 1795 but this is now doubted.

[iv] Donald Tovey, *Ludwig van Beethoven* in: *The classics of music,* Michael Tilmouth editor, 2001, pp. 333–4.

[v] Derived from the Augener Edition No. 8030 of *Beethoven's piano sonatas* (undated). Augener gives the date of publication as 22 December but other authorities (Thayer-Forbes and Cooper) give 21 December.

[vi] For a complete list of the works of Beethoven, published by T. Mollo and Co., see: Peter Clive, 2001, pp. 236–7.

[vii] A facsimile of Mollo's First Edition of Beethoven's Op. 14 Piano Sonatas is reproduced on the Beethoven House website, Digital Archives Library Document Jean Van der Spek C Op. 14.

[viii] The biographies of Braun and his wife are documented in: Peter Clive, 2000, pp. 43–5.

[ix] The circumstances of the Dedication are discussed by Barry Cooper, 2000, pp. 88–90.

[x] Stewart Gordon, 1996, p. 160.

[xi] Charles Rosen, 2002, p. 144.

[xii] Edwin Fischer, 1959, pp. 48–9.

[xiii] Paul Bekker, 1925, p. 103.

[xiv] Denis Matthews, 1985, p. 83.

[xv] Anton Schindler, 1860, English edition: Donald MacArdle, 1966, p. 406.

[xvi] Harold Truscott is one authority who considers Schindler's remarks to be somewhat fanciful, given Beethoven's reluctance to give detailed interpretations of his compositions. See: Harold Truscott, *The piano music* [of Beethoven], in: Denis Arnold and Nigel Fortune, editors, 1973, p. 102.

xvii Konrad Wolff, 1990, p. 157.

xviii William Newman, 1963, p. 515.

xix From the recollections of Carl Czerny, see: Paul Badura-Skoda, editor, 1970, p. 16.

PIANO SONATA
IN E MAJOR,
OP. 14, NO. 1

'Op. 14, No. 1 is the only sonata Beethoven ever
arranged for string quartet, and his decision to
undertake the transcription in 1802 was surely
motivated by the special affinity of this sonata to
the quartet medium.'

William Kinderman, Liner notes to *Beethoven: The Complete Sonatas*, Philips 446 909-2, 1996, p. 26.

Sketches for the Piano Sonata Op. 14, No. 1 are found in two collections of documents; the Kafka Miscellany that preserve Beethoven's musical thoughts for the period 1786–99, and the related sketch-drafts called the Fischhof Miscellany that date from about 1790 to 1799. Beethoven's first thoughts for the sonata may have their origin in 1795 when he was completing work on his Piano Concerto in

B-flat major, Op. 19.[ii] Serious work on the sonata, however, dates from the summer of 1798 when Beethoven was also working on his Violin Sonatas Op. 12.[iii] Of particular interest is that in 1802 he was prevailed upon to arrange his Piano Sonata Op. 14, No. 1 for string quartet. This was despite his misgivings over such an undertaking, as he made clear in a letter to the music publisher Breitkopf and Härtel of Leipzig. He writes: 'The *unnatural mania*, now so prevalent, for transferring even *pianoforte compositions* to stringed instruments, instruments which in all respects are utterly different from one another, should really be checked.' Beethoven was firmly of the opinion that 'only *Mozart* could arrange for other instruments the works he composed for the pianoforte; and *Haydn* could do this too.'[iv] [Beethoven's italics] Notwithstanding these reservations, as is implicit in our opening quotation, the transcription is generally considered to be successful and, more importantly, the work in question well suited to the undertaking.

Despite making the protests we have just cited, Beethoven undertook a number of transcriptions of chamber and orchestral works for the piano, or collaborated with others in their creation; these include the Seventh Symphony and his celebrated four-hand arrangement of the Grosse Fuge — completed on his deathbed.[v] The arrangement of the Piano Sonata Op. 14, No. 1 is, however, unique in being the only piano sonata Beethoven arranged for string quartet.[vi] Given the extent to which the two versions of the music are, so to speak, intertwined, rather than merely make passing reference to the string-quartet version we will consider it here in some detail.

The string-quartet arrangement was published in May 1802 by the *Bureau des Arts et d'Industrie*, known also as the *Kunst-und Industrie-Comptoir*. A founder member of this firm was Joseph Sonnleithner who, a few years later, supplied Beethoven with the libretto for his opera *Leonora* (*Fidelio*). The string quartet was the first of Beethoven's works to be published by the *Bureau* and was soon followed by a succession of major compositions in what was to become one of the composer's most creative periods. As was the custom of the day, the quartet was issued in parts for the individual players; remarkably, it was not published in full score until 1910. Like the original Piano Sonata Op. 14, No. 1, Beethoven dedicated the string quartet to Baroness Josephine von Braun.

The suggestion of writing in the medium of the string quartet was originally made to Beethoven by the Hungarian Count Anton von Apponyi, sometime in 1795, at one of Prince Lichnowsky's morning concerts. Apponyi was a friend of Prince Esterhazy and had previously (1793) commissioned from Haydn the six celebrated String Quartets that the composer divided between his Op. 71 and Op. 74. Beethoven did not respond to the Count's proposals but they may have subconsciously influenced the style of his writing for the Piano Sonata Op. 14, No. 1. Denis Matthews, for example, remarks how 'the quartet texture, common enough in Beethoven's piano music, *stares up from the opening lines* [present author's italics]'. As we have already noted in our prefatory quotation, William Kinderman is amongst those who believe: '[Beethoven's] decision to undertake the transcription in 1802 was surely motivated by the special affinity of this sonata to the quartet medium.'

We should refer more correctly to the string quartet as being an arrangement rather than a note-for-note transcription of the piano score. In making the quartet arrangement, Beethoven had to rewrite parts of the piano sonata to give further consideration to such specific quartet properties as sonority, blending and timbre that differ inherently from those of the pianoforte. He also had to bear in mind the practical limits of the five-octave keyboard for which the piano sonata was conceived. In the piano sonata, the high G sharp and high A that Beethoven required were beyond the compass of the contemporary keyboard; by transposing the key a semitone higher, from E to F, high passages were reinstated for the first violin. Furthermore, Beethoven was also able to give added resonance in the bass by placing the low C within the cello's reach, thereby putting the dominant as low down as possible.[xii]

Although Beethoven's string-quartet arrangement has not entered the string quartet repertoire, it has enduring value as vigorously affirmed by Donald Tovey: 'Beethoven's wonderful arrangement of this sonata as a string quartet should be in the hands of every student ... A good rehearsal of it by competent players is a lesson in style such as no other piece can give.' Of the piano sonata itself he remarks: 'We have here a unique demonstration of what the pianoforte can do better than strings, what qualities of bowed instruments it can really imitate, what qualities it can suggest without imitating, and in what characteristics it is ... totally opposite to the string quartet.'[xiii]

The first movement of the sonata exhibits passages that are particularly suggestive of string quartet, part-writing.[xiv] A Mozartian influence is discernible 'in the skilful arrangement of distinct yet related material'.[xv] Carl Czerny describes the mood as being 'of a serene and noble character'; notwithstanding, he encourages the performer to be 'lively' and to regard the movement as comprising a sequence of ideas that 'alternate in a picturesque, poetical manner and form a small, but rich picture'.[xvi] For Tovey, the prevailing mood is 'reflective' and for Edwin Fischer it is 'elegiac in character'.[xvii] [xviii] Eric Blom considers Beethoven's *Allegro* artfully conceals depths of 'profound feeling' that are both restrained yet penetratingly suggested.[xix]

Czerny perceived in the second-movement *Allegretto* 'a kind of sad humour' requiring it to be played 'in an earnest but lively manner, though by no means humorously or capriciously'.[xx] Does this movement, 'gently touched with melancholy' and animated with 'softly swaying motion', perhaps anticipate the coming of the Piano Sonata in E minor, Op. 90?[xxi] Tovey considered this movement 'wonderful', not least for the 'soft full chords' of the pianoforte; he thought the writing here in the sonata to be more beautiful than in the string quartet whose spareness he likens to a 'line drawing ... starved of material'.[xxii] Visual imagery is at the heart of Egerton Lowe's analysis of this movement. He asks: 'Should we *always* think of pictures or stories, of churches, cathedral, or ruins, of scenes of nature and such like, when listening to or performing real abstract music such as we find in Beethoven's sonatas?' He acknowledges musical interpretation it often assisted by our having 'a picture in the mind' but, he argues, there are certain movements, such as this *Allegretto*, that 'put one in a mood no poet or painter can invoke'. His conclusion is disarming: 'Let us enjoy the sweet simplicity of music for its own art-sake alone.'[xxiii]

Humour abounds in the *Rondo* finale with some characteristic Beethovenian surprises 'such as the virtuosic central section'.[xxiv] 'Very gay and lively' is Czerny's estimation, with the encouragement to the performer to interpret the music 'with a certain playful facility'.[xxv] Romain Rolland though did not consider Beethoven's Piano Sonata Op. 14, No. 1 to be one of the composer's strongest works. He was won over though by the final movement, commending it for its 'great beauty and finish'.[xxvi] Fischer concludes his survey of this work in the same spirit: 'And so we leave this lovely, warm piece in E major, the key to which Beethoven entrusted so many of his happiest movements.'[xxvii]

i   For a discussion of Beethoven's surviving sketchbooks for the period of composition of the Piano Sonatas Op. 14, see: Barry Cooper, 1991, p. 185.

ii   Eric Blom, 1938, pp. 67–8 and Thayer-Forbes, 1967, p. 214.

iii   Douglas Johnson, 1985, pp. 81–2.

iv   Emily Anderson, 1961, Vol. 1, Letter No. 59, pp. 74–5.

v   The score of this was considered lost but came to light in an American seminary in recent times. Beethoven only made the transcription because he was dissatisfied by the efforts of others to whom he had first entrusted the assignment.

vi   Perhaps as many as a dozen of Beethoven's other piano sonatas were arranged for string quartet in his lifetime, most of them anonymously – and usually to the composer's displeasure!

vii   The origins of the string quartet arrangement are discussed in: Robert Winter and Robert Martin, editors, 1994, pp. 145–8. The string quartet parts were discovered in 1903 by Dr. W. Altmann who created the score that was published in 1910 (Eulenberg Miniature Score), see: John Shedlock, 1918, p. 29.

viii   Thayer-Forbes, 1967, p. 262.

ix   Denis Matthews, 1967, p. 22.

x   William Kinderman, Liner Notes to *Beethoven: The complete sonatas,* Philips 446 909-2, 1996.

xi   These considerations are discussed in detail by Lewis Lockwood, in: Sieghard Brandenburgh, editor, 1998, pp. 175–180.

xii   See, for example: Barry Cooper, 2000, p. 115; Eric Blom 1938, pp. 67–8; and Denis Matthews, 1985, p. 83.

xiii   Harold Craxton and Donald Francis Tovey, *Beethoven: Sonatas for pianoforte, Piano Sonata in E major, Op. 14, No. 1*, p. 192, [1931].Donald Tovey, 1931.

xiv   Discussed by Stewart Gordon, 1996, p. 160.

xv   William Kinderman, Liner Notes to *Beethoven: The complete sonatas,* Philips 446 909-2, 1996.

xvi   From the recollections of Carl Czerny, see: Paul Badura-Skoda, editor, 1970, p. 34.

xvii   Harold Craxton and Donald Francis Tovey, *Beethoven: Sonatas for pianoforte, Piano Sonata in E major, Op. 14, No. 1*, p. 192, [1931].

xviii   Edwin Fischer, 1959, pp. 48–9.

xix   Eric Blom, 1938, pp. 67–8.

xx   From the recollections of Carl Czerny, see: Paul Badura-Skoda, editor, 1970, p. 34.

xxi   This is the opinion of Paul Becker, 1925, p. 103.

xxii   Harold Craxton and Donald Francis Tovey, *Beethoven: Sonatas for pianoforte, Piano Sonata in E major, Op. 14, No. 1*, p. 192, [1931].

xxiii   Egerton Lowe, 1929, p. 53.

xxiv   William Kinderman, Liner Notes to *Beethoven: The complete sonatas,* Philips 446 909-2, 1996.

xxv   From the recollections of Carl Czerny, see: Paul Badura-Skoda, editor, 1970, p. 34.

xxvi   Romain Rolland, 1917, p. 145. He likens the theme of the final movement to that of a hunting song.

xxvii   Edwin Fischer, 1959, p. 50.A performance of the Piano Sonata in E major, Op. 14, No. 1 has been recorded by Malcolm Binns on a fortepiano of 1802 by Matthäus Stein. Source L'Oiseau-Lyre: D 183 D3.

PIANO SONATA IN G MAJOR, OP. 14, NO. 2

'The G major Sonata, Op. 14, No. 2, is a charmingly sensuous and tightly integrated work, whose outer movements are linked by motivic and rhythmic connections.'

William Kinderman, Liner Notes to *Beethoven: The Complete Sonatas*, 1996, Philips 446 909-2.

Little is known of the creation origins of Beethoven's Piano Sonata Op. 14, N0. 2. However, given Beethoven's propensity to work on a number of compositions together, it seems probable the piece evolved within the same, or closely related, timescale as that of its companion the Piano Sonata Op. 14, No. 1. Beethoven's Op. 14, No. 2 is one of his most genial works, and serves to remind us the composer was an artist of many moods. Edwin Fischer likens the spirit prevailing throughout the sonata to that of a 'sunlit forest scene' that calls to mind '[Beethoven's] love of the fresh, open country [and] his delight in long ambling walks'. William Kinderman, whom we have cited above, further describes the piece as being possessed of a 'gentle lyrical character' but which is also seized by 'episodes of surprising dramatic power'. In this work, together with its E major companion, Kinderman sees Beethoven absorbing 'the spirit of Mozart' whom he considers exerted a profound influence on the young composer and, as he reminds us, would in turn influence his melodically gifted young contemporary Franz Schubert.

Carl Czerny considered this sonata to be 'one of the most lovely and agreeable compositions' and encourages the performer to play the piece 'with delicacy and tender feeling, but still lively'. In his systematic study of all Beethoven's piano sonatas, Donald Tovey singles out Op. 14, No. 2 for not only being an 'exquisite little work' but cites it as one which, being largely free of technical difficulties, is amenable to performance by the younger student with small hands. Also with the performer in mind, Egerton Lowe enthuses: 'Banish sorrow and care, philosophy and worldliness ... be lissom, contented and gay, abandoned to the happy joy of being alive with such a music-treasure rippling its happy course.'

Beethoven displays his sense of humour in the opening movement in a manner that recalls Haydn's writing for the piano. The movement as a whole has been likened to 'growth from a single germ'. As in the case of the companion piece Op. 14, No. 1, Beethoven once more encountered the limitations of the five-octave keyboard; in this case it precluded him from letting the music rise to the desired high A flat. With the performer in mind, Fischer further invokes the imagery of a forest scene: 'The *Allegro* of the first movement should not be taken too fast in order to give the little birds in the right hand time to sing their songs'.

The slow movement is marked *Andante* and is based around a set of variations that are cast 'in an ostentatiously simple style' which recalls 'many of the modest sets of Mozart'. This is the first example of the variation form in a Beethoven piano sonata. Here, the miniature set of variations is consistent with the 'confiding' and 'affectionate' character of the sonata. A march theme is 'sometimes draped decoratively, sometimes broken by syncopation [and] sometimes broken up into syncopated harmonies'. These simple procedures foreshadowed even mightier things to come; consider, for example, the Piano Sonata Op. 57 – the *Appassionata*. Fischer regards Beethoven's syncopated chords as being *Schumannesque*. Concerning their interpretation, Tovey has typically acerbic advice for the performer: 'The syncopated counterpoint in the *Right Hand* should deliver its repeated notes like a nightingale, not a hen.' We can almost imagine Beethoven remonstrating in such a manner with one of his own errant pupils. Beethoven maintains the musical tension and humour to the very end of the movement; 'pouncing loud chords are paired with scurrying gestures of rapid passage work in a game of cat and mouse'. He approaches the final chord very softly (*pp*) and then proclaims it very loudly (*ff*) in a spirited gesture reminiscent of the famous musical joke in the *Andante* of Haydn's *Surprise* Symphony, No. 94.

Beethoven designates the final movement *Scherzo*, synonymous with *Jest* and in musical terms *spirited* and *playful*. He sanctioned this expression sparingly in the piano sonatas and in his Op. 14, No. 2 it is used to signify 'wit and humour' with a main theme that is 'rhythmically disorientating' and 'is never quite sure whether it has two or three beats in a bar'. Regarding Beethoven's use of the scherzo form,

145

a conversation between Beethoven and Anton Schindler is of interest. It is known in later life Beethoven wished to have a complete edition of his works published and plans for such were considered in 1816 and again 1823. According to Schindler, intrigues frustrated and prevented such an edition. Concerning the piano sonatas, he recalls how Beethoven wondered whether this edition might achieve a greater unity if some of the earlier four-movement sonatas should be reworked to a three-movement form. Apparently, Beethoven also wanted to reconsider some of his scherzos — and perhaps have them published separately. Schindler ends his reminiscence: 'However, this desire on Beethoven's part did not go uncontested, for everyone in our circle had his favourite *scherzo* or other movement, and would not countenance its being removed from the place it had so long occupied.'[xii]

Czerny's performance instructions here are: 'Very humorous and serenely gay, and therefore to be played lively and fluently.'[ix] Beethoven sustains the jovial spirit 'by the use of short motives that end in staccato'.[xi] Fischer reverts to his forest-scene imagery once more and refers to these motives as being like playful insects that 'dart about in the clear air of this G major'.[xii] A 'pastoral', even 'rustic' style is also evident with perhaps a drone of bagpipes wafting through the air 'kin to some of the more humorous bagatelles Beethoven wrote both early and late in life'.[xiii] '[The] dancing merriment of the scherzo-rondo says the last word and rounds off the whole.'[xiv]

---

[i] See, for example: Thayer-Forbes, 1967, pp. 214 and Barry Cooper, 2000, p. 245.

[ii] Edwin Fischer, 1959, p. 50.

[iii] William Kinderman, Liner Notes to *Beethoven: The complete sonatas,* Philips 446 909-2, 1996, pp. 27–8. Regarding Franz Schubert, his teacher Antonio Salieri remarked: 'I can teach him nothing, he knows it all already; God has taught him!'

[iv] From the recollections of Carl Czerny, see: Paul Badura-Skoda, editor, 1970, p. 45.

[v] Donald Tovey, *Piano Sonata Op. 14, No. 2*, 1931, p. 207.

[vi] Egerton Lowe, 1929, p. 55.

[vii] Discussed by Charles Rosen, 2002, p. 146 and Donald Tovey, *Piano Sonata Op. 14, No. 2*, 1931, p. 207. Tovey also refers here to Beethoven's 'certain ornateness of style'.

[viii] Romain Rolland, 1917, p. 145.

[ix] Donald Tovey, *Piano Sonata Op. 14, No. 2*, 1931, p. 207. The limitation is felt in particular at bar 102.

[x] Edwin Fischer, 1959, p. 51.

[xi] Charles Rosen, 2002, p. 147.

[xii] Denis Matthews, 1967, p. 22.

[xiii] Paul Becker, 1925, p. 104.

[xiv] Edwin Fischer, 1959, p. 51.

[xv] Donald Tovey, *Piano Sonata Op. 14, No. 2*, 1931, p. 207.

[xvi] Stewart Gordon, 1996, p. 160.

[xvii] Barry Cooper, 2000, p. 86.

[xviii] Matthew Rye, BBC Radio Three website: *Beethoven experience*, 3 June 2005.

[xix] Anton Schindler, 1860, English edition: Donald MacArdle, 1966, pp. 402–3.

[xx] From the recollections of Carl Czerny, see: Paul Badura-Skoda, editor, 1970, p. 45.

[xxi] Stewart Gordon, 1996, p. 160.

[xxii] Edwin Fischer, 1959, p. 51.

[xxiii] Charles Rosen, 2002, p. 147.

[xxiv] Paul Becker, 1925, p. 104. A performance of the Piano Sonata in G major, Op. 14, No. 2 has been recorded by Malcolm Binns on a fortepiano of 1802 by Matthäus Stein. Source: L'Oiseau-Lyre: D 183 D3

PIANO SONATA IN B-FLAT MAJOR, OP. 22

'[This] sonata, in its beautifully contrasting and associated movements, unites in a very original way, brilliant and vigorous qualities, qualities that are solemn and moving, cheerful, pleasing and turbulently grand or sublime.'

Allgemeine musikalische Zeitung, 6 August 1807.

Beethoven's Piano Sonata in B-flat major, Op.22 is the composer's eleventh piano sonata, in the series bearing an opus number, and made its appearance more-or-less contemporaneously with several other of his major compositions. These include: Pianoforte Concerto in C (Op. 15), Quintet for Piano and Wind (Op. 16), Sonata for Pianoforte and Horn (Op. 17), Six String Quartets (Op. 18), Pianoforte Concerto in B flat (Op. 19), Septet (Op. 20), and Symphony

No. 1 (Op. 21). This body of work is testimony to Beethoven's creative development and growing experience in composition. Concerning the Piano Sonata Op. 22, it is a large-scale work with a performing time of about 25 minutes; perhaps for this reason Beethoven gave it the sub-title *Grande Sonate*. He was particularly pleased with this creation and regarded it as being 'really something' — or words to that effect (see below). Notwithstanding, the rather conservative writing Beethoven employed in the working-out of the sonata has led to it being regarded as one of his more conventional piano works — with subsequent relative neglect in recital programmes. Together with the previous piano sonatas, this work constitutes a form of 'epilogue' or 'farewell' to the standard high Classic sonata and stands at 'a transition toward a new line of development' — a process that would continue and be realized right up to Beethoven's final years.[i]

Donald Tovey refers to the musical form in Piano Sonata Op. 22 as being 'the most conventional of all Beethoven's works'.[ii] In a later commentary he elaborates this point of view stating Beethoven was well aware of the virtues of 'dramatic force' and 'originality' but that it was also 'a fine thing to achieve smoothness also and to show that he was no longer inferior to Mozart in Mozart's own line'.[iii] Harold Truscott endorses this assessment with a play on words: '[It] is as though Beethoven were determined to show just how extraordinary ordinary things can be.'[iv] In similar vein, Denis Matthews views Beethoven's Op 22 as 'a work of consolidation rather than adventure' in which its 'decorum' and 'respectability' lead to 'a certain predictability in form and mood' but also 'gathering strength from convention'.[v]

Beethoven's newest sonata must have seemed far from 'conventional' and 'predictable' at the time of its appearance as is evident from a contemporary review: 'Beethoven's inexhaustible genius gives each of his works an entirely new character, one cannot easily be compared with the other.' Other commentators have been equally fulsome in their acknowledgement of the virtues of Beethoven's Op. 22. Romain Rolland is unequivocal: 'This sonata is the finest since the Opus 10, No. 3 in D ... full of characteristic vigour for its own sake.' Paul Bekker is like-minded: 'The whole work pulsates with energy and conscious power, disregarding troublesome doubts. Few of Beethoven's works display such a confident, conscious joy in existence.' Edwin Fischer recognizes Beethoven's 'graceful, florid piano-writing' whilst acknowledging the work as a whole may be 'less dramatic' than some of his other works and may account for its reduced popularity today. On this subject, Glenn Gould pays fulsome tribute to the virtues of Beethoven's early sonatas, recognizing 'Beethoven's senses of structure, fantasy, variety, thematic continuity, harmonic propulsion and contrapuntal discipline' all of which, he asserts, 'were absolutely, *miraculously* in alignment'. But of the Piano Sonata Op. 22 he proclaims: '[Much] as I love the early sonatas — and I really *do* love them there is one dud in the batch ... the Op. 22'! Charles Rosen is more restrained; he accepts Op. 22 may not enjoy the popularity of other of Beethoven's sonatas, but considers it to be 'one of [Beethoven's] most accomplished works' and 'a demonstration of his compositional powers'. Alfred Brendel supports the belief that, with the Piano Sonata in B flat major of 1800, Beethoven had reached 'the end of a period in his sonata writing'. He remarks: 'You can feel that he has mastered a certain manner: it comers too easily for him.' William Newman expresses related thoughts. He cites the writings of the nineteenth-century musicologist Wilhelm von Lenz who was the first to suggest the musical style and development of Beethoven's compositions can be divided into three characteristic periods as elaborated in his — *Beethoven et ses trois styles.* Within this context he comments: '[The] Op. 22 in B flat is the sonata that Lenz regarded as ending the first of Beethoven's "three periods" — the last one, that is, in the direct line of Mozart and Haydn and the last one within the bounds of a Classically abstract concentration of main ideas.'ᵢᵢᵢ Tovey is in broad agreement but interjects words of caution: '[The] Op. 22 is far from being a Mozartian work ... Many works lie between this and the complete establishment of Beethoven's "second style" but this is the last that has removed all younger traces of conflict without anticipating new conflicts or new issues.'ₓᵢᵥ

Before continuing our discussion of the Piano Sonata Op. 22, we briefly consider Beethoven's growing reputation in the context of Vienna at the dawn of the new century. In April 1800 he gave his first public concert in Vienna; the venue was the *Royal Imperial Court Theatre.* He premiered one of his piano concertos (probably the Op. 15), the First Symphony and the Septet — the success of which proved so popular it plagued the composer in later life. These works, and Beethoven's improvisation at the piano, prompted the correspondent of the *Allgemeine musikalische Zeitung* to report: 'Herr Beethoven took over the theatre and this was truly the most interesting concert in a long time.'ᵥ Beethoven's star was rising and publisher's would soon be eager to accept his works — largely on his financial terms. Doubtless, in recognition of the composer's rising accomplishments, Beethoven's patron Prince Karl Lichnowsky conferred on his protégée an annuity, in effect a stipend, of 600 florins — about sixty pounds sterling. The Prince's intention was to provide Beethoven with some financial security until he obtained a secure post. The payments continued for several years until, as we shall later discuss, he received a more secure annuity in 1809 from three of

Vienna's most notable citizens. Of Lichnowsky's support, Schindler remarks: 'The great love this princely family felt for Beethoven was constant and unwavering.' He adds: 'In fact, for ten to twelve years, nearly all Beethoven's works were first tried out in the music circle of Count Lichnowsky.'[xv]

An article in the *Allgemeine musikalische Zeitung* for the year 1800 places the value of Beethoven's annuity in its contemporary context – and also reveals how little the average musician received for his labours. A player in an orchestra could expect to earn from 200 to 300 gulden (about 20–30 pounds sterling). In the Austro-Hungarian Empire at this time the gulden was a standard unit of currency and was the equivalent of the Austrian silver florin (about two English shillings or a half-crown, depending on currency values). Violinists were in the worst position, because, the article states, 'they are expected to play for nothing since ten dilettante can readily be found who will do so with great pleasure'. A teacher of pianoforte could earn a decent living but 'must possess enough self-denial to serve willingly the houses that support him' and, furthermore, 'to give lessons 'morning, noon and night'. On a more positive note, the article concludes: 'But as there are exceptions ... amongst musicians, so there are worthy houses to which the above complaints do not apply.'[xvi] Clearly, the household of Prince Lichnowsky was one of these and Beethoven was fortunate to secure a patron who valued his gifts so highly.

For the summer of 1800, Beethoven took quarters for himself and a manservant in a house in Unterdöbling, a district of Döbling located in the wooded slopes to the northeast of Vienna. In Beethoven's day it was about an hour's walk from the city centre. Here Beethoven could escape the oppressive summer heat of the city, stroll the woodland paths and devote his mind to composition. As

Thayer remarks, with typical eloquence: 'Throughout this period of Beethoven's life, each summer is distinguished by some noble composition, completed, or nearly so, so that on his return to the city it was ready for revision and his copyist.'[xviii] The work of May-August, 1800 was devoted to composing the Piano Sonata Op. 22 and, as was the composer's habit, of working simultaneously on other compositions. Part of Beethoven's sketchbook for the summer of 1800 survives. It is a typical makeshift effort of Beethoven's own creation, stitched together from leftover sheets of manuscript paper.[xix] It reveals sketches for the Piano Sonata Op. 22 and thoughts for the Violin Sonata Op. 23. Other sketches indicate Beethoven was also at work on the companion Violin Sonata Op. 22 and the String Quartets Op. 18.[xx] The sketches were originally owned by the book dealer Richard Wagener and were later purchased by the Royal Berlin Library (Staatsbibliothek).[xxi] Analysis by Paul Mies, amongst others, reveals the many sides of Beethoven's creativity; the sketches, for example, show Beethoven searching for the appropriate keys to convey his required feelings of pathos and passion.[xxii]

The growing interest in Beethoven on the part of music publishers has been mentioned. Illustrative of this is an approach made to Beethoven by the music publisher and composer Anton Hoffmeister. He had been in the music business since 1784 and had published several of Mozart's compositions; devotees of Mozart remember him today for his association with the *Hoffmeister* String Quartet (K. 499).[xxiii] In 1800, Hoffmeister established the *Bureau de musique* in Leipzig with his partner Ambrosius Kühnel and approached Beethoven with a request to publish more of the composer's works; in 1799 he had already brought out an edition of the Sonata *Pathétique*. Beethoven, resident once more in Vienna, replied to Hoffmeister in a letter of

15 December 1800. He first addresses Hoffmeister as 'Most beloved and worthy brother'; this was Beethoven's favourite, and rather florid, salutation he reserved for use when addressing fellow composers and others whom he considered devoted their lives to the promotion of music. He apologised for the delay in writing and added, with typical humour, that he preferred to write musical notes than letters of the alphabet. He lists several compositions that are ready for publication, most of those referred to above, and 'a grand solo sonata' — namely the Piano Sonata Op. 22. He suggested Hoffmeister should set the prices to be paid for the various compositions, concluding 'no doubt we shall come to an agreement'.xxiv

Early in the New Year (1801), Beethoven wrote once more to Hoffmeister; he dates the letter 15 January 'or thereabouts' — illustrative of his neglect of everyday matters. This time Beethoven suggested prices himself for his compositions: twenty ducats (about ten pounds sterling) for the Septet, which was already becoming popular, and the same for the First Symphony; the Piano Concerto Op. 19 was offered at half price (ten ducats), Beethoven giving the reason: 'I do not consider it to be one of my best concertos.' He also asks for twenty ducats for the Piano Sonata Op. 22 describing it as 'a first-rate composition'. Beethoven tells Hoffmeister how much he dislikes the business-side of a composer's life and laments: 'There ought to be in the world *a market for art* [Beethoven's italics] where the artist would only have to bring his works and take as much money as he needed.' He then takes a swipe at the Leipzig music critics: 'Just let them talk ... they will certainly never make anyone immortal, nor will they ever take immortality away from anyone upon whom Apollo has bestowed it' — Beethoven clearly considered himself to be one so favoured by the gods.xxv

Later in the year (21 June), Beethoven wrote once more to Hoffmeister to confirm his obligations to the publisher. Under the copyright arrangements of the day Hoffmeister received exclusive rights to publish the Piano Sonata Op. 22 and to benefit from the proceeds.[xxvi] Beethoven had to wait almost a year before the sonata was finally published in March 1802. The outcome, however, pleased him: 'My sonata is beautifully engraved – but it took a nice long time.' With this in mind he gently exhorts Hoffmeister: 'Do send my Septet into the world a little more quickly, because the rabble is waiting for it.'[xxvii] The Title Page to the first edition of the Piano Sonata Op. 22 reads: '*Grande Sonate pour le Piano Forte, composée et dédiée à M. le Comte de Browne, Brigadier en Service de S. M. I. de toute la Russie, par Louis van Beethoven. Oeuvre 22. Leipzig, Kühnel.*'[xxviii] The dedicatee, Count Johann Georg von Browne, has been mentioned previously in relation to the Piano Sonatas Op. 10.

With his Piano Sonata Op. 22, Beethoven returned to the four-movement structure he had pioneered so successfully in the Op. 2 set, the Op. 7 and the strikingly original Op. 10, No. 3. In these works, 'Beethoven had raised the level of ... treatment of the four-movement sonata concept to a very high level'. As remarked above, the Op. 22, notwithstanding its expansive four-movement form, is essentially a work of consolidation of this achievement and does not represent the composer 'penetrating new frontiers'.[xxix] The composer's creative powers are, however, very much in evidence. Discussing the construction of Beethoven's Op. 22, Konrad Wolff first reminds us that 'musical material has no value *in itself* [Wolff's italics] ... aesthetically, the only thing that matters is what the composer does with it'. He adds it is because Beethoven understood 'the importance of the thematic substance for his oeuvre' and was aware 'the individualization of a new work takes time and effort' that he constantly made sketches and revisions of his compositions. Through this process, Wolff concludes, Beethoven shaped 'the ideal principal motive' leading to, in the case of the B-flat major Piano Sonata, Op. 22, 'the miracles of the opening measures of the first movement'.[xx] Rosen also draws attention to the opening of the Op. 22 Sonata and finds a parallel with it and Beethoven's other piano sonata in B-flat major, the majestic *Hammerklavier*. He suggests the Op. 22 begins as the *Hammerklavier* but '*on a miniature scale*' [Rosen's italics]. Elsewhere, Rosen adds: 'There are interesting coincidences, as certain tonalities seem to develop different and individual qualities.'[xxi] Whereas the *Hammerklavier* has 'heroic ambitions', in the first movement of the Op. 22 Beethoven uses material of a 'neutral character', the intrinsic interest being in how he handles this material. Rosen sums up: 'The first movement is not picturesque, and neither tragic nor humorous, and it lays no claim to lyricism. It is content to be masterly.'[xxii]

In the original notice of the Piano Sonata Op. 22, published in 1807, the reviewer declared: 'The first movement, *Allegro con brio*, is full of powerful motion and proclaims the restless effects of an energetic heart in all traces of a now rising, now falling passion.'[xxiii] Ninety years later, commentators were disposed to comment in similar fashion: 'The first movement ... is distinguished by energy and strong youthful vitality; a fresh pulse of life beats through these tones, a joyful, courageous feeling pervades the whole.'[xxiv] Rolland finds Beethoven's resolution of spirit and originality in the first movement the hallmarks of which he considers are 'the purity of its strength and the austerity of its brilliance'.[xxv] 'The energy of this movement 'derives from the opening snatch of a motif' and is progressively rendered more resonant in passage work that employs 'sonorous doublings in thirds, sixths and octaves'.ᵡᵡᵛⁱ Michael Broyles considers the 'motion and character' of the composition as 'overtly symphonic' in its 'rhythmic drive, overall tone, melodic simplicity ... and phrase structure'. He praises Beethoven's writing for being 'particularly brilliant in pianistic effect, not so much because it makes extraordinary demands upon the performer but because the material is so well suited to the keyboard'.ᵡᵡᵛⁱⁱ Perhaps Beethoven is recalling some of the brilliance of his Op. 2, No. 3 'but with considerably more subtly'.ᵡᵡᵛⁱⁱⁱ Bekker regards the first movement of the Op. 22 as being 'written for the pianist' and being 'full of musical vitality ... so indeed is the whole work'.ᵡᵡⁱˣ This is consistent with Carl Czerny's advice to the performer: 'To be played with energy and decision.'ˣˡ

The second movement, marked *Adagio con molta espressione*, has been likened to an 'Italianate aria' enriched with 'arresting harmonic complexes';ˣˡⁱ notwithstanding, the full flowing melody is 'surrounded with a romantic haze that is essentially Teutonic'.ˣˡⁱⁱ Earlier commentators found this slow movement particularly affecting: Egerton Lowe considered 'it must rank as one of [Beethoven's] very fine slow movements';ˣˡⁱⁱⁱ Romain Roland thought the long drawn out *Adagio* 'possess great charm';ˣˡⁱᵛ and for Ernst von Elterlein — 'A deep yearning breathes through the theme, a pleasant calm and atmosphere of romance pervade the entire movement.'ˣˡᵛ For one modern-day musicologist, Beethoven's expansiveness calls to mind 'Dussek's wonderful slow movement from his C minor Sonata Op. 35, No.3'.ˣˡᵛⁱ Another observer feels: 'The marvellously spiritual tuneful E-flat *Adagio* [is] a foretaste of the nocturne of the Romantic period.'ˣˡᵛⁱⁱ William Newman finds in the mood of the *Adagio*, 'a new pre-Mendelssohnian charm and grace' possessing affinities with the composer's Fourth Symphony, written, some six years later in the same key of B flat.ˣˡᵛⁱⁱⁱ Czerny's directions to the performer, perhaps recalling Beethoven's own interpretation, are: 'The melody [to be] extremely *cantabile* and the bass *legato* ... The character of the whole [to be] soft, mild and tranquil.'[xlix]

The *Minuetto* of the third movement looks back to the style of the '*ancien regime*' with 'the poet-composer in non-controversial mood'.[l] 'Graceful lyricism' abounds with 'occasional bursts of irritation; the results are highly individual.'[li] Truscott goes further and asserts 'no eighteenth-century composer ever wrote a minuet like this ... in the manner of accompaniment ... a wide-ranging base ... [and] texture'. 'Here' he asserts, 'is the really original Beethoven, bringing forward the most basic things in conjunctions no one had thought of before.'[lii] However, as so often in Beethoven, what, in the final version, may seem 'self-evident' and 'natural' was frequently the outcome of much creative thought and rejection of initial ideas. His Piano Sonata Op. 22 is no exception. Mies's study of the surviving sketches for the sonata reveal typical Beethovenian processes of refinement bearing upon the working out of the melodic line, the use of ornamentation, the filling out of moods of pathos and passion and even the choice of key.[liii]

The final movement adopts the rondo form Beethoven had used so effectively in the preceding Piano Sonatas Opp. 2, No. 2, Op. 7, Op. 13 and Op. 14, No.1. Bekker characterizes the treatment of this as 'flexible' and 'decorative', being based on 'simple harmonies' that are 'graceful without being superficial'. The music's 'deeper stirrings are repressed to allow a peaceful, joyful mood to bear'. Beethoven would use the rondo in other of his piano sonatas (Opp. 28, Op. 31, No1, Op. 49, No. 1 and Op. 53) but regarding the B flat Sonata Bekker adds: 'The Rondo of Op. 22 is the last and most exquisite expression of a period of intensely conscious happiness.'[liv] (Beethoven's hearing was worsening and the realization of this would soon cause him great anguish.) Edwin Fisher considered the Rondo of the Op. 22 to be the sonata's most significant movement, 'significant by virtue of its wealth of ideas, thematic relationships and blend of variational and contrapuntal technique'.[iv] Truscott has pointed out how much larger the variation form is worked in this sonata than in earlier rondos and all 'cunningly extracted from the final note of a shake' (ornament). This idea, Truscott further observes, so appealed to Beethoven that he used it once more in the Rondo of the Violin Sonata Op. 24.[lvi] Beethoven's sketches for the piano sonata further reveal the composer's facility for working on a number of compositions at the same time and being prepared to exchange material between them. Barry Cooper's study of these reveals an advanced sketch of over fifty bars showing the final movement conceived in A major, prompting him to conjecture 'perhaps in this case Beethoven was considering transferring the theme to another work but then decided against it'.[lvii]

Tovey regarded Beethoven's skilful ending of his Op. 22 as a '*tour de force* in punctuality'. He likens the composer's proficiency to the adroitness of an oarsman's last stroke that 'brings his boat to the landing stage and enables him to ship skulls, throw in the painter [bowline] to the waterman, and step on shore in the same moment'.[lviii] An anecdote from the memoirs of Sergey Prokofiev is of interest. At the age of fourteen he was a student at the Conservatory at St. Petersburg and wished to be considered for entry to the 'special piano class' — an endeavour known to be demanding. His teacher at the time was Alexander Winkler who asked his youthful protégé if he knew Beethoven's Piano Sonata Op. 22. 'By heart', was Prokofiev's reply. He subsequently performed the piece before 'eight or nine examiners' — all grim-faced — but who, two hours later, told him he was accepted. Winkler's response was to say: 'To start with we'll work on techniques to strengthen your fingers. It'll be a bit boring at first, but there's nothing we can do about it!'[ix]

We close with three evaluations of this delightful and sometimes neglected work. Stewart Gordon writes: 'Although it is true that Beethoven presents us with few or no experimental features in the Op. 22, his musical thinking, nevertheless, is on very solid ground throughout the work. The sonata deserves higher marks than it has been accorded in many quarters.'[x] Charles Rosen's summary-remarks are: 'Opus 22 demonstrates Beethoven's control of all the conventions of Viennese style. The works that follow are more openly radical. This sonata is his farewell to the eighteenth century.'[xi] Our final words of appreciation are left to the doyen of Beethovenians, Donald Tovey: 'Only a very great composer could have written this sonata, and a good performance of it promises a capacity for presenting the greater things that followed it.'[xii]

[i] This is the first recognised published review of the Piano Sonata Op. 22. The text and translation are derived from: Wayne M. Senner, et al, 1999, p. 173.

[ii] Discussed by Maynard Solomon, 1977, pp. 104–5 and p. 115.

[iii] Donald Tovey, 1944, p. 106.

[iv] Donald Tovey, 1949, p. 274.

[v] Harold Truscott *The piano music* in: Denis Arnold and Nigel Fortune, editors, 1973, pp. 102–3.

[vi] Denis Matthews, 1985, p. 83.

[vii] Wayne M. Senner, et al, 1999, p. 173.

[viii] Romain Rolland, 1917, p. 146.

[ix] Paul Bekker, 1925, p. 104.

[x] Glenn Gould in conversation with Tim Page, see: Tim Page, 1992, pp. 100–1.

[xi] Charles Rosen, 2002, p. 147.

[xii] David Dubal in conversation with Alfred Brendel, see: David Dubal, 1985, p. 103.

[xiii] William Newman, 1963, p. 515.

[xiv] Harold Craxton and Donald Francis Tovey, *Beethoven: Sonatas for pianoforte, Piano Sonata Op. 22*, 1931, p. 81.

[xv] Thayer-Forbes, 1967, pp. 254–5.

xvi   Anton Felix Schindler, *Beethoven as I knew him*, edited by Donald W. MacArdle and translated by Constance S. Jolly from the German edition of 1860, 1966, p. 50.

xvii   Cited in Piero Weiss and Richard Taruskin, 1984, p. 325.

xviii   Thayer-Forbes, 1967, p. 259.

xix   The facsimile of a surviving bifolium (double-format page) can be viewed at: Beethoven-House Bonn, Digital Archives, Library Document HCB BSk 25/73.

xx   For a discussion of this creative period see: Barry Cooper, 1990, p. 88 also Barry Cooper, 2000, p. 95 and Thayer-Forbes, pp. 266–7.

xxi   Douglas Johnson, 1985, pp. 96–7. The sketches also indicate Beethoven was revising passages of the Piano Concerto in C major, Op. 15.

xxii   Paul Mies, 1929. Mies makes numerous references to the Op. 22 Piano Sonata throughout his text.

xxiii   Hoffmeister's relationship with Beethoven is documented by Peter Clive, 2001, pp. 166–7.

xxiv   Emily Anderson, 1961, Vol. 1, Letter No. 41, pp. 42–3. A facsimile of the original letter can be viewed on the Beethoven House Website: Beethoven-House Bonn, Digital Archives, Library Document NE 181.

xxv   Emily Anderson, 1961, Vol. 1, Letter No. 44, pp. 47–8. Beethoven's description of the Piano Sonata Op. 22 translates more literally as 'This sonata has really washed itself'! Donald Tovey suggests the equivalent idiomatic translations: 'This sonata takes the cake' or 'That's the way to do it'. See: Harold Craxton and Donald Francis Tovey, *Beethoven: Sonatas for pianoforte, Piano Sonata Op. 22*, 1931, p. 81.

xxvi   Emily Anderson, 1961, Vol. 1, Letter No. 50, pp. 55–7. A facsimile of the original letter can be viewed on the Beethoven House Website: Beethoven-House Bonn, Digital Archives, Library Document HCB BBr 33. The date is given as 22 or 23 June.

xxvii   Emily Anderson, 1961, Vol. 1, Letter No. 57, pp. 73–4. A facsimile of the original letter can be viewed on the Beethoven House Website: Beethoven-House Bonn, Digital Archives, Library Document NE 197.

xxviii   Beethoven House Website: Beethoven-House Bonn, Digital Archives, Library Document C 22/12.

xxix   Stewart Gordon, 1996, p. 161.

xxx   Konrad Wolff, 1990, pp. 113–4.

xxxi   Charles Rosen, 1976, p. 422.

xxxii   Charles Rosen, 2002, p. 147.

xxxiii   The review quoted from the *Allgemeine musikalische Zeitung* is derived from: Wayne M. Senner. et al, 1999, Vol. 1, p. 173.

xxxiv   Ernst von Elterlein, 1898, p. 62.

xxxv   Romain Rolland, 1937, pp. 121–2.

xxxvi   Denis Matthews, 1985, p. 83.

xxxvii   Michael Broyles, 1987, p. 59.

xxxviii   Philip Radcliffe, *Piano music* in: *The age of Beethoven, The new Oxford history of music, Vol. VIII*, Gerald Abraham, editor, 1988, pp. 340–1.

xxxix   Paul Bekker, 1925, p. 104.

xl   From the recollections of Carl Czerny, see: Paul Badura-Skoda, editor, 1970, p. 35.

xli   Denis Matthews, 1985, p. 83.

[xlii] Philip Radcliffe, *Piano music* in: *The age of Beethoven, The new Oxford history of music, Vol. VIII*, Gerald Abraham, editor, 1988, pp. 340–1.

[xliii] Egerton Lowe, 1929, p. 61.

[xliv] Romain Rolland, 1917, p. 146.

[xlv] Ernst von Elterlein, 1898, p. 64.

[xlvi] Harold Truscott *The piano music* in: Denis Arnold and Nigel Fortune, editors, 1973, pp. 102–3.

[xlvii] Paul Bekker, 1925, p. 105.

[xlviii] William Newman, 1963, p. 515.

[xlix] From the recollections of Carl Czerny, see: Paul Badura-Skoda, editor, 1970, p. 36.

[l] Paul Bekker, 1925, p. 104.

[li] Philip Radcliffe, *Piano music* in: *The age of Beethoven, The new Oxford history of music, Vol. VIII*, Gerald Abraham, editor, 1988, pp. 340–1.

[lii] Harold Truscott *The piano music* in: Denis Arnold and Nigel Fortune, editors, 1973, pp. 102–3.

[liii] Paul Mies, 1929, p. 178.

[liv] Paul Bekker, 1925, pp. 104–5.

[lv] Edwin Fischer, 1959, p. 51.

[lvi] Harold Truscott *The piano music* in: Denis Arnold and Nigel Fortune, editors, 1973, pp. 102–3.

[lvii] Barry Cooper, 1990, p. 124.

[lviii] Donald Tovey, 1944, p. 110.

[lix] Sergey Prokofiev, 1979, pp. 89–9.

[lx] Stewart Gordon, 1996, p. 124.

[lxi] Charles Rosen, 2002, p. 149.

[lxii] Harold Craxton and Donald Francis Tovey, *Beethoven: Sonatas for pianoforte, Piano Sonata Op. 22*, 1931, p. 81.A performance of the Piano Sonata in B flat, Op. 22 has been recorded by Jörg Demus on a fortepiano of 1825 by Nanette Streicher: source Harmonia Mundi 30 469 K. The sonata has also been recorded on Beethoven's own Conrad Graf pianoforte of 1825 – more correctly, the instrument was on loan to him. The performance is by Elly Ney. Source: Colosseum Mst 1015.

PIANO SONATA IN A-FLAT MAJOR, OP. 26

'Op. 26 marks a significant progress in Beethoven's efforts to give unmistakable individuality to each new work, as if he were not simply writing a new sonata but redefining the genre each time.'

Charles Rosen, *Beethoven's Piano Sonatas: a Short Companion*, 2002, p. 150.

In the context of Beethoven's creative development, the Piano Sonata in A-flat major, Op. 26 may be considered alongside his two contemporary piano sonatas that form the composer's Op. 27. All three works derive from around the year 1800 and, more importantly, the compositions may be considered experimental in nature insofar as through them 'the sonata concept is adjusted in various ways'. These sonatas take a decidedly different turn after the achievement of Op. 22. They share several features including, 'a more individualized poetic feeling, particularly in the outer movements, a more vocal-rhetorical tone, an improvisatory quality, and a much greater flexibility of motion'. The Piano Sonata Op. 26, is the first of Beethoven's thirty-two piano sonatas to have no example of what would be later considered 'a standard sonata form'. With this work, '[Beethoven] struck out in a radically new direction'. It is a creative and imaginative 'hybrid', made so by the order and character of the movements that are 'new and thoroughly romantic'. 'An *andante con variazioni* takes the place of the customary *allegro* of cyclic form; then follows a *scherzo, molto allegro,* going like the wind, instead of the usual *adagio;* then an intensely sombre slow movement, the *Marcia funebre sulla morte d'un Eroe,* and then a rushing finale.'.

Donald Tovey describes Piano Sonata Op. 26 as a 'divertimento' in the sense Haydn would have called a work 'in sonata style with a preponderance of light sectional forms'. Maynard Solomon groups the Piano Sonatas Op. 26 and Op. 27 Nos. 1 and 2 and remarks how, in these works, 'Beethoven appeared to take leave of the traditional sonata-cycle form in favour of a more flexible construction — the *fantasy sonata*'. This, he adds, 'permitted the freer expression of improvisatory ideas and displaced the climax of the final movement'. Philip Radcliffe finds a parallel between Beethoven's Op. 26 Piano Sonata and Mozart's Piano Sonata in A, K 331: 'In spite of much fine music, the work as a whole ... gives the impression of a suite rather than a sonata.' He suggests Beethoven might have called it, as he did its companion Piano Sonatas of Op. 27, '*Sonata quasi una fantasia*'. Denis Matthews regards what he calls 'the order of events' as being 'unusual in the extreme', citing, as already mentioned, variations for the first movement, scherzo second, a funeral march third and 'a rippling finale in sonata-rondo form'.[i] Carl Dahlhaus views Beethoven's 'irregular order of movements', with a slow movement first, as one of the composer's 'typical characteristics', representative of what he regards as Beethoven's 'transitional period'.[ii] Concerning such matters, Harold Truscott introduces a note of caution with his observation: 'There is nothing notably indicative of a new period in either the first or the last movement, both of which could have been written a few months earlier.' In a more general aside he reminds us, there are no 'hard and fast lines of demarcation' that characterise a composer's change of outlook; such things, he contends, happen gradually 'and of which the composer is usually unaware until it has happened'.[iii] As Matthews observes, concerning Beethoven's new achievements: 'Whether we view them as *late early* or *early middle* Beethoven is unimportant as it is more vital to note their flexibility of form in relation to Op. 22.'[iv] Less equivocal is that at the period of composition of his Piano Sonata Op. 26, Beethoven, at the age of thirty, was possessed of 'an immense force within himself' that disposed him in the next decade to 'a dizzy course of creativity'. In the genre of writing for the keyboard he gave expression to this with the group of seven piano sonatas — Op. 26, Op. 27, Nos. 1—2, Op. 28 and Op. 31, Nos. 1—3 — all of which were written between 1800 and 1802. However, to progress any further 'thematic conflict and tension of development' were not enough; 'the sonata as an entity had to be considered'.[v]

Beethoven's 'second compositional phase', frequently styled as his 'heroic period', is best exemplified in the *Eroica* Symphony of 1803—4. Matthew Rye though suggests the slow movement of the Op. 26 Piano Sonata shows thoughts 'expressing a kind of Romantic heroism in his music' were in the composer's mind as early as 1800.[vi] Marion Scott also considers Beethoven's Sonata in A-flat major, Op. 26 'was a marked departure towards romanticism'. From then onwards she believes 'through most of the sixteen sonatas of his middle period, it seems as if he were intent on enriching classic sonata form with the romantic elements in music'. She quotes from Sir Hubert Parry's *Beethoven* of 1886: 'The imagination and the reason must both be satisfied, but above all things the imagination.' Scott concludes: 'To unify two apparently opposite principles, without the loss of any essential good, was a task after Beethoven's heart.'[vi] Also close to Beethoven's heart was his growing fame and success with Vienna's music publishers, to which we now make passing reference before considering the Op. 26 Piano Sonata in greater detail.

On 21 May 1801, the Leipzig music publisher Gottfried Christoph Härtel wrote to Beethoven in encouraging terms. He states how pleased his publishing house would be 'to do everything that circumstances allow' to further his compositions, especially 'piano sonatas without accompaniment, or with accompaniment of violin, or of violin and violincello'. Härtel adds a touch of flattery, doubtless to secure the composer's commissions: 'The fame of your talents is established firmly enough.' Härtel concludes by requesting where Beethoven's portrait may be seen so that a likeness could be taken for its publication alongside his series of 'the most prominent composers'. An engraving of Beethoven duly appeared in Volume 6 of the *Allgemeine musikalische Zeitung* (October 1803 – September 1804). Johann Neidl created this from a drawing by the artist Gandolph Stainhauser – made sometime in 1800.[vii]

In June 1801 Beethoven had occasion to write to Franz Gerhard Wegeler, his close friend from schooldays in Bonn; it is one of Beethoven's longest and most moving letters. The first part is full of optimism. He tells his friend about his benefactor Prince Karl Lichnowsky who, the year previously, had settled upon him an annual sum of 600 gulden 'on which', he writes, 'I can draw until I obtain a suitable appointment'.[viii] He adds: 'My compositions bring me in a good deal, and I may say that I am offered more commissions than it is possible for me to carry out.' Moreover, Beethoven's standing with Vienna's music publishers was high as he further explains: '[For] every composition I can count on six or seven publishers, and even more, if I want them; people no longer come to arrangement with me, I state the price and they pay. So you see how pleasantly situated I am.' However, towards the end of the letter Beethoven discloses his inner feelings to Wegeler regarding his health: '[That] jealous demon, my wretched health, has put a spoke in my wheel … for the last three years my hearing has become weaker and weaker … Heaven alone knows what is to become of me.'[ix] We consider the rest of this letter and its implications later. For the present, our concern is with Beethoven's inclination to romanticism and the creation and reception of his Piano Sonata Op. 26.

The composition of the sonata may have been influenced by the German-borne, London-based piano virtuoso and composer Johann Baptist Cramer. He was resident in Vienna in the winter of 1799-1800 and, according to Carl Czerny: 'He caused a great stir by his playing three sonatas dedicated to Haydn [*Trois Grandes Sonates pour le Pianoforte*].'[x] It is perhaps no coincidence that the first of these is in the key of A-flat major — that chosen by Beethoven for his Op. 26. Although at times pianistic rivals, a measure of mutual admiration appears to have existed between Cramer and Beethoven. Cramer considered Beethoven to be 'the supreme improviser' and, according to Beethoven's pupil Ferdinand Ries: 'Cramer was the only pianist whom Beethoven had praised as being truly excellent.'[xxi] The Viennese music cognoscenti were captivated not only by Cramer's playing of his own works but also by those of his teacher Muzio Clementi. As a consequence, it has been suggested 'Beethoven felt the need to compete with this virtuosity and wrote a number of works that began to break away form the more Classically oriented sonatas of the 1790s, towards the mature second-period style'.[xxii] Thayer suggests when Beethoven was writing his Piano Sonata in A flat, Op. 26, 'there is purposely a reminder of ... Clementi-Cramer passage work in the finale'.[xxiii] Later in life Beethove admired Cramer's *Instructions for the Pianoforte* (*Grosse Pianoforteschule*), published in 1815 that are still in use today.[xxiv]

With the Piano Sonata Op. 26, Beethoven returned to a four-movement structure but, as remarked, making departures from the traditional sonata form. Barry Cooper comments: 'It was this more flexible approach to the overall structure which was to pave the way for the great diversity in late works.'[xxv] The Op. 26 opens with a slow movement (*Andante con variazioni*). Beethoven then places the *Scherzo* in the second movement so as to separate the first-movement slow variations from the sombre third movement (*Marcia funebre sulla morte d'un eroe*). The piece concludes with an animated fourth-movement *Allegro*. The overall effect is to achieve 'a poetic quality' in the manner in which 'the movements hang together'.[xxvi] Edwin Fischer goes further and considers the sonata belongs to the category of Beethoven's 'psychological works'. He elaborates: 'In this sonata we meet for the first time one of those creations which I should like to call *psychological composi-tions* since they are intimately personal utterances, strictly speaking, represent transitional stages in Beethoven's development.' Fischer cites the 'freer' and 'more unconventional' forms, although 'closely worked and strictly controlled', the change in the normal sequence of movements and, not least, 'the demands made on the interpreter'.[xxvi] Fischer's distinguished pupil Alfred Brendel endorses these views with insights of his own: '[Beethoven's] musical material is condensed into a few motivic units feeding the entire piece.' Brendel acknowledges not all Beethoven's sonatas are composed like this: 'There are exceptions where I can see only a loose motivic relationship between the movements, and where it is necessary to explain the sequence of movements in a purely psychological way — for example in Op. 26.'[xxvii]

The Sonata Op. 26 had its origins in the year 1800.[xxix] Sketches for the work are found in the so-called Landsberg Sketchbook that covers the period August 1800–March 1801.[xxx] Thirteen pages of sketches exist for the Op. 26 interwoven, in Beethoven's typical creative fashion, with sketches for his Op. 18, No. 1 (String Quartet in F major), Op. 23 (Violin Sonata in a minor), Op. 24 (Violin Sonata in F major) and his Op. 36 (Second Symphony).[xxxi] On the basis of his study of Beethoven's surviving sketches, Cooper comments on the difficulty of charting the composer's precise compositional progress but he suggests the Piano Sonatas Opp. 26, 27 and 28 were 'probably composed ... in numerical order, [Beethoven] working on all of them at some stage during the summer [of 1801]'.[xxxii] Publication of the Piano Sonata Op. 26 was announced in the *Vienna Journal* of 3 March 1802. The Title Page states: '*Grande Sonate pour le Clavecin ou Piano Forte, composée et dédiée à Son Altesse Monseigneur le Prince Charles de Lichnowsky, par Louis van Beethoven. Oeuvre 26, à Vienne, chez Jean Cappi.*'[xxxiii] The publisher mentioned here was Giovanni Cappi. He arrived in Vienna in 1773 and twenty years later became a partner in the famous publishing house of Artaria & Co. In 1801 he established his own publishing business under the name Johann Cappi, Beethoven being one of his first customers. In 1894 a forgery came to light purporting to be an original Beethoven sketch for the Op. 26 — evidence of the commercial value, even then, of Beethoven memorabilia.ᵐ The authentic Autograph Score of the sonata was originally in the possession of the manuscript collector Friedrich Grasnick. On his death, it was purchased by the Berlin Royal Library — now the Staatsbibliothek.ᵐ

In 1802 reviews of Beethoven's Op. 26, together with the two Piano Sonatas Op. 27, were published in Issue No. 4 of the *Allgemeine musikalische Zeitung*. As was then the custom, the reviewer based his comments not, as would be the case today, upon hearing the music performed in concert, but upon personally reading through the published score; some reviewers it should be noted were accomplished performers. The three works were published separately but the reviewer comments upon them collectively: 'These are the three piano compositions with which Herr v[an]. B[eethoven] recently enriched a selected few cultivated musicians and accomplished pianists. I say enriched, because they are truly an enrichment and belong among those few works of art of the present day that will scarcely ever grow old; certainly number three [the *Moonlight*] can never grow old.'ᵐ The reviewer also hints at the technical challenges posed by the compositions: 'Less educated musicians, and those who expect nothing more from music than a facile entertainment, will pick up these works in vain.'ᵐ

One who did struggle with these works was Beethoven's amanuensis Anton Schindler. As a performing musician Schindler was primarily a violinist but the conversation books from Beethoven's later years bear witness to the fact that he studied the piano sonatas with the composer. An entry from mid-September 1820, reads: 'Sundays and holidays I am always at home busily working on the sonatas. Now I have the *Pathétique* [as well as] Opus 26, and two others in hand ... When I am able to come again I shall play some of them for you and show you what I have learned, but it is always a struggle with the notes.'[xxviii]

In the intervening years, the universal popularity of the Op. 27 Sonatas – and in particular that of No. 2 the *Moonlight* – has somewhat eclipsed the qualities of the Op. 26 Sonata, despite its celebrated *Funeral March*. For example, on the occasion of Beethoven's death-centenary (1927), the music critic Fuller-Maitland, writing about the composer's sonatas, comments: 'The A flat Sonata, with the funeral march in it, is another not very frequently heard in the present day.' The only performance he could recall in those years was by the gifted child pianist Max (later Mark) Hambourg.[xxix] Some years previously, Bernard Shaw had heard Hambourg play at the Steinway Hall in London and remarked, prophetically, 'this Russian lad might astonish the world one day'. Even the ardent Beethoven champion Donald Tovey had to concede, in a lecture given on 10 October 1922: '[The] Sonata Op. 26, the sonata with the *Funeral March*, [is] probably the most despised of Beethoven's popular works.' He adds, with typical provocation, 'rightly very popular indeed, very light, very slight, with little serious form in it at all except in its tiny little finale'.[xl] Admiration in the nineteenth century for Beethoven's Piano Sonata Op. 26 did, however, come from an unexpected quarter.

We learn from Beethoven's early biographer Wilhelm von Lenz that by 1828 three of the composer's piano sonatas had 'found acceptance in France'. These were the Piano Sonata Op. 26, the *Moonlight* and the *Appassionata*.[xli] Perhaps it was by this circumstance, doubtless amongst others, that they came to the attention of Frederick Chopin. History has conferred upon Chopin the reputation for being somewhat reserved in his attitude towards Beethoven but it is known he admired, and even performed, the Op. 26. A reminiscence from von Lenz, who was a pupil of Chopin, confirms this. Lenz recalls how one day he accompanied Chopin to the residence of Countess Cheremetiev (a distinguished lady-in-waiting) where he had undertaken to play the A-flat major Sonata. He relates: '[Chopin] played admirably. I was wonderstruck but *only* by the beauty of the sound, by the touch, by the charm and by so pure a style ... It was not Beethoven. It was too light, too feminine!' Lenz's view of Chopin's interpretation is interesting. Chopin was himself physically slight and this, combined with his insidious consumption, may have disposed him to conserve his energy in performance. Be this as it may, on the journey home Lenz gave Chopin his frank opinion of his master's performance. Chopin replied: 'I only indicate, suggest and leave it to my hearers to complete the picture.'[xlii] [xliii]

A further reminiscence takes us further afield – to *The Altenburg* a few miles outside Weimer. From 1848 this was the home of Franz Liszt where he had established his ménage – controversially for the period – with Princess Carolyne von Sayn-Wittgenstein (the two had spurned the conventions of a formal marriage). In October 1854 the music critic and amateur composer Richard Pohl was privileged to visit Liszt where the great man showed him some of his prized possessions. These included Beethoven's Broadwood piano – to which we will make reference in our discussion of the composer's later works – and Mozart's clavichord of 1772 by the maker C. E. Friederici. Lost in wonderment, Phol had no more time to feast his gaze on other of the treasures that had been heaped upon his distinguished host; Liszt was already seated at a giant instrument, the capabilities of which he was eager to demonstrate. This was a three-keyboard harmonium built to Liszt's own specification by the French maker Alexander & Fils — now on display at the Kunsthistorisches Museum, Vienna. His performance included the *Funeral March* from the Piano Sonata in A flat. Phol recalls: '[At] one moment with sounds ghostly, soft, celestial and far-off, at the next mighty, convulsing, swelling masses of tone, revealing to us the full greatness and range of sonority of the instrument whose effects are truly surprising in the highest degree.'[xliv]

We conclude these introductory comments concerning Beethoven's Piano Sonata Op. 26 with the estimation of a pianist from our own times. Glenn Gould could on occasions be aloof in his estimation of Beethoven — even eccentrically so — but he has nothing but praise for the composer's 'transitional sonatas' (as he called them) which include the Opus 26: 'All in all, I'd have to say that Beethoven's most consistently excellent works are those from his early period ... Almost all of those early piano works are immaculately balanced — top to bottom, register to register. In these pieces, Beethoven's sense of structure, fantasy, variety, thematic continuity, harmonic propulsion and contrapuntal discipline were absolutely, miraculously, in alignment.'[xlv]

The opening movement of the Piano Sonata Op. 26, marked *Andante con variazioni*, shows Beethoven 'restlessly experimenting with inherited procedures' and presenting 'a dazzling array of unorthodox abstractions upon the original material'.[xlvi] As a young composer newly arrived in Vienna, Beethoven had established his reputation as a virtuoso pianist and had further enhanced it with several sets of published variations in which his powers of improvisation are evident.[xlvii] With the public in general, but notably on the part of Vienna's many pianists and amateurs, the piano-variation form was an established and popular genre but one from which 'little of substance or originality was expected' — with occasional noteworthy exceptions from such great masters as Haydn and Mozart. Beethoven's many sets of variations, written between 1793—1801, are for the most part considered to be variously 'entertaining, brilliant, and deliberately superficial' — although few are without beautiful moments. However, in his piano sonatas, 'Beethoven was progressing from the external variation-manner to more complex and imaginative principles of variation technique'.[xlviii] Moreover, Beethoven's choosing to begin his Op. 26 with a set of variations may also be seen as part of his attempt to 'expand away from the traditional confines of the sonata'.[xlix] Other composers before Beethoven had used the concept of developing a theme and variations for the opening movement of a piano sonata. Haydn employed such an arrangement in his late sonata (Hoboken No. 42, L. 56) as did Mozart in his A major Sonata K. 331. Beethoven himself had included a set of variations in his Piano Sonata Op. 14, No. 2 and would do so again in the Piano Sonata Op. 57 (*Appassionata*), Op. 109 and Op. 111 — the last two 'raising the art to its sublimest level'. Concerning Op. 26, the slow written-out trill pattern that characterizes the florid final variation, has a texture 'that is a foreshadowing of the extended trills that the composer is to use in the variation movements of the Opp. 109 and 111'.[l]

Earlier writers have adopted moving word-imagery to describe the feelings invoked by the first movement of Piano Sonata Op. 26. Ernst von Elterlein remarks: 'The theme [of the variation] breathes an ardent longing, arising ... out of a deep yearning, exalted feeling ... The feeling intensifies and is diversified at every step, the aspiring motive is worked up higher and higher till ... it sinks back timidly and reservedly into its native regions.'[li] Writing twenty years later, Romain

174

Rolland felt similarly disposed saying: 'The opening *Andante* is beautiful, and in the variations the theme breathes as it were through a thin lovely veil.'[ii] Perhaps it was these same sentiments, or at least Beethoven's theme, that appealed to the young Franz Schubert when he was composing his celebrated Impromptu in A flat major; it has 'a certain likeness' to Beethoven and is in the same key.[iii] Concerning influences, Fischer believes Beethoven's second variation 'is an anticipation of the brilliant violin variation in the *Kreutzer* Sonata'.[iv] Regarding performance he comments: 'It should be played loosely and softly.'[v]

Nearer our own time, commentators have been no less discerning of Beethoven's sonata innovation and musicological achievement found in the first movement of the Op. 26. Harold Truscott describes the variations as 'a beautiful melodic set, with a hint in the final variation of the persistent shakes [ornaments] above or below a melody of which he was fond in later life'. He also considers Beethoven's variations — in particular the short coda — 'strikingly anticipates for a few bars a passage in the *Arietta* variations of Op. 111'.[vi] Philip Radcliffe similarly finds interesting connections with Beethoven's A flat Piano Sonata and other of his compositions: 'The variations with which Op. 26 opens have, like the *Adagio* of the *Pathétique*, a broadly flowing lyricism which reappears, on a higher plane, in the slow movement of the Quartet in E flat, Op. 74; it is perhaps significant that all three pieces are in the key of A flat.'[vii] For his part, Cooper draws our attention to the manner in which, in the Op. 26 Piano Sonata, Beethoven conveys a sense of movement towards the finale by what he describes as 'the pacing of the previous movements', beginning with the theme and variations and 'reserving the dramatic character of a full sonata movement until the finale'.[viii]

Returning to the views of more distant writers, Czerny,

with the performance of the opening theme in mind, observes: '[The] whole art of sustained, harmonious *legato*, and of fine touch, must be called forth, in order to worthily display the noble, and almost religious character of the same.'[lix] Also with questions of refinement of performance in mind, the ever-vigilant Tovey is characteristically unequivocal: 'Slovenly chords and stumbling rhythm in this intensely aristocratic set of variations would be as impossible as shabby clothes and slouching attitudes at Court'![lx]

In placing the *Scherzo: Allegro molto* as the second movement of the sonata, Beethoven showed he had no hesitation 'in sacrificing convention to aesthetic demands'. Moreover, this procedure serves to separate the reflective mood of the opening variations from the sombre atmosphere of the *Funeral March*, thereby preserving the work's overall 'poetic plan'.[lxi] The music here, whose rhythms Tovey describes as 'witty',[lxii] continues with 'the fieriest scherzo in the sonatas so far'[lxiii] and some of the most 'lively keyboard counterpoint which had not appeared in the sonatas since the finale of Op. 10, No. 2'.[lxiv] The surviving sketches for the *Scherzo* offer an interesting glimpse into Beethoven's creative process and insights into his varied thoughts, adaptations and rejections.[lxv]

Czerny encourages the performer to play the *Scherzo* 'quick, gay and smartly'.[lxvi] In a lecture on the Piano Sonata Op. 26, Tovey stated he considered Beethoven's writing in the *Scherzo* anticipates the style of Schumann: 'In the present stage of musical fashion I venture to assert that one could take about half-a-dozen trios out of Beethoven's early *scherzos* and *allegrettos* and publish them as posthumous pianoforte pieces of Schumann.'[lxvii]

The underlying idea of the third movement is the death of a hero – *Marcia funebre sulla morte d'un eroe*. Already in his Bonn days Beethoven had given expression in music to the feelings associated with death in his Funeral Cantata *On the death of Joseph II* (WoO 87); the wider themes of suffering, death and the celebration of a hero would soon become 'a prime component of Beethoven's musical vocabulary'. The sombre slow movement of the Piano Sonata Op. 26 is evident in such works as *Christ on the Mount of Olives*, the *Eroica* Symphony (composed to celebrate 'the memory of a great man'), *Fidelio*, and the incidental Music to Goethe's *Egmont*.[lviii][lix] Cooper suggests Beethoven's disposition to heroism, and its expression in music of a profound, celebratory nature, may have been intensified by the return of war heroes from the campaigns against Napoleon. In support of this suggestion, we recall Beethoven had contributed to a charity concert in aid of the war-wounded in January 1801 and, later in life, he participated in several other concerts for the widows and orphans resulting from military conflict. Cooper also draws attention to the probable influence on Beethoven, when composing the Piano Sonata Op. 26, of the pianism of Daniel Steibelt. As we have previously remarked at the time of Steibelt's stay in Vienna, in 1800, Beethoven had decisively defeated Steibelt in an informal pianistic contest. However, Beethoven, always ready to learn from a gifted fellow musician — even a defeated one — appears to have absorbed something of Steibelt's keyboard style into his own writing. Cooper remarks: '[A] most striking feature [of the third movement] is the recurring combination of tremolando and crescendo. Beethoven may have derived the idea of tremolandos from Daniel Steibelt, whose use of them at the famous contest between him and Beethoven the previous year was said to have been entirely new.'[lx] Also of interest concerning the mood prevailing throughout the movement, is Beethoven's juxtaposition of the keys of A-flat minor and that of B minor. According to the scheme of musical aesthetics prevailing at the period, the former key denoted 'difficult struggle' and the latter 'patience'.[lxi] These ideas were propounded by Beethoven's contemporary Christian Schubart and are known to have been of particular interest to the composer.[lxii]

A possible source of influence on Beethoven, in deciding to include a funeral march in his Piano Sonata Op. 26, may have been the opera *Achilles* by the composer Ferdinand (Ferdinando) Paer. This work, a melodrama, celebrates the central character Achilles, Homer's renowned hero of the Trojan Wars. It was premiered on 6 June 1801 at the *Kärntnertor-Theater* where Paer was then Music Director. Writing about this nearly forty years later, Beethoven's pupil Ferdinand Ries states: 'The Funeral March in A flat minor in the sonata dedicated to Prince Lichnowsky (Opus 26) originated in the great praise Paer's funeral march in his opera *Achilles* received from Beethoven's friends.'[lxiii] Czerny, who had become a pupil of Beethoven at the time of the premiere of *Achilles*, also makes brief mention of Paer's opera with regard to Beethoven's Op. 26.[lxiv] [lxv] It is probable Beethoven did not have a particular hero in mind for the subject of his Funeral March; doubtless he was intent upon giving more generalised musical expression to the feelings of loss associated with mourning. Egerton Lowe's eloquence is relevant here: 'It has never been discovered who was the hero whose death evoked this wonderful Funeral March, an elegy of sorrow, hope, and resignation which must for all time remain a work of outstanding uniqueness.' Concerning Beethoven's choice of key, Lowe adds: 'The close in the tonic major A flat (claimed by C. F. D. Schubart to be the most beautiful of all the keys) gives a sublime effect of peace and resignation.'[lxvi] Rolland's estimation of the march is in similar vein with additional insights into how Beethoven conveys instrumental effects through the medium of the keyboard: 'It is not a lamentation but rather a tragic, elegiac picture set in an impressive frame. One feels the throb of brass, the blare of trumpets, the roll of muffled drums, the impressive pageantry of death.'[lxxvii] [lxxviii] In his later writings, Rolland detects the composer's 'subconscious preparation for the *Eroica*'.[lxxix]

The march has been described as having 'the grandiose manner of the opening of the *Pathétique*' but being 'more advanced harmonically'.[lxxx] Truscott remarks how the Funeral March, although on a much smaller scale than that of the later *Eroica* Symphony, achieves similar effects 'without the colour of an orchestra and with the severest restraint in harmony, plus a theme which is for the most part only a rhythm'. He considers Beethoven's originality 'shines by reducing the music and its technique to basic elements' and concludes, 'the muffled grief which spreads its pall by this means is as moving as the most impassioned oratory and as austere as the Cenotaph'.[lxxxi]

The *marcia funebre* functions as the sonata's 'centre of gravity' and is characterised by 'rugged pianistic writing'.[lxxxii] Moreover, with economy of means and in a space of only eight bars, 'Beethoven's uses of register, theme, sonority, and musical rhetoric are combined with utmost ingenuity'.[lxxxiii] Czerny's notes to the Piano Sonata Op. 26 state: 'This movement must be performed with a certain grandeur, which is expressed not only by the slow time, but also by a heavy pressure of the chords.'[lxxxiv] Rosen views the movement as being 'laconic, sober and dramatic' and, concerning performance, urges against too slow a tempo — dismissed as 'a modern prejudice' — with the muffled drum rolls to be played with the pedal and 'the brass interjections ... to be played dryly'.[lxxxv] Fischer also cautions the performer not to overstate the imagery by, for example, overstating the drum rolls. He finds a parallel with the *Pastoral* Symphony and cites Beethoven's own words 'not painting, but the expression of feeling'.[lxxxvi]

Concerning performance it is salutary to bear in mind, as Solomon remarks, in Vienna at the turn of the century public performances of solo keyboard works were rare. Piano Sonata Op. 26 has the distinction of being one of the very few of his sonatas to be played in public but it had to wait until 1819, the performance taking place in Boston.[lxxxvii] In the published review of 1802, to which reference has already been made, the Funeral March is described as 'the truly great, solemn, and magnificent chordal section'. The reviewer offers the following encouragement for correct performance: '[In] this section all the weight and wealth of this music must be fully expressed.'[lxxxviii] Elsewhere the reviewer adds, 'of the truly great, gloomy, and magnificent work of *harmony* ... everything difficult and artistic is part of the expression and therefore the essential point'.[lxxxix]

Contemporary records show the Funeral March was well received by the discerning music-public and publishers, three of whom — Kuhn (Berlin), Simrock (Bonn) and the *Bureau de Musique* (Leipzig) — each published the movement separately as did the original publisher Cappi who brought out an edition of his own in the same year as the complete piano sonata.[xc] In 1815 Beethoven himself arranged the Funeral March for orchestra as part of the music he composed to accompany Johann Duncker's tragedy *Leonore Prohaska*, the heroine of which has no connection with the composer's Leonore in his opera *Fidelio.* Duncker, a Prussian civil servant, had accompanied King William III to the Congress of Vienna the previous year and is known to have met Beethoven and came on friendly terms with him.[xci] Duncker may have acquainted Beethoven with the remarkable circumstances of Leonore Prohaska (Eleonore Prochaska). Disguised as a man, she enlisted in the Prussian army in the Wars of Liberation against Napoleon; serving as an infantryman she was mortally wounded and only then was discovered to be a woman. Such a tale, with its overtones of 'glorification of political freedom', was guaranteed to appeal to Beethoven's own nature and indomitability of spirit and doubtless stirred him to compose the music to Duncker's drama (WoO 96).[xcii] The subject, however, proved too subversive for the public Censor and no performances materialized. In his orchestration, Beethoven transposed the march up to the key of B minor, for the benefit of the wind instruments; the resulting scoring is for string instruments, two flutes, two clarinets in A, two bassoons, two horns in D, two horns in E, and kettle drums.[xciii]

Twelve years later, on the death of Beethoven, musicians and writers once more had occasion to make use of the music from the third movement of the composer's Piano Sonata in A-flat major. The poet and physician Alois Jeitteles, who supplied the verses for Beethoven's song cycle *An die ferne Geliebte*, was moved to write the poem *Beethoven's Begräbnis* ('Beethoven's Funeral') which was set for four voices and piano by Ignaz von Seyfried – a pallbearer at the funeral. Further public expression of Beethoven's funeral music was given on the day of the composer's internment. The service was held in the Trinity Church of the Minorites. From eyewitness accounts Thayer records: 'When the procession turned into the Alsergasse [close by the church], a brass band played the *Marcia funebre* from the Op. 26 ... The relatives and friends of the master succeeded only with difficulty to get inside the church.'[xciv] [xcv] One of the chief participants in the funeral was the young Franz Schubert who within a year also passed away and was laid to rest by the side of the composer who, in life, he had so much admired.

The transition from the sombre imagery of the Funeral March to the lively animation of the final movement juxtaposes contrary emotional feelings that, in Fischer's words, 'seem ... to be irreconcilably opposed to one another'. In his psychological interpretation of the sonata, he invites both performer and listener to imagine the funeral cortege and mourners are gone and the churchyard is now empty: 'It is as if a shower of rain fell after the funeral, veiling the burial ground in a consoling grey mist.' Fischer's 'shower of rain' is a reference to the scatter of semiquavers with which the *Allegro* final movement opens. 'Nature has the last word', remarks Fischer, and he draws a parallel with Beethoven's animated resolving finale and the *Presto* finale of Chopin's celebrated Piano Sonata No. 2 in B flat minor.[xcv] Czerny refers to Beethoven's animation here as 'that uniform, perpetual moving style' and suggests Beethoven may have derived this from Cramer (see above).[xcvi] It is open to question whether Beethoven was attempting to upstage Cramer with his own dextrous keyboard writing, or merely that he intended to make a more whimsical 'reminiscence' of his rival's style.[xcvii] Whatever, 'the finale ... flows along with apparent detachment in its context and in almost unbroken semiquavers: its patterns, and its many exchanges between the hands, give it added bonus as a study, though it ends on a gently poetic note'.[xcviii] With the psychology of the music in mind, and evoking similar imagery to Fischer, Brendel offers the following guidance to the performer: 'The pianist should ... play this finale not as an étude, but a little in the manner of the Finale of Chopin's Sonata in B-flat minor: like a wind — although in this case a warm breeze — going over the graves.'[ci]

We draw to a close with anecdotes concerning two musicians who might have benefited from Brendel's guidance — one of them at least. In 1851, Modest Mussorgsky, then aged twelve, had made such good progress in piano at the St Petersburg Conservatory that his teacher, Professor Anton Herke, nominated him to play a Concert Rondo at the home of a lady-in-waiting to the Russian Empress. Herke, a demanding teacher and 'always critical in evaluating his students', was so impressed on this occasion that he made a present to Mussorgsky of Beethoven's Piano Sonata in A flat major.[i] Erik Satie appears to have been a more errant pupil than Mussorgsky. He attended the Paris Conservatoire in the early 1880s where a fellow pupil was Paul Dukas; the records of its students still survive in the *Archives Nationales*, Paris. Satie's teacher, Émile Descombes, described Satie as 'gifted but indolent' and 'quite simply the laziest student in the Conservatoire'. For his last examination, on 15 June 1882, Satie was required to play the finale of Beethoven's A flat Piano Sonata, Op. 26. 'The general response of the examiners was lukewarm and Satie's studies were eventually terminated.'[ii]

It is only fitting we should close our account of Beethoven's Piano Sonata in A flat, Op. 26 in a more uplifting way with the words of a musician, and musicologist, of acknowledged standing: 'The four movements of this sonata are all relatively modest and unpretentious forms, and the work is pure chamber music rather than a grand public work ... With this work, Beethoven needed only breadth of movement to achieve a large-scale rhythm in the relatively small forms.'[iii]

[i] Stewart Gordon, 1996, p. 161. Gordon is one of several commentators to perceive a creative link between the Piano Sonata Op. 26 and the two Piano Sonatas of Op. 27.

[ii] Michael Broyles, 1987, p. 61. Broyles also considers the Piano Sonata Op. 28 extends Beethoven's 'new piano-sonata style'.

[iii] Charles Rosen, 2002, p. 150.

[iv] Leon Plantinga, 1984, p. 29.

[v] Marion Scott, 1940, pp. 137–8.

vi Harold Craxton and Donald Francis Tovey, *Beethoven: Sonatas for pianoforte, Piano Sonata Op. 26*, [1931], p. 11. Tovey remarks how the Piano Sonata Op. 26 is 'technically more difficult than it looks'.

vii Tovey also remarks how many of Haydn's early piano sonatas were published under the title *Divertimento*, denoting a composition formed from 'a group of small movements in sectional forms'. See: Harold Craxton and Donald Francis Tovey, *Beethoven: Sonatas for pianoforte, Piano Sonata Op. 26*, [1931], p. 11.

viii Maynard Solomon, 1977, p. 105.

ix Philip Radcliffe, *Piano music* in: *The age of Beethoven, The new Oxford history of music, Vol. VIII*, Gerald Abraham, editor, 1988, pp. 341.

x Denis Matthews, 1967, p. 24.

xi Carl Dahlhaus, 1989, p. 21.

xii Harold Truscott, *The Piano music* in: Denis Arnold and Nigel Fortune, editors, 1973, p. 103.

xiii Denis Matthews, 1972, p. 174 and 1985, p. 83.

xiv Giorgio Pestelli, 1984, p. 233.

xv *Matthew* Rye, BBC Radio Three, *Beethoven experience*, 3 June 2005.

xvi Marion Scott, 1940, p. 137.

xvii Theodore Albrecht, 1996, Vol. 1, Letter No. 34, pp. 63–4.

xviii In Vienna at the turn of the century, the gulden was the equivalent of the Austrian florin. The practical value of Beethoven's annuity can be estimated from the following: The *Wiener Zeitung* of 28 January 1792 recorded the appointment of Salieri's pupil, Joseph Weigl, as 'Kapellmeister and Composer to the Royal Imperial National Court Theatre with a salary of 1,000 florins'. Allowing for inflation, Beethoven's 600 florins was the equivalent of about two-thirds of the annual salary of a professional musician. Derived from Thayer–Forbes 1967, p. 150.

xix Beethoven's letter to Wegeler is translated in Emily Anderson, 1961, Vol. 1, Letter No. 51, pp. 57–62. A facsimile of the original document can be viewed on the Beethoven House Website: Beethoven House Bonn, Digital Archives, Library Document Sammlung Wegeler, EW. 17.

xx From the recollections of Carl Czerny, see: Paul Badura-Skoda, editor, 1970, p. 9.

xxi Peter Clive, 2001, pp. 77–8. Clive's citation of the views of Ferdinand Ries is derived from Ries's study *Beethoven Biographische Notizen*.

xxii Matthew Rye, BBC Radio Three, *Beethoven experience*, 3 June 2005.

xxiii Thayer-Forbes, 1967, p. 296.

xxiv Biographical information, and a portrait of Cramer, can be seen on the Beethoven House Website, Beethoven House Bonn, Digital Archives, Library Document B. 1254.

xxv Barry Cooper, 1991, p. 241.

xxvi David Dubal in conversation with Alfred Brendel: see: David Dubal, 1985, p. 103.

xxvii Edwin Fischer, 1959, p. 58.

xxviii Alfred Brendel, 2002, pp. 112–3. Brendel is here in conversation with Martin Mayer. Elsewhere, in conversation with the writer on music David Dubal, Brendel likens Beethoven's Piano Sonata Op. 26 to 'a new departure' but one 'that goes back to older models'. See: David Dubal, 1985, p. 103.

xxix Thayer Forbes, 1967, p. 296.

xxx Barry Cooper, 1990, p. 88 and 1991, p. 185.

xxxi Douglas Johnson, *et al*, 1985, p. 106 and p. 116.

xxxii Barry Cooper, 2000, pp. 106–8.

xxxiii Beethoven House, Digital Archives, Library Document Sammlung H. C. Bodmer, HCB C Op. 26 (a).

xxxiv Beethoven House, Digital Archives, Library Document NE 190.

xxxv Douglas Johnson, *et al*, 1985, pp. 33–4.

xxxvi Anton Schindler, 1860, English edition, Donald MacArdle, 1966, p. 93. The *AmZ* review, with commentary, is also reproduced in Wayne M. Senner, *et al*, 1999, pp. 176–7.

xxxvii Robin Wallace, 1986, p. 10.

xxxviii Donald MacArdle commenting on Schindler in: Anton Schindler, 1860, English edition, Donald MacArdle, 1966, p. 446 and note 319.

xxxix John A. Fuller-Maitland, *Notes to the Beethoven sonatas* contributed to the Special Issue of *The Musical Times*, Vol. VIII, No. 2, 1927, pp. 218–23. The special Issue was published in book form.

xl Donald Tovey, *Eight lectures on Beethoven* in: *The classics of music*, Michael Tilmouth, editor, 2001, pp. 418–9.

xli Harold C. Schonberg, 1964, p. 92.

xlii As related in: Wanda Landowska, 1926, pp. 157–8.

xliii Commenting upon Chopin's attachment to Beethoven's Piano Sonata Op. 26, Charles Rosen observes: 'The exquisite lyricism of the opening *Andante* ... may account for Chopin's preference even more than his natural interest in the Funeral March.' Charles Rosen, 2002, pp. 150–1.

xliv As recounted by Adrian Williams, 1990, pp. 308–13.

xlv Glenn Gould in conversation with Tim Page in: Tim Page, editor, 1987, pp. 102–3.

xlvi Leon Plantinga, 1984, p. 29.

xlvii From the many sets of piano variations, contemporary with the Piano Sonata Op. 26, may be cited WoO 73, WoO 75 and WoO 76, composed in 1799, based on melodies derived from popular operas of the day.

xlviii Maynard Solomon, 1977, p. 98.

xlix Matthew Rye, BBC Radio Three, *Beethoven experience*, 3 June 2005.

l The use of the variation form in the development of the piano sonata is briefly discussed by Dennis Matthews, 1967, p. 24 and Stewart Gordon, 1996, p. 161 – from both of whom the quoted passages are derived. See also: Barry Cooper, 1991, p. 241 and Dennis Matthews, 1985, p. 83.

li Ernst von Elterlein, 1898, pp. 65–6.

lii Romain Rolland, 1917, p. 147.

liii Dennis Matthews, 1967, p. 24.

liv The reference here is to the Violin Sonata in A major, Op. 47 that Beethoven dedicated to Rudolph Kreutzer, one of the most celebrated violin virtuosos of his time. Beethoven said of him: '[He] was a good and nice person, it was indeed a pleasure to be with him.' See: Beethoven House, Bonn; Digital Archives, Library Document, B 2001.

lv Edwin Fischer, 1959, p. 59.

lvi Harold Truscott, *The Piano Music* (of Beethoven) in: Denis Arnold and Nigel Fortune, editors, 1973, p. 103.

lvii Philip Radcliffe, *Piano music* in: *The age of Beethoven, The new Oxford history of music, Vol. VIII*, Gerald Abraham, editor, 1988, pp. 341.

lviii Barry Cooper, 1991, p. 207.

lix From the recollections of Carl Czerny, see: Paul Badura-Skoda, editor, 1970, p. 37.

lx Harold Craxton and Donald Francis Tovey, *Beethoven: Sonatas for pianoforte, Piano Sonata Op. 26*, [1931], p. 11.

lxi Considered by Marion Scott, 1940, pp. 137–8 and Dennis Matthews, 1967, p. 25.

lxii Harold Craxton and Donald Francis Tovey, *Beethoven: Sonatas for pianoforte, Piano Sonata Op. 26*, [1931], p. 11.

lxiii Dennis Matthews, 1985, p. 83.

lxiv Philip Radcliffe, *Piano music* in: *The age of Beethoven, The new Oxford history of music, Vol. VIII*, Gerald Abraham, editor, 1988, pp. 341.

lxv An audio version of Beethoven's sketches can be heard on the website, *The Unheard Beethoven*/Compositions/Piano Works/Piano Sonata Op. 26/ Biamonti 256.

lxvi From the recollections of Carl Czerny see: Paul Badura-Skoda, editor, 1970, p. 9.

lxvii Donald Tovey, *Eight lectures on Beethoven* in, *The classics of music*, Michael Tilmouth, editor, 2001, pp. 418–9.

lxviii Quoted, with adaptations, from Maynard Solomon, 1977, p. 51.

lxix A year before the Piano Sonata Op. 26 was published Beethoven's ballet *Die Geschöpfe des Prometheus* was performed in Vienna on 28 March 1801. This ballet contains the theme the composer later used in the *Funeral March* of the *Eroica* Symphony. 'This has been regarded by some as [Beethoven's] second outcome ... the slow movement of the Sonata [Op. 26] may, justifiably, be regarded as a kind of sketch or exercise for the greater one in the Symphony.' Eric Blom, 1938, pp. 93–4.

lxx Barry Cooper, 2000, pp. 106–8.

lxxi As remarked upon by Leon Plantinga, 1999, p. 298.

lxxii Christian Schubart outlined his views in: *Ideen zu einer Aesthetik der Tonkunst* (1806). He considered A-flat minor implied 'difficult struggle' and 'wailing lament' and B minor suggested 'patience' and 'calm awaiting one's fate'. In comparison, C major was the key with the connotation 'completely pure'.

lxxiii Ferdinand Ries in: Franz Wegeler, 1838, English edition 1988, p. 70.

lxxiv In a commentary to Czerny's text, Paul Badura-Skoda identifies Paer's aria *Sieh, wie vom Tod entstellet* and also remarks: 'Beethoven's march was already begun *before* (author's italics) the performance of *Achilles.*' From the recollections of Carl Czerny, see: Paul Badura-Skoda, editor, 1970, endnote 35.

lxxv Alfred Brendel briefly mentions Paer's music in relation to Beethoven's Piano Sonata Op. 26 in his conversations with the writer David Dubal. See: David Dubal, 1985, pp. 103–4.

lxxvi Egerton Lowe, 1929, p. 65. Lowe gives one of the most detailed published accounts of the structure of Beethoven's Piano Sonata Op. 26.

lxxvii Romain Rolland, 1917, p. 147.

lxxviii Dennis Matthews expresses similar views to those of Romain Rolland: See Dennis Matthews 1967, p. 25 and 1985, pp. 83–4.

lxxix Romain Rolland. 1937, p. 125.

lxxx Philip Radcliffe, *Piano Music* in: *The age of Beethoven, The new Oxford history of music, Vol. VIII*, Gerald Abraham, editor, 1988, pp. 341.

[lxxi] Harold Truscott, *The piano music* in: Denis Arnold and Nigel Fortune, 1973, p. 104.

[lxxii] Giorgio Pestelli, 1984, p. 233.

[lxxiii] Barry Cooper, 2000, pp. 106–8.

[lxxiv] From the recollections of Carl Czerny, see: Paul Badura-Skoda, editor, 1970, p. 37.

[lxxv] Charles Rosen, 2002, p. 152.

[lxxvi] Edwin Fischer, 1959, p. 59.

[lxxvii] Maynard Solomon, 1977, p. 128.

[lxxviii] Cited in Anton Schindler, 1860, English edition, Donald MacArdle, 1966, p. 94.

[lxxxix] Wayne Senner, *et al*, 1999, Vol. 1, pp. 176 –7.

[xc] *Ibid*, derived from note 2 to the text.

[xci] Peter Clive, 2001, p. 96.

[xcii] See: Eric Blom, 1938, p. 94.

[xciii] Derived from Paul Mies, 1929, p. 181. Mies provides some discussion of Beethoven's sketches to Piano Sonata Op. 26.

[xciv] Thayer-Forbes, 1967, p. 1054.

[xcv] Some authorities suggest four trombonists performed the Funeral March. See the text accompanying the facsimile of Franz Stoeber's watercolour portraying the composer's funeral: Beethoven House Website, Beethoven House Bonn, Digital Archives, Library Document B 209.

[xcvi] Edwin Fischer, 1959, p. 59.

[xcvii] From the recollections of Carl Czerny, see: Paul Badura-Skoda, editor, 1970, p. 38.

[xcviii] Marion Scott suggests Beethoven is giving a 'reminiscence' of Clementi. Marion Scott, 1940, pp.137–8.

[xcix] Dennis Matthews, 1985, p. 84.

[c] Romain Rolland describing the final movement writes: 'The final *Rondo* bubbles with life ceaselessly until it disappears in a faint whisper.' Romain Rolland, 1917, p. 147.

[ci] Alfred Brendel, 2002, pp. 112–3.

[cii] As recounted by Alexandra Orlova, 1983, p. 51.

[ciii] As recounted by Alan M. Gillmor, 1988, pp. 10–11.

[civ] Charles Rosen, 2002, p. 152. A performance of the Piano Sonata in A flat, Op. 26 has been recorded by Elly Ney on Beethoven's Graf fortepiano of 1825 – more correctly the one on loan to him. Source: Colosseum MSt 1015.

PIANO SONATAS
OP. 27, NOS. 1–2

'[These] sonatas show the composer emancipating himself from the classical sonata pattern and doing it as drastically as possible by substituting pieces in a freely chosen form for the traditional first movement that was always the most important part of a sonata, though not invariably in what we now call sonata form. In the first sonata of Op. 27 Beethoven may be said to be looking back, in his opening movement, to the old suite form, in the second forward to that of the Schubertian impromptu or even the Mendelssohn song without words.'

Eric Blom, *Beethoven's Pianoforte Sonatas Discussed* 1938, p. 102.

'Each of [the piano sonatas] in Op. 27 is ... designed to be played without a break between movements. The order of the movements is dictated by their poetic content; they have the glamour that hangs over a magnificent extemporization, yet their aesthetic structure is masterly.'

Marion M. Scott, *Beethoven, The Master Musicians* 1940, p. 138.

'An essential change is to be observed in the two sonatas Op. 27. We are at the beginning of the nineteenth century, not far from the time of composition of the *Eroica* Symphony. Beethoven was fully conscious of the freedom of these sonatas (E-flat major and C-sharp minor): he inscribed both *Sonata quasi una fantasia.*'

Oskar Bie, *A History of the Pianoforte and Pianoforte Players* 1966, p. 175.

The composition and publication of the Piano Sonatas Op. 27, Nos. 1 and 2 belong to the period 1800–02 when Beethoven was in his early thirties. He had by then secured the patronage of Prince Karl Lichnowsky, one of Vienna's foremost patrons of the arts, who had settled on him an annuity of 600 gulden (about 60 pounds sterling). Moreover, Beethoven's reputation was now extending beyond the confines of the salons where, on taking up residence in Vienna, he had been lionized as a virtuoso pianist. For example on 2 April 1800 Beethoven gave an *Akademie* (benefit concert) at the *Burgtheater* (Royal Imperial Court Theatre) — his first public appearance as such. On this occasion, he premiered his Symphony No. 1

in C and 'a grand Concerto for the pianoforte' (unidentified) and improvised at the piano. The correspondent of the contemporary journal *Allgemeine musikalische Zeitung* (*AmZ*) considered the concert to be 'truly the most interesting for a long time'. He found in the symphony 'considerable art, novelty and a wealth of ideas', the piano concerto to be 'written with a great deal of taste and feeling', and Beethoven's improvisation to be 'masterly'.[ ]

Beethoven's success with the musically minded public was consolidated further when, in January of the following year, he was commissioned to collaborate with the Italian ballet master and choreographer Salvatore Viganò in a production of *Die Geschöpfe des Prometheus* ('The Creatures of Prometheus'). The ballet was subsequently performed in March to general acclaim, although Beethoven's music was too original for some. For instance Joseph Rosenbaum, secretary of the Esterhazy family — who the reader will recall, were Haydn's employers — attended the concert and recorded in his diary: 'The ballet did not please at all, the music a little ... at the end the ballet was more hissed than applauded.'[ ] Beethoven, however, was undeterred and in June of the same year he dedicated a pianoforte arrangement (Op. 43) of his music to Princess Lichnowsky, the wife of his patron.[ ]

In our consideration of Beethoven at the period of composition and publication of the Op. 27 Piano Sonatas, brief mention should be made of his extraordinary creativity as manifest in other of his contemporary works. These include: sketches for the String Quartets Op. 18, the Septet Op. 20 (revised later by Beethoven as his Trio Op. 38), the sonata for violin and piano Op. 24 (whose genial warmth has earned it the nickname *Spring*), sketches for the Piano Sonata Op. 28 (similarly imbued with genial warmth and earning it the nickname *Pastorale*), the String Quintet Op.

29, work on the Bagatelles for piano Op. 33, work on the Second Symphony Op. 36 and sketches for the Piano Concerto No. 3, Op. 37. It is little wonder that in January 1801 Beethoven should feel impelled to write to his Vienna publisher Franz Hoffmeister about his recent labours. He opens his letter with the salutation, 'Dear Brother in Art' — Beethoven's way of greeting a fellow artist. He expresses relief 'that tiresome business has now been settled', by which he means the complex and time-consuming procedures he had had to transact with Hoffmeister to see his works in print. Beethoven calls it tiresome because, as he remarks, 'he should like such matters to be differently ordered in this world'. He goes on to say: 'There ought to be in the world *a market for art* [Beethoven's italics] where the artist would only have to bring his works and take as much money as he needed.' He laments how he has to be both an artist and 'to be to a certain extent a business man as well, and how can he manage to be that — Good Heavens!'.

Notwithstanding the demands Beethoven's creative work imposed upon him, he did not neglect his responsibilities as a teacher of piano — irksome as he often considered such work to be. Carl Czerny, reflecting on the instruction he received from Beethoven as this period, remarks: 'During the first lessons Beethoven kept me altogether on scales in all the keys and showed me (something at the time still unknown to most players) the only correct position of the hands and fingers and, in particular, how to use the thumb ... Then, he went over the studies belonging to this method with me and, especially, called my attention to the *legato*, which he himself controlled to such an incomparable degree.'.

Before resuming our discussion of the Piano Sonatas Op. 27, mention should be made of the *jealous demon* — Beethoven's expression — that was now haunting him and which was to transform both his future existence and his relationship with his art — namely, the onset of deafness. This was to initiate a period of what has been described as 'Crisis and Creativity'. Beethoven's hearing had begun to deteriorate significantly from about 1798 and by 1800 he was consciously avoiding social gatherings, 'fearing his disability would become common knowledge'. In his despair he confided his circumstances to the physician Dr. (later Prof.) Franz Gerhard Wegeler, a close friend from his schooldays in Bonn. In a letter of 29 June 1801 — one of the most poignant in cultural history — he explains how for the last three years his hearing has become weaker and weaker and how his ears 'continue to hum and buzz day and night' (a characteristic of tinnitus — a disease of the inner ear). He confesses to leading a miserable life and cannot bring himself to say to people: 'I am deaf.' He admits even to cursing his Creator and his very existence. But, with characteristic Beethovenian defiance, he resolved to accept his fate adding: 'I live entirely in my music; hardly have I completed one composition when I have already begun another.'

A few days later (July 1 1801) he wrote in similar terms to his close friend the theologian and amateur violinist Karl [Carl] Amenda. He tells Amenda of the success he is having with his compositions, and of his relative financial security — the combined income from his works and from Prince Lichnowsky's annuity — but he then discloses the circumstances of his increasing deafness and the tribulations it is causing. He writes: 'We must wait and see whether my hearing can be restored ... I must hope, but I hardly think it possible ... Oh, how happy should I be now if I had perfect hearing.' Later in the year (November) Beethoven wrote again to Wegeler asking if he considered if galvanism might benefit his hearing. Only ten years previously (1791) Luigi

Galvani had published his treatise on what he termed 'biological electricity' with sensational claims of its alleged powers to animate the muscles of dead limbs — including those of human beings (derived from the corpses of criminals). The reader will recall this innovation was the genesis of Mary Shelly's *Frankenstein*. It is a measure of Beethoven's desperation concerning his hearing that he was prepared to contemplate such new and untested procedures. His letter to Wegeler, however, reveals how love and his indomitability of spirit were helping him to conquer his *jealous demon*. He tells Wegeler he is 'leading a slightly more pleasant life' and mixing more with his 'fellow creatures'. Hitherto, he explains, how his poor hearing had haunted him everywhere 'like a ghost' and had made him seem to be 'a misanthrope' which he insists he is 'far from being'. This more positive transformation in his life, and outlook, had been brought about by 'a dear charming girl who loves me and whom I love'. Beethoven even contemplated marriage in the hope it might bring him further happiness. He recognized, however, this was impossible since 'unfortunately [the lady in question] is not of my class'. In any event, Beethoven concluded, he could not marry at the present moment on the grounds: 'For me there is no greater pleasure than to practice and exercise my art.'[xiii]

The 'dear charming girl', to whom Beethoven makes reference, was Countess Gillette Guicciadi. She would eventually receive the dedication of the second of the Piano Sonatas Op. 27 — the *Moonlight*. We consider these circumstances in greater detail later. For the moment, it will be helpful to recall Beethoven's powers of improvisation at the keyboard, since it is widely acknowledged it is the spirit of improvisation that permeates the two sonatas Op. 27 and imparts to them something of the nature of a *fantasia* — as Beethoven himself was to describe them. As a pianist

Beethoven had his equals in speed and dexterity in what may be described as conventional keyboard attainments — such as the transaction of scales, arpeggios, trills and the like — but in the realm of improvisation those privileged to hear him perform attest to Beethoven being without equal. Some accounts of Beethoven's playing, often recalled many years after the event, should perhaps be read with caution — bearing in mind the tendency in human nature to exaggerate. Even after making such allowances, one is left with an indelible impression of his artistry and powers of imagination.

Ignaz von Seyfried, who conducted the première of the original version of Beethoven's opera *Fidelio* (1805) — and whose judgment therefore should carry some weight — recalls, albeit in a somewhat florid style: 'When once he began to revel in the infinite world of tones, he was transported also above all earthly things ... Now his playing tore along like a wildly foaming cataract, and the conjurer constrained his instrument to an utterance so forceful that the stoutest structure was scarcely able to withstand it ... Again the spirit would soar aloft, triumphing over transitory terrestrial sufferings.'

Baron Louis Trèmont, a French nobleman, met Beethoven when he (Trèmont) was a young man and recalled several years later: 'I admired his genius and knew his works by heart ... he arranged several meetings with me during my stay in Vienna, and would improvise an hour or two alone for me ... I fancy that to these improvisations of Beethoven's I owe my most vivid musical impression. I maintain that unless one had heard him improvise well and quite at ease, one can but imperfectly appreciate the vast scope of his genius.'

A summation of the eyewitness accounts and the aural memories of Beethoven's powers of improvisation, suggest they were precursors to Beethoven's developing *quasi una fantasia* compositional style. In particular may be identified four singular characteristics: 'elaborate virtuoso figuration; irregular melodies suggesting recitative style; cantabile melodies analogous to aria styles; and strict contrapuntal style'.[xvi] Beethoven's growing confidence in the possibilities of innovating with the medium of the piano-based sonata form, doubtless also owed much to the 'boldness and freedom'[xvii] he had expressed in his earlier Piano Sonata Op. 26 — characterized by its pioneering 'unmistakable individuality' and 'redefinition of the genre'.[xviii] As a consequence of these innovations, the *difference* ('emphatic, volatile quality about the fast movements') and the *newness* ('romance and pathos about the slow ones') of a Beethoven piano sonata — compared with that of one by other composers — must have been immediately apparent (sometimes shocking) to the more traditionally-minded members of a Viennese audience.[xix]

In this regard acknowledgement should be made of the pioneering efforts of Haydn and Mozart in establishing the link between *fantasy* and sonata form — of which Beethoven himself was fully aware. Wilfrid Mellers reminds us how Haydn, in his Keyboard *Fantasy* in C (1794), displays 'wild modulations' and 'gestural anarchy'.[xx] Similarly, the indefatigable H. C. Robbins Landon observes how Haydn had often shown 'a willingness to produce a kind of raw bravura in his piano writing'. He cites Haydn's last three piano sonatas, in particular the opening of the very last sonata, 'with its arpeggiated full chords, contrast between *forte* and *piano*, double thirds — a masterly integration of medium and message'.[xxi] Mellers, in his further consideration of the 'expressive immediacy' of the fantasy style', cites Mozart's C minor *Fantasy* (K. 475) — a work Beethoven is known to have admired. In this Mellers finds anticipations of Beethovenian connotations of 'the free fantasy in terms of violence of expression, strangeness of effect and formal freedom, shared with the sonata [within] a more prescribed tonal and metrical framework'.ᵛⁱⁱⁱ Such stylistic developments were in part in response to the developing sonority of the piano — to which Beethoven responded throughout his life. In the ten years since Mozart's death in 1792, the piano had been enlarged with regard to its physical strength (and thereby its sonority), its mechanism, its capacity for more subtle dynamic gradation and the compass of its keyboard — both in the upper and lower octaves.ˣⁱⁱⁱ

The two Piano Sonatas Op. 27 are the first of Beethoven's works in the genre to be given the subtitle *Sonata quasi una fantasia.* In selecting this expression it is as though the composer was preparing the listener for his unorthodox procedures — rather as Franz Schubert was to do twenty years later in designating the expression *Wanderer Fantasie* for what would be his most virtuosic and technically challenging piece for the keyboard.ˣⁱᵛ With the Op. 27 Piano Sonatas, Beethoven was not merely 'departing from the traditional sonata structure'ˣᵛ but was also 'emancipating himself from the classical sonata pattern — and doing it as drastically as possible'.ˣᵛⁱ Romanticism is also evident in these two works with regard to the order of their movements, their shapes, passion of expression and changes of mood.ˣᵛⁱⁱ As remarked, the spirit of improvisation is also manifest. We recall how contemporaries of Beethoven who heard him improvise, remark he would initially strike out a few simple notes or chords and then elaborate upon them consistent with his mood and the dictates of his imagination.ˣᵛⁱⁱⁱ With this in mind, an entry in one of his sketchbooks is of interest. He writes: 'One improvises actually only when one doesn't pay attention to what one plays, so if one would extemporize in the best, truest way in public, it is necessary to give oneself up freely to one's inclinations.'ˣⁱˣ When embodied within the piano sonata form, as in the case of the Op. 27 Piano Sonatas, the effect of these innovations could be startling – even to Beethoven's admirers. As Mellers observes, the piano sonata of the late eighteenth-century had premeditated characteristics, within a 'multi-movement' structure, of 'formal constraints' and 'unified character'. The new sound-world Beethoven was exploring was distinguished by a quite different personality embracing 'improvisation', 'formal freedom', and 'varied character', within a 'single movement format'.[xxx]

When embarking on his Op. 27 Piano Sonatas, Beethoven was well aware that the ears of his audience were conditioned, anchored even, to late eighteenth-century expectations. As he set out 'to push his audience's under-standing to its limit' (Mellers) they would need to be prepared for his innovations. His sub-title *Sonata quasi una fantasia* suggests this was Beethoven's way of preparing his audience, and the performers of his work, for the departures he was contemplating from the conventional sonata form. Alexander Thayer, the first authoritative chronicler of Beethoven, affirms this in his observation: 'Both [the Piano Sonatas Op. 27] are designated *Quasi una fantasia* which plainly indicates a departure from the customary structure.'[xxxi] Moreover, since both sonatas share the same designation, *Sonata quasi una fantasia*, it is clear Beethoven felt they shared close affinities of mood and style and that he wanted them to appear as a set. However, as William Newman (amongst others) has remarked: 'Certainly their fates have been different. Op. 27, No. 1 is one of the least played or sympathetically regarded of Beethoven's sonatas, while Op. 27, No. 2, or at least the first movement, is one of the best known of all musical works, let alone sonatas.'[xxxii]

The autograph manuscript of the Piano Sonata in E flat Op. 27, No. 1 is lost. That of its more famous companion, the Piano Sonata in C-sharp minor Op. 27, No. 2, although largely intact, is missing its first and last leaves – and the clean copy that Beethoven prepared for publication (the process that vexed him so much as he repeatedly had to expunge copyists' errors) is also lost.[xxiii] What do survive, however, are many of Beethoven's sketches in which the origins of both works can be traced. We consider these in more detail later. For now we confine ourselves to some general remarks.

Nicholas Cook comments on the 'enormous repertoire of compositional sketches and other materials' Beethoven has bequeathed to musicologists as a consequence of his working method – putting his thoughts down in sketch form as distinct from working directly at the piano. This process he suggests was Beethoven's way of 'using paper to improvise'. Beethoven would write something down, perhaps when out on one of his walks in the country – which he found so stimulating to his personal wellbeing and creativity – and then, back at his writing desk, he would, in Cook's memorable phrase, 'let the paper speak back to him'.[xxiv] The assembly of the many sketches – usually only after much effort – finally resolved in the finished composition, calling to mind Alfred Brendel's description of a typical Beethoven structure: 'From the beginning of a piece, Beethoven places stone upon stone, constructing and justifying his edifices as it were in accordance with the laws of statics.'[xxv] As cultural artifacts Beethoven's sketches have long been the object of veneration; from the time of the auction of his effects following his death they have been sought by collectors. Musicologists have equally valued them as providing insights into Beethoven's creative process. In this context we are indebted to Paul Lang who has drawn our attention to the imagery of William Wordsworth in his verses *The Prelude*, and their bearing on the sometimes arcane appearance of the composer's sketches: 'There is a dark/Inscrutable workmanship that reconciles/Discordant elements, making them cling together.'[xxxvi]

Beethoven began collating his thoughts in sketchbook form in the late 1790s. Before then he had recourse to individual manuscript sheets.[xxxvii] During much of 1801 (April to December) he made use of a single sketchbook now known as the Sauer Sketchbook after the name of the Viennese music dealer Ignaz Sauer who purchased it after Beethoven's death. This contains sketches for the finale of the Piano Sonata Op. 27, No. 2.[xxxviii] Mellers suggests: 'It is possible that sketches for the other movements of the Op. 27 Sonatas were entered in some of the leaves from the lost opening section of the sketchbook.'[xxxix] Sauer subsequently dismembered the sketchbook and sold individual leaves to collectors and souvenir hunters. Before the horrors of the Second World War had scattered or, worse, destroyed the archives of many European libraries, the French writer and Beethoven devotee Romain Rolland had the privilege of consulting the Sauer Sketchbook when it was in the possession of the then Prussian State Library (now the Berlin State Library). It was catalogued as *The Sketchbook F 91*. He remarks: 'The first sketches for the *Sonata quasi una fantasia*, Op. 27, No. 1 [appear] *with all its social grace*.' [italics added][xl]

Beethoven's surviving sketches reveal him striving to find a new form for the structure of the piano sonata to serve as a vehicle for his developing ideas. By designating the Op. 27 Sonatas '*Quasi una fantasia*', he was in effect announcing he was 'infiltrating the most characteristic field of musical rationalism with new values'.[xli] A process of 'disintegration' of the sonata form is evident that would find ultimate expression, as regards the form and shape of movements, in such later piano sonatas as Op. 106 and Op. 109.[xlii] In the

Op. 27 Piano Sonatas Beethoven's self-imposed challenge becomes one of reinventing the integrative process of making 'the various parts of a multi-movement work fit together' such that each sonata becomes, in a manner of speaking, 'greater than the sum of its movements'.[xliii] By adopting the 'fantasy style' of sonata, Beethoven allowed himself 'freer expression of improvisatory ideas and displaced the climax ... to the final movement'.[xliv] Both the Op. 27 Piano Sonatas are 'weighted' towards the finale. The *Presto agitato* of the second in the set is presented on the largest scale undertaken by Beethoven up to this point — 'making use of all the technical possibilities, thick chords, an improvisatory cadenza and expanded cantabile writing ... driven forward with unusual rapidity'.[xlv]

The Viennese Publisher Giovanni Cappi published the Op. 27 Piano Sonatas on 3 March 1802.[xlvi] Various other editions appeared in Beethoven's lifetime. In Vienna the publishing house Breitkopf & Härtel, the world's oldest, published an edition in 1809. In Paris Ignaz Pleyel brought out an edition of the C-sharp minor Sonata in 1823 and the E flat Sonata the following year. Pleyel had met Beethoven in 1805 before moving to Paris where he founded his publishing firm and what was to become France's — and the world's — oldest maker of keyboard instruments.[xlvii] The London Firm of Monzani and Hill issued both sonatas at about the same time. After Beethoven's death Carl Czerny, who had learned several of Beethoven's piano sonatas under the composer's own direction, entered into a collaboration in 1828 with Ignaz Moscheles — to whom Beethoven had entrusted the preparation of the piano score of his opera *Fidelio.* Their intention was a projected complete edition of all Beethoven's piano sonatas but this enterprise was not fulfilled. However, numerous other editions of the sonatas appeared in the mid and late nineteenth century in which subsequent editors added 'their own interpretive layer' to the texts revealing, thereby, what they thought concerning 'performance practice' – bearing upon such considerations, for example, as the realization of Beethoven's tempi and expression marks.[xviii]

Notwithstanding that both of the Piano Sonatas Op. 27 now form part of the repertoire of many of today's concert pianists, their fortunes, as previously noted, have varied. Reassuringly the position today is not as unjust as formally. Witness the observations of the music critic and scholar John Fuller-Maitland – writing on the occasion of Beethoven's death centenary – when he felt obliged to remark: 'I seek in vain for any performance of the E flat Sonata that is worth remembering, and I can hardly think of any great player whom I have not heard in the C-sharp minor.'[xix] We consider their differences and similarities in the texts that follow.

---

[i] Thayer-Forbes, 1967, pp. 254–5.

[ii] Beethoven's growing reputation at this period is considered by Wilfrid Mellers, 1957, p. 11.

[iii] From the Diary of Joseph Carl Rosenbaum, 27 March 1801, cited in: H. C. Robbins Landon, 1970, p. 80.

[iv] From a letter of Beethoven to Franz Hoffmeister, in: Emily Anderson, 1961, Vol.1, Letter No, 47, pp. 50–51.

[v] This creative period of Beethoven's life is considered in some detail by: Thayer-Forbes, 1967, Chapters XIII and XIV; Wilfrid Mellers, 1957; Denis Matthews, 1985; and Glenn Stanley, 2000. Beethoven's letter to his publisher Franz Hoffmeister also sheds light on the many compositions he had in hand at this time, see: Emily Anderson, 1961, Vol. 1, Letter No, 41, pp. 42–3.

[vi] From a letter of Beethoven to Franz Hoffmeister, in: Emily Anderson, 1961, Vol.1, Letter No, 44, pp. 47–8. Worthy of note is that Beethoven's gifted contemporary Franz Schubert, in the years of his maturity, gave expression to just such frustrated sentiments as those expressed by Beethoven in his letter to Hoffmeister.

[vii] Carl Czerny, cited in: George Oscar Sonneck, 1927, p.27.

[viii] Taken from William Kinderman, 1997, p. 73.

[ix] The bearing of these circumstances on Beethoven's frame of mind is discussed by Wilfrid Mellers, 1957, p. 12.

[x] From a letter of Beethoven to Franz Gerhard Wegeler, in: Emily Anderson, 1961, Vol.1, Letter No, 51, p.57 and p.62. Later in life Wegeler became

Rector of the University of Bonn, both Wegeler's and Beethoven's home-town.

x Amenda was a gifted violinist who, in a typical act of generosity, received a copy of Beethoven's first version of his String Quartet, Op. 18, No. 1. See: Peter Clive, 2001. pp. 4–5.

xii From a letter of Beethoven to Karl [Carl] Amenda, in: Emily Anderson, 1961, Vol.1, Letter No. 53, pp. 63–5. For a facsimile of this letter see: Beethoven House Digital Archives Library Document, Bodmer HCB:BBr:1.

xiii From a letter of Beethoven to Franz Gerhard Wegeler, in: Emily Anderson, 1961, Vol. 1 Letter No. 54, pp. 66–8.

xiv Thayer-Forbes, 1967, pp. 206–7.

xv Paul. Nettle, 1975, pp. 278–80 and Thayer-Forbes, 1967, p. 466.

xvi These are the summations of Wilfrid Mellers, 1957, p. 58.

xvii This aspect of Beethoven's developing innovation of the piano-sonata form is considered by Eric Blom, 1938, p. 93.

xviii Charles Rosen, 2002, p. 150.

xix The words in quotation marks are derived from the commentary on the Op. 27 Piano Sonatas by Conrad Wilson, 2003, p. 20.

xx Wilfrid Mellers, 1957, p. 61.

xxi H. C. Robbins Landon, 1988, p. 282.

xxii Wilfrid Mellers, 1957, p. 59.

xxiii H. C. Robbins Landon, 1970, p. 56. An anecdote may be added here. In the summer of 1801, the Viennese firm of Streicher sold a piano to Beethoven's friend Karl Amenda – Streicher's instruments were among the best available. As a gesture of goodwill Beethoven reportedly sent copies of his latest piano compositions inside the case when it was shipped to Amenda's hometown in Latvia. See: Theodore Albrecht, 1996, Letter No. 31, pp. 56–8, Vol. 1, note 1.

xxiv Denis Matthews, 1985, p. 84. Schubert, unlike Beethoven, was not a virtuoso pianist and his *Wanderer Fantasie* was beyond his own pianistic powers: 'Let the Devil play it!' he once exclaimed.

xxv Barry Cooper, 1991, p. 241 and 2000, p. 107.

xxvi Eric Blom, 1938, p. 102.

xxvii Adapted from Harold Truscott, *The piano music* [of Beethoven] in: Denis Arnold and Nigel Fortune, editors, 1973, p. 104.

xxviii Eric Blom, 1938, p. 102.

xxix Cited by William Kinderman on *Beethoven's creative process*, in: Scott G. Burnham and Michael P. Steinberg, editors, 2000, p. 194.

xxx Wilfrid Mellers, 1957, p. 56.

xxxi Thayer-Forbes, 1967, pp. 296–7.

xxxii William S. Newman, 1963, p. 517.

xxxiii Wilfrid Mellers, 1957, pp. 19–20.

xxxiv Nicholas Cook, in: Michael Oliver, 1999, p. 224.

xxxv Alfred Brendel, 2001, p. 3.

xxxvi Paul Henry Lang, 1997, p. 242.

xxxvii For a detailed discussion see: Barry Cooper, *The compositional act: sketches and autographs*, in: Glenn Stanley, editor, 2000, pp. 32–42; and Joseph Kerman, *Beethoven's early sketches*, in: Paul Henry Lang, 1971, p. 24.

xxxviii For a discussion of the Sauer sketchbook, together with a facsimile of selected pages, see: Beethoven House, Digital Archives, Library Document HCB

BSk 10/58.

[xxxix] Wilfrid Mellers, 1957, pp.19–20.

[xl] Romain Rolland, *A Beethoven Sketchbook of 1800*, in: Romain Rolland, 1937, pp. 293–5.

[xli] Giorgio Pestelli, 1984, p. 233.

[xlii] John South Shedlock, 1895, p. 176.

[xliii] Barry Cooper, 1991, pp. 205 –6.

[xliv] Maynard Solomon,1977, pp. 105–6.

[xlv] Giorgio Pestelli, 1984, p. 233.

[xlvi] For a discussion of the date of publication of the Op. 27 Piano Sonatas, in their wider context, see: Thayer-Forbes, 1967, p. 323; Paul. Nettle, 1975, p. 23; and Barry Cooper, 1991, p. 193.

[xlvii] Portraits of Ignaz Pleyel, combined with related historical information, can be see at the Beethoven House, Digital Archives, Library Documents B 187, B 2131 and B2281. The celebrated piano maker Pleyel closed on 13 November 2013 after almost two hundred years of continuous activity.

[xlviii] With acknowledgement to the survey of the publication of Beethoven's piano sonatas as compiled by Wilfrid Mellers, 1957, pp. 34–5.

[xlix] John A. Fuller-Maitland writing in *Music & Letters, Beethoven: Special Number*, 1927, p. 219.

PIANO SONATA IN E-FLAT MAJOR, OP. 27, NO. 1 QUASI UNA FANTASIA

'This sonata, which is one of Beethoven's most impassioned, is also extremely considerate for the player, not too difficult to learn, and the character so clearly expressed, that no pianist can [overlook] it who possesses the necessary facility and vigour.'

Carl Czerny, *On the Proper Performance of all Beethoven's Works for the Piano*, In: Paul Badura-Skoda, editor, (1846), 1970, p. 39.

'Undoubtedly this is one of the most neglected of Beethoven's sonatas and also one of his most subtle masterpieces.'

Harold Truscott, *The Piano Music* in: *The Beethoven Companion*, Denis Arnold and Nigel Fortune, editors, 1973, p. 105.

> 'I've often played it and I admire it very much indeed. It is one of the most original of Beethoven's sonatas, and it already sets some of the patterns for the later works. If you compare it with Op. 101 you will find a few features in common. He called it a "fantasy sonata", and he set out to give a new unity to the movements; they interlock and interact in a way that has not been attempted before, to my knowledge.'

Alfred Brendel in conversation with David Dubal in: *The World of the Concert Pianist*, David Dubal, 1985, p. 104.

Reference has been made previously to the various compositions upon which Beethoven was engaged in the period preceding work on his Op. 27 Piano Sonatas. In considering Op. 27, No. 1 it will be useful to briefly recall the composer's commission to write the music for the ballet *The Creatures of Prometheus* — and how it may have shaped his outlook in the writing of music having a dramatic and *fantasy* character. In Greek mythology Prometheus was the benefactor who brought the gift of fire to mankind by theft from Olympus and against the will of Zeus — ruler of the Olympians. For this Prometheus was doomed to eternal punishment. From antiquity this fable has been the source of inspiration to sculptors, artists and poets. Beethoven's ballet includes scenes in which Prometheus flees from the gods and brings statues to life with fire from his torch. It is not surprising such a dramatic subject should have seized his imagination.

Wilfrid Mellers has made comparisons between the music Beethoven wrote for *Prometheus* and that for the Piano Sonata Op. 27, No. 1. He suggests several parallels can be drawn between the ballet music and that of the piano sonata. First, he draws attention to the ballet's 'narrative structure' that may have prompted Beethoven 'to treat [musical] forms in unconventional ways'. Second, he observes Beethoven makes use of such expression marks as *attacca subito* — usually taken to mean without any break between the current movement and the next — a characteristic of the sonata in question (see later). Third, Mellers draws attention to the manner in which both the ballet and the sonata share such characteristics as 'sudden and extreme changes of tempo [and] cadenza-like gestures'. Although Mellers concludes too much should not be made of these similarities, it is the case that the music Beethoven composed for *Prometheus* exerted a continuing influence on him. He used the theme of the ballet's finale in the seventh of his so-called *Contradanses* (WoO 14, 1800–2); it served as the theme for his epic *Variations and Fugue* Op. 35 — the '*Eroica* Variations'; and he adapted the theme once more in the finale of his epochal Third Symphony, Op. 55 — *The Eroica.*

Sketches for the Piano Sonata Op. 27, No. 1 are preserved in the Landesberg Sketchbook; named after the collector of manuscripts Ludwig Landesberg, he purchased it some time after Beethoven's death. These sketches date from August 1800 to March 1801. The originality emerging in the E-flat major Piano Sonata is evident in the manner in which the movements 'interpenetrate each other'. The performer is directed, as remarked, to link each movement by Beethoven's instruction *attacca subito* — which was his first use of this expression in this way. Notwithstanding the degree of unity this confers on the work as a whole, the movements are, as Charles Rosen comments, 'well-formed, independent ... completely rounded structures that are, nevertheless, unintelligible played on their own'. Rosen goes further and suggests, as indeed do other performers and musicologists, that Mozart's *Fantasia* in C minor K. 475 may have provided an inspirational model for Beethoven with its dramatic key changes that confer different moods throughout its slow-fast sections. ▪

In his study of the relationships between Beethoven's piano sonatas and those of his older contemporary Jan Dussek, Alexander Ringer believes close parallels can be found in the first movement of Dussek's Piano Sonata Op. 9, No. 2 and that of Beethoven's Piano Sonata Op. 27, No. 1. In particular, Lang cites bars 39–41 (Dussek) and bars 43–5 (Beethoven). Ringer is convinced, and the evidence is compelling, that Beethoven made a direct transfer from Dussek of what he describes as 'typically "Beethovenian" exchanges of clearly defined material and decorative figuration between the two hands'.▪ A century ago Romain Rolland in his discussion of Piano Sonata Op. 27, No. 1, reminds us 'the term *fantasia* by no means implies formlessness but rather a departure from the ordinary sonata form'.▪ He viewed the work as: 'This noble musical plaything, already vivified by the genius of Mozart and Haydn ... typical of a genre of early Beethoven sonatas ... Learned yet not pedantic, sensitive yet not doting, gathering at its choice the flowers of feeling but lingering over none of them, this exquisite art is for the lovely butterflies of the salon and is made in their image.'▪ Perhaps it was Beethoven's departure from the strict sonata-form convention, alluded to by Romain, that prompted William Newman, in his discussion of the sonata in the classical era, to suggest Op. 27, No. 1 'may be less accessible for the very reason that it has more real, improvisatory fantasy in it'.[vii]

Although the four movements are to be played without a break, they are, as it were, 'chained together in one whole' (Rolland) and result as a consequence is a terse, compressed work that has a playing time of about fifteen minutes. Notwithstanding the cohesion imparted by the 'chaining together' of the movements, from moment to moment the musical continuity is threatened by such devices as, 'cadenza-like passages and disjunctions of tonality, tempo, idea, register and texture'.[viii] In Beethoven's laying aside the strict sonata form, the nineteenth-century musicologist Ernst von Elterlein finds the character of Op. 27, No. 1 seems 'like a mixture of song, rondo, fantasia and sonata' since all these forms enter into it in such a manner that 'each has an equal and none a special prominence'. In Elterlein's words, there is 'a want of formal organic unity', but combined with a 'visible striving after a definite character and meaning', a 'heterogeneity of expression [and] a want of uniformity of sentiment' and 'abrupt transition from one phase of feeling to another' — the hallmarks of 'a free fantasia'.[ix] Egerton Lowe, writing in the 1920s, considers Op. 27, No. 1 to be 'a unity' in which 'Beethoven continually [preserves] a continuity of purpose throughout the whole work'. He likens the psychological effect of the evolving music to the 'unravelling of [a] picture'.[x] Barry Cooper endorses these thoughts and goes further. He regards the innovation of 'linking consecutive movements in a multi-movement work' to be 'one of Beethoven's most persistent ideas'. In this context he regards Op. 27, No. 1 to be 'an early exercise along this line of exploration'. From about 1804 Cooper further observes how Beethoven, in other of his works, would link his finales to the preceding movement without a break. He sees this as a step in the composer's developing creativity that would find expression in such compositions as the song cycle *An die ferne Geliebte* – a pioneering work in the genre of the *lied* in which each song follows on from what has gone before and is then linked to the next song. Cooper also cites what he describes as 'the extraordinary relationships' in the String Quartet Op. 131.[i] Perhaps the ultimate expression of Beethoven's use of the device of thematic linkage is to be found in his majestic final trilogy of piano sonatas, namely, the Opp. 109, 110 and 111. The present writer recalls, from more than fifty years ago, attending a piano recital in which these three works were played continuously, without a break – in support of the performer's contention they constitute a single, integral whole. The experience presented a supreme challenge to the performer – and the audience.

Publication of the Piano Sonata Op. 27, No. 1 was announced in the *Vienna Journal* of 3 March 1802 as being available from the Printing House of Giovanni Cappi: '*Sonata, quasi una Fantasia per il Clavicembalo e Piano Forte. Composta e dedicata a Sua Altezza la Principessa GIOVANNI LIECHTENSTEIN, Nata Langravia Fürstenberg, da Luigi van Beethoven, Opera 27, Nr. 1'.*[ii] The dedicatee, whose maiden name was (Countess) Josephine Sophie zu Fürstenberg-Weytra, had married General Field Marshall Prince Johann von Liechtenstein. He was from an old aristocratic family, of great wealth, who possessed a mansion in Vienna and various properties elsewhere. Liechtenstein used much of his fortune acquiring works of art. Beethoven became acquainted with Princess Liechtenstein at the Vienna residence of his patron, Prince Karl Lichnowsky, where he performed at morning recitals. There is speculation she may for a period have been one of his pupils.[iii] Be this as it may, Beethoven had a close friendship with Josephine – insofar as their different social positions allowed. This is evident since he wrote to her 'most illustrious Princess' (September 1805) requesting financial support for another of his pupils — Ferdinand Ries. Ries, notwithstanding his vocation as a pianist and composer, had been conscripted into the army, or, as Beethoven puts it in his letter, 'Ries ... must shoulder his musket'.[xiv]

A review of the two Piano Sonatas Op. 27 appeared in the *Allgemeine musikalische Zeitung* (*AmZ*) — issue No. 4, 30 June 1802 — together with that for the Piano Sonata Op. 26. The reviewer considered these three piano sonatas 'of Herr van Beethoven' had 'enriched the selected company of educated musicians and skilled keyboard players'. He enthused: 'They are true enrichment and belong among the few products of the present year that will hardly ever become obsolete.' Beethoven's daring did not, however, go unchallenged. The reviewer liked the first three movements of Op. 27, No. 1 but the concluding *Presto* (about twenty bars) proved too much for him, being likened to the 'thundering conclusion in Italian opera arias that are written for grandiose effects'.[xv]

Although at this period Beethoven had growing confidence in his creative powers, he was nonetheless sensitive to what he considered to be unfair criticism. Earlier (April 22 1801) he had occasion to write to the publishers of the *AmZ* protesting about what he considered to be the unduly critical reception of his first two piano concertos: 'Advise your reviewers to be more circumspect and intelligent, particularly in regard to the productions of younger composers.' On this occasion, however, he characteristically dismissed the reviewers on the grounds: 'They don't know anything about music.'[xvi] With the passing of time Beethoven would become indifferent to critical carping as his art led him into realms of creative endeavour ever more in advance of convention.

We conclude these general remarks concerning Piano Sonata Op. 27, No. 1 with two anecdotes from our own time. The first concerns the English conductor Sir Adrian Boult. He first pursued his musical studies at Christ Church, Oxford (where he scraped a 'pass' degree) and then at the Leipzig Conservatoire. His youthful diaries provide insights into English music-making at the period just before the Great War. An entry in his Diary for June 1908 records he attended a piano recital given by the great Polish pianist and statesman Ignacy (Ignaz) Paderewski. Boult recalls: 'The Beethoven Sonata in E flat, Op. 27 impressed me wonderfully.' He was in thrall to Paderewski's playing and his 'magnetism [that] holds one spellbound'. Notwithstanding, it was Beethoven who triumphed. Boult's entry concludes: '[It] was the Beethoven [piano sonata] — never the Paderewski — that attracted me, so great is its power.'[vii] Paderewski's reputation does not however appear to have suffered since, thirty years later, he was persuaded to come out of retirement to give a filmed performance of the companion piece Op. 27, No. 2. The film was distributed in the UK with the appropriate title *The Moonlight*. The following year it was released in the United States where, doubtless to give it added popularity, it was released as *The Charmer*. It is unclear whether this epithet was intended for Beethoven or for Paderewski — given the latter's striking appearance enhanced by his mass of flaming red hair.

Our second anecdote calls to mind the truism that in times of adversity and sorrow we turn to music for comfort and solace. This was doubtless in mind when, with the onset of the Second World War (and until its close), London's National Gallery hosted a series of much-loved and well-attended lunch-time recitals. The Executive Committee included composer Dr. Vaughan Williams, pianist Dame Myra Hess (herself a regular performer) and the Director of the National Gallery Sir Kenneth Clark. Beethoven's Piano Sonatas Op. 27 featured no fewer than on twenty-two occasions: pride of place went, inevitably, to No. 2, *The Moonlight*, with thirteen performances but No. 1 achieved a respectable nine performances.[xviii]

We turn now to a consideration of the Sonata's individual movements.

Beethoven's use of the subtitle *Sonata quasi una fantasia* 'sets the stage', in the words of musicologist Stewart Gordon, for the 'improvisatory characteristics' and 'multiple tempo pattern' that abound in the sonata as a whole.[xix] Here the performer encounters the musical injunction *attacca subito*, previously mentioned, to ensure the work's four movements are inter-connected. Dennis Matthews characterizes Beethoven's Op. 27, No. 1 as 'this strangely personal sonata' and cites the somewhat high-minded view of past critics who have found the opening movement 'commonplace' and 'childlike'. Matthews' rejoinder is that Beethoven's music here has 'the deceptive simplicity of Mozart's later works'.[xx] This remark calls to mind the aphorism of the celebrated pianist Artur Schnabel: 'Mozart is too easy for children and too difficult for adults.'

In the first movement's *Andante-Allegro*, Beethoven's 'fantasy-like exploration ... sets up richly ambiguous patterns'.[xxi] Matthew Rye, discussing Op. 27, No. 1 in his contribution to the 2006 *BBC Experience* — in which *all* of Beethoven's works were performed within a single week — remarks: 'Despite being outwardly in four standard movements, [the sonata] is more of a continuous whole, with speed and mood-changes within movements and a more fluid approach to key, thematic development and form.'[xxii] In his commentary to the work, Lowe draws attention to what he regards as the 'capricious contrasting effects of the *Andante* and *Allegro* subjects' in the first movement and finds in them the essential features that justify Beethoven's use of the expression *fantasia*.[xxiii] This is consistent with

Cooper's views about the innovatory nature of the movements in this sonata. With regard to the first, he cites the manner in which Beethoven 'inserts an allegro in C between two andante sections in E flat'.[xxiv]

Donald Tovey describes Op. 27, No. 1 as being 'a very remarkable sonata' and then, almost by way of contradiction, he cites the opinion of the German conductor Hans von Bülow who considered the first movement of this E flat Sonata 'unworthy of Beethoven'. Tovey concedes: 'It would be idle to pretend that the beginning of Op. 27, No. 1 is "powerful," ' but he rebukes those who find it 'childish' and argues that in its simplicity it is more 'childlike', the first bars of which may be compared with 'the opening of a nursery rhyme'. He suggests in the first movement Beethoven may be 'fooling' but is quick to add 'there is no fooling in the rest of the sonata'.[xxv] Tovey discussed the Op. 27, No. 1 at some length in a series of public lectures he gave on Beethoven in 1922. Concerning the first movement he goes so far as to propose Beethoven 'absolutely refuses to do anything serious at all' but elects, instead, to put together 'the squarest and simplest of tunes' — tunes, he suggests, 'even Schuman in his most naïve moments would have thought somewhat platitudinous'. However Tovey, the most eminent Beethoven musicologist of his day, recognised how 'Beethoven is reducing everything to the most childish statements in order to give due weight to the harmonic facts that interest him'. He enlarges on this observation and advances the proposition that here we have 'an extreme case', in one of Beethoven's earlier works, of a 'musical statement' forming the basis for 'a fruitful musical idea'.[xxvi] In his guide to the performance and interpretation of Beethoven's piano sonatas, Tovey cautions the student 'to beware of the first movement' since, although it may seem childish it becomes 'formidable as it proceeds' and, in its 'playfulness' and its 'sentimentality', it is, nonetheless, 'laughing at something'.ˣˣᵛⁱ He suggests, resorting to his typical imagery, that 'behind the ostentatiously silly graces ... a hidden power lurks, and makes itself dimly suspected in bright gleams and dark shadow'.ˣˣᵛⁱⁱⁱ

Rolland, in his study of Beethoven written twenty years prior to the words just quoted, is in agreement with Tovey and considers the *Andante* of the first movement to be 'full of light and shade'.ˣˣⁱˣ Countering criticism that the opening theme is trivial, Mellers is of the opinion: 'Beethoven's critics have perhaps concentrated too much on the melody and not enough on the interplay between the treble and the bass.'ˣˣˣ This remark calls to mind the technical challenges posed when performing this sonata. Notwithstanding Czerny's encouragement that it is 'not too difficult to learn' (recall our opening quotation) — and bearing in mind that at the age of *ten* Czerny could perform *all* of Mozart's published works for the piano — Beethoven's Piano Sonata Op. 27, No. 1 is difficult enough. With this in mind, Tovey has advice to offer. Concerning the passage in question — relating to the bars written in chords — he suggests: 'If any of the right hand stretches are beyond your reach, take care that the thumb falls on the beat ... chords treated so will soon become satisfactory.'ˣˣˣⁱ In this context the views of Czerny himself are of interest and serve as a guide to interpretation and performance. Czerny had the privilege of learning a number of Beethoven's piano sonatas directly from the composer and, later in life, premiered some of them when Beethoven's deafness precluded this — the formidable *Hammerklavier Sonata* being one of them. Regarding the movement as a whole, Czerny encourages the performer to regard it as being 'highly poetical'. He suggests it is descriptive of 'a night scene in which the voice of a complaining spirit is heard at a distance'. Such imagery is unusual in

Czerny's writing. His utterances on music, in common with his personal life, are somewhat austere; he never married and declined the career of a virtuoso since he thought he lacked the personality required. He requests the whole movement to be played 'in moderate andante time'. His following remarks are of particular interest for those performing on restored or reproduction instruments: 'The prescribed pedal must be re-employed at each note in the bass; and must be played *legatissimo [to be performed as smoothly and connectedly as possible].' Czerny concludes:* 'In *forte*, the shifting pedal is also relinquished, which otherwise Beethoven was accustomed to employ throughout the whole piece.'[xxii]

In his concluding remark, concerning the 'shifting pedal', Czerny is referring to the knee-lever device typical of the fortepiano of the early 1800s. By application of this the instrument's dampers could be raised to fulfil the composer's direction *senza sordini* – 'without dampers'.[xxiii] Translating Beethoven's instructions into modern-day performance-practice must of course take into consideration the greater strength of today's instruments and their increased sustaining power. The instruments of Beethoven's day could be lifted easily by two men like a piece of furniture – which is just as well given how many times Beethoven changed his lodgings!

Taking the two Piano Sonatas Op. 27 together, musicologist Harold Truscott is of the view: 'No movement in these two sonatas shows [a] romantic mixture more than the first in the E flat Sonata.' Alongside other commentators, some of whom we have cited, he considers Beethoven 'on the surface ... seems to have almost reverted to childhood' but acknowledges how the movement develops 'an extraordinarily mature and romantic sound as it progresses'. Truscott enthuses, this may even be the first use of a musical form 'so dear to Schuman in his earlier music' — namely 'the classical, sectional-rondo, romantically adapted'.[xxviii]

Given the various quasi-metaphorical references we have cited, relating to the imagery of childhood bearing on the character to be found in the first movement of Piano Sonata Op. 27, No. 1, it is perhaps fitting we should conclude our opening remarks with an anecdote told by the distinguished interpreter of Beethoven, Edwin Fischer — relating to actual childhood. He recalls the occasion when he was due to give a performance of the Op. 27, No. 1 'in a small town' — he does not say where but we can infer it was isolated and remote. Fischer had been reflecting on the unusual sequence of episodes in the first movement — *andante, allegro, andante* — and asked himself: 'Where is the subject's true centre of gravity?' The answer came from an unexpected source — and in a most enchanting way. In search of an answer, and wanting to practice, he enquired where he might find a piano — and was duly directed to the local grocer! He called on him and was shown into a pleasant room where there was a grand piano — and a girl of about fourteen years of age. She opened the lid and stood by ready to play. The coincidence that followed is quite remarkable. He asked her to play something. Fischer then recalls: 'Without a word she sat down and played Op. 27, No. 1 with a naturalness, gentleness, equanimity and sadness that suggested that this was the true expression of hidden suffering.' Fischer continues: 'She new nothing about "subjects" ... or editors' "metronome marks" but inside her beat the heart of the Beethoven who composed this sonata.' Deeply moved by her playing, Fischer concludes: 'I had found the answer to my problems.'[xxix]

The second movement, *Allegro molto e vivace,* 'with its rash, unstable hurrying character and ... its humour ... already clearly bears the stamp of the Beethoven *scherzo*'.[xxx]

This interpretation of feeling in this movement is endorsed by Fischer who describes it as being 'a genuine Beethoven *scherzo*, of the demonic kind [whose] motifs ... scurry ghost-like over the keys'.ˣˣˣᵛⁱⁱ Likewise, Rolland found the *Allegro* passages to be 'full of imagination and vigour'.ˣˣˣᵛⁱⁱⁱ Gerald Abraham goes further and suggests: 'The *scherzo* has something in common with that of the Fifth Symphony, the mysteriously foreboding main section being contrasted with a rather grotesque trio.'ˣˣˣⁱˣ Czerny, whom we recall learned the work at Beethoven's hands, is more cautious. With performance in mind he acknowledges the *scherzo* 'is certainly lively' but requires it to be played 'agreeably' rather than with 'gaiety'. Excessive 'humorous mirth' would, he considers, 'contrast too greatly with the first movement'.ˣˡ

Charles Rosen, considering the form of the *Allegro*, regards it as being 'conventional' but draws attention to 'the contrast of texture' he regards as 'exceedingly original and complex'.ˣˡⁱ Mellers shares this outlook and elaborates, 'the *Andante's* rhythmic patterns refer unmistakably to the gavotte' which he reminds us was a dance-form of 'the high style' associated in the late eighteenth century with the aristocracy. He extends this viewpoint by conjecturing when at work on this movement Beethoven was perhaps recalling works recently composed by his former teacher Haydn. He cites 'the harmonic stasis' of the trio section with its 'off-beat arpeggios' that for him recall the *Presto* of Haydn's Op. 76, No. 6 String Quartet, published in Vienna in December 1799, and the Trio of Op. 77, No. 1, published around the same time as Beethoven's Op. 27, No.1 in 1802.ˣˡⁱⁱ In similar vein Cooper finds the trio section of Piano Sonata Op. 27, No.1 has several features in common with Beethoven's own Bagatelle Op. 33, No. 7 that is contemporaneous with the sonata in question. He cites their shared keys of A-flat major and their 'fast triple time, with a repeated left-hand chord and the texture spreading into the treble clef only towards the end of the phrase'.ᵡˡⁱ Tovey, with interpretation in mind, refers to these chords and urges the performer to adopt a tempo that 'should not be too fast for a significant delivery of the bass'. He maintains, with a touch of his typical imagery, 'side drums cannot be more stirring than the short chords of the *Trio* when properly played'.ˣˡⁱᵛ

The third movement is designated *Adagio con espressione* and follows on directly from the second movement, as directed by Beethoven, without a pause. Thereby: 'It stands midway between a separate movement and an introduction to the finale.' With the melody often expressed in double octaves 'the sonority is exceptionally rich, even thick'.ˣˡᵛ Here the piano writing has been described as being 'cast in the true Beethoven mould and displays depth and warmth of feeling'.ˣˡᵛⁱ It may even be suggestive of the mood prevailing in the composer's Third Piano Concerto.ˣˡᵛⁱⁱ Mellers recalls how the composer's admirers were moved by the eloquence of his own adagio playing and suggests this movement 'may embody something of Beethoven's own pianism'.ˣˡᵛⁱⁱⁱ Also with reference to the composer, and the innovatory nature of the movements in this sonata, Cooper draws attention to both the expressive feeling in the *Adagio* and also to the manner in which 'a part of it reappears just before the end of the finale' reminiscent, as he observes, of procedures Beethoven adopts in the finale of his String Quartet, Op. 18, No. 6 – published in 1801.ˣˡⁱˣ Gordon also reflects here on Beethoven's compositional procedures. He suggests the composer's varied tempo marking and contrasting of sections – shaped within an overall unity – anticipate in some measure the closing passages of the Piano Sonata Op. 110, composed some twenty years later.ˡ

The fourth movement, *Allegro vivace,* follows directly from the third, again, as directed by the composer.

In his researches into the origins of this movement, Maynard Solomon believes Beethoven may have looked back to the three quartets for piano and strings that he wrote in 1785 — when he was age fifteen. Solomon adds it was not inspiration Beethoven was seeking but potential 'raw material'. Beethoven never published these early compositions, in part because he realised they were apprentice works but also, perhaps, because of his over-reliance on the works of Mozart that he had adopted as his models (see related endnote). Solomon remarks: '[Beethoven] evidently held them dear, however, for they contain a number of original melodic ideas upon which he drew in Vienna for the finale of Op. 27, No. 1.'[i] For Eric Blom the finale of this sonata 'is at once the support and the chief aesthetic feature of its structure'.[ii] In strict musicological terms the closing movement 'approximates more to conventional sonata form' within 'a sonata-allegro structure'.[iii] Cooper remarks how the sonata-rondo form is found in the finales of both the two Piano Sonatas Op. 27 and, thereby, 'the drama and inherent tension in the sonata have been transferred from the beginning to the end of the works'.[iv] Rosen also expresses similar views. Not only does he affirm how, in the final movement, Beethoven displaces 'some of the weight of the work from the opening to the finale' but he maintains: 'With this sonata Beethoven began an experiment to which he continued to return and develop through the years.'[v]

We close with further thoughts regarding performance. Czerny characterises the final movement as being 'extremely impetuous' and to be played 'with a powerful, clear and brilliant touch'.[vi] Tovey, however, cautions the performer from taking the movement at too rapid a tempo. He maintains: 'Like the finale of the F major Quartet, Op. 59, No. 1, this movement loses all energy if taken at a dangerous pace.'[vii] Fischer, responding to the pianistic-delight and listener-pleasure Beethoven has enshrined within his Piano Sonata Op. 27, No.1, concludes: 'After a number of performances, the player will become joyfully aware of the work's unity when nearing the end, and will be able to communicate this feeling to his audience.'[viii]

[i] Wilfrid Howard Mellers, 1957, pp. 18–9.

[ii] The sketchbook origins of Piano Sonata Op. 27, No. 1 are discussed by Elliot Forbes, editor, 1967, p. 296 and Barry Cooper, 1990, p. 185. For a detailed analysis of the Landesberg Sketchbook, containing references to Piano Sonata Op. 27, No. 1, see: Douglas Porter Johnson, editor,1985, pp. 101–112.

[iii] Charles Rosen, 2002. p. 153.

[iv] Alexander A. Ringer *Beethoven and the London pianoforte school* in: *The creative world of Beethoven*, Paul Henry Lang, editor, 1971, pp.250–1.

[v] Romain Rolland, 1917, p. 27.

[vi] Romain Rolland, 1937, p. 120.

[vii] William S. Newman, 1983, p. 517.

[viii] Wilfrid Howard Mellers, 1957, p. 66.

[ix] Ernst von Elterlein, 1898. p. 67.

[x] C. Egerton Lowe, 1929, p. 70.

[xi] Barry Cooper, 1990, p. 73.

[xii] See: Beethoven House Digital Archives, Library Documents Cappi and Czerny 879 and C27/58.

[xiii] For the context of the dedication, and references to those cited, see: Peter Clive, 2001, p. 208 and Eric Blom, 1938. p. 102.

[xiv] Emily Anderson, 1961, Vol. 1, Letter No. 121, p. 140. A facsimile of Beethoven's letter to Ries can be seen at the Beethoven House, Digital Archives, Library Document Sammlung H. C. Bodmer, HCB Br. 171.

[xv] Wayne M. Senner, Robin Wallace and William Meredith, editors, 1999, p. 176.

[xvi] Emily Anderson, editor and translator, 1961, Vol. I, Letter No. 48, pp. 52–3.

[xvii] Michael Kennedy, 1987, p. 35.

[xviii] National Gallery (Great Britain), 1948.

[xix] Stewart Gordon, 1996, pp. 162–3. The short phrases quoted are from Gordon's more detailed commentary.

[xx] Denis Matthews, 1967, p. 25.

[xxi] Wilfrid Howard Mellers, 1957, p. 66.

[xxii] Matthew Rye, 2006. BBC Website *Beethoven Experience.*

[xxiii] C. Egerton Lowe, 1929, p. 68.

[xxiv] Barry Cooper, 2000, p. 8.

[xxv] Donald Francis Tovey, 1944, p. 35.

[xxvi] Michael Tilmouth, editor, 2001, p. 421.

[xxvii] Harold Craxton and Donald Francis Tovey, [1931], p. 32.

[xxviii] Donald Francis Tovey, 1931, revised by Barry Cooper, 1998, p. 96.

xxix Romain Rolland, 1917, p. 27.

xxx Wilfrid Howard Mellers, 1957, p. 68.

xxxi Harold Craxton and Donald Francis Tovey, [1931], p. 32.

xxxii Carl Czerny in: Paul Badura-Skoda, editor, 1970, p. 39.

xxxiii Denis Matthews, 1967, p. 26. Matthews briefly discusses the interpretation of Beethoven's piano sonatas in the context of his expression marks and modern-day performance-practice.

xxxiv Harold Truscott in: Denis Arnold and Nigel Fortune, editors, 1973, p. 105.

xxxv Edwin Fischer, 1959, pp. 60–1.

xxxvi Ernst von Elterlein, 1929, p. 69.

xxxvii Edwin Fischer, 1959, p 61.

xxxviii Romain Rolland, 1917, p. 27.

xxxix Gerald Abraham, editor, 1982, p. 341.

xl Carl Czerny in: Paul Badura-Skoda, editor, 1970, p. 39.

xli Charles Rosen, 2002, p. 153.

xlii Wilfrid Howard Mellers, 1957, pp. 70–2.

xliii Barry Cooper, 1990, pp. 65–6.

xliv Harold Craxton and Donald Francis Tovey [1931], p. 32.

xlv Charles Rosen, 2002, p. 155.

xlvi Ernst von Elterlein, 1898, p. 68.

xlvii Denis Matthews, 1967, p. 25.

xlviii Wilfrid Howard Mellers, 1957, p. 72.

xlix Barry Cooper, 2000, p. 107.

l Stewart Gordon, 1996, p. 163.

li Maynard Solomon, 1977, p. 47. The compositions cited by Solomon, as providing the models for Beethoven's youthful exploration of the medium of the string quartet, are Mozart's Violin Sonata K. 379 and the Piano Sonatas K.296 and K.380.

lii Eric Blom, 1938, p. 102.

liii Stewart Gordon, 1996, p. 164.

liv Barry Cooper, 1991, p. 241.

lv Charles Cooper, 2002, p. 156.

lvi Carl Czerny in: Paul Badura-Skoda, editor, 1970, p.39.

lvii Harold Craxton and Donald Francis Tovey, [1931], p. 33.

lviii Edwin Fischer, 1959, p. 62. A performance of the Piano Sonata in E flat, Op. 27, No. 1 has been recorded by Jörg Demus on a fortepiano of 1825 by Nanette Streicher. Source Harmonia Mundi 30 469 K.

PIANO SONATA IN C-SHARP MINOR OP. 27, NO. 2 THE MOONLIGHT

'This sonata, so rich in ideas, is one of the most interesting though not one of the easiest.'

Carl Czerny: *On the Proper Performance of all Beethoven's Works for the Piano*, in: Paul Badura-Skoda, editor, [1846], 1970, p. 50.

'I cannot explain it. The form is unique. I think Wagner must have loved it as an unending melody, one of the very early cases of that procedure.'

Alfred Brendel in: David Dubal, *The World of the Concert Pianist*, 1985, p. 104.

'Sonata Op, 27, No. 2 (the so-called *Moonlight* Sonata), although comprising three superficially disparate movements, is a masterpiece of intuitive organization. As opposed to the *Pathétique*, which recedes emotionally from the belligerence of its opening *Allegro* to the more modest claims of its concluding *Rondo*, the *Moonlight* Sonata escalates from first note to last ... because of its cumulative zeal, the *Moonlight* Sonata is deservedly high on the all-time eighteenth-century hit parade.'

Glen Gould in: Tim Page, *The Glenn Gould Reader*, 1987 p. 52.

'[Sonatas] ... such as the Sonata *Pathétique* and the Sonata in C-sharp minor (Op. 27, No. 2), are among the most popular and successful compositions in this genre composed by Beethoven or anyone else for that matter. They share a fortunate combination of qualities: they are large concert pieces in which Beethoven's particular motivic type of theme and consequent thematic development appear in association with virtuoso exploitation of the piano. This combination has proven to be potent.'

F. E. Kirby, *Music for Piano: a Short History*, 1995, p. 123.

'Beethoven's persistent desire to create unity, continuity, and forward thrust throughout a whole work finds a new manner of realization in this sonata.'

Barry Cooper, *Beethoven: The Master Musicians Series*, 2000, p. 108.

> 'Beethoven's achievement in the *Moonlight* was to merge fantasy and sonata into a unity, greatly to the work's advantage, and in doing so he paved the way for the compressed sonata-like format of Schubert's *Wanderer Fantasy*.'

Conrad Wilson, *Notes on Beethoven: 20 Crucial Works*, 2003, p. 21.

The opening bars of Beethoven's Piano Sonata Op 27, No.2 *The Moonlight* have been compared, in their familiarity, with the opening words Shakespeare gives to Hamlet in his celebrated Soliloquy. Just as Shakespeare's words *To be or not to be* are memorable, instantly recognisable, and are known throughout the world, so too are the opening bars of Beethoven's *Moonlight* Piano Sonata, even to those who know little about classical music and nothing at all about Beethoven — such has become the world-wide popularity of the opening of this particular sonata. Although the designation *Moonlight* (or its equivalent in translation) is universally adopted, the description is not Beethoven's. The composer was cautious in the extreme in conferring titles on his music. We can infer this from an anecdote left by his pupil Ferdinand Ries. He recalls how Beethoven acknowledged when he was composing, 'he frequently had a certain subject in mind'; consider, for example, the second movement of his Sixth Symphony, *The Pastoral*, in which the flute sings like a nightingale, the oboe, like the quail and the clarinet like the cuckoo. More generally, however, '[Beethoven] often laughed at and inveighed descriptive music, particularly the frivolous sort'.

The title *Moonlight* was conferred on the sonata by the German poet, novelist and music critic Ludwig Rellstab. Rellstab is known to *Schubertians* for the text of the first seven songs of Franz Schubert's posthumous song cycle *Schwanengesang*. The poet originally offered his verses to Beethoven when he met the composer in 1825. He was too unwell, however, to make the settings and they were subsequently passed on to Schubert by Beethoven's self-appointed assistant Anton Schindler. Rellstab's meeting with Beethoven was heartfelt; he admired the composer greatly and recorded the impressions of his meeting with him that were eventually published after his (Rellstab's) death in 1861. Long before then his sobriquet *Moonlight* (*Mond-schein*, 'Moonshine', in German) had become well established in both popular culture and in German and English-language publications.

Rellstab is said to have been inspired to confer the title *Moonlight* on Beethoven's C-sharp minor Sonata when contemplating moonlight reflected off Lake Lucerne. Critics — at least some — have been quick to dismiss this as misplaced romanticism. A closer examination of Rellstab's imagery, now somewhat overlooked, invites a more sympathetic view of the poet's fancy. He *originally* imagined the sight of two lovers drifting in a rowing boat, bathed in moonlight, and being gently swayed by the ripples on the surface of the lake. The latter piece of the poet's invention was doubtless prompted by the rhythm Beethoven adopts in the opening bars of the first movement of the sonata. Romain Rolland' s estimation, of the mood prevailing in the music here, brings him into close proximity with Rellstab's poetic imagery: 'By an innovation that appears to be unique, the *Moonlight* begins with a monologue without words, a confession, veracious and poignant, such as one rarely hears in music.' Later on we examine further aspects of the influence of the *Moonlight* Sonata on other writers and artists. For the present, we consider the origins of the composition and the circumstances bearing on Beethoven's personal life at the period of the work's creation.

The C-sharp minor Sonata is the only piano sonata by Beethoven in this key. The autograph score survives, although it is lacking its first and last leaves. No 'clean copies', as required for the publisher to make his engraving, are known. This was the intermediary stage undertaken by the long-suffering copyist, who had to 'translate' Beethoven's often-challenging manuscript into recognisable musical notation. Between the summer of 1800 and the spring of 1801, Beethoven, adopting his usual practice of outlining his preliminary musical thoughts in sketchbook form. The so-called Sauer Sketchbook, to which previous reference has been made, may have contained about ninety-six leaves of which some twenty-two have been identified. Five of the extant leaves contain sketches for the finale of the *Moonlight* Sonata. It is conjectured sketches for other movements of the sonata may have been committed to the lost pages of the sketchbook. On the centenary of Beethoven's death in 1927, Donald Tovey contributed a study of the surviving sketches for the opening movement of the Piano Sonata, Op. 27, No. 2 in a special issue of *The Musical Times.* The reconstruction and interpretation of the Sauer Sketchbook, and others originally in Beethoven's possession, continues to occupy the attention of scholars and musicologists.

Publication of the Piano Sonata Op. 27, No. 2 was announced, in the *Vienna Journal* on 3 March 1802, as being from the printing House of Giovanni Cappi in the following terms: '*Sonata, quasi una Fantasia per il Clavicembalo e Piano Forte. Composta e dedicate Alla Damigella Contessa GIULIETTA GUICCIARDI DA Luigi van Beethoven Opera 27, Nr. 2.*' The year of composition of the sonata (1801) has been described as 'the happy year of the composer [for his] love of the Countess Giulietta Guicciardi' — the dedicatee of the composition.[xi] Giulietta Guicciardi was a member of a distinguished Austrian aristocratic family to a number of whose members Beethoven gave piano lessons commencing some time in 1800. For many years she was considered to be the object of Beethoven's much-conjectured *Immortal Beloved* — as described in a love letter preserved in the composer's possessions and only discovered after his death.[ix] Giulietta, at age nineteen, eventually married the musically trained Count Wenzel Robert Gallenberg who was a year older than herself. A year after publication of the *Moonlight* Sonata the two emigrated to Italy and would not return to Vienna until 1822.[x] With regard to Giulietta's love for Beethoven, it should be born in mind that in his early thirties he was not the grim-faced demigod as portrayed in later painting and sculpture, but was a well-dressed, slim-waisted young man with his hair cut short in the then fashionable Bonapartist style.[xi]

In 1866 when Alexander Wheelock Thayer completed the first of the three volumes of his celebrated *Life of Beethoven*, he gave consideration to the circumstances bearing upon the public's reception of the Piano Sonata Op. 27, No. 2. He was disposed to caution regarding the love between Beethoven and the Countess, remarking: 'As Beethoven's relationship to the Countess was exaggerated, so also more significance was attached to this sonata than is justified from a sober point of view.'[xii] Thayer was clearly inferring that the musically-inclined public of the day were already attaching 'extra-musical' associations to this composition.[xiii]

In our own time, Wilfrid Mellers (with others) has expressed similar views. He accepts Beethoven may have been in love with Giulietta Guicciardi in 1801, but concludes 'rather too much has been made of the dedication of Op.27, No.2'.* In short, Giulietta was not the inspiration for the work. By way of support for this point of view Mellers cites the Countess's recollections as she recalled them to Otto Jahn — musicologist and biographer (notably of the life of Mozart).

In 1852 Jahn had a meeting with Giulietta Guicciardi who recalled the time when Beethoven had been her teacher of piano. What she has to say is initially of interest beyond the confines of the Piano Sonata, Op. 27, No. 2. She related how in his own performance Beethoven 'made a point of playing without effort' and chose to improvise rather than to play his own compositions. In her lessons Giulietta told Jahn how the Beethoven 'was extremely severe' until 'she achieved an interpretation correct in its very least detail'. Consistent with the popular view of Beethoven, as an irascible genius, she affirms how he was 'prone to excite-ment' and disposed at times to fling down the music and to tear it up. Concerning the sonata in question, Giulietta reported to Jahn that Beethoven had initially intended to dedicate to her his Rondo in G, Op. 51, No. 2. However, finding he needed a suitable composition to dedicate to the sister of his Patron Karl Lichnowsky (Henrietta by name) he asked for the return of the Rondo, that was then in Giulietta's possession. He resolved to confer upon her, instead, the dedication to the Piano Sonata Op. 27, No. 2. In so doing he unwittingly conferred upon his pupil lasting immortality.*

In the past musicologists have been tempted to overlay the sonata with a variety of extra-musical associations bearing on the character of the first movement. For example the German composer and musicologist Friedrich Bernard Marx stated: 'Disappointed affection was the moving cause of this composition which is dedicated to *Alla Damigella Giulietta Guicciardi.'* The nineteenth-century musicologist Ernst von Elterlein shared this outlook: 'Beethoven shows ... in his immortal C-sharp minor Sonata, that love — a secret flame burning itself out in the consuming fire of insatiable desire — lived in his heart.'[xvi] The Swiss-born British musicologist Eric Blom is dismissive of such interpretations allegedly based upon 'inner meanings'. He considers somewhat provocatively (with a pun thrown in on the German-language) that *Moonshine* is all that may legitimately be sought in connection with the work'[xvii]

Pianist and teacher Edwin Fischer makes an observation with reference to a circumstance that appears to have received little attention in Beethoven literature. He refers to a manuscript of Beethoven's that contains a few lines from Mozart's opera *Don Giovanni* — a work Beethoven is known to have admired. The passage in question occurs at the moment when Don Giovanni has killed the Commendatore. Fischer comments: 'Underneath, Beethoven has transposed the passage into C-sharp minor, and the absolute similarity of this with the first movement of Op. 27, No. 2 is quite unmistakable.' He further cites the occasion when Beethoven improvised at the piano to lament the passing of a friend. Combining these two circumstances, Fischer concludes 'there is no romantic moonlight in this movement: it is rather a solemn dirge'.[xviii] In this context, William Newman is more sympathetic. He argues, whilst there is no reason for identifying the sonata with moonlight, what justification is there, he asks, for rejecting this descriptive title? Newman's own position is unequivocal: '[As] a description of mood *Moonlight* is a no less plausible title for, at least the first movement of Op. 27, No. 2, than, say, *Clair de lune* is for Debussy's almost as well-known piece.'[xix]

Given Beethoven's undoubted affection for Countess

Giulietta Guicciardi, it is only fitting we should close this section of our remarks by taking leave of her with the following observation; upon the composer's death, discovered amongst his most personal possessions, was an ivory-painted miniature portrait of Giulietta that he had kept safe all his life.^x

According to Carl Czerny the *Moonlight* Sonata became very popular in Beethoven's own lifetime — somewhat to the composer's irritation. Speaking to Otto Jahn years after the composer's death, he recalled Beethoven remarking: 'Everybody is talking about the C-sharp minor Sonata! Surely I have written better things. There is the Sonata in F sharp — that is something very different.'^x However, not all of Beethoven's piano sonatas appear to have fared so well in popularity. Indeed, Anton Schindler informs us, what seems incredible today — given the universal admiration now felt for these works — that within ten years or so of Beethoven's death 'almost all of Beethoven's piano music had disappeared from the Vienna repertoire'. He adds how, even in Beethoven's lifetime, by the 1820s 'the sonatas, the vehicles of the deepest poetry, existed no longer'.^{xii}

A pianist who, in Beethoven's lifetime, did perform the composer's piano sonatas (to considerable acclaim) was Baroness Dorothea von Ertmann. She received lessons from Beethoven and so earned his respect as to be known by him as 'Dorothea *Cecilia*' (Cecilia being of course the patron saint of music). In 1817 he dedicated to her his Piano Sonata in A Major, Op. 101. The German composer and music critic Johann Friedrich Reichardt heard Dorothea perform Beethoven in the winter of 1808–09. He comments on her noble manner and beautiful face 'full of deep feeling'^{xiii} and, regarding her interpretation following a performance of 'a great Beethoven sonata' (he does not say which) he remarks: 'I have never seen such power and innermost tenderness combined in even the greatest virtuosi.'[xxiv]

Further testimony to the popularity in Beethoven's lifetime of the Piano Sonata Op. 27, No. 2 is evident from circumstances concerning the German composer and musician Georg Christoph Grosheim. These are somewhat protracted in the telling but are worthy of our attention. Grosheim was the author of several books on music and was a particular admirer of the work of the German poet Johann Gottfried Seume. Beethoven also respected Seume's work and an anecdote illustrates the personal regard he had for the poet. In 1811 Beethoven spent the summer at the spa town of Teplitz where he was seeking relief from illness (abdominal pains) but, nonetheless, he made the effort to visit Seume's grave – the poet had died at Teplitz the previous year.[xxv] Following Beethoven's own death two volumes of Seume's works were found amongst the composer's possessions – further evidence of his respect for Seume.[xxvi] Grosheim was aware of Beethoven's interest in Seume's work and wrote to him in this connection on 10 November 1819. He first expressed his appreciation 'for the manifold delights' that Beethoven's labours had given him. He then proceeded to suggest how Beethoven 'might impart to the world your marriage with Seume (I mean the *Fantasia* in C-sharp minor [Op. 27, No. 2] and *Die Beterin*).'[xxvii] Seumer's poem, *Die Beterin*, in translation meaning *The Pleader*, describes a young woman kneeling at an altar in prayer for the recovery of her gravely ill father. Her petitions for his recovery are duly answered as angels come to her aid and the face of the supplicant 'glows in the transfiguring light of hope'.[xxviii] Although Beethoven did not respond to Grosheim's suggestion – that we can imagine would have so fired the imagination of his young contemporary Franz Schubert – we can infer from this episode the extent to which the mood and atmosphere suggested by the opening movement of the Piano Sonata Op. 27, No. 2 was starting to exert its influence on the minds of poetically inclined, kindred-spirits such as Grosheim — an influence, moreover, that would endure throughout the rest of the 19th century down to our own time. An early example of this is to be found in a transcription for voices of the first movement of the piano sonata, dated 1831, of the poem *Resignation* by the celebrated German poet Friedrich von Schiller. This came from the publishing house of Breitkopf and Härtel that had collaborated closely with Beethoven in his lifetime. Perhaps it was the morose tone of Schiller's verses, which include such lines as *Once blooms, and only once, life's youthful May,* that disposed the arranger to find a sombre correlation with Beethoven's music.[xix]

Almost from the time of its creation Beethoven's Piano Sonata Op. 27, No. 2 has been embraced by fellow musicians — including composers, performers, editors and transcribers — and, in popular culture, by artists, illustrators and even sculptors. With these considerations in mind we reflect for a moment on selected aspects of these responses to Beethoven's music drawn from various times down to the present.

The Title Page of an early Viennese edition of the Piano Sonata Op. 27, No. 2 referred to the work as the *Laubensonata* (*Arbour* Sonata) in response to the rumour, prevailing at the time, that Beethoven had composed the music seated in an arbour. A similar anecdote, that cast its influence on German artists for many years, has Beethoven moved by the plight of a blind girl; he is portrayed playing to her by the light of the moon. Moritz Müller, known for his painting in watercolours of landscapes and romantic scenes, was one of the earliest to give expression to this image. He depicts Beethoven performing at the piano whilst the blind girl, the subject of his sympathy, is seated near a window through which the moonlight slants. The portrait painter Lorenz Vogel created a similar scene in which the blind girl stands at Beethoven's side whilst family members look on in silent contemplation. A variant on the same subject came from the hand of the artist Fritz Herman Armin, noted for his illustrations of magical and fantastic scenes. His painting was inspired by an anecdote prevalent at the time. It tells how Beethoven when out on an evening walk was seized by the sounds of a blind girl playing the piano. Gazing in at the room where she was playing, the romance invites us to believe he was so moved by her plight he seated himself at the instrument and played for her the first movement of his Piano Sonata in C minor. Kurt von Rozynski, known for his depiction of Richard Wagner at the keyboard, is another artist who embraced the 'moonlight imagery'. In his version Beethoven plays the piano whilst the blind young woman stands nearby enraptured. Finally, in this brief selection (from very many) of the works of German artists who sought to capture the essence of the music expressed in Beethoven's *Moonlight* Sonata, mention should be made of the work of Franz Stassen — known more generally for his designs of Wagnerian stage sets. Perhaps it was as a consequence of his collaboration with Wagner that inspired him to portray the muse of Beethoven hovering over a moonlit scene whilst receiving inspiration to write his celebrated music.^{xxx}

As the nineteenth century unfolded the *Moonlight* Sonata entered the repertoire of many pianists and exerted its influence on other musicians. We trace its progress with reference to the lives of a selected number of these individuals.

On June 22 1830 the twenty-one year old Felix Mendelssohn had occasion to write to Carl Friedrich Zelter — his music teacher and a friend of Germany's celebrated man-of-letters Johann Wolfgang Goethe. Mendelssohn was then resident in Munich and he relates how Goethe wanted to learn more about how music was developing and to gain an idea of the works of different composers. Apparently Goethe, who had once met Beethoven, 'seemed rather wary' of his former illustrious contemporary but, undeterred, Mendelssohn played through a piano-reduction of the C minor Symphony 'which [Goethe] liked very much'. He then mentions a soirée given by a Countess (unnamed) who asked Mendelssohn to play. He duly obliged with the C-sharp minor Piano Sonata and writes: 'When I had finished I noticed that the impression had been enormous; the ladies were weeping, the gentlemen hotly discussing the importance of the work.' In response to the enthusiasm his performance received, Mendelssohn then had to write down the details of a number of other Beethoven sonatas 'for the female pianists who wanted to play them'.[xxi]

Mendelssohn spent the following summer in Milan where he discovered Dorothea von Ertmann to whom we have made previous reference. Mindful that Beethoven had dedicated to her his Piano Sonata Op. 101, and aware of her reputation as an interpreter of the composer's works, he resolved to pay her a visit — which resulted in a further performance of the C-sharp minor Sonata. He described the experience to his gifted sister Fanny in a long letter dated 14 July 1831. Dorothea had married Captain Stefan Ertmann, now elevated to the status of a General, who was in the habit of going about their palatial residence in full-dress uniform — complete with medals! The youthful Mendelssohn tells Fanny how he was 'seized with a sudden panic' on contemplating the splendid vaulted hall to which he was admitted. The General at first received him somewhat frostily but Dorothea bestowed upon him 'much courtesy'. She later performed the Piano Sonata, Op. 27, No. 2 for

Mendelssohn which 'quite enchanted' the General who, at the end of the performance, 'had tears of delight in his eyes'. Of her interpretation of Beethoven, Mendelssohn told Fanny he thought she rather exaggerated the expression 'dwelling too long on one passage and then hurrying the next'. However, he generously concluded: 'I think I have learned something from her.'ˣˣⁱⁱ

It was probably during his stay in Italy when Mendelssohn was befriended by the eminent German orientalist Baron Christian von Bunsen. He was invited to perform at his home — an experience that subsequently tested the young composer's patience. We learn that after Mendelssohn had performed several pieces, the *Moonlight* Sonata was called for and how 'All was silence and delight; no one moved, no one breathed aloud.' Alas, in the middle of the *Adagio*, a 'stately dowager', sitting in the front row, was so carried away by the rhythm of the music that she began to waft her fan 'by letting it open and shut with each bar'. Despite the glares of those around her she persisted. Mendelssohn generously kept going until he could stand the intrusion no longer. His response was to repeat the last bar in arpeggios 'again and again' following the movements of the fan until, at last, the lady in question took the hint, let her fan fall silent, and Mendelssohn 'went on playing as if nothing had happened'.ˣˣⁱⁱⁱ

The legendary pianist Franz Liszt is the subject of our next illustration of the adoption of the C-sharp minor Piano Sonata into cultural history. Regarding his keyboard skills, Liszt was, in a sense, a direct descendant of Beethoven; he had been a pupil of Carl Czerny, who, in turn, as we have remarked, learned Beethoven's sonatas directly from the master himself. It was Liszt's championing of Beethoven's piano sonatas, especially in his early years as a concert pianist, which did much to raise them from their relative neglect and to place them at the forefront of the pianists' repertoire. By all accounts Liszt, ever the dazzling virtuoso and lion of the keyboard, was willing to condone the taking of liberties with Beethoven's music — at least in his early years. For example, sometime around 1830 he gave a performance of the Piano Sonata, Op. 27, No. 2 to which he added 'trills and tremolos and *impassioned chords* to the first movement'. On another occasion he combined the first movement of the Piano Sonata, Op. 26, which he played on the organ, with that of the final movement of the *Moonlight* that he played on the piano.[xxiv] At a concert in Paris in 1835, the first movement of the Piano Sonata, Op. 27, No. 2 was performed in an arrangement for orchestra that Liszt then completed unaccompanied on the piano. The occasion was considered so memorable it was later depicted in various paintings and lithographs.[xxv]

As Liszt's career as a virtuoso pianist progressed, so did his theatricality. Henry Reeve attended a recital given by Liszt when he was on a concert tour in Scotland in 1841; he performed in Glasgow and in Edinburgh's fashionable Assembly Rooms. Reeve was Editor of the *Edinburgh Review,* an intellectually inclined journal established in 1802 by men-of-letters — 'to gather all the rays of culture into one' (the Journal's motto). Reeve's account of the concert records the hall being very full and Liszt's person as being 'slight and tall, a delicate frame ... perpetually strained by the flow of animated thoughts'. Liszt played a *Fantasia* of his own followed by Beethoven's C-sharp minor Piano Sonata. On completion of the Beethoven, Reeve took the platform, grasped Liszt's hand and 'thanked him for the divine energy that he had shed forth'. As the concert continued, as a consequence of the emotional stresses Liszt was suffering at the time — 'he fainted at the keyboard and had to be escorted from the hall'![xxvi]

The French dramatist Ernest Legouvé has left a similar

account of the emotional effect Liszt's playing could have on individuals. The occasion in question was a private soiree attended by a small, but highly select, audience of connoisseurs. Legouvé describes how Liszt took his place at the piano and, as he puts it, 'began the funereal and heart-rending *Adagio* of the Sonata in C-sharp minor'. Legouvé himself was seated in an armchair and was disturbed by 'stifled sobs and moans'. He turned to look, only to see they came from non other than Hector Berlioz.[xxvii] We find Berlioz in a similar state of emotional catharsis as he confided in a letter to his sister Nanci. Writing to her from Paris on 28 December 1829, he describes his meeting with his friend the German composer and conductor Ferdinand Hiller. Hiller had been with Beethoven when he passed away and had secured a lock of the composer's hair.[xxviii] The two frequently had lunch together following which Hiller, an accomplished pianist, liked to play Bach fugues that Berlioz compared, somewhat irreverently, 'to the sound a kitten might make walking across the keys'! It was a different matter though when he performed the *Adagio* from the C-sharp minor Piano Sonata. Berlioz told his sister: 'Hiller ... plays to perfection ... When it's finished, if one of us is not in tears, we look at each other for a moment without saying anything ... A deep sigh ... A long silence ... and we go our separate ways.'[xxix]

Dmitri Shostakovich provides a further, and more sober, recollection of Franz Liszt in the context of our discussion of the adoption and interpretation of the Piano Sonata, Op. 27, No. 2. He recalls memories of Alexander Glazunov who was his teacher and mentor when he attended the Saint Petersburg Conservatory. Glazunov was an admirer of Liszt, whom he had met in Weimer, and had the privilege of hearing the great pianist perform at a private gathering. Liszt played the C-sharp minor Piano Sonata and, according to

Glazunov, 'his manner differed vastly from what we are used to imagining ... When we hear the name we usually picture banging and ballyhoo, gloves tossed in the air, and so on'. On this occasion, Liszt 'played simply and accurately and transparently' and 'with [such] control that the tempos were extremely moderate'. Glazunov especially liked the manner in which Liszt revealed 'all the inner voices'.

The name Hallé is one we ordinarily associate with the famous British orchestra. In consequence of which we are inclined to overlook that its originator, Sir Charles Hallé, was a gifted pianist and something of a child prodigy — at the age of four, for example, he performed a sonatina in public. His training in Paris, as a concert pianist, brought him into contact with such renowned keyboard executants as Chopin and Liszt. In England he gave regular recitals, at first (1850) privately from his own home and later (1861) publicly from St. James Hall, Piccadilly. It was at these recitals he became the first pianist, in England, to perform the entire series of Beethoven piano sonatas. During the concert season of 1870–1 (by which time Hallé was better known to the public as a conductor), in fulfilment of a personal resolution he gave a performance of the C-sharp minor Piano Sonata on the anniversary of Beethoven's death — which fell on 17 December 1870. In the event the concert had to be given on 15 December and included so many other works of Beethoven's it did not finish until 11.00 p.m.

Hallé regularly took the family for their summer holiday on the Isle of Wight, where they had a cottage at Cowes. His son recalls, affectionately, the delight of sitting in the garden on summer nights 'hearing the *Moonlight* and other divine sonatas played as only my father could play them'.

Felix Weingartner, like Charles Hallé, originally trained as a pianist — and was a pupil of Liszt. He is remembered today primarily as a distinguished conductor; he was the first

238

such to make commercial recordings of all nine Beethoven symphonies and, thereby, made their appreciation available to a wider public. Recalling his childhood he tells how, whilst still only in his third year at the Gymnasium, he was 'thoroughly well acquainted with all Beethoven's symphonies'. He relates how one day the musically inclined inhabitants of Graz, where he was then living, were stirred by the news that Anton Rubinstein — a pianist of known formidable powers — was shortly to perform in the Styrian capital. Weingartner describes how the concert hall (*The Rittersal*) was crammed. 'Then came Beethoven's Sonata in C-sharp minor. Like a lovely song the first movement, like an elemental storm the last!' The young budding musician rushed home and went straight to the piano and, child as he was, 'attempted to imitate the master's touch'.[xlii]

The youthful Weingartner was not the only one to be captivated by Rubinstein's powers. The contemporary music critic Eduard Hanslick refers to his 'untapped natural strength' ad capacity to 'play like a god'. This was manifest at a memorable recital when Rubinstein opened with the *Moonlight* Sonata and then followed it in succession with the *Tempest* (Op. 31, No.2), the *Waldstein* (Op. 53), the *Appassionata* (Op. 57), the E minor (Op. 90), the A major (Op. 101), the E major (Op. 109) and the C minor (Op. 111)! Little wonder, the audience left with their ears ringing and, notwithstanding their admiration for Rubinstein — and Beethoven — were left wondering if it is indeed possible to have too much of a good thing![xliii]

We turn now to citations of the *Moonlight* Sonata, with references to selected musicians and writers that draw us nearer to our own time.

To supplement his income the Austrian composer Hugo Wolf devoted much of his career to music criticism, contributing to such respected Journals as the *Vienna*

Salonblatt. His reviews are frequently acerbic and he soon gained a reputation for his independence of mind and the strength of his convictions. Writing about him in *The Musical* Times (1 August 1912) the English music critic Ernest Newman conceded Wolf had 'a sharp pen', but acknowledged how 'he wrote about everybody with perfect frankness'. We sense this in a review of Wolf's following a recital by the Italian pianist Luisa Cognetti — another pupil of Franz Liszt. On 24 February 1884 she performed the C-sharp minor Piano Sonata in the very same hall where only the previous day Anton Rubinstein — to whose prodigious abilities we have just made reference — had performed the same work. The unfortunate Signorina's interpretation incurred Wolf's wrath. He remarks how Rubinstein's art had 'made our hearts tremble' but Luisa Cognetti's rendering prompted Wolf to expostulate how 'one would gladly have had [Beethoven's] ears cut off' rather than suffer 'such indignities'.xliv

In his autobiography, Sergey Prokofiev recalls his earliest memories were of lying in bed drifting off to sleep listening to his (highly gifted) mother playing Beethoven. It was from her he received his first lessons but in 1902, at the age of eleven, he received more formal instruction from the Russian composer-pianist Reinhold Glière. The youthful prodigy — who by now had already written two operas — was set to work by Glière to learn 'one of Beethoven's G major sonatas' (probably Op. 14 No. 2). He was then required to learn Op. 27, No. 2 whose 'stormy dramatic finale' he particularly liked. Shortly after, Prokofiev moved to the Saint Petersburg Academy to study with the renowned Alexander Glazunov, but he always remembered his studies with Glière with affection: 'Our relationship was such that I would willingly come to him with all kinds of questions about music and would always receive a thoughtful answer.'xliv

During the time when he was living in London, the American poet Ezra Pound wrote occasional music reviews to supplement his income — rather like Hugo Wolf. And, also like Wolf, he adopted an uncompromising stance regarding anything to which he took exception. This is evident from an account he wrote in *The New Age* (8 August 1918) of a recital he attended in *The Steinway Hall*. The pianist was Harold Craxton. We usually associate his name with musicology, particularly in collaboration with Donald Tovey, but Craxton had trained with Tobias Matthay (famed for his studies of the hand position at the keyboard) and had a successful career as an accompanist. At the recital Pound attended, Craxton played the *Moonlight* Sonata; Pound was not impressed by the sonata. He remarks disparagingly: 'The Beethoven *Adagio* is *soft*, in the bad sense. People are scared of the great name of Beethoven, and suppose it to be above question ... There is a cheap opening to the *Allegretto*, and the *Presto agitato* is largely a shindy ... It has no real passion, or, at most, a mere trace towards the finale.' Pound concludes his uncompromising review with the defence: 'A critic must take the risk of such iconoclastic judgements now and then if he is not to sink into utter inutility from cowardice. At any rate, the sonata was a bore.'*

In his survey of the manner in which certain iconic pieces of music have been absorbed into popular literature, Richard Hudson cites the *Moonlight* Sonata as portrayed in the novel *The Moonlight* by Joyce Cary (1946). The scene in question has a seventy-four year old woman playing the first movement of the sonata. He describes her 'old fash-ioned style' with its 'exaggerated rubato, her swayings, murmurings [and] tosses of the head'. The author accepts that whilst all this might amuse a modern audience — or even find it distasteful — he defends her mannered interpretation on the grounds: 'She had been taught to regard music as a poetry of the elemental feelings in which, while she performed, she was required, like a poet, to lose herself.'[xlvi]

The Russian cellist Alexander Ivashkin is known, amongst his many attainments, for his readings of the works of his fellow countryman the composer Alfred Schnittke. In conversation with him he remarked how apparently unrelated subjects can mutually enhance each other. This prompted Schnittke to make the generalisation that 'facts and phenomena, apparently from different sources, for some reason coincide as though they shared a single unified basis'. He substantiates this remark with reference to a scene from the work of the Russian film maker Marlen Khutsiev. This depicted 'gliders in beautiful flight' to which Khutsiev added background music. The piece chosen was the first movement of the *Moonlight* Sonata prompting Schnittke to make the further observation: 'One had the impression that, independently one of the other, the film and the music followed the same structure-pattern, a pattern one could not express in concrete language.'[xlvii]

From what is a veritable mountain of references to the *Moonlight* Sonata, as referred to in popular culture, we conclude with a final illustration that is somewhat removed from the, for the most part, respectful observations that have gone before — but, we trust, the reader will find no less endearing.

In his book *Am I too Loud?* the highly respected, and affectionately remembered, accompanist Gerald Moore recalls his years of performing with many of the world's leading singers of his generation. However, as a young teenager he served his apprentice years performing in some unlikely places. He tells how at the age of fifteen he was part of a trio then performing in a small downtown picture theatre in Toronto. This was the era of the silent movie when musical accompaniment was required to underscore the events unfolding on the screen. Moore recalls how he and his companions 'enjoyed themselves hugely' by scrambling through Beethoven (and other composers) 'often regardless of what was happening on the silver screen' complete with 'wrong notes and false entries'. Clearly, as Moore himself observes, their endeavours were 'not quite in the class of Cortot–Thibaud–Casals' (the celebrated Trio of the period). Notwithstanding their limitations, Moore and his fellow musicians appear to have found their vocation when music of a melodramatic kind was required. On such occasions, Moore and his companions had frequently to press into service the *Moonlight* Sonata. For example, whenever a deathbed scene or a heart-rending farewell appeared, the Leader would call out '*Moonlight*' and instantly the three would break out into an adaptation of passages from the opening movement.

Two other of Moore's recollections, with a Beethoven connection, are worthy of note. The three innovative musicians once attempted to play the composer's *Archduke* Trio (Op. 97) but their efforts were so bad they decided to leave it alone — as Moore remarks, 'to ripen'! Finally, came the evening when they decided to give the *Moonlight* Sonata a rest and to play instead an ethereal passage from the slow movement of Beethoven's *Ghost* Trio (Op. 70). The circumstance calling for this was the plight of pale-faced captives, huddled in their waggons as warring Red Indians encircled them. The theatre manager, however, clearly did not share his intrepid ensemble's predilection for Beethoven. They had not got very far before he hissed from the wings — 'Stop that racket'!xviii

It is only fitting we should close our survey-remarks bearing on this celebrated composition, by quoting from words of a more elevated and respectful kind. For these we can cite Gerald Moore once again, recalling the occasion when he heard the celebrated Polish pianist Ignaz Paderewski play the C-sharp minor Sonata. He writes: 'His *Adagio* ... [was] marvellously eloquent and made the more moving when you glimpsed the lined melancholy countenance of the player.'

Finally we turn to reviews of the Piano Sonata, Op. 27, No. 2 that were published shortly after it made its appearance in 1802. A reviewer, writing in the *Allgemeine musikalische Zeitung (AmZ)*, acknowledged Beethoven's gift not only as a composer but also as 'a creative personality whose idiosyncrasies are valued in their own right'. Another reviewer writing a little later in the *AmZ* of 30 June enthused: 'This *Fantasia* is one solid whole from beginning to end; it arises all at once from an undivided, profound, and intimately excited heart and is cut, as it were, from one block of marble.'

We turn now to a consideration of the sonata's individual movements.

With regard to the first movement, marked *Adagio sostenuto*, we should bear in mind as Barry Cooper observes how: 'The popularity of the first movement can easily distract from its remarkable originality.' Other composers had begun a sonata with a slow movement (Mozart for example) but Cooper draws attention to the particular 'sonority and texture' in Beethoven's music and how 'highly novel for a sonata' they were at this period. Writing in the 1930's Blom was similarly disposed, remarking: 'As a *new departure* [italics added] in sonata form, the work is one of extreme interest.' In this context he comments on the innovatory manner in which what he calls 'the big sonata movement' comes at the end with the slow movement placed first. By so doing Beethoven, in the words of William Kinderman, 'shapes the three movements into a directional sequence leading from a soft, improvisatory *Adagio soste-*

nuto to a turbulent *Presto agitato* finale, whose sonata design reinterprets the thematic substance of the opening movement'.[iv] Denis Matthews, concert pianist turned scholar-academic, suggests Beethoven's use of the term *fantasia*, in the Piano Sonata Op. 27, No. 2, refers only to this 'unusual juxtaposition of moods' on the grounds 'the *Adagio* is sonata form, and so is the explosive finale whose urgent drama has no place for rondo returns'.[v] The *newness* of Beethoven's creation was certainly not lost on the reviewer of the *Allgemeine musikalische Zeitung* who remarked: 'It is not possible that any human being, to whom nature has not denied inner-music, should not be stirred by the first *Adagio*.'[vi]

In his discussion of the possible creative origins of the first movement, Gerald Abraham cites Beethoven's powers of improvisation at the keyboard and suggests these may have been a source of an inspired improvisation that he later adapted into the sonata 'with its single theme and slow, deliberate harmonic motion'.[vii] Writing of Beethoven's pianistic abilities, at about the period of composition of the *Moonlight* Sonata, the composer's first biographer Johann Alloys Schlosser informs us: 'People marvelled at the facility with which he executed difficult passages. His playing may not always have been delicate, and at times may have lacked clarity, but it was extremely brilliant. He excelled at free improvisation.'[viii] Reflecting on Rellstab's *Moonlight* title, Matthews comments that although it was bestowed on the sonata after the composer's death, 'it is apt enough for the nocturnal calm of the first movement'. Elsewhere he adds: 'The veiled opening *Adagio* makes its hypnotic effect through the utmost restraint and shows, more than any previous music, the sustained eloquence of the piano's singing tone at its quietest levels.'[ix] [x] Barry Cooper likens the first movement to a *cavatina*, generally taken to mean a solemn, elegiac melody — of the kind Beethoven was to employ to such moving effect in the celebrated slow movement to his String Quartet Op. 130. In the Piano Sonata Op. 27, No. 2, Cooper finds in the slow movement 'an aria-like melody, accompanied by patterned figuration, all swathed in a misty background'. He further observes how, in his reading of the work, the beginning 'has surprisingly much in common with the funeral march in the Piano Sonata Op. 26' with its similar feeling of 'profound tragedy'.[lxi]

The distinguished physician and musicologist Anton Neumayr is known for his evaluation of clinical and psychological data and its role in elucidating patterns of behaviour as revealed by diseases and mental disorders. In his study of Beethoven's many illnesses, in the context of the first movement of the Piano Sonata, Op. 27, No. 2, he asks: 'Could [the prevailing mood] be related somehow to the deep shadows beginning to be cast, at this time, over his spirits by his hearing disorder?' He also draws attention to 'the despairing eighth-note triplets' from the death-scene music given to the Commendatore, in Mozart's *Don Giovanni,* which, as we have previously suggested, may have been transposed by Beethoven into the *Moonlight* Sonata.[lxii] Writing about the sonata at the close of the nineteenth century, von Elterlein stated similar views, although expressed in more florid language: 'We hear soft, low, plaintive tones, such as arise from a troubled heart. The intense pain reaches a climax ... but closely blended with this heart-trouble is a sense of quiet submission to the inevitable ... a comforting ray of light penetrates the sonata.'[lxiii] Neumayr's suggestion of pain being in the music is also implicit in Oskar Bie's evaluation of the first movement as being 'a unique expression of melancholy'.[lxiv] Rolland was in no doubt as to the extent to which 'personal emotion governs the construction' with the consequence: 'Here the sentiment breaks the usual tonal links of the melody ... [Beethoven] deliberately rejects the symmetry of fixed periods ... he is subject to all the surprises of passion.'[lv]

Over a period of several years the German philosopher and musicologist Theodor Adorno assembled a mass of notes — what have been described as 'a wealth of tantalizing fragments' and 'disparate material' — bearing on the philosophy implicit in Beethoven's music. With regard to Op. 27, No. 2, (first movement) he asserts: 'Beethoven ... bears within himself the whole of Romanticism — not merely in its "mood" but its "cosmos of forms".' He later adds: 'The first movement, of what became popular as the *Moonlight* Sonata Op. 27, No. 2, can be seen as a prototype of the nocturne later to be cultivated by Chopin.'[lvi] In much the same spirit, Beethoven's biographer Marion Scott affirms: 'The first movement, *Adagio*, with its mist of slow-moving triplets and its melody rising from "monotone on a prevalent rhythmic figure" is as impressionistic as anything in Debussy.'[lvii]

Blom's estimation of the first movement embraces references to a number of composers. He finds parallels with some of the 'non-polyphonic preludes' in Bach's *Well-tempered Clavier* but at the same time he remarks how, for the period, it was 'distinctly modern' looking forward in some respects 'to the impromptus of Schubert and to the songs without words of Mendelssohn'. Concerning the latter, Blom detects 'sets [of] songful phrases of a distinctly vocal character over figures of accompaniment that keep to the same pattern throughout'. There are echoes here of Georg Grosheim's letter to Beethoven inviting him to set Seume's words to this movement of the sonata. Finally, Blom also comments that in some ways 'this movement also anticipates the type of Chopin's nocturne'.[lviii]

The Australian born Percy Granger is commonly associated with folksong settings, to the detriment of his reputation and considerable gifts as a concert pianist. By the age of thirteen he had left his native Melbourne to study in Frankfurt at the *Hoch Conservatory* and later had lessons with the titan of the keyboard Ferruccio Busoni. It must be conceded he did not hold Beethoven in high regard – he thought he was 'greatly overvalued as a craftsman and perfectionist' but he did acknowledge him to be a 'transcending personality'. He accepted the *Moonlight* Sonata possessed 'a perfect slow movement evincing a *sustained rapturous mood'* [italics added] but followed with a sting in the tail – 'albeit the only example of a perfect slow movement to be found in all the Beethoven piano sonatas'.[lix]

Today the Spanish composer Isaac Albéniz has a reputation, as with Percy Ganger, for his transcriptions of folk idioms, an assessment, however, that overlooks his youthful pre-eminence as a considerable pianist. He studied at the Leipzig Conservatory, was a pupil of Franz Liszt and went on concert tour throughout Europe for the period 1889-92. At one of his recitals he performed the first movement of the *Moonlight* Sonata that clearly fulfilled the expectations of the reviewer in the *Vanity Fair* of 21 February 1891: 'His excellence lies in the power to play softly ... He can preserve a special shade of tone for a very long time without the slightest fluctuation or variety.' In particular, the reviewer praises Albéniz for his control of the power of the modern-day concert grand piano and his 'appropriate absence of *blurred sound'* [the reviewer's italics]. He concludes: 'This skilful executant has entirely subdued the hard metallic ring which is almost inseparable from the pianoforte, and by his wonderful art produces tones which resemble the ripple of water, and which charm the ear by their delicate softness.'[lxx]

Few would take issue with the view of Denis Matthews who refers to the *Adagio sostenuto* as 'probably the most celebrated single movement Beethoven ever wrote'. He cites the manner in which the music makes its effect 'through restraint' and, thereby, how well Beethoven 'understood the singing qualities of the piano at its quietist levels'.[lxxi] In this context Carl Czerny's instructions to the performer are relevant: 'The first movement [to be] tranquil, not dragging, but with expression ... the melody well sustained.'[lxxii] Charles Rosen expresses similar modern-day words of caution: 'We tend to play Beethoven's adagio's more slowly than they were played during his lifetime.' Classical music he maintains has become a part of high culture and on occasions can become pretentious. He suggests 'playing a Beethoven adagio very slowly is a way of making the public aware they are undergoing a deeply spiritual experience'. He believes such tendencies are encouraged by the greater sustaining power of today's powerful instruments: '[The] slower tempo for an adagio is encouraged ... by the modern piano, which not only makes [slow playing] possible but even tempting ... [The] thicker sound and stiffer action of the modern piano also induce slower speeds.'[lxxiii]

The eminent German Marxist philosopher Ernst Bloch, venturing into musicology, also has words of caution for the performer. First, he likens each note to 'an instrument of the orchestra' with a capacity 'to bring out an inner voice' or 'to play a passage as a melody with accompaniment'. He then asks the question: 'Why does the first movement of Beethoven's Sonata *quasi una Fantasia* Op. 27, No. 2 seem intolerably sentimental if the melody is made unduly prominent in performance?' Adopting his philosopher's stance he provides the answer: 'Is it not because a temporary implicit agent has been mistakenly converted into one that, by its insistence, seems permanent?'ᴸˣⁱᵛ Gordon Stewart acknowledges the spirit of Beethovenian improvisation in the *Moonlight* Sonata 'may be suggested by the introduction to the first movement'. For him though the key is the manner in which 'the persistent use of the triplet figure' in the composer's writing achieves 'a high degree of unity' through its unrelenting effect with the consequence 'One mood is thus sustained and unbroken throughout the movement, thereby establishing a serene but intense emotionalism'.ᴸˣᵛ

With regard to considerations of establishing the correct mood in Beethoven's Piano Sonata Op. 27, No.2, as indeed in other of his works for the keyboard, a challenge confronting the interpreter intent on fulfilling the composer's written intentions is, as we have just noted in the remarks of Charles Rosen, the much-increased sustaining power of today's instruments over those available to Beethoven in his lifetime. At the head of the composition Beethoven writes: *Si deve suonare tutto questo pezzo delicatissimamente e senza sordino* – 'The entire piece must be played as delicately as possible and without dampers.' Strict adherence to this instruction, by pianists playing on modern-day instruments, may result in an excessively reverberant sound. In his social history of the piano Dieter Hildebrandt remarks: 'How the pianist resolves the question, possibly by keeping the pedal halfway down, or releasing it every time the harmony changes is one of those trade secrets.' Commenting on Beethoven's pedal markings he observes, with a touch of humour: 'The trouble is that this instruction cannot be carried out to the letter on a modern piano, for the result would not be a cloud of sound but a full-scale smoke-screen'! He quotes the acknowledged 'poet of the piano' Frederick Chopin who once remarked: '[The] proper use of the pedal was the study of lifetime.'[lxxvi] With regard to such considerations we cite Rosen once more. He invites us to consider the proposition: 'Composers are not infallible judges of the best form of interpretation of their own works. Like anyone else they need the experience of performance to refine their ideas of execution. When the composition is exceedingly original, even revolutionary, the composer may not have evolved a style of performance suited to the new conceptions.'[lxxvii]

We give further consideration to questions of performance and the interpretation of Beethoven's pedal markings later. For the moment we can observe that proponents of historically informed performance have recourse to playing on period or period-reproduction instruments. The reader for whom these considerations are of particular interest will find rewarding the interpretations of the Singapore-born British pianist Melvyn Tan — noted for his study of historical performance-practice. In particular, mention may be made of his recording of Beethoven on the fortepiano given to him by the celebrated English maker Thomas Broadwood.[lxxviii] (See also the remarks we have compiled at the close of our references to this composition.)

For Rosen the *Moonlight* Sonata is 'a unique essay in tone colour'. With this in mind, he supports the practice of achieving what he describes as 'a slight blurring' in order to achieve Beethoven's the required 'wonderful atmospheric sonority'. This requires 'exercising great care, with half changes and delayed changes of the pedal'.[lxxix] Elsewhere he explains the use of the 'half-pedal' with reference to performing on a modern concert instrument. To achieve 'a very delicate blur at the change of harmony' he advocates 'raising the dampers just slightly so that they still remain in contact with the strings, but not enough to cut off all the resonance when the keys are released'.[lxxx]

251

With performance in mind we give the last words on this subject to Denis Matthews. He observes pragmatically: 'People will continue to argue over the degree of compromise required on a modern concert-grand.' He comments on how some pianists are disposed to ignore 'Beethoven's long-held pedal effects' and how others take them literally 'as indicating a veiled, cloudy texture'. Supreme amongst the latter is the Austrian pianist Artur Schnabel. He went to great lengths to edit a scholarly performing-edition of Beethoven's sonatas and was the first to record the entire cycle of thirty-two sonatas (HMV) in 1935 – prompting the musicologist Harold C. Schonberg to dub Schnabel as 'the man who invented Beethoven'! As Matthews concludes – with a witty pun at the end: 'It is up to the individual to decide when half-pedalling is desirable, but any changes dictated by the slow-moving harmonies of the *Moonlight* should be imperceptible: daylight, in fact, should not be let in.'[lxxxi]

Turning now to the second movement, titled *Allegretto*, in his attempt to distinguish its character from that of the two outer movements, Franz Liszt described it as *une fleur entre deux abîmes* – 'a flower between two chasms'.[lxxxii][lxxxiii] The change of mood from that of the opening movement is certainly pronounced. By writing *Attacca subito* at the close of the *Adagio*, Beethoven clearly wants the performer to proceed directly to the *Allegretto* so as not to dispel the mood he has so far engendered. The effect of the suddenness of this procedure prompted von Elterlein to comment – writing at the close of the nineteenth century: 'I feel a shock to my feelings in being suddenly snatched from the poetic spell of the *Adagio*, and transported from the profoundest soul depths into a light, fleeting, easy-going sort of world. I may be mistaken ... to me, however, it is a mystery.'[lxxxiv] Cooper feels processes of 'musical integration' and 'rebirth' are at work throughout the entire sonata[lxxxv] in which the second movement serves to provide 'a sharp contrast of mood' that acts as 'a brief interlude before the angry and agitated finale'.[lxxxvi] This is close in spirit to the views of Kinderman for whom the middle movement represents 'a kind of interlude that connects the almost static opening movement with the rapid, agitated finale'.[lxxxvii] In strictly formal terms the *Allegretto* fulfils the function of a minuet and trio and has been described as 'a bewitching little movement'.[lxxxviii]

With regard to interpretation, Carl Czerny is succinct: 'The second movement [to be] quick and brilliant.'[lxxxix] Donald Tovey urges the performer here to play the movement with a lilt, if not he contends 'it will never be played either truthfully or tenderly'.[xc] The music critic Conrad Wilson cautions against the second movement being taken too fast. He feels when Beethoven's *allegretto* marking is respected the minuet character of the music is better preserved and, thereby, 'some of the trancelike nature of the opening movement remains'.[xci]

The third and final movement is marked *Presto agitato*. Its powerful nature has disposed Nicholas Marston to characterise the sonata as a whole as being a 'finale-weighted work' in which the energy and drive of the piece are reserved for its closing pages.[xcii] In Cooper's words: 'The drama and inherent tension in the sonata [has] been transferred from the beginning to the of the end of the [work].'[xciii]

Musicologists and pianists writing about the closing movement of the Piano Sonata Op. 27, No. 2, are at one in their adoption of vivid word-imagery to describe the mood that prevails. Von Elterlein leads the way with his high-flown romanticism: 'In the last movement ... the spirit of the tone-poet bursts forth in gloomy passionate agitation, the pent-up wrath breaks boldly into free channels, a frightful storm begins to rage, as if some volcano were rolling out glowing lava from its thundering depths.' Not satisfied he asks: 'Could this be represented more finely than in the opening motive, and in the succession of wildest harmonies and modulations which surge like tempestuous billows?'[xciv] Rolland cannot resist adopting similar word-imagery in his depiction of the character of the *Presto*: 'Then the wild night-squalls come again, but now with redoubled rage — a cyclone; fiery arpeggios that surge up from the depths to the heights, frantic convulsions ...'.[xcv] Fischer is more restrained: 'The last movement depicts a storm.'[xcvi] Gordon remarks on the manner in which the 'tranquil intensity' of the first movement has been held in check only to be 'unleashed and [to] mushroom into wild frenzy in the final movement'. Even the quieter moments he adds 'are used to set the stage for yet another outburst'.[xcvii] For Kinderman 'the finale is of unremittingly tragic character' and provides a fitting culmination to the entire work.[xcviii] Wilson invokes some of the imagery just quoted and describes the minor-key finale as an 'eruption' that is 'so sudden and unprecedentedly violent that, if the music can be called nocturnal at all, it is in its evocation of thunder and lightning in a night sky'. He also remarks on the originality of Beethoven's writing here: 'Nothing like its hammering chords and streaking arpeggios had been written for the piano before.'[xcix]

In his evaluation of the emotional feeling implicit in the final movement Matthews asks — recalling Beethoven's love for Countess Giulietta Guicciardi: '[Does] the *agitato* Finale express Beethoven's rage at being jilted?' He promptly answers his own question: 'The music transcends the importance of such localised conjectures.'[c] Lowe is more dispassionate here in his discussion and is content to observe: 'The last movement is in true sonata form.'[ci] Rolland, analysing Beethoven's musical structure, detects three primary elements, namely, 'the first melodic, the second dolorous [with] expressive chords [and] the third a souvenir of the first'. He then enters into the impassioned-manner of appreciation and concludes: 'The *Coda* is one of the most deeply expressive things Beethoven has ever written. It ends with a powerful gust of unspent passion.'[cii]

Oskar Bie, who the reader will recall found pain in the first movement, also detects suffering in the last — albeit alongside the composer's originality: 'A new and grand expression of pain is the last movement of the *Moonlight* Sonata ... which is full of invigoration. The threatening strokes of the quaver chords which sharply define each repetition of the stormy motive-passages, the quivering secondary theme, the unrestful rests, the melodies, which seem to calm down the seething bass; all this was a world of seriousness which the clavier had not yet learned to know.'[ciii]

Notwithstanding the high praise heaped upon Beethoven for this movement, he is not without his critics. Harold Truscott is one such. He regards the finale of the work to be its 'comparatively weak part' in which 'the passionate drama seems, in no matter how fine a performance, some-what leaden-footed and never gets off the ground'. He attributes this to the nature of the two main themes which to him seem to be 'clogged and hampered in their attempt at flight'. Analysing Beethoven's writing he cites what he regards as the composer's 'very static harmony' and consid-ers 'the low-pitched *Alberti* chords' to be in the wrong place. For Truscott the movement that is meant to sound fast 'succeeds only in sounding as though it is *trying to be fast*' [Truscott's italics].[civ]

The latter remark raises questions of performance-interpretation that in turn obligese us to note Tovey's stricture: 'It is vital to the colour of the main theme here that the arpeggios should be without pedal and that the staccato bass make its *dramatic menace* [italics added] without disguise.'* In his guidance Czerny is characteristically pithy and succinct: 'The third movement [is] a scherzo of a highly animated character ... The melody [to be] performed almost impetuously ... The quick time must be strictly preserved throughout ... The conclusion [to be] very fast.'*

As we draw to a close it is fitting we should call to mind once more the recollection of a performance of Beethoven's Piano Sonata Op. 27, No. 2 as interpreted by Franz Liszt – who doubtless was more than willing to comply with Czerny's injunction to play 'very fast'. This is provided by a further reminiscence from the memoirs of the youthful Charles Hallé. He heard Liszt perform the *Moonlight* Sonata sometime in 1837. He first provides a description of the great virtuoso that is consistent with the portraits we have of him: 'He is tall and very thin, his face very small and pale, his forehead remarkably high and beautiful; he wears his perfectly lank hair so long that it spreads over his shoulders, which looks very odd, for when he gets a bit excited and gesticulates, it falls right over his face.' Liszt's playing left Hallé 'speechless' and for a whole hour afterwards he was in 'a stupor of amazement – such execution, such limitless – truly limitless – execution no one else can possess.'*

Beethoven's *Moonlight* Piano Sonata has the unique distinction of being both a staple of the concert-pianists' repertoire and also, as we have remarked, of having been absorbed into popular culture. We take leave of this celebrated work with reference to a musician who may also be described as having been absorbed into popular culture, namely, Sir Henry Wood – co-founder of the ever-popular London *Promenade Concerts*. It was Wood who established that 'Friday night is Beethoven night'; a tradition that endured for decades – as the present writer fondly recalls. It is however with Wood's perception of the final movement

256

of the Piano Sonata Op. 27, No. 2 in mind that we conclude
our survey. Apparently, of its closing bars, the eminent
conductor was given to say: 'They rush to their doom!'[cviii]

---

[i] Ferdinand Ries as recalled in: Franz Wegeler and Ferdinand Ries, London,
   1988 (reprint), pp. 67–8.

[ii] See, for example: Peter Clive. London, 2001, pp. 283–4. These circumstances
   have been outlined by various writers. The other two poets Schubert set
   were Heinrich Heine (seven songs) and Johann Seidal (one song).

[iii] Romain Rolland, 1937, pp. 130–1.

[iv] Derived from Wilfrid Howard Mellers, London, 1957, pp. 19–20 and Barrie
   Cooper, 1990 p. 52. A facsimile reproduction of the cover of the Sauer
   Sketchbook can be seen at Beethoven House, Digital Archives, Library
   Document H. C. Bodmer, HCB BSk 10/58.

[v] Donald Francis Tovey in: *The Musical Times*, London, Vol. VIII, No. 2, 1927,
   p. 8.

[vi] See, for example, in relation to the *Moonlight* Sonata: Douglas Porter Johnson,
   editor, 2001, p. 40.

[vii] A facsimile reproduction of the cover of the First Edition of the *Moonlight*
   Sonata can be seen at: Beethoven House, Digital Archives, Library Document Cappi 879.

[viii] Romain Rolland, London, 1968, p. 58.

[ix] The letter was written between 6–7 July 1812. For a detailed discussion of the
   women who have been proposed as the intended recipient of the letter that
   Beethoven never sent, see: Wikipedia, *Beethoven: Immortal Beloved*.

[x] These circumstances are discussed by, amongst others: Peter Clive, 2001, pp.
   142–3; Barry Cooper, 2000, p. 110; and Paul Nettl, 1975, p. 69 and p. 74.

[xi] See, for example, the portraits of Beethoven from this period by Christian
   Horneman (1803) and Joseph Willibrod Mähler. For depictions of
   Beethoven in later years, and *numerous* depictions of him as portrayed
   throughout the 19th century by artists and sculptors, see: Beethoven House,
   Digital Archives *Beethoven's Appearance*.

[xii] Thayer-Forbes, 1967, p. 297.

[xiii] 'Extra-musical influence' is the expression used by Barry Cooper in his
   discussion of the *Moonlight* Sonata. He remarks how it is difficult to assess
   the extent to which such an influence affected Beethoven's output 'since any
   answer is bound to involve some speculation'. See: Barry Cooper, 1990, pp.
   42–3.

[xiv] Wilfrid Howard Mellers, 1957, pp. 62–3.

[xv] Otto Jahn's recollections are preserved in Oscar George Theodore Sonneck,
   1927, p. 33. In his documentary study, H. C. Robbins Landon also records
   details of Otto Jahn's meeting in later life with Countess Giulietta Guicciadi.
   See: H. C. Robbins Landon, 1970, p. 83.

[xvi] Ernst von Elterlein, 1898, p. 69. The quotation from Marx is also derived from
   this source.

[xvii] Eric Blom, 1938, p. 108.

[xviii] Edwin Fischer, 1959, pp. 62–3. Mention is also made of these circumstances
   in the Beethoven House Digital Archives, *Beethoven and the Moonlight
   Sonata*.

xix   William S. Newman, 1963, p. 518. Newman concludes his observation: 'At any rate, an association [with moonlight] that has lasted so long and held so widely is not likely to die easily, however logical the objections.'

xx   The miniature was painted by an unknown artist and is reproduced in many sources, see, for example: H. C. Robbins, Landon, 1970, p. 81.

xxi   Czerny's recollections to Otto Jahn were collected by Alexander Wheelock Thayer as quoted in: Thayer-Forbes, 1967, p. 297. The sonata to which Beethoven was directing attention is the Piano Sonata Op. 78.

xxii   Anton Felix Schindler, 1966, p. 408. Schindler's remarks were in part prompted by the further observations on the performance of Beethoven's piano sonatas recalled by Carl Czerny.

xxiii   Dorothea's portrait is reproduced in the Beethoven House Digital Archives, Library Document B 486/b.

xxiv   Reichardt's reminiscences were recalled by Alexander Wheelock Thayer as published in Thayer-Forbes, 1967, p. 412.

xxv   Beethoven had originally planned to travel to Italy where he hoped to take the waters on account of his poor health and failing hearing. However, his physician Dr. Johann Malfatti overruled this. In any even, such an extended trip was beyond the composer's means following the devaluation of money after the collapse of the Austrian economy. See: Beethoven House, Digital Archives, Library Document H. C. Bodmer, HCB Br 93.

xxvi   For a more detailed commentary on Beethoven's relationship with Georg Christoph Grosheim, see: Paul Nettl, 1975, p. 78.

xxvii   Derived from Theodor Albrecht, 1996, Vol. 2, Letter No. 263, pp. 169–170. These circumstances are also discussed by Alexander Wheelock Thayer in Thayer-Forbes, 1967, p. 297.

xxviii   The paraphrase of Seume's verses is derived from Henry Edward Krehbiel, 1971, p. 164. The reference to the *Laubensonata* that follows is also derived from the same source.

xxix   As discussed by Wilfrid Howard Mellers, 1957, p. 39. This is an early example in Beethoven of what Barrie Cooper describes as 'musical metamorphosis'.

xxx   The images described here, together with their related interpretive texts, can be viewed at the Beethoven House Digital Archives, *Müller*, Library Document B 924; *Vogel*, Library Document B 2430; *Armin*, Band VIII, No. 107; *Rozynski*, Library Document B 1966; and *Stassen*, Library Document B 388. A resolutely determined sculptural representation of Beethoven, associated with the *Moonlight* Sonata, is also reproduced at the Beethoven House Digital Archives, Library Document B 716/b. For a more comprehensive survey of the manner and extent to which the *Moonlight* Sonata continues to exert its influence in literature, music and television, see: Wikipedia *The Moonlight Sonata in Popular Culture*. For the last few years *alone* more than one-hundred citations have been listed.

xxxi   As related in: Sam Morgenstern, editor, 1956, p. 135.

xxxii   Felix Mendelssohn, as recollected in: *Letters from Italy and Switzerland*, London: Longman, Green, Longman, and Roberts, 1862, pp. 199–206. Concerning Mendelssohn's opinion of Dorothea's playing it should be borne in mind she was then aged fifty and had not regularly practised the piano. The views of Dorothea's husband, Stefan, are also of interest; he told Mendelssohn there was no public enthusiasm in Milan at this time (1830) for Beethoven's music.

xxxiii   As recalled by Roger Nichols, 1997, p. 197.

   As recounted by Hugh Macdonald, editor, *Berlioz: Selected letters*, 1995, p.

xxxiv Derived from Alain Frogley in: Glen Stanley, editor, 2000, p. 24.

xxxv As recalled by William S. Newman, 1963, p. 518. The artworks to which he makes reference can be found in the Beethoven House Digital Archives.

xxxvi As recalled by Adrian Williams, 1990, p. 66. Details of Liszt's concert tour in Scotland are described in: *Liszt Society Journal* 13 (1988) pp. 65–9. Liszt fainting at the keyboard is worthy of the Hollywood biographical film romance *Song Without End: The Story of Franz Liszt*, in which the matinee idol Dirk Bogarde portrayed the celebrated pianist-composer.

xxxvii As recalled in: Alan Walker, 1983. Vol. 1, p. 182. Berlioz's emotional temperament was tested on a similar occasion following one of the first performances in France of Beethoven's Fifth Symphony. When I friend suggested to Berlioz the work merely 'showed talent', Berlioz had to be restrained from attacking him!

xxxviii This is now preserved at San Jose State University following its sale at Sotheby's in 1994.
63.

xl As recalled by Dmitri Shostakovich in: Solomon Volkov, editor, 1981, p. 71. Glazunov's recollections derive from late in Liszt's life when his declining energies may have disposed him to impose more control over his abundant artistry. Some confirmation of the growing restraint in Liszt's playing, as a consequence of his increasing years, is afforded by the recollections of the Russian pianist Alexander Siloti – a pupil of the great interpreter of Beethoven, Nikolai Rubinstein. Siloti heard Liszt play the C-sharp minor Piano Sonata in 1883 – when Liszt was 72. Liszt managed to complete the first two movements but had to leave off in the third saying 'he was too old and had not the strength for it'. In our own time we recall Alfred Brendel announce he would no longer perform the taxing *Hammerklavier* Piano Sonata in public, doubtless for much the same reason.

xli Michael Kennedy, 1960. The information cited is derived from a general reading of this source. The quotation is taken from p. 81.

xlii Felix Weingartner, 1937, p. 41.

xliii In a subliminal way Rubenstein's performances were assisted by the fact that he bore an uncanny resemblance to Beethoven. There were those of his contemporaries who seriously entertained the thought he must be the composer's illegitimate son despite this not being chronologically possible!

xliv Sergey Prokofiev,1979, pp. 30–1.

xlv Ezra Pound as cited in: R. Murray Schafer, editor, 1978, p. 116.

xlvi Quoted by Richard Hudson in: Blair Sullivan, editor, *The echo of music: essays in honor of Marie Louise Göllner*. Warren, Michigan: Harmonie Park Press, 2004, p. 179.

xlvii Alfred Schnittke, 2002, p. 24.

xlviii Gerald Moore, 1962, p. 28.

xlix Gerald Moore, 1983, p. 51.

l Quoted in: Robin Wallace, 1986, p. 10.

li Derived from Wayne M. Senner, Robin Wallace and William Meredith, editors. 1999, Vol. 1, p. 176.

lii Barry Cooper, 2000, pp. 107–8.

liii Eric Blom, 1938, p. 108.

liv William Kinderman in: Glenn Stanley, editor, 2000, pp. 117–8.

lv Denis Matthews, 1972, p. 174.

li Cited in: Wayne M. Senner, Robin Wallace and William Meredith, editors, 1999, Vol. 1, p. 176.

lvii Gerald Abraham, editor, 1982, p. 341.

lviii Johann Aloys Schlosser, as recounted in: Barry Cooper, editor, 1996, p. 79. Cooper discusses the origins of the quotation cited in its more extended form in note 39 to Schlosser's text.

lix Denis Matthews, 1985, p. 84.

l Denis Matthews, 1972, p. 174.

li Barry Cooper, 2000, p. 108.

lii Anton Neumayr, 1994–7. p. 244.

liii Ernst von Elterlein, 1898, p. 69.

liv Oskar Bie, 1966, p. 175.

lv Romain Rolland, 1937, p. 133.

lvi Theodor W. Adorno, 1998, p. 26 and p. 81.

lvii Marion M. Scott, 1940, p.138.

lviii Eric Blom, 1938, p. 108.

lix Adapted from Malcolm Gillies and David Pear, editors, 1994, pp. 115–6.

lx Quoted in: Walter Aaron Clark, 1999, p. 82.

lxi Denis Matthews, 1967, p. 26.

lxii Carl Czerny as quoted in: Paul Badura-Skoda, editor, 1970, p. 50.

lxiii Charles Rosen, 2002, pp. 105–6.

lxiv Ernst Bloch cited in: Edward T. Cone, 1974, p. 99. Quoted also in: Walter Aaron Clark, 1999, p. 82.

lxv Stewart Gordon, 1996, p. 165.

lxvi Dieter Hildebrandt, 1988, p. 149. The Chopin quotation is derived from his writings as collected and published by Willi Reich in *Chopin, Briefe und Dokumente* 1995, p. 216. Hildebrandt remarks that Beethoven's instruction *sempre pianissimo e senza sordini* was so innovatory for the period in question as to prompt the editor of an early English edition (unspecified) to explain that the pedal was *only* to be used when required by the harmony. In his wider considerations of composers introducing pedal markings in their music, Hildebrandt also makes acknowledgement to the pioneering achievements of Beethoven's contemporary Daniel Steibelt.

lxvii Charles Rosen, 2002, p. 81.

lxviii Beethoven received the Broadwood piano in 1818. It had been specially selected for him in London by, amongst others, Ferdinand Ries and J. B. Cramer who signed the instrument. Franz Liszt once owned it. In recent years it has been restored – at considerable cost – and now resides in the Hungarian National Museum. Melvyn Tans' recording was issued by EMI Classics on CDC 7 54526 2, 1992.

lxix Adapted from Charles Rosen, 2002, p. 108. Rosen adds how 'pedalled sound [was at this period] still a special effect for Beethoven, as it was for Haydn, and he used it above all for contrast'.

lxx Charles Rosen, 1995, p. 20.

lxxi Denis Matthews, 1967, p. 26. Although, as stated in the main text, it is not our intention to discuss the relative merits of the (many) different recordings of Beethoven's Piano Sonatas, the reader is directed to: Conrad Wilson, *Notes on Beethoven,* 2003. Wilson reviews interpretations by Alfred Brendel, Wilhelm Kempff and Artur Pizarro. See also: Wilfrid Mellers, 1957; Mellers makes a wide-ranging survey of Beethoven pianists and their interpretations (pp. 46–54).

lxxxii As quoted in Donald Francis Tovey, 1944. p. 80.

lxxxiii As quoted in Alfred Brendel, 2001, p. 71.

lxxxiv Ernst von Elterlein, 1898, p. 71.

lxxxv Barry Cooper, 1991, p. 206.

lxxxvi Barry Cooper, 2000, p. 108.

lxxxvii William Kinderman, 1997, p. 73.

lxxxviii C. Egerton Lowe, 1929, p. 73.

lxxxix Carl Czerny in: Paul Badura-Skoda, editor, 1970, p. 50.

xc Harold Craxton and Donald Francis Tovey, [1931], p. 51.

xci Conrad Wilson, 2003, p. 22.

xcii Nicholas Marston in: Glenn Stanley, editor, 2000, p. 93.

xciii Barry Cooper, 1991, p. 241.

xciv Ernst von Elterlein, 1898, p. 71.

xcv Romain Rolland, 1937, p. 137.

xcvi Edwin Fischer, 1959, p. 3.

xcvii Stewart Gordon, 1996, p. 165.

xcviii William Kinderman, 1997, p. 73.

xcix Conrad Wilson, 2003, p. 23.

c Denis Matthews, 1967, p. 26.

ci C. Egerton Lowe, 1929, p. 74.

cii Romain Rolland, 1917, pp. 148–9.

ciii Oskar Bie, 1966, p. 170.

civ Harold Truscott in: Denis Arnold and Nigel Fortune, editors, 1973, pp. 105–6.

cv Harold Craxton and Donald Francis Tovey, [1931], p. 51.

cvi Carl Czerny in: Paul Badura-Skoda, editor, 1970, p. 50.

cvii As quoted in: Adrian Williams, 1990, pp. 84–5.

cviii Derived from Denis Matthews, 1967, p. 27. A performance of the Piano Sonata in C-sharp minor, Op. 27, No. 2 has been recorded by Ernst Gröschel on Beethoven's Conrad Graf fortepiano of 1825 (more correctly the one on loan to him) source: Colosseum M 2004. Joseph Kerman, in his accompanying text to the liner notes *Contemplating Music* (sub-title page) remarks: 'No one who has heard Beethoven's *Moonlight* Sonata or the Sonata in D Minor, Op. 31, No. 2, well played on the fortepiano will ever be entirely happy with them again on the modern piano.' In the notes accompanying her fortepiano recording of the *Moonlight* Sonata, Ella Sevskaya, remarks: 'The use of the moderator [soft pedal] in this *Rondo* is ... justified, even if it lends the movement a slightly *folky* flavour. This brings it a little closer in line with the late eighteenth and early nineteenth century rondos of a light and cheerful character.' Source: Ella Sevskaya, Quil 303. In his discussion of the performance of the *Moonlight* Sonata, Derek Melville, himself an accomplished performer, remarks how modern-day editors have changed the *sordino* into the plural *sordini*, i.e. with the dampers raised or with the sustaining pedal held down. He adds: 'Some people have tried, or imagined, taking these instructions literally which is unfortunate.' He quotes Donald Tovey (Associated Board, II, p. 50): '[As] for *senza sordini*, this simply means "with raised dampers", and on the feeble instruments of 1802 there was no reason for changing the pedal at all in this instrument, for the sound of the undamped strings did not out-last its slow changes of harmony.' Melville endorses Tovey's comments and adds, drawing upon his own experience of having played the *Moonlight* Sonata on two of Beethoven's pianos: 'It is true that in order to play the work correctly the *dampers* must be raised from the strings or the right-hand pedal held down all the time *except* for the split-second damping that is necessary at changes of harmony.' See: Derek Melville *Beethoven's Pianos*, in: Denis Arnold and Nigel Fortune, editors, *The Beethoven companion*, London: Faber and Faber, 1973, p. 52.

PIANO SONATA
IN D MAJOR, OP. 28
THE PASTORAL

'The sonata always awakens in my mind feelings akin to those works like the *Pastoral* Symphony call forth.'

Ernst von Elterlein, *Beethoven's Pianoforte Sonatas: Explained for the Lovers of the Musical Art*, 1898, p. 72.

'[Op. 28] has been called the *Pastoral* Sonata, a name which neither belies, nor yet fully expresses, its content. It would be hard to find any short title to fit this dreamy, reflective, meditative work.'

Paul Bekker, *Beethoven*, 1925, p. 113.

'It is a lyrical piece throughout, and I think the

nickname *Pastoral* is well chosen. It takes a lot of imagination and poetic ability on the part of the player to keep the tension. In some ways it looks back to earlier periods.'

Alfred Brendel in: David Dubal, *The World of the Concert Pianist*, 1985, pp. 104–5.

'[In] terms of melodic character it is one of Beethoven's most innovative works to that time [1801–2]. More than any composition in these years, it presages the new stylistic directions that appear in the later Op. 50s and Op. 60s.'

Michael Broyles, *Beethoven: The Emergence and Evolution of Beethoven's Heroic Style*, 1987, p. 70.

B eethoven's Piano Sonata Op. 28 has been described as 'the cheerful, happy, much less known neighbour of the C-sharp minor Sonata'. Although composed in 1801, in close proximity to the C-sharp minor Sonata, it nevertheless 'differs fundamentally from that work'. This illustrates Beethoven's capacity, and preference, to work simultaneously on compositions of a strikingly different character, or, in the words of William Newman: '[It] is typical of Beethoven's tendency to alternate a passionate and driving work with a calm and restful one.' Maynard Solomon also offers a similar interpretation of Beethoven's creative working-process at this period. He affirms how the Op. 28 Piano Sonata 'celebrates the peace that comes from fulfillment of a difficult creative effort'. This is a reference to the emotional and intellectual energy the composer had expended on the three previous highly experimental and innovatory compositions, the C-sharp minor Piano Sonata and the Piano Sonatas Op. 26 and Op. 27.

In the Piano Sonata Op. 28 Solomon sees Beethoven withdrawing 'to a relative traditionalism' from which he 'will gain strength for a new creative urge'. Part of this traditionalism is Beethoven's adoption of the four-movement sonata format, with its relatively equal 'distribution of emotional weight and emphasis'. Only seldom in the medium of the piano sonata, would Beethoven revert to this musical structure. In his later piano sonatas he would embrace other movement-combinations in his 'exploration of the possibilities of expressing new impulses and ideas'. For the present he was content to explore the 'calm reflective attributes' of piano writing that permeate the Piano Sonata Op. 28.[iv]

Others, expressing their views on the emotional and musical character of Beethoven's *Pastoral* Sonata, offer similar thoughts to those just outlined. Barry Cooper finds Beethoven benefiting from turning to a work of a more 'relaxed' and 'less experimental' kind.[v] He notes Beethoven's 'complete contrast' of style in the Op. 28 with its 'lengthy, relaxed, totally unheroic, and pastoral ... mood'. He also pays tribute to Beethoven's remarkable ability 'to produce four such different sonatas so quickly' — a unique feat he considers in the composer's thirty-two, piano-sonata sequence.[vi] Likewise, Stewart Gordon remarks on Beethoven's capacity to shift his musical thinking from 'the experimental fantasy' of the Op. 27 set to the 'self-contained expressiveness' and 'more traditional structure' of the Op. 28.[vii] In similar vein, Michael Broyles reminds us how, with the Op. 26 and Op. 27 Piano Sonatas, 'Beethoven had challenged tradition at its structural foundations' but in his Op. 28 he was content to revert to a more 'classical pattern ... conforming precisely to the standard overall ordering and structure of movements'.[viii]

Peter Clive, quoting musicologist Alexander Ringer,

suggests Muzio Clementi may have influenced Beethoven in his Piano Sonata Op. 28. Daniel Coren adds force to this belief, citing how Beethoven's opening bears 'a striking similarity' to Clementi's Piano Sonata, Op. 40, No. 2 that is also in the key of D major; moreover, both sonatas were published in 1802.ᵢ Beethoven certainly held Clementi in high regard as a pianist. He was given to say: 'They who thoroughly study Clementi, at the same time make themselves acquainted with Mozart.' Later in life Beethoven considered Clementi as a possible teacher of piano for his nephew Karl. As Clive reminds us, Beethoven not only admired Clementi's prowess at the keyboard but also thought highly of his piano sonatas — 'following the Italian master's lead not merely in matters of pianistic style but in thematic inspiration as well'.ᵢ Clive, quoting Ringer once more, also considers Jan Dussek's piano writing of the period may also have exerted its influence on Beethoven in the composition of his Piano Sonata Op. 28.ᵢ

Matthew Rye, writing on the occasion of the BBC's *Beethoven Experience* — when all of the composer's works were performed within a single week — suggests, with his D major Piano Sonata, 'Beethoven appears to step back again with the next work in the medium [of the piano sonata]'. To avoid misinterpretation, however, he qualifies his observation by adding that any thoughts of 'regression' would be misplaced; Beethoven, he adds, was merely electing to revert 'to the classical four-movement model'.ᵢ

In her pioneering popular study of Beethoven, intended for the typical classical music-lover, Marion Scott describes the Piano Sonata Op. 28 as 'a felicitous work, more-or-less of a reversion to classic order'.ᵢ There is a note of reservation in Eric Blom's estimation of Beethoven's Op. 28: 'The present sonata, it must be confessed, is in no sense an advance upon Op. 27.' He does though concede: 'It contains a good deal that is fanciful and imaginative [but] nothing that is particularly prophetic.' The reader interested in learning about the inner-workings of what Blom finds 'fanciful and imaginative' is well served by the analysis of this sonata undertaken by Donald Tovey (more recently revised and updated by Barry Cooper).

In his discussion of Beethoven's development in the medium of the piano sonata, Paul Bekker considers how the composer's achievements to date reveal his frame of mind: 'They are great works and show Beethoven, self-confident [and] happy in the work as man and artist.' He does though acknowledge the threat of the 'passing shadows', then hovering about Beethoven, to which we will shortly make further reference. In his analysis, of what we may describe as the 'inner-workings' of Beethoven's mind, Cooper draws attention to what he refers to as the 'extra-musical factors' bearing on the composer's compositional process — especially in terms of the 'contrasts' to be found between works written at about the same time. Cooper maintains, 'such contrasts were a necessary and inevitable part of [Beethoven's] creative process, and sometimes changes in the mood of the music were very rapid'. In support of this contention, he quotes from Beethoven's own words: 'The artist must often be able to assume all humours.' He cites the sketches Beethoven drafted for the Piano Sonata Op. 28, finding in them evidence of Beethoven at work simultaneously on the slow movement, 'a sad and delicate one in D minor' and then, as Cooper's observes, 'almost with the same stroke of the pen he moved on to a sketch for the exuberant finale'. Cooper further maintains how a number of Beethoven's compositions which share the same key, often share similar 'common features' and the same, or similar, 'complex interrelationships' — especially to be found in works composed at or around the same time. This is the case Cooper considers with the *Pastoral* Sonata and the Second Symphony; both share the same key of D and both derive from 1801.[xvii]

Before we proceed to further consideration of the *Pastoral* Sonata and its 'sunlit world of summer air and the scent of flowers', we should pause for a moment to consider the 'passing shadows' to which Bekker (see above) alludes. He is, of course making reference to Beethoven's growing awareness of the onset of deafness. This was the 'demon monster' that would be no mere 'passing shadow' but constitute a permanent impairment to his most precious faculty. In Electra Yourke's memorable phrase: 'The gate of music is the ear.' As she elucidates, our faculties of musical perception, and the ability to perform music, depend upon 'the perfection of our auditory apparatus'. By 1801 Beethoven's hearing was rapidly deteriorating as we have noted in our previous remarks relating to other of Beethoven's piano sonatas dating from this period. It is to mankind's eternal benefit that, by drawing upon his indomitability of spirit, Beethoven protected his creative imagination in the form of 'a dome of sound' such that his *inner ear* remained intact; '[Beethoven] no longer needed external stimuli to organize ... sounds into melodies or harmonies'.[xviii]

The cost to Beethoven's composure imposed by his loss of hearing was high. We have noted previously (Piano Sonatas Op. 27) how he recognised his affliction was not only incurable but also 'had implications for his social and artistic life'.[xix] We have also noted that he confided his growing anguish to his close friend Franz Gerhard Wegeler (letter of 29 June 1801)[xx] and to Karl Amenda (letter of 1 July 1801)[xxi]. The following year these circumstances would reach a point of psychological crisis for Beethoven when he gave expression to his innermost thoughts in the so-called *Heiligenstadt Testament*. In this highly personal document, he reflects on his despair at his increasing deafness but, with characteristic fortitude, he resolved to transcend his physical and emotional tribulations in order to fulfil his artistic destiny.[xxii] These are circumstances for later consideration. For the present, we consider the origins of the title *Pastoral* Sonata and its musical implications.

Tradition holds that the German publisher August Cranz conferred the title *Pastoral* on Beethoven's Piano Sonata Op. 28. However, it is now known the soubriquet derives from the London publishers Broderip and Wilkinson who had already published a number of the composer's works dating from his early years in Vienna.[xxiii] The English edition may have preceded the German one by about three years.[xxiv] Irrespective of such claims for priority over the actual naming of the Op. 28 Piano Sonata, it is almost universally accepted as being appropriate to the genial mood of the composition. For Romain Rolland 'the whole work is exceeding happy in mood, the last two movements almost boisterously so, the Finale being a mad gallop home'.[xxv] Denis Matthews cannot resist the pun of finding *moonlight,* in the Op. 27 and *sunlight,* in the Op. 28.[xxvi] Edwin Fischer detects 'a feeling of nature' in the music with 'a presence of the god Pan such as we find only in the *Pastoral* Symphony itself'. However, he makes a clear distinction between the two works. He reminds us how, in the Symphony, the themes are clear cut and well delineated viz. — *Awakening of cheerful feelings upon arriving in the countryside, Scene by the brook* ... etc. — whereas, in the piano sonata, Fischer considers Beethoven is content merely to create an atmosphere. Nonetheless, he is fulsome in his recognition of this remarking: '[There] is a shimmering as of summer air, a murmuring of bees and fragrance; one can almost feel the warm sun on one's skin. All our instincts are aroused, and, in a trance, natural man within us feels at one with mother earth.'[xxvii] Donald Tovey expresses similar views, attributing to the sonata 'attributes of peacefulness and picturesqueness'. He too finds 'vivid contrasts' between the *Pastoral* Symphony and the *Pastoral* Sonata, contrasts he considers reveal the piano sonata to be 'a much more difficult work than it seems to be'.[xxviii] [xxix]

Tovey's observations lead us to a consideration of the musical structures Beethoven deploys which have earned the piano sonata its enduring, and endearing, nickname. Matthews draws attention to Beethoven's use in the outer movements of repeated bass-notes in their opening themes, a device he reminds us was considered 'rustic' at the period in question.[xxx] In his identification of the procedures Beethoven uses to establish a rustic character in the piano writing, William Newman cites the composer's use of 'pedal points at the beginning of the first and last movements and occasional bagpipe fifths'.[xxxi] William Kinderman also remarks on these features and suggests how the rustic character of the music is enhanced by 'the cadential theme in the first movement', an 'internal episode' in the slow movement and the *Scherzo* itself having a rustic character.[xxxii] Broyles finds and compares features shared between the Piano Sonata Op. 28 and the Second Symphony Op. 36, which, as we have remarked, share the same key and were written in close proximity. He makes reference to Beethoven's 'placement of specific harmonic functions at analogous structural positions in different movements'. He also finds similarities between the two works relating to their 'overall structure and outward characteristics'. That said, he comments how 'different stylistically' the two compositions are; the piano sonata being 'decidedly non-symphonic' but essentially 'of melodic character'. He goes further and asserts: '[It] is one of Beethoven's most innovative works to that time. More than any composition, in these years, it presages the new stylistic directions that appear in the later Op. 50s and Op 60s'.[xxiii] Daniel Coren has devoted an entire essay titled *Structural relations between Op. 28 and Op. 36.* He convincingly demonstrates the extent to which Beethoven's compositional procedures, between the two works, are 'intimately connected'.[xxiv]

Beethoven's Piano Sonata Op. 28 had its compositional origins in sketches that were once collated in the so-called Sauer Sketchbook. Beethoven used this through the spring of 1801 to late summer, possibly to early autumn.[xxv] As remarked in our earlier accounts, the Viennese art and music dealer Ignaz Sauer purchased the sketchbook at the auction of the composer's effects that took place shortly after his death (see the Op. 27 Piano Sonatas). Following Sauer's reduction of the sketchbook to single leaves and their subsequent sale to collectors, the surviving pages allow only a partial reconstruction and interpretation of the sketchbook to be made.[xxvi] Nevertheless, seven leaves have been identified that are devoted to the *Pastoral* Sonata. Although, for reasons stated, the sketches are incomplete 'all four movements are thoroughly represented'.[xxvii] For example, one of the leaves, now held in the archives of the Beethoven House in Bonn, exemplifies the richness of Beethoven's imagination and his ability to both conceive, and work on, divergent musical thoughts at the same time. The leaf in question contains sketches for all four movements of the sonata. On the recto there are sketches for the first movement, and on the verso there are sketches for the other three movements.[xxviii] The reader for whom such matters are of particular interest, relating to the Op. 28 Piano Sonata, will find the study of Beethoven's sketches by Paul Mies invaluable.[xxix]

Beethoven's Piano Sonata Op. 28 was announced for the first time in the *Vienna Journal* of 14 August 1802, as:

'*Grand Sonata pour le Piano Forte, composée et dediée à Monsieur Joseph Noble de Sonnenfels, Conseiller aulique et Secrétaire perpetual de l' Academie des beaux arts, par Louis van Beethoven. Oeuvre 28'*. The publisher was the Bureau des Arts et d'Industrie or, as it was known in Germany, the Kunst-und Industrie-Comptoir. From 1802 this publishing house replaced Artaria & Co, Beethoven's previous publisher, and remained his principal publisher until 1808. The Piano Sonata Op. 28, together with Beethoven's own arrangement for string quartet of the Piano Sonata Op. 14, No. 1, were the first works to be published by the Kunst-und Industrie-Comptoir. Beethoven signed the publication contract in October 1801.

The Title Page designation is of interest insofar as it indicates the piano sonata as being intended exclusively for the *Piano Forte*. Hitherto, Beethoven's piano sonatas had been promoted as being suitable also for the *clavecin*, or harpsichord. Beethoven clearly wanted his latest keyboard composition to benefit from the increased power and sonority that was becoming available with the newer instrument — the *pianoforte* (in modern-day terminology). The improved action of the newer instrument, in which the strings are struck by felt hammers, gave the performer greater control to manipulate the required sound — soft or loud — according to the strength of touch of the performer. Doubtless these considerations were in Beethoven's mind, given the serene nature of his new composition and the style of interpretation it requires. The older instrument, in which the strings are plucked or twanged by plectrums, would not provide the range of tone colours and expressive feeling Beethoven was seeking which, as we have seen, soon earned for the work the epithet *Pastoral.*

The recipient of the sonata's dedication, Joseph von Sonnenfels, was a figure of high standing in Viennese society.

He was by then a seventy-year old grandee, a professor of political science at the University of Vienna — where he was also Rector — was President of the Academy of Sciences and, furthermore, had been ennobled a baron. Curiously, Beethoven does not appear to have been on close personal terms with Sonnenfels. It is possible Beethoven may have met his distinguished contemporary at one of the private concerts given by his former benefactor the Baron Gottfried von Swieten. The publisher of the *Pastoral* Sonata itself, the Kunst-und Industrie-Comptoir, may also have been a possible source of contact between the two men.[xliii] Alexander Thayer comments, cryptically: 'The dedication was probably nothing more than a mark of respect for the man of brains with whose ideas Beethoven was in sympathy.'[xliv] The latter aspect of Thayer's observation is worthy of further remark since it casts light on Beethoven's developing social and political outlook.

Sonnenfels was by training and vocation a lawyer. He was liberal by nature at a time when censorship in Vienna was widespread, especially in the arts and the theatre. Even so eminent a figure as Beethoven was not exempt from the long reach of the public censor. For example, he had to tailor his opera *Leonora* (later *Fidelio*) in compliance with theatre-censorship demands. At this period the police also had powers to obtain information by process of severe interrogation and even torture. None were exempt; the young Franz Schubert and some of his friends — a circle of free-thinking writers and poets — were once taken-in for questioning in the mistaken belief they were promulgating subversive views. Beethoven himself had cause to write to his friend, the publisher, Nikolaus Simrock: 'You dare not raise your voice here or the police will take you into custody.'[xlv] Sonnenfels was instrumental in bringing about much-needed reforms in the spirit of the newly emerging

Age of Enlightenment. He wrote extensively on art, literature, and politics and was a champion of Christoph Gluck
who had himself for many years been advocating the need
for reform in the lyric theatre.[xlvi] Maynard Solomon suggests
that, by conferring his dedication upon Sonnenfels,
Beethoven was in effect 'deflecting his rebellious impulse
into art' — and, thereby, was identifying himself with a
kindred spirit who recognized the sanctity of the individual.[xlvii]

Four months after publication of the Piano Sonata Op.
28, the work was reviewed in the 8 December Issue of the
Allgemeine musikalische Zeitung. By now Beethoven's
reputation for daring and innovation were beginning to earn
the reviewer's respect: 'Beethoven remains faithful to his
character and manner ... an artist like B[eethoven] can really
do nothing better than remain faithful to himself.' Of the
music the reviewer adds: '[Op. 28] is on a very large scale
and is peculiar to the extent of being strange and adventurous, particularly the first and third movements.'[xlviii] Then
comes a sting in the tail, as Anton Schindler cites in his
selection from the *AmZ's* review: 'The part can be very
pleasant and constitute an interesting whole but still not a
perfect work with a pervading unity and intelligence that will
be comprehended by those for whom the music has
meaning.'[xlix]

The Piano Sonata did have meaning for Ferdinand Ries,
one of Beethoven's piano pupils at this period. We have
introduced him already (Piano Sonatas Opp. 26, 27) and,
at about the period of composition of the sonata in question,
we find him writing to the publisher Simrock: 'Beethoven
takes more pains with me than I shall ever have believed
possible. I have three lesson a week, usually from one
o'clock till half past two.' This is testimony to the composer's
generosity with his time, notwithstanding the demands that
working on his compositions must have imposed. Years later

Ries, perhaps recalling his study of the *Pastoral* Sonata, prepared an arrangement of the music for string quartet.

We draw our prefatory remarks to a close with selected anecdotes relating to the Piano Sonata Op. 28 derived from the nineteenth century and some from nearer to our own time.

On 21 August 1857 Clara Schuman had occasion to write to the great violinist Joseph Joachim, with whom she was on familiar terms. When only twelve years old Joachim had made his London debut, under the baton of Felix Mendelssohn, playing Beethoven's Violin Concerto — for which he had written out his own cadenzas. In playful manner she reprimands Joachim: 'I am very angry with you about one thing: you listened to my *Pastoral Sonata*, disliked my reading, and said nothing about it to me, for fear I should be offended!' Later in the letter she adds: 'Johannes has told me all his thoughts about the *Pastoral Sonata*, and now I play it differently.' Clara is, of course, referring to Johannes Brahms, with whom she had an intimate relationship and who, the reader may recall, had received assistance from Joachim in the writing-out of his Violin Concerto in D. Regrettably, Clara does not reveal what Brahms had to say about the Op. 28.

The Russian composer and pianist Elena Gnesina was a student contemporary of Sergei Rachmaninoff at the Moscow Conservatory. She recalls the autumn of 1888 when he gave two student recitals; Rachmaninoff was then eighteen years old. One of his recitals included the first movement of the *Pastoral* Sonata. Even at this young age Gnesina recalls how 'his blossoming pianistic prowess was beginning to attract attention'. She adds: 'Whenever it became known that Rachmaninoff was going to play at a students' evening, everyone would lead for the hall to listen to him.'

In our survey of the *Moonlight* Sonata we encountered

Charles Hallé in the role of concert pianist. We learn of him once more in the *Special Issue* of the *Musical Times,* celebrating Beethoven's *Death Centenary* (1927). The contributor John Alexander Fuller-Maitland (music critic and contributor to *The Times*), first reviewed the London performances of Beethoven's piano sonatas for that season and then adds: 'The so-called *Pastoral* Sonata, Op. 28, in D is another which calls up memories of Hallé, this time as a marvellously clear executant'.[liii]

We have also previously recalled the performances of Beethoven's piano sonatas given at the lunchtime recitals held at the National Gallery, London, during wartime. The records reveal the *Pastoral* Sonata was played three times[liv]. We can but trust its calm and reflective character helped to sooth the troubled nerves of the members of the audience on the occasions when it was performed. It is to a consideration as to how Beethoven establishes this character, within the work's individual movements, that we now direct our attention.

The first movement opens with nine bars of repeated low notes, 'a gentle tapping tonic pedal' in the bass, expanding over twenty-four bars as the rhythm rises to a higher register; 'a splendid specimen of development by elimination and condensation'. Later, in the middle section, 'the phrase seems almost to disappear into thin air'.[lv] A later variant, in octaves, exhibits a type of *drone bass*. Rosamond Harding suggests Beethoven may here be drawing on a musical form fashionable at the time of Carl Philipp Emanuel Bach, who calls it '*Trommel-Bass*'. She remarks how *pastorales* were written for every type of solo instrument and cites, by way of illustration, the *Pastorale for Guitar*, of about 1790, by Césare Mussolini. She also instances the contemporary popularity of depicting the bagpipe and shepherd's pipe on the spinet.[lvi] Ernst von Elterlein, yielding to nineteenth-century romance, asks rhetorically: 'Is there not a gentle, fresh spring-breeze breathing through the first movement ... This is surely a sunny-bright and expressive picture of life, pleasing, richly coloured, and full of charming changes?'. Gordon finds 'lyricism' throughout the themes in the exposition of the opening movement that 'blend into a texture of gentle contours'. Kinderman also detects 'lyric warmth' in the opening pages of this movement, upheld by Beethoven's favourite device of foreshortening 'whereby segments from the opening theme are progressively compressed into smaller units'.

Bekker discerns in Beethoven's pastoral enchantment, 'thoughts [that] flow almost imperceptibly into one another'. They contribute: 'A mood of restful content [that] pervades the movement ... [A single broad theme] proceeds in circular motion and ends at the point where it began.' Broyles also perceives movement, initially in the form of the repeated notes in the bass, which establish their 'relaxed pulse', expanding so as to convey 'a sense of a spacious, easy-going motion [that] permeates the melodic nature of the movement'. He asserts: '[This] is perhaps the single most important feature separating it from Beethoven's more typical earlier works.' Theodor Adorno refers to Beethoven's 'stillness through motion' with its implicit idea of 'expressing tranquility through motion', qualities he also suggests are evident in the G major Piano Concerto and the Violin Concerto. Phillip Radcliffe finds cause here to pay tribute to Beethoven's ability to 'sustain a single mood throughout a fully developed sonata without monotony'. He singles out the concluding stages of the development that he regards as being 'particularly imaginative, owing to the skillfully prolonged harmonic suspense'.

Harold Truscott calls attention to the originality of the main theme in the first movement 'with its veiled subdominant harmony at its very beginning'. He elaborates enthusiastically: '[It] is perhaps the most individual thing Beethoven had yet written, and the furthest flight he had taken away from the eighteenth century.' In offering this opinion he draws attention to the composer's possible debt to Muzio Clementi, to whom we have made previous reference. Clementi, virtuoso pianist, composer, founder of a publishing house and, later in his career, instrument maker, exerted an influence on many of his contemporaries, not least through the medium of his celebrated keyboard studies; his Op. 44, *Gradus ad Parnassum* is still held in high regard. Some find traces of Clementi's pianistic effects in Mozart's piano variations K. 500 dating from 1786. Concerning Beethoven, his biographer Anton Schindler informs us: 'Even though his hearing made it impossible for him to apply Clementi's principles himself, he was still able to recommend Clementi to others eager for instruction.'[liv] With regard to the main theme of the first movement of the *Pastoral* Sonata, Truscott comments: '[It] is astonishing how much of Beethoven's theme is suggested by [the] short opening phrase of Clementi's Sonata in D, Op. 10, No. 2, published in 1783.' In Beethoven's hands, however, it becomes something much more, no less, in Truscott's estimation, than 'a huge and hitherto unforeseen extension of eighteenth-century principles' and a further insight into the 'secret of Beethoven's originality'. In Truscott's opinion, it would have to await the endeavours of such composers as Schubert, Brahms and Bruckner before others would show 'they were capable of maintaining one harmony for so many bars without a break'.[lv]

Beethoven's opening movement may not aspire to the 'heavenly lengths' that Robert Schuman assigns to many of Franz Schubert's piano-sonata movements, but it is nonetheless on an extended scale, spanning across some 461 bars.

This allows the composer to call into play a number of pianistic devices by means of which to achieve a 'sense of joy and happiness'. Fischer remarks on how the left hand contributes a great deal of the 'calm tranquility' by the use of the low bass D that is repeated some sixty times. He also draws attention to the shape of the music with its 'gradual rising and falling of the melody in small intervals' and 'the repetition of similar phrases'. All these elements he maintains give the work 'a sense of wideness and peace'. Perhaps in the central section Fischer suggests 'there is the impression of a brief afternoon storm' and of a fleeting 'merry sunbeam'.[lxvi] Notwithstanding the rustic character of the music, Matthews reminds us of the 'intellectual strength' that is to be found in the development of the first movement. This he considers shares 'similar tonal features and manipulations with the Second Symphony whose close affinities with the *Pastoral* Sonata we have already noted.[lxvii]

With regard to the interpretation required in this opening movement, Carl Czerny will be allowed the last words: 'All very *legato* even the bass. Although in a lively time, the character of this movement is still tranquil and kindly fervent.'[lxviii]

For von Elterlein the romantic atmosphere in the second movement 'evokes a feeling like that which comes over us when light film-clouds veil the sun, making a beautiful landscape shine in fallow light, the cloud only breaking a little now and then to admit kindly beams'.[lxix] Matthews discerns a 'melancholy' and 'plaintive song' that is sustained over 'a quasi-pizzicato bass'.[lx] These sentiments are close in spirit to those expressed by Oskar Bie who regards the *Pastoral* Sonata as standing 'on that indefinable borderline between the comic and the tragic' enshrined in music that is 'the most perfect of Nature prayers, a *Pastoral* Symphony on the pianoforte'.[lxxi]

In Kinderman's imagery the D minor *Andante* 'has a processional, ballade-like atmosphere' in which 'the melodic inflections of its main theme seem suggestive of speech'.[lxii] Bekker finds 'resignation' here in the minor key passages combined with what he describes as 'a graceful, rhythmical major *intermezzo*' that introduces 'a more cheerful mood' that in turn is supplanted by 'gentle melancholy' as the movement nears its close.[lxiii] Alfred Brendel considers that in both the Op. 28 and the Op. 53 Piano Sonatas, Beethoven is inviting the listener 'to share in the composer's musical communion with nature' — as he was to do even more fulsomely a few years later in the *Pastoral* Symphony.[lxiv]

Extending the idea of the listener communing with nature, Brendel comments on how 'the listener's enjoyment of country life ... incorporates two thunderstorms' (a reference to the movement's more agitated passages), then experiences moods alternating between 'stern composure and sighing lamentation' and is engaged with surprise in the form of 'a bucolic scene in the major mode' that is imbued with 'the quality of innocence [that] remains wholly untouched by melancholy or fear'.[lxv] Truscott does not regard this movement as being one of Beethoven's 'deep, broad movements' of the kind with which he had already experimented, nevertheless he enthuses 'there are few more fascinating or more haunting sounds than the lovely main melody, with its persistent bass'. Analyzing the composer's workmanship here he considers it to be 'another of Beethoven's miracles, fashioned from a bit of rhythm and broken chord'.[lxvi] Broyles, taking a wider view, calls to mind how this slow movement has particular affinities — 'specific motivic connection' — with those of the Second Symphony. In both of these compositions Beethoven was perhaps recalling the musical innovation, prevalent in the eighteenth century, in which in both the piano sonata and the symphony the slow movement was 'a point of poetic repose, usually of a more tender or lyrical character than the first'.[lxxvii] In Gordon's estimation much of the second movement presents 'a quartet-like texture with a staccato bass line', recalling Beethoven's similar procedures in the second movement of his Piano Sonata Op. 2, No. 2.[lxxviii]

Although by its very nature the Piano Sonata Op. 28 is not one of Beethoven's more dramatic compositions, there is evidence it received a measure of recognition in Beethoven's lifetime. Evidence for this derives from the biography of the horn player and composer Friedrich Starke. He met Beethoven sometime in 1812 and established a friendly relationship with him. He had a particular aptitude for making wind band arrangements – which included an adaptation of Beethoven's Overture *Egmont.* Between 1819–21 Starke published a piano tutor for which he commissioned contributions from Vienna's leading composers; Beethoven contributed his five Bagatelles Op. 119. Not satisfied, Starke added to his collection the *Andante* and *Rondo* from the *Pastoral* Sonata and at the same time paid tribute to Beethoven with the encomium – 'a star of the first magnitude in the musical firmament'.[lxxix]

Turning now to questions of interpretation, Tovey lays emphasis on the performer needing a 'fine legato' in the melody and chords.[lxxx] Fischer encourages the artist with a note of optimism: 'Provided one exactly follows Beethoven's directions, *staccato* and *legato*, the idea of the movement will emerge of its own accord.'[lxxxi] Czerny recounts that Beethoven himself was very fond of playing this movement and apparently needed little encouragement to take it up. Having heard his teacher perform the work on several occasions, it is only fitting therefore that we close this section with a summary of Czerny's own performance instructions. 'The right hand very *legato* and *cantabile*. The bass very short, light, and remarkably staccato ... The middle subject ... with tender delicacy, rather in the march style, and therefore in strict time ... This *Andante* ... is like a simple narration — a ballad of former times — and must be so interpreted.'[lxxxii]

The third movement is a Beethoven scherzo that functions here as a minuet — 'one of [the composer's] happiest'[lxxxiii] and one that is 'perfectly regular in form'.[lxxxiv] Subtlety prevails throughout the movement that is structured around 'one simple melodic four-bar phrase played, with repeats, eight times, with changing harmony'.[lxxxv] 'Naïve humour' is also present that may also be thought of as 'rustic'.[lxxxvi] Perhaps we can find here in Beethoven's humour traces of the kind that both exasperated and fascinated his contemporaries — changes of mood, variations in tempo, quirky points of emphasis and the like. Nevertheless: 'The trio is decidedly a humorous tour de force.'[lxxxvii] Perhaps Beethoven was subliminally paying homage to the humour his former teacher Joseph Haydn infiltrated into some of the minuets of his late string quartets, such as that of the Quartet in F, Op. 77, No. 2.[lxxxviii]

We find Beethoven enjoying 'the simplicity of four repeated notes, descending through the registers of the piano'[lxxxix] with a simple motive of 'four single F sharps in descending order'.[xc] The movement is 'full of gay, teasing humour' and is characterised 'through its succession of octaves, thirds and sixths'.[xci] The teasing humour is 'set to a mood of high-spirited jest' that Bekker identifies as being in the folk-song manner and, moreover, 'one of the most delightful examples of the type'.[xcii]

With regard to performance and interpretation Konrad Wolf singles out Beethoven's Piano Sonata Op. 28 for particular mention, in the context of questions of tempo as determined by the prevailing room acoustics. He emphasizes how the tempi, selected by the performer, are in large measure subtly interdependent with 'the acoustic circumstances created by the hall or room as well as by the piano'. Towards the end of his life Beethoven became interested in such devices as metronome makings, by mean of which to provide the performer with a more secure guide to interpretation. However, as Wolf observes he left many decisions 'to the pianist's own judgment'. In this regard Wolf further suggests: '[Beethoven] saw the piano primarily as an instrument of improvisatory qualities, in which the personality of the performer is interposed between the composer and the listener.' Fifteen years after Beethoven's death (1842) Czerny published a comprehensive set of metronome markings that he later revised (1850). In both cases he was 'trying to state what he knew of Beethoven's own tempo choices, especially in the early works'.[xciii] With regard to the *scherzo* of the *Pastoral* Sonata Czerny is succinct, requesting the interpretation to be 'lively and humorous'.[xciv] To achieve this interpretation the Tovey-Craxton partnership affirm 'all the humour of the *scherzo* must find expression in a tempo not too fast'.[xcv]

In strictly formal terms the final movement is a sonata-rondo that Beethoven uses 'so that we can renew acquaintance with ... its opening pastoral dance, which returns with subtle and delightful variants'.[xcvi] The movement is headed with the instruction *Allegro, ma non troppo* (to be played allegro — brisk-lively — but not too much so). This was Beethoven's first use of this expression not only in his piano sonatas but also in all of his published works. The instruction clearly had special significance for him as he explores various artful and adventurous episodes that require different moods, rhythms, and harmonic texture. Rolland finds in these 'the joy of field and forest'[xcvii] and Bie the 'delight in the chase' as the music moves to its 'joyous conclusion'.[xcviii]

Von Elterlein is even more fulsome, suggesting the music conveys thoughts of 'lusty sons of nature boisterously jesting and romping, seizing each other and running away'. For him, Haydn and Mozart appear 'very clearly in their more playful moods'.[xcix]

Worthy of reiteration is that the movement as a whole is founded on a repeating, rhythmic bass figuration suggestive of the drone of the bagpipe, imparting thereby the rustic and pastoral character to the work.[c] Tovey initially enters into the spirit of things, finding the sonata as a whole 'full of elaborate beauty in its various phrases of meditation, humour, melancholy, and wit'. He acknowledges all this is 'intensely poetical' but in the final analysis he concludes: '[On] the whole [it is] about as pastoral as Jane Austen'![ci] In his later writing about the sonata he is less censorious, praising the opening of the *Rondo* for its 'uniqueness' and being endowed with 'so gloriously naïve a collection of ideas'.[cii]

Amidst the praise for Beethoven's achievement in his D Major Piano Sonata, there is one dissentient voice, namely that of Paul Bekker. He does not regard the final movement to be one the composer's happiest efforts 'despite certain beauties of diction'. He recognizes Beethoven shows his hand in the 'pastoral bass rising above a pedal note' and the 'mysterious opening of the coda'. That said, he finds the underlying thought 'fails to add anything fresh to the preceding movements'. He asks: 'Was the four-part design a mistake?' He believes the rondo feeling Beethoven hinted at in his first D major Piano Sonata, Op. 10, No. 3 serves as a better 'counterbalancing factor', to what has gone before, than is achieved in the Op. 28. As the work stands he considers 'it ends as a mere display of virtuosity'.[ciii]

The virtuosity required in the final pages of the *Pastoral* Sonata should not be underestimated. The keyboard skills Beethoven's writing demands enters the realms of the professional pianist with, for example, 'some brilliant figuration in the right hand over the initial bagpipe drone-bass played in octaves'. The movement closes 'with eighteen bars of virtuosity' that Rolland refers to as 'a mad gallop home'. Gordon comments on how, in what has so far been a 'calm sonata', Beethoven 'sets the stage for a surprising burst of energy ... which provides a flourish of unexpected brilliance with which to end the work'. Even Tovey, not given to expressing himself in extremes, refers here to 'this very difficult passage'. With encouragement to the performer he adds if taken at 'quite a reasonable pace' the passage 'will become brilliant'. This same spirit is at the heart of Fischer's exhortation: 'The final *Presto* should be played with brilliance.' And likewise from Czerny: 'The conclusion very quick and brilliant, and with bravura.'

Shortly after completing his D major Piano Sonata Op. 28, Beethoven expressed dissatisfaction over his piano writing to date. He confided this sometime in 1803 to his close friend, the mandolin and violin player Wenzel Krumpholz — he was an accomplished performer and a member of Prince Nikolaus Esterhazy's orchestra. We learn of Beethoven's feelings concerning his piano music through an interesting chain of events that are as follows. Krumpholz conveyed Beethoven's expression of dissatisfaction with his work to Carl Czerny — who was also an intimate friend of Krumpholz. Years later (1842) Czerny left an account of Beethoven's remarks in a short autobiography he made of his life which was later deposited in the archives of the *Gesellschaft der Musikfreunde* at Vienna. Czerny's account only came to light in 1870 when the keeper of the archives published it in his *Annual Report* to coincide with the celebrations planned for that year — Beethoven's Birth Centenary. In 1880 Czerny's account of Beethoven's conversation with Krumpholz was eventually published by the musicologist Ludwig Nohl — to whom, amongst other things, posterity owes a debt for discovering the lost autograph of one of Beethoven's most cherished miniature compositions, his bagatelle *Für Elise.*

Back in1803 Beethoven had apparently exclaimed to Krumpholz: 'God knows why my piano music still makes the worst impression on me.' But, with characteristic resolution he confided to his sketchbook how he 'intended to make a fresh start'. This would shortly include the Piano Sonatas Op. 31 to which we next direct our attention.

i Harold Truscott in: Denis Arnold and Nigel Fortune, editors, 1973, pp. 106–7.
ii Edwin Fischer, 1959, pp. 64–5.
iii William S. Newman, 1963, p. 519.
iv The words quoted are derived from Maynard Solomon, 1977, pp. 106–7.
v Barry Cooper, 1991, p. 241.
vi Barry Cooper, 2000, p. 108.
vii Stewart Gordon, 1996, p. 165.
viii Michael Broyles, 1987, p. 70.
ix Daniel Coren, *Structural relations between Op. 28 and Op. 36*, in: Alan Tyson, *Beethoven studies 2*, 1977, p. 74.
x Peter Clive, quoting Alexander L. Ringer, 2001, p. 74.
xi *Ibid*, p. 249.
xii Matthew Rye, Notes to the BBC *Radio Three Beethoven experience* Friday 10 June 2005. www.bbc.co.uk/radio3/Beethoven
xiii Marion M. Scott, 1940, p. 138.
xiv Eric Blom, pp. 112–3.
xv Donald Francis Tovey, [1931], revised by Barry Cooper, 1998, pp. 108–9.
xvi Paul Bekker, 1925, p. 113.
xvii Barry Cooper, 1990. p. 44 and p. 66.
xviii Electra Yourke, 2003–5, Vol. 4, p. 150.
xix William Kinderman, 1997, p. 61. Discussed in the Chapter: *Crisis and creativity.*
xx For a facsimile reproduction and annotated text see: Beethoven House, Digital Archives, Library Document Sammlung W 17.
xxi For a facsimile reproduction and annotated text, see: Beethoven House Digital Archives Document Sammlung H. C. Bodmer, HCB BBr. William Kinderman also discusses this period in Beethoven's life. See: *Crisis and creativity* in: *Beethoven*, 1997, p. 61.
xxii We catch a glimpse of the despair Beethoven must have felt from a letter Gabriel Fauré wrote to his wife when he too realized he was loosing his hearing: 'I am overwhelmed by the affliction that has struck me in what is most important I should preserve intact ... I am constantly weighed down by a frightful cloak of misery and discouragement.' As quoted in: Madeleine Goss, 1945, p. 51.

xxiii See, for example: [*Beethoven*] *Piano sonatas Vol. 2. Nos. 9–15*, Alfred Music Publishing, editor Stewart Gordon, *Masterworks, piano collection*. [undated].

xxiv As remarked by William S. Newman, 1963, p. 519. For a brief mention of this topic see also: Denis Matthews, 1985, p. 84.

xxv Romain Rolland, 1917, p. 150.

xxvi Denis Matthews, 1967, p. 27.

xxvii Edwin Fischer, 1959, pp. 64–5.

xxviii Harold Craxton and Donald Francis Tovey, [1931], p. 68.

xxix For a modern-day interpretation of how Beethoven may have appeared, when composing out of doors in the countryside, see the illustrations by the artist-sculptor Donna Dralle reproduced in the website text: *The Unheard Beethoven* to the texts 'Twelve German Dances' and '3 Part Fugue, Hess 237 nr. 4'.

xxx Denis Matthews, 1967, p. 27. See also: Denis Matthews, 1985, p. 84.

xxxi William S. Newman, 1963, p. 519.

xxxii William Kinderman, 1997, pp. 73–4.

xxxiii Michael Broyles, 1987, p. 70.

xxxiv Daniel Coren, *Structural relations between Op. 28 and Op. 36*, in: Alan Tyson, *Beethoven studies 2*, 1977, pp. 76–83.

xxxv See: Barry Cooper, 1990, p. 88 and Barry Cooper, 1991, p. 183. Cooper suggests the Sauer Sketchbook may have been used in 1801 by Beethoven as early as April and as late as November.

xxxvi It is thought the surviving leaves of the Sauer Sketchbook may now reside in as many as sixteen different locations; those for the Op. 28 Piano Sonata are held in the Bonn (Beethoven House) and Berlin (State Library) archives. See: Wilfrid Howard Mellers, 1997, p. 19.

xxxvii Douglas Porter Johnson, editor, 1985, p. 72 and pp. 114–16.

xxxviii Beethoven House, Digital Archives, Library Document Sammlung H. C. Bodmer, HCB 10/58. A similar sketch-leaf is illustrated in Library Document Sammlung H. C. Bodmer, HCB Mh 68.

xxxix Paul Mies, 1929 (Reprint, 1969). Mies makes a wide-ranging study of Beethoven's Sketchbooks. His study of the Op. 28 Piano Sonata is found at p. 108.

xl The Title Page of the first edition is reproduced at Beethoven House Digital Archives, Library Document Sammlung, J. van der Spek C Op. 28/15. For a discussion of contemporary related circumstances, see: Elliot Forbes, 1997, p. 297.

xli These circumstances are discussed in: Peter Clive, 2001, pp. 200–1.

xlii Egerton C. Lowe, 1929, p. 76.

xliii As suggested in the text to Sonnenfels in: Beethoven House Digital Archives, Library Document BH 61.

xliv See: Elliot Forbes, editor, 1967, p. 297.

xlv Emily Anderson, editor and translator, 1961, Letter No. 11, pp. 17–19.

xlvi Peter Clive, 2001, pp. 340–1. See also: Beethoven House Digital Archives Library Document BH 61.

xlvii Maynard Solomon, 1988, pp. 193–204.

xlviii Wayne M. Senner, Robin Wallace and William Meredith, editors, 1999, Vol. 1, pp. 180–1.

xlix Felix Anton Schindler, edited by Donald W. MacArdle and translated by

l Peter Clive, 2001, p. 285.

Constance S. Jolly from the German edition of 1860, 1966, p. 94.
^{li} Bertold Litzman, editor, 1971, Vol. II, pp. 150–1.
^{lii} Barrie Martyn, 1990, p. 371.
^{liii} John Alexander Fuller-Maitland, *The Musical Times*, London: Vol. VIII, No. 2, 1927, p. 218.
^{liv} National Gallery (Great Britain), London: Privately printed, 1948.
^{lv} Romain Rolland, 1917, p. 150.
^{lvi} Rosamond E. M. Harding, 1938, p. 48.
^{lvii} Ernst von Elterlein, 1898, p. 72.
^{lviii} Stewart Gordon, 1996, p. 165.
^{lix} William Kinderman, 1997, pp. 60–1.
^{lx} Paul Bekker, 1925 , p. 113.
^{lxi} Michael Broyles, 1987, pp. 70–1.
^{lxii} Theodor W. Adorno, 1998, p. 21, p. 26 and p. 88.
^{lxiii} Phillip Radcliffe in: Gerald Abraham, editors, 1982, p. 342.
^{lxiv} Anton Schindler in: Donald W. MacArdle, editor and translated by Constance S. Jolly from the German edition of 1860, 1966 p. 414.
^{lxv} Harold Truscott in: Denis Arnold and Nigel Fortune, editors, 1973, pp. 106–7.
^{lxvi} Edwin Fischer, 1959, p. 65.
^{lxvii} Denis Matthews, 1985, p. 84.
^{lxviii} Carl Czerny in: Paul Badura-Skoda, editor, 1970, p. 51.
^{lxix} Ernst von Elterlein, 1898, p. 73.
^{lxx} Denis Matthews, 1967, pp. 27–8 and, 1985, p. 84.
^{lxxi} Oskar Bie, 1966, p. 174
^{lxxii} William Kinderman, 1997, pp. 73–4.
^{lxxiii} Paul Bekker, 1925, p. 113.
^{lxxiv} Alfred Brendel, 2001, p. 74.
^{lxxv} *Ibid*, pp. 73–4.
^{lxxvi} Harold Truscott in: Denis Arnold and Nigel Fortune, editors, 1973, pp. 106–7.
^{lxxvii} Michael Broyles, 1987, pp. 72–3.
^{lxxviii} Stewart Gordon, 1996, p. 165.
^{lxxix} Peter Clive, 2001, pp. 348–9.
^{lxxx} Harold Craxton and Donald Francis Tovey, [1931], p. 69.
^{lxxxi} Edwin Fischer, 1959, p. 65.
^{lxxxii} Carl Czerny in: Paul Badura-Skoda, editor, 1970, p. 51. See also: Dennis Matthews, 1967, p. 27.
^{lxxxiii} Romain Rolland, 1917, p. 150.
^{lxxxiv} Stewart Gordon, 1996, p. 165.
^{lxxxv} Harold Truscott in: Denis Arnold and Nigel Fortune, editors, 1973, pp. 106–7.
^{lxxxvi} Denis Matthews, 1985, p. 84.
^{lxxxvii} Charles Rosen, 2002, p. 162.
^{lxxxviii} Phillip Radcliffe in: Gerald Abraham, editor, 1982, p. 342.
^{lxxxix} Matthew Rye, Notes to the BBC Radio Three *Beethoven experience* Friday 10 June 2005. www.bbc.co.uk/radio3/Beethoven
^{xc} Egerton C. Lowe, 1929, p. 79.
^{xci} Ernst von Elterlein, 1898, p. 73.
^{xcii} Paul Bekker, 1925, p. 113.
^{xciii} Konrad Wolff, 1990, p. 152.
^{xciv} Carl Czerny in: Paul Badura-Skoda, editor, 1970, p. 51.
^{xcv} Harold Craxton and Donald Francis Tovey, [1931, p. 69.
^{xcvi} Denis Matthews, 1967, p. 28. See also: Egerton C. Lowe, 1929, p. 80.
^{xcvii} Romain Rolland, 1917, p. 150.
^{xcviii} Oskar Bie, 1966, p. 174.

[xcix] Ernst von Elterlein, 1898, p. 74.
[c] Edwin Fischer, 1959, p. 65. See also: Charles Rosen, 2002, p. 162.
[ci] Harold Craxton and Donald Francis Tovey, [1931], p. 68.
[cii] Donald Francis Tovey, 1944, p. 78.
[ciii] Paul Bekker, 1925, p. 113.
[civ] Charles Rosen, 2002, p. 162.
[cv] Romain Rolland, 1917, p. 150.
[cvi] Stewart Gordon, 1996, p. 165.
[cvii] Harold Craxton and Donald Francis Tovey, [1931, p. 69.
[cviii] Edwin Fischer, 1959, p. 65.
[cix] Carl Czerny in: Paul Badura-Skoda, editor, 1970, p. 51.
[cx] Derived in part from: Ludwig Nohl, 1880, p. 48; Peter Clive, 2001, p. 197; and Denis Matthews, 1997, p. 2.A performance of the Piano Sonata in D, Op. 28 has been recorded by Paul Badura-Skoda on a fortepiano of 1815 by John Broadwood. Source BASF KHF-20326.

BIBLIOGRAPHY

The author has individually consulted all the publications listed in this bibliography and can confirm that each makes reference, in some way or other, to Beethoven and his works. It will be evident from their titles which of these are publications devoted exclusively to the composer. Others that make only passing reference to Beethoven and his compositions, nevertheless unfailingly bear testimony to his genius and humanity. The diversity of the titles listed also testifies to the centrality of Beethoven to western culture and, indeed, beyond; the mere survey of these should be of itself a rewarding experience for the typical lover of so-called classical music. The entries are confined to book publications only, reflecting the scope of the author's researches. The cut-off date for this was 2007; consequently no works after this date are listed, notwithstanding the author is mindful that Beethoven musicology, and related publication, continue to be a major field of endeavour.

Abraham, Gerald. *Beethoven's second-period quartets*. London: Oxford University Press: Humphrey Milford, 1944.

Abraham, Gerald. *Essays on Russian and East European music*. Oxford: Clarendon Press: New York: Oxford University Press, 1985.

Abraham, Gerald, Editor. *The age of Beethoven, 1790-1830*. London: Oxford University Press, 1982.

Abraham, Gerald. *The tradition of Western music*. London: Oxford University Press, 1974.

Abse, Dannie and Joan. *The Music lover's literary companion*. London: Robson Books, 1988.

Adorno, Theodor W., Translator. *Alban Berg: master of the smallest link*. Cambridge: Cambridge University Press, 1991.

Adorno, Theodor W. *Beethoven: the philosophy of music; fragments and texts*. Cambridge: Polity Press, 1998.

Albrecht, Daniel, Editor. *Modernism and music: an anthology of sources*. Chicago; London: University of Chicago Press, 2004.

Albrecht, Theodore, Translator and Editor. *Letters to Beethoven and other correspondence*. Lincoln, New England: University of Nebraska Press, 3 vols., 1996.

Allsobrook, David Ian. *Liszt: my travelling circus life*. London: Macmillan, 1991.

Anderson, Christopher, Editor and Translator. *Selected writings of Max Reger*. New York; London: Routledge, 2006.

Anderson, Emily, Editor and Translator. *The letters of Beethoven*. London: Macmillan, 3 vols.,1961.

Anderson, Martin, Editor. *Klemperer on music: shavings from a musician's workbench*. London: Toccata Press, 1986.

Antheil, George. *Bad boy of music*. London; New York: Hurst & Blackett Ltd., 1945.

Appleby, David P. *Heitor Villa-Lobos: a bio-bibliography*. New York: Greenwood Press, 1988.

Aprahamian, Felix, Editor. *Essays on music: an anthology from The Listener*. London, Cassell, 1967.

Armero, Gonzalo and Jorge de Persia. *Manuel de Falla : his life & works*. London: Omnibus Press, 1999.

Arnold, Ben, Editor. *The Liszt companion*. Westport, Connecticut; London: Greenwood Press, 2002.

Arnold, Denis and Nigel Fortune, Editors. *The Beethoven companion*. London: Faber and Faber, 1973.

Ashbrook, William. *Donizetti*. London: Cassell, 1965.

Auner, Joseph Henry. *A Schoenberg reader: documents of a life*. New Haven Connecticut; London: Yale University Press, 2003.

Avins, Styra, Editor. *Johannes Brahms: life and letters*. Oxford: Oxford University Press, 1997.

Azoury, Pierre H. *Chopin through his contemporaries: friends, lovers, and rivals*. Westport, Connecticut: Greenwood Press, 1999.

Badura-Skoda, Paul. *Carl Czerny: On the Proper Performance of all Beethoven's Works for the Piano*. Universal Edition: A. G. Wien, 1970.

Bailey, Cyril. *Hugh Percy Allen*. London: Oxford University

Press, 1948.

Bailey, Kathryn. *The life of Webern.* Cambridge: Cambridge University Press, 1998.

Barenboim, Daniel. *A life in music.* London: Weidenfeld & Nicolson, 1991.

Barlow, Michael. *Whom the gods love: the life and music of George Butterworth.* London: Toccata Press, 1997.

Barrett-Ayres, Reginald. *Joseph Haydn and the string quartet.* New York: Schirmer Books, 1974.

Bartos, Frantisek. *Bedrich Smetana: Letters and reminiscences.* Prague: Artia, 1953.

Barzun, Jacques. *Pleasures of music: an anthology of writing about music and musicians.* London: Cassell, 1977.

Bauer-Lechner, Natalie. *Recollections of Gustav Mahler.* London: Faber Music, 1980.

Bazhanov, N. Nikolai. *Rakhmaninov.* Moscow: Raduga, 1983.

Beaumont, Antony, Editor. *Ferruccio Busoni: Selected letters.* London: Faber and Faber, 1987.

Beaumont, Antony, Editor. *Gustav Mahler, letters to his wife.* London: Faber and Faber, 2004.

Beecham, Thomas. *A mingled chime: an autobiography.* New York: Da Capo Press, 1976.

Bekker, Paul. *Beethoven.* London: J. M. Dent & Sons, 1925.

Bellasis, Edward. *Cherubini: memorials illustrative of his life.* London: Burns and Oates, 1874.

Bennett, James R. Sterndale. *The life of William Sterndale Bennett.* Cambridge: University Press, 1907.

Benser, Caroline Cepin. *Egon Wellesz (1885–1974): chronicle of twentieth-century musician.* New York: P. Lang, 1985.

Berlioz, Hector. *Evenings in the orchestra.* Harmondsworth: Penguin Books, 1963.

Berlioz, Hector. *The musical madhouse (Les grotesques de la musique).* Rochester, New York: University of Rochester Press, 2003.

Bernard, Jonathan W., Editor. *Elliott Carter: collected essays and lectures, 1937-1995.* Rochester, New York; Woodbridge: University of Rochester Press, 1998.

Bernstein, Leonard. *The joy of music.* New York: Simon and Schuster, 1959.

Bertensson, Sergei. *Sergei Rachmaninoff: a lifetime in music.* London: G. Allen & Unwin, 1965.

Biancolli, Louis. *The Flagstad manuscript.* New York: Putnam, 1952.

Bickley, Nora, Editor. *Letters from and to Joseph Joachim.* London: Macmillan, 1914.

Bie, Oskar. *A history of the pianoforte and pianoforte players.* New York: Da Capo Press, 1966.

Blaukopf, Herta. *Mahler's unknown letters.* London: Gollancz, 1986.

Blaukopf, Kurt and Herta. *Mahler: his life, work and world.* London: Thames and Hudson, 1991.

Bliss, Arthur. *As I remember.* London: Thames Publishing, 1989.

Block, Adrienne Fried. *Amy Beach, passionate Victorian: the life and work of an American composer, 1867–1944.* New York: Oxford University Press, 1998.

Bloch, Ernst. *Essays on the philoso-*

phy of music. Cambridge: Cambridge University Press, 1985.

Blocker, Robert. *The Robert Shaw reader*. New Haven; London: Yale University Press, 2004.

Blom, Eric. *A musical postbag*. London: J. M. Dent, 1945.

Blom, Eric. *Beethoven's pianoforte sonatas discussed*. London: J. M. Dent, 1938.

Blom, Eric. *Classics major and minor: with some other musical ruminations*. London: J. M. Dent, 1958.

Blum, David. *The art of quartet playing: the Guarneri Quartet in conversation with David Blum*. London: Gollancz, 1986.

Blume, Friedrich. *Classic and Romantic music: a comprehensive survey*. London: Faber and Faber, 1972.

Boden, Anthony. *The Parrys of the Golden Vale: background to genius*. London: Thames Publishing, 1998.

Bonavia, Ferruccio. *Musicians on music*. London: Routledge & Kegan Paul, 1956.

Bonds, Mark Evan *After Beethoven: imperatives of originality in the symphony*. Cambridge, Massachusetts; London: Harvard University Press, 1996.

Bonis, Ferenc, Editor. *The selected writings of Zoltán Kodály*. London; New York: Boosey & Hawkes, 1974.

Bookspan, Martin. *André Previn: a biography*. London: Hamilton, 1981.

Boros, James and Richard Toop, Editors. *Brian Ferneyhough: Collected writings*. Amsterdam: Harwood Academic, 1995.

Boulez, Pierre. *Stocktakings from an apprenticeship*. Oxford: Clarendon Press, 1991.

Boult, Adrian. *Boult on music: words from a lifetime's communication*. London: Toccata Press, 1983.

Boult, Adrian. *My own trumpet*. London, Hamish Hamilton, 1973.

Boult, Adrian with Jerrold Northrop Moore. *Music and friends: seven decades of letters to Adrian Boult from Elgar, Vaughan Williams, Holst, Bruno Walter, Yehudi Menuhin and other friends*. London: Hamish Hamilton, 1979.

Bovet, Marie Anne de. *Charles Gounod: his life and his works*. London: S. Low, Marston, Searle & Rivington, Ltd., 1891.

Bowen, Catherine Drinker. *Beloved friend: the story of Tchaikowsky and Nadejda von Meck*. London: Hutchinson & Co., 1937.

Bowen, Meiron, Editor. *Gerhard on music: selected writings*. Brookfield, Vermont: Ashgate, 2000.

Bowen, Meirion. *Michael Tippett*. London: Robson Books, 1982.

Bowen, Meiron, Editor. *Music of the angels: essays and sketchbooks of Michael Tippett*. London: Eulenburg, 1980.

Bowen, Meiron, Editor. *Tippett on music*. Oxford: Clarendon Press, 1995.

Bowers, Faubion. *Scriabin: a biography*. Mineola: Dover; London: Constable, 1996.

Boyden, Matthew. *Richard Strauss*. London: Weidenfeld & Nicolson, 1999.

Bozarth, George S., Editor. *Brahms studies: analytical and historical* perspectives; papers delivered at the International Brahms Conference, Washington, DC, 5-8 May 1983. Oxford: Clarendon Press, 1990.

Brand, Juliane, Christopher Hailey and Donald Harris, Editors. *The Berg-Schoenberg correspondence: selected letters.* Basingstoke: Macmillan, 1987.

Brandenbugh, Sieghard, Editor. *Haydn, Mozart, & Beethoven: studies in the music of the classical period: essays in honor of Alan Tyson.* Oxford: Clarendon Press, 1998.

Braunstein, Joseph. *Musica Æterna, program notes for 1961–1971.* New York: Musica Æterna, 1972.

Braunstein, Joseph. *Musica Æterna, program notes for 1971-1976.* New York: Musica Æterna, 1978.

Brendel, Alfred. *Alfred Brendel on music: collected essays.* Chicago, Iliinois: A Cappella Books, 2001.

Brendel, Alfred. *The veil of order: Alfred Brendel in conversation with Martin Meyer.* London: Faber and Faber, 2002.

Breuning, Gerhard von. *Memories of Beethoven: from the house of the black-robed Spaniards.* Cambridge: Cambridge University Press, 1992.

Briscoe, James R., Editor. (Brief Description): *Debussy in performance.* New Haven: Yale University Press, 1999.

Brott, Alexander Betty Nygaard King. *Alexander Brott: my lives in music.* Oakville, Ontario; Niagara Falls, New York: Mosaic Press, 2005.

Brown, Alfred Peter. *The symphonic repertoire. Vol. 2, The first golden age of the Viennese symphony: Haydn, Mozart, Beethoven, and Schubert.* Bloomington, Indiana: Indiana University Press, 2002.

Brown, Maurice John Edwin. *Schubert: a critical biography.* London: Macmillan; New York: St. Martin's Press, 1958.

Broyles, Michael. *Beethoven: the emergence and evolution of Beethoven's heroic style.* New York: Excelsior Music Publishing Co., 1987.

Brubaker, Bruce and Jane Gottlieb, Editors. *Pianist, scholar, connoisseur: essays in honor of Jacob Lateiner.* Stuyvesant, N.Y., Pendragon Press, 2000.

Buch, Esteban. *Beethoven's Ninth: a political history.* Chicago; London: University of Chicago Press, 2003.

Burk, John N., Editor. *Letters of Richard Wagner: the Burrell collection.* London: Gollancz, 1951.

Burnham, Scott G. *Beethoven hero.* Princeton, New Jersey: Princeton University Press, 1995.

Burnham, Scott G and Michael P. Steinberg, Editors. *Beethoven and his world.* Princeton, New Jersey; Oxford: Princeton University Press, 2000.

Burton, William Westbrook, Editor. *Conversations about Bernstein.* New York; Oxford: Oxford University Press, 1995.

Busch, Fritz. *Pages from a musician's life.* London: Hogarth Press, 1953.

Busch, Hans, Editor. *Verdi's Aida: the history of an opera in letters and documents.* Minneapolis:

University of Minnesota Press, 1978.

Busch, Hans, Editor. *Verdi's Falstaff in letters and contemporary reviews*. Bloomington: Indiana University Press, 1997.

Busch, Marie, Translator. *Memoirs of Eugenie Schumann*. London: W. Heinemann, 1927.

Bush, Alan Dudley. *In my eighth decade and other essays*. London: Kahn & Averill, 1980.

Busoni, Ferruccio. *Letters to his wife*. Translated by Rosamond Ley. New York: Da Capo Press, 1975.

Byron, Reginald. *Music, culture, & experience: selected papers of John Blacking*. Chicago: University of Chicago Press, 1995.

Cairns, David. *Responses: musical essays and reviews*. New York: Da Capo Press, 1980.

Cardus, Neville. *Talking of music*. London: Collins, 1957.

Carley, Lionel. *Delius: a life in letters*. London: Scolar Press in association with the Delius Trust, 1988.

Carley, Lionel. *Grieg and Delius: a chronicle of their friendship in letters*. London: Marion Boyars, 1993.

Carner, Mosco. *Major and minor*. London: Duckworth, 1980

Carner, Mosco. *Puccini: a critical biography*. London: Duckworth, 1958.

Carroll, Brendan G. *The last prodigy: a biography of Erich Wolfgang Korngold*. Portland, Oregon: Amadeus Press, 1997.

Carse, Adam von Ahn. *The life of Jullien: adventurer, showman-conductor and establisher of the Promenade Concerts in England, together with a history of those concerts up to 1895*. Cam-

bridge England: Heffer, 1951.

Carse, Adam von Ahn. *The orchestra from Beethoven to Berlioz: a history of the orchestra in the first half of the 19th century, and of the development of orchestral baton-conducting*. Cambridge: W. Heffer, 1948.

Casals, Pablo. *Joys and sorrows: reflections by Pablo Casals as told to Albert E. Kahn*. London: Macdonald, 1970.

Casals, Pablo. *The memoirs of Pablo Casals as told to Thomas Dozier*. London: Life en Español, 1959.

Chappell, Paul. *Dr. S. S. Wesley, 1810–1876: portrait of a Victorian musician*. Great Wakering: Mayhew-McCrimmon, 1977.

Chasins, Abram. *Leopold Stokowski, a profile*. New York: Hawthorn Books, 1979.

Charlton, Davi, Editor and Martyn Clarke Translator. *E.T.A. Hoffmann's musical writings: Kreisleriana, The Poet and the Composer*. Cambridge: Cambridge University Press, 1989.

Chávez, Carlos. *Musical thought*. Cambridge: Harvard University Press, 1961.

Chesterman, Robert, Editor. *Conversations with conductors: Bruno Walter, Sir Adrian Boult, Leonard Bernstein, Ernest Ansermet, Otto Klemperer, Leopold Stokowski*. Totowa, New Jersey: Rowman and Littlefield, 1976.

Chissell, Joan. *Clara Schumann: a dedicated spirit; a study of her life and work*. London: Hamilton, 1983.

Chua, Daniel K. L. *The "Galitzin" quartets of Beethoven: Opp.127, 132, 130*. Princeton: Princeton

University Press, 1995.

Citron, Marcia, Editor. *The letters of Fanny Hensel to Felix Mendelssohn*. Stuyvesant, New York: Pendragon Press, 1987.

Clark, Walter Aaron. *Enrique Granados: poet of the piano*. Oxford, England; New York, N.Y.: Oxford University Press, 2006.

Clark, Walter Aaron. *Isaac Albéniz: portrait of a romantic*. Oxford; New York: Oxford University Press, 1999.

Clive, Peter. *Beethoven and his world*. Oxford University Press, 2001.

Closson, Ernest. *History of the piano*. Translated by Delano Ames and edited by Robin Golding. London: Paul Elek, 1947.

Cockshoot, John V. *The fugue in Beethoven's piano music*. London: Routledge & Kegan Paul, 1959.

Coe, Richard N, Translator. *Life of Rossini by Stendhal*. London: Calder & Boyars, 1970.

Coleman, Alexander, Editor. *Diversions & animadversions: essays from The new criterion*. New Brunswick, New Jersey; London: Transaction Publishers, 2005.

Colerick, George. *From the Italian girl to Cabaret: musical humour, parody and burlesque*. London: Juventus, 1998.

Coleridige, A. D. *Life of Moscheles, with selections from his diaries and correspondence by his wife*. London: Hurst & Blackett, 1873.

Colles, Henry Cope. *Essays and lectures*. London: Humphrey Milford, Oxford University Press, 1945.

Cone, Edward T., Editor. *Roger Sessions on music: collected essays*. Princeton, New Jersey: Princeton University Press, 1979.

Cone, Edward T. *The composer's voice*. Berkeley; London: University of California Press, 1974.

Cook, Susan and Judy S. Tsou, Editors. *Cecilia reclaimed: feminist perspectives on gender and music*. Urbana: University of Illinois Press, 1994.

Cooper, Barry. *Beethoven*. The master musicians series. Oxford: Oxford University Press, 2000.

Cooper, Barry. *Beethoven and the creative process*. Oxford: Clarendon Press, 1990.

Cooper, Barry. *Beethoven's folksong settings: chronology, sources, style*. Cambridge: Cambridge University Press, 1991.

Cooper, Barry. *The Beethoven compendium: a guide to Beethoven's life and music*. London: Thames and Hudson, 1991.

Cooper, Martin. *Beethoven: the last decade, 1817–1827*. London: Oxford University Press, 1970.

Cooper, Martin. *Judgements of value: selected writings on music*. Oxford; New York: Oxford University Press, 1988.

Cooper, Martin. *Ideas and music*. London: Barrie and Rockliff, 1965.

Cooper, Victoria L. *The house of Novello: the practice and policy of a Victorian music publisher, 1829–1866*. Aldershot, Hants: Ashgate, 2003.

Coover, James. *Music at auction: Puttick and Simpson (of London), 1794–1971: being an annotated, chronological list of sales of musical materials*. Warren, Michigan: Harmonie Park Press, 1988.

Copland, Aaron. *Copland on music.* London: Deutsch, 1961.

Corredor, J. Ma. *Conversations with Casals.* London: Hutchinson, 1956.

Cott, Jonathan. *Stockhausen: conversations with the composer.* London: Picador, 1974.

Cottrell, Stephen. *Professional music making in London: ethnography and experience.* Aldershot: Ashgate, 2004.

Cowell, Henry. *Charles Ives and his music.* New York: Oxford University Press, 1955.

Cowling, Elizabeth. *The cello.* London: Batsford, 1983.

Crabbe, John. *Beethoven's empire of the mind.* Newbury: Lovell Baines, 1982.

Craft, Robert. *An improbable life: memoirs.* Nashville: Vanderbilt University Press, 2002.

Craft, Robert, Editor. *Stravinsky: selected correspondence.* London: Faber and Faber, 3 Vols. 1982–1985.

Craw, Howard Allen. *A biography and thematic catalog of the works of J. L. Dussek: 1760–1812.* Ann Arbor: Michigan, 1965.

Crawford, Richard, R. Allen Lott and Carol J. Oja, Editors. *A Celebration of American music: words and music in honor of H. Wiley Hitchcock.* Ann Arbor: University of Michigan Press, 1990.

Craxton, Harold and Tovey, Donald Francis. *Beethoven: Sonatas for Pianoforte.* London: The Associated Board, [1931].

Crichton, Ronald: Editor. *The memoirs of Ethel Smyth.* New York: Viking, 1987.

Crist, Stephen A. and Roberta M.

Marvin, Editors. *Historical musicology: sources, methods, interpretations.* Rochester, New York: University of Rochester Press, 2004.

Crofton, Ian and Donald Fraser, Editors. *A dictionary of musical quotations.* London: Croom Helm, 1985.

Crompton, Louis, Editor. *Shaw, Bernard: The great composers: reviews and bombardments.* Berkeley; London: University of California Press, 1978.

Csicserry-Ronay, Elizabeth, Translator and Editor. *Hector Berlioz: The art of music and other essays: (A travers chants).* Bloomington: Indiana University Press, 1994.

Curtiss, Mina Kirstein. *Bizet and his world.* London: Secker & Warburg, 1959.

Cuyler, Louise Elvira. *The symphony.* New York: Harcourt Brace Jovanovich, 1973.

Dahlhaus, Carl. *Ludwig van Beethoven: approaches to his music.* Oxford: Clarendon Press, 1991.

Dahlhaus, Carl. *Nineteenth-century music.* Translated by J. Bradford Robinson. Berkeley; London: University of California Press, 1989.

Daniels, Robin. *Conversations with Cardus.* London: Gollancz, 1976.

Daniels, Robin. Conversations with Menuhin. London: Macdonald General Books, 1979.

Day, James. *Vaughan Williams.* London: Dent, 1961.

Davies, Peter Maxwell. *Studies from two decades.* Selected and introduced by Stephen Pruslin.

London: Boosey & Hawkes, 1979.

Dean, Winton. *Georges Bizet: his life and work.* London: J.M. Dent, 1965.

Deas, Stewart. *In defence of Hanslick.* London: Williams and Norgate, 1940.

Debussy, Claude. *Debussy on music.* London: Secker & Warburg, 1977.

Delbanco, Nicholas. *The Beaux Arts Trio.* London: Gollancz, 1985.

Demény, Janos, Editor. *Béla Bartók: letters.* London: Faber and Faber, 1971.

Dent, Edward Joseph. *Selected essays.* Edited by Hugh Taylor. Cambridge; New York: Cambridge University Press, 1979.

Deutsch, Otto Erich. *Schubert: a documentary biography.* London: J.M. Dent, 1946

Deutsch, Otto Erich. *Schubert: memoirs by his friends.* London: Adam & Charles Black, 1958.

Dibble, Jeremy. *C. Hubert H. Parry: his life and music.* Oxford: Clarendon Press, 1992.

Dibble, Jeremy. *Charles Villiers Stanford: man and musician.* Oxford: Oxford University Press, 2002.

Donakowski, Conrad L. *A muse for the masses: ritual and music in an age of democratic revolution, 1770–1870.* Chicago: University of Chicago Press, 1977.

Dower, Catherine. *Alfred Einstein on music: selected music criticisms.* New York: Greenwood Press, 1991.

Downs, Philip G. *Classical music: the era of Haydn, Mozart, and Beethoven.* New York: W.W. Norton, 1992.

Drabkin, William. *Beethoven: Missa Solemnis.* Cambridge: Cambridge University Press, 1991.

Dreyfus, Kay. *The farthest north of humanness: letters of Percy Grainger, 1901–1914.* South Melbourne; Basingstoke: Macmillan, 1985.

Dubal, David, Editor. *Remembering Horowitz: 125 pianists recall a legend.* New York: Schirmer Books, 1993.

Dubal, David. *The world of the concert pianist.* London: Victor Gollancz, 1985.

Dvořák, Otakar. *Antonín Dvořák, my father.* Spillville, Iowa: Czech Historical Research Center, 1993.

Dyson, George. *The progress of music.* London: Oxford University Press, Humphrey Milford, 1932.

Eastaugh, Kenneth. *Havergal Brian: the making of a composer.* London: Harrap, 1976.

Edwards, Allen. *Flawed words and stubborn sounds: a conversation with Elliott Carter.* New York: Norton & Company, 1971.

Edwards, Frederick George. *Musical haunts in London.* London: J. Curwen & Sons, 1895.

Ehrlich, Cyril. *First philharmonic: a history of the Royal Philharmonic Society.* Oxford: Clarendon Press, 1995.

Einstein, Alfred. *A short history of music.* London: Cassell and Company Ltd., 1948.

Einstein, Alfred. *Essays on music.* London: Faber and Faber, 1958.

Einstein, Alfred. *Mozart: his character, his work.* London: Cassell and Company Ltd., 1946.

Einstein, Alfred. *Music in the Romantic era.* London: J.M.

Dent Ltd., 1947.

Ekman, Karl. *Jean Sibelius, his life and personality*. New York: Tudor Publishing. Co., 1945.

Elgar, Edward. *A future for English music: and other lectures*, Edited by Percy M. Young. London: Dobson, 1968.

Elkin, Robert. *Queen's Hall, 1893–1941*. London: Rider, 1944.

Ella, John. *Musical sketches, abroad and at home: with original music by Mozart, Czerny, Graun, etc., vocal cadenzas and other musical illustrations*. London: Ridgway, Vol. 1., 1869.

Ellis, William Ashton. *The family letters of Richard Wagner*. Edited and translated by William Ashton Ellis and enlarged with introduction and notes by John Deathridge. Basingstoke: Macmillan, 1991.

Ellis, William Ashton. *Richard Wagner's prose works: Vol. 1, The art-work of the future*. Edited and translated by William Ashton Ellis. London: Kegan Paul, Trench, Trübner, 1895.

Ellis, William Ashton. *Richard Wagner's prose works: Vol. 2, Opera and drama*. Edited and translated by William Ashton Ellis. London: Kegan Paul, Trench, Trübner, 1900.

Ellis, William Ashton. *Richard Wagner's prose works: Vol. 3, The theatre*. Edited and translated by William Ashton Ellis. London: Kegan Paul, Trench, Trübner, 1907.

Ellis, William Ashton. *Richard Wagner's prose works: Vol. 4, Art and politics*. Edited and translated by William Ashton Ellis. London: Kegan Paul, Trench,

Trübner, 1895.

Ellis, William Ashton. *Richard Wagner's prose works: Vol. 5, Actors and singers*. Edited and translated by William Ashton Ellis. London: Kegan Paul, Trench, Trübner, 1896.

Ellis, William Ashton. *Richard Wagner's prose works: Vol. 6, Religion and art*. Edited and translated by William Ashton Ellis. London: Kegan Paul, Trench, Trübner, 1897.

Ellis, William Ashton. *Richard Wagner's prose works: Vol. 7, In Paris and Dresden*. Edited and translated by William Ashton Ellis. London: Kegan Paul, Trench, Trübner, 1898.

Ellis, William Ashton. *Richard Wagner's prose works: Vol. 8, Posthumous*. Edited and translated by William Ashton Ellis. London: Kegan Paul, Trench, Trübner, 1899.

Elterlein, Ernst von. *Beethoven's pianoforte sonatas: explained for the lovers of the musical art*. London: W. Reeves, 1898.

Engel, Carl. *Musical myths and facts*. London: Novello, Ewer & Co.; New York: J.L. Peters, 1876.

Eosze, László. *Zoltán Kodály: his life and work*. London: Collet's, 1962.

Etter, Brian K. *From classicism to modernism: Western musical culture and the metaphysics of order*. Aldershot: Ashgate, 2001.

Ewen, David. *From Bach to Stravinsky: the history of music by its foremost critics*. New York, Greenwood Press, 1968.

Ewen, David. *Romain Rolland's Essays on music*. New York: Dover Publications, 1959.

Fay, Amy. *Music-study in Germany: from the home correspondence of Amy Fay.* New York: Dover Publications, 1965.

Fenby, Eric. *Delius as I knew him.* London: Quality Press, 1936.

Ferguson, Donald Nivison. *Masterworks of the orchestral repertoire: a guide for listeners.* Minneapolis: University of Minnesota Press, 1954.

Fétis, François-Joseph. *Curiosités historiques de la musique: complément nécessaire de la Musique mise à la portée de tout le monde.* Paris: Janet et Cotelle, 1830.

Fifield, Christopher. *Max Bruch: his life and works.* London: Gollancz, 1988.

Fifield, Christopher. *True artist and true friend: a biography of Hans Richter.* Oxford: Clarendon Press, 1993.

Finson, Jon and R. Larry Todd, Editors. *Mendelssohn and Schumann: essays on their music and its context.* Durham, N.C.: Duke University Press, 1984.

Fischer, Edwin. *Beethoven's pianoforte sonatas: a guide for students & amateurs.* London: Faber and Faber, 1959.

Fischer, Edwin. *Reflections on music.* London: Williams and Norgate, 1951.

Fischer, Hans Conrad and Erich Kock. *Ludwig van Beethoven: a study in text and pictures.* London: Macmillan; New York, St. Martin's Press, 1972.

Fischmann, Zdenka E. *Janáček-Newmarch correspondence.* 1st limited and numbered edition. Rockville, MD: Kabel Publishers, 1986.

Fitzlyon, April. *Maria Malibran: diva of the romantic age.* London: Souvenir Press, 1987.

FitzLyon, April. *The price of genius: a life of Pauline Viardot.* London: John Calder, 1964.

Forbes, Elliot, Editor. *Thayer's life of Beethoven.* Princeton, New Jersey: Princeton University Press, 1967.

Foreman, Lewis, Editor. *Farewell, my youth, and other writings by Arnold Bax.* Aldershot: Scolar Press, 1992.

Foreman, Lewis, Editor. *Farewell, my youth, and other writings by Arnold Bax.* Aldershot: Scolar Press, 1992.

Foster, Myles Birket. *History of the Philharmonic Society of London, 1813–1912: a record of a hundred years' work in the cause of music.* London: Bodley Head, 1912.

Foulds, John. *Music today: its heritage from the past, and legacy to the future.* London: I. Nicholson and Watson, limited, 1934.

Frank, Mortimer H. *Arturo Toscanini: the NBC years.* Portland, Oregon: Amadeus Press, 2002.

Fraser, Andrew Alastair. *Essays on music.* London: Oxford University Press, H. Milford, 1930.

Frohlich, Martha. *Beethoven's Appassionata' sonata.* Oxford: Clarendon Press, 1991.

Gal, Hans. *The golden age of Vienna.* London: Max Parrish & Co. Limited, 1948.

Gal, Hans. *The musician's world: great composers in their letters.* London: Thames and Hudson, 1965.

Galatopoulos, Stelios. *Bellini: life,*

times, music. London: Sanctuary, 2002.

Garden, Edward and Nigel Gottrei, Editors. *'To my best friend': correspondence between Tchaikovsky and Nadezhda von Meck, 1876–1878.* Oxford: Clarendon Press, 1993.

Geck, Martin. Beethoven. London: Haus, 2003.

Gerig, Reginald. *Famous pianists & their technique.* Washington: R. B. Luce, 1974.

Gilliam, Bryan. *The life of Richard Strauss.* Cambridge: Cambridge University Press, 1999.

Gilliam, Bryan, Editor. *Richard Strauss and his world.* Princeton, New Jersey: Princeton University Press, 1992.

Gillies, Malcolm and Bruce Clunies Ross, Editors. *Grainger on music.* Oxford; New York: Oxford University Press, 1999.

Gillies, Malcolm and David Pear, Editors. *The all-round man: selected letters of Percy Grainger, 1914–1961.* Oxford: Clarendon Press, 1994.

Gillies, Malcolm, Editor. *The Bartók companion.* London: Faber and Faber, 1993.

Gillmor, Alan M. *Erik Satie.* Basingstoke: Macmillan Press, 1988.

Glehn, M. E. *Goethe and Mendelssohn : (1821–1831).* London: Macmillan, 1874.

Glowacki, John, Editor. *Paul A. Pisk: Essays in his honor.* Austin, Texas: University of Texas, 1966

Gollancz, Victor. *Journey towards music: a memoir.* London: Victor Gollancz Ltd., 1964.

Good, Edwin Marshall. *Giraffes, black dragons, and other pianos: a technological history from Cristofori to the modern concert grand.* Stanford, California: Stanford University Press, 1982.

Gordon, David. Musical visitors to Britain. London: Routledge, 2005.

Gordon, Stewart. *A history of keyboard literature: music for the piano and its forerunners.* Schirmer Books: New York: London : Prentice Hall International, 1996.

Gorrell, Lorraine. *The nineteenth-century German lied.* Portland, Oregon: Amadeus Press, 1993.

Goss, Glenda D. *Jean Sibelius: the Hämeenlinna letters: scenes from a musical life, 1875–1895.* Esbo, Finland: Schildts, 1997.

Goss, Madeleine. *Bolero: the life of Maurice Ravel.* New York: Tudor, 1945.

Gotch, Rosamund Brunel, Editor. *Mendelssohn and his friends in Kensington: letters from Fanny and Sophy Horsley, written 1833–36.* London: Oxford University Press, 1938.

Gounod, Charles. *Charles Gounod; autobiographical reminiscences: with family letters and notes on music; from the French.* London: William Heinemann, 1896.

Grabs, Manfred, Editor. *Hanns Eisler: a rebel in music; selected writings.* Berlin: Seven Seas Publishers, 1978.

Grace, Harvey. *A musician at large.* London: Oxford University Press, H. Milford, 1928.

(La) Grange, Henry-Louis de. *Gustav Mahler.* Oxford: Oxford University Press, 1995.

Graves, Charles L. *Hubert Parry: his life and works.* London: Macmillan, 1926.

Graves, Charles L. *Post-Victorian music: with other studies and sketches*. London: Macmillan and Co., limited, 1911.

Graves, Charles L. *The life & letters of Sir George Grove, Hon. D.C.L. (Durham), Hon. LL.D. (Glasgow), formerly director of the Royal college of music*. London: Macmillan and Co., Ltd.; New York: The Macmillan Co., 1903.

Gray, Cecil. *Musical chairs, or, between two stools: being the life and memoirs of Cecil Gray*. London: Home & Van Thal, 1948.

Gregor-Dellin and Dietrich Mack, Editors. *Cosima Wagner's diaries: Vol. 1, 1869 – 1877*. London: Collins, 1978-1980.

Griffiths, Paul. *Modern music: the avant-garde* since 1945. London: J. M. Dent & Sons Ltd., 1981.

Griffiths, Paul. *Olivier Messiaen and the music of time*. London: Faber and Faber, 1985.

Griffiths, Paul. *Peter Maxwell Davies*. London: Robson Books, 1988.

Griffiths, Paul. *The sea on fire: Jean Barraqué*. Rochester, New York: Woodbridge: University of Rochester Press, 2003.

Griffiths, Paul. *The string quartet*. London: Thames and Hudson, 1983.

Grout, Donald Jay and Claude V. Palisca, Editors. *A history of Western music*. London: J. M. Dent, 1988.

Grove, George. *Beethoven and his nine symphonies*. London: Novello, Ewer, 1896.

Grover, Ralph Scott. *Ernest Chausson: the man and his music*.

London: The Athlone Press, 1980.

Grover, Ralph Scott. T*he music of Edmund Rubbra*. Aldershot: Scolar Press, 1993.

Grun, Bernard. *Alban Berg: letters to his wife*. Edited and translated by Bernard Grun. London: Faber and Faber, 1971.

Gutman, David. *Prokofiev*. London: Omnibus Press, 1990.

Hadow, William Henry. *Collected essays*. London: H. Milford at the Oxford University Press, 1928.

Hadow, William Henry. *Beethoven's Op. 18 Quartets*. London: H. Milford at the Oxford University Press, 1926.

Haggin, Bernard H. *Music observed*. New York: Oxford University Press, 1964.

Hailey, Christopher. *Franz Schreker, 1878–1934: a cultural biography*. Cambridge: Cambridge University Press, 1993.

Hall, Michael. *Leaving home: a conducted tour of twentieth-century music with Simon Rattle*. London: Faber and Faber, 1996.

Hall, Patricia and Friedemann Sallis, Editors. (Brief Description): *A handbook to twentieth-century musical sketches*. Cambridge: Cambridge University Press, 2004.

Hallé, C. E. *Life and letters of Sir Charles Hallé: being an autobiography (1819–1860) with correspondence and diaries*. London: Smith, Elder & Co., 1896.

Halstead, Jill. *The woman composer: creativity and the gendered politics of musical composition*. Aldershot: Ashgate, 1997.

Hamburger, Michael, Editor and Translator. *Beethoven letters, journals, and conversations.* New York: Thames and Hudson, 1951.

Hammelmann, Hanns A. and Ewald Osers. *The correspondence between Richard Strauss and Hugo von Hofmannsthal.* London: Collins, 1961.

Hanson, Lawrence and Elisabeth Hanson. *Tchaikovsky: the man behind the music.* New York: Dodd, Mead & Co, 1967.

Harding, James. *Massenet.* London: J. M. Dent & Sons Ltd., 1970.

Harding, James. *Saint-Saëns and his circle.* London: Chapman & Hall, 1965.

Harding, Rosamond E. M. *Origins of musical time and expression.* London: Oxford University Press, 1938.

Harman, Alec with Anthony Milner and Wilfrid Mellers. *Man and his music: the story of musical experience in the West.* London: Barrie & Jenkins, 1988.

Harper, Nancy Lee. *Manuel de Falla: his life and music.* Lanham, Maryland; London: The Scarecrow Press, 2005.

Hartmann, Arthur. *'Claude Debussy as I knew him' and other writings of Arthur Hartmann.* Edited by Samuel Hsu, Sidney Grolnic, and Mark Peters. Rochester, New York; Woodbridge: University of Rochester Press, 2003.

Haugen, Einar and Camilla Cai. *Ole Bull: Norway's romantic musician and cosmopolitan patriot.* Madison: The University of Wisconsin Press, 1993.

Headington, Christopher. *The Bodley Head history of Western music.* London: The Bodley Head, 1974.

Heartz, Daniel. *Music in European capitals: the galant style, 1720–1780.* New York; London: W. W. Norton, 2003.

Hedley, Arthur, Editor. *Selected correspondence of Fryderyk Chopin: abridged from Fryderyk Chopin's correspondence.* London: Heinemann, 1962.

Heiles, Anne Mischakoff. *Mischa Mischakoff: journeys of a concertmaster.* Sterling Heights, Michigan: Harmonie Park Press, 2006.

Henderson, Sanya Shoilevska. *Alex North, film composer: a biography, with musical analyses of a Streetcar named desire, Spartacus, The misfits, Under the volcano, and Prizzi's honor.* Jefferson, N.C.; London: McFarland, 2003.

Henschel, George. *Personal recollections of Johannes Brahms: some of his letters to and pages from a journal kept by George Henschel.* Boston: R G. Badger, 1907.

Henze, Hans Werner. *Bohemian fifths: an autobiography.* London: Faber and Faber, 1998.

Henze, Hans Werner. *Music and politics: collected writings 1953–81.* London: Faber and Faber, 1982.

Herbert, May, Translator. *Early letters of Robert Schumann.* London: George Bell and Sons, 1888.

Heyman, Barbara B. *Samuel Barber: the composer and his music.* New York: Oxford University Press, 1992.

Heyworth, Peter. *Otto Klemperer,*

his life and times. Cambridge: Cambridge University Press, 2 Vols. 1983–1996.

Hildebrandt, Dieter. *Pianoforte: a social history of the piano.* London: Hutchinson, 1988.

Hill, Peter. *The Messiaen companion.* London: Faber and Faber, 1995.

Hill, Peter and Nigel Simeone. Messiaen. New Haven Connecticut; London: Yale University Press, 2005.

Hiller, Ferdinand. *Mendelssohn: Letters and recollections.* New York: Vienna House, 1972.

Hines, Robert Stephan. *The orchestral composer's point of view: essays on twentieth-century music by those who wrote it.* Norman: University of Oklahoma Press, 1970.

Ho, Allan B. *Shostakovich reconsidered.* London: Toccata Press, 1998.

Hodeir, André. *Since Debussy: a view of contemporary music.* New York: Da Capo Press, 1975.

Holmes, Edward. *The life of Mozart: including his correspondence.* London: Chapman and Hall, 1845.

Holmes, John L. *Composers on composers.* New York: Greenwood Press, 1990.

Hopkins, Antony. *The concertgoer's companion.* London: J.M. Dent & Sons Ltd., 1984.

Hopkins, Antony. *The seven concertos of Beethoven.* Aldershot: Scolar Press, 1996.

Holt, Richard. *Nicolas Medtner (1879–1951): a tribute to his art and personality.* London: D. Dobson, 1955.

Honegger, Arthur. *I am a composer.*

London: Faber and Faber, 1966.

Hoover, Kathleen and John Cage. *Virgil Thomson: his life and music.* New York; London: T. Yoseloff, 1959.

Horgan, Paul. *Encounters with Stravinsky: a personal record.* London: The Bodley Head, 1972.

Horowitz, Joseph. *Conversations with Arrau.* London: Collins, 1982.

Horowitz, Joseph. Understanding Toscanini. London: Faber and Faber, 1987.

Horwood, Wally. *Adolphe Sax, 1814–1894: his life and legacy.* Bramley: Bramley Books, 1980.

Howie, Crawford. *Anton Bruckner: a documentary biography.* Lewiston, N.Y.; Lampeter: Edwin Mellen Press, 2002.

Hueffer, Francis. *Correspondence of Wagner and Liszt.* New York: Greenwood Press, 2 Vols.1969.

Hughes, Spike. *The Toscanini legacy: a critical study of Arturo Toscanini's performances of Beethoven, Verdi, and other composers.* London: Putnam, 1959.

Hullah, Annette. *Theodor Leschetizky.* London and New York: J. Land & Co., 1906.

Le Huray, Peter and James Day, Editors. *Music and aesthetics in the eighteenth and early-nineteenth centuries.* Cambridge: Cambridge University Press, 1988.

D' Indy, Vincent. *César Franck.* New York: Dover Publications, 1965.

Jacobs, Arthur. *Arthur Sullivan: A Victorian musician.* Aldershot: Scolar Press, 1992.

Jahn, Otto. *Life of Mozart.* London: Novello, Ewer & Co., 1882.

Jefferson, Alan. *Sir Thomas Beecham: a centenary tribute.* London: World Records Ltd., 1979.

Jezic, Diane. *The musical migration and Ernst Toch.* Ames: Iowa State University Press, 1989.

Johnson, Douglas Porter, Editor. *The Beethoven sketchbooks: history, reconstruction, inventory.* Oxford: Clarendon, 1985.

Johnson, Stephen. *Bruckner remembered.* London: Faber and Faber, 1998.

Jones, David, Wyn. *Beethoven: Pastoral symphony.* Cambridge: Cambridge University Press, 1995.

Jones, David Wyn. *The life of Beethoven.* Cambridge: Cambridge University Press, 1998.

Jones, David Wyn. *The symphony in Beethoven's Vienna.* Cambridge: Cambridge University Press, 2006.

Jones, J. Barrie, Editor. *Gabriel Fauré: a life in letters.* London: Batsford, 1989.

Jones, Peter Ward, Editor and Translator. *The Mendelssohns on honeymoon: the 1837 diary of Felix and Cécile Mendelssohn Bartholdy, together with letters to their families.* Oxford: Clarendon Press, 1997.

Jones, Timothy. *Beethoven, the Moonlight and other sonatas, Op. 27 and Op. 31.* Cambridge; New York, N.Y.: Cambridge University Press, 1999.

Kalischer, A. C., Editor. *Beethoven's letters: a critical edition.* London: J. M. Dent, 1909.

Kárpáti, János. *Bartók's chamber music.* Stuyvesant, New York: Pendragon Press, 1994.

Keefe, Simon P. *The Cambridge companion to the concerto.* Cambridge, New York, N.Y.: Cambridge University Press, 2005.

Keller, Hans. *The great Haydn quartets: their interpretation.* London: J. M. Dent, 1986.

Keller, Hans, Editor. *The memoirs of Carl Flesch.* New York: Macmillan, 1958.

Keller, Hans, and Christopher Wintle. *Beethoven's string quartets in F minor, Op. 95 and C minor, Op. 131: two studies.* Nottingham: Department of Music, University of Nottingham, 1995.

Kelly, Thomas Forrest. *First nights at the opera: five musical premiers.* New Haven: Yale University Press, 2004.

Kennedy, Michael. *Adrian Boult.* London: Hamish Hamilton, 1987.

Kennedy, Michael. *Barbirolli, conductor laureate: the authorised biography.* London: Hart-Davis, MacGibbon, 1973.

Kennedy, Michael, Editor. *The autobiography of Charles Hallé; with correspondence and diaries.* London: Paul Elek, 1972.

Kennedy, Michael. *Hallé tradition: a century of music.* Manchester: Manchester University Press, 1960.

Kennedy, Michael. *The works of Ralph Vaughan Williams.* London: Oxford University Press, 1964.

Kemp, Ian. *Tippett: the composer and his music.* London; New York: Eulenburg Books, 1984.

Kerman, Joseph. *The Beethoven quartets.* London: Oxford University Press, 1967, c1966.

Kerman, Joseph. *Write all these down: essays on music.* Berkeley, California; London: University of California Press, 1994.

Kildea, Paul, Editor. *Britten on music.* Oxford: Oxford University Press, 2003.

Kinderman, William. *Beethoven.* Oxford: Oxford University Press, 1997.

Kinderman, William. *Beethoven's Diabelli variations.* Oxford: Clarendon Press; New York: Oxford University Press, 1987.

Kinderman, William, Editor. *The string quartets of Beethoven.* Urbana, Ilinois: University of Illinois Press, 2005.

King, Alec Hyatt. *Musical pursuits: selected essays.* London: British Library, 1987.

Kirby, F. E. *Music for piano: a short history.* Amadeus Press: Portland, 1995.

Kirkpatrick, John, Editor. *Charles E. Ives: Memos.* New York: W.W. Norton, 1972.

Knapp, Raymond. *Brahms and the challenge of the symphony.* Stuyvesant, N.Y.: Pendragon Press, c.1997.

Knight, Frida. *Cambridge music: from the Middle Ages to modern times.* Cambridge, England.: New York: Oleander Press, 1980.

Knight, Max, Translator. *A confidential matter: the letters of Richard Strauss and Stefan Zweig, 1931–1935.* Berkeley; London: University of California Press, 1977.

Kok, Alexander. *A voice in the dark: the philharmonia years.* Ampleforth: Emerson Edition, 2002.

Kopelson, Kevin. *Beethoven's kiss: pianism, perversion, and the mastery of desire.* Stanford, California: Stanford University Press, 1996.

Kostelanetz, Richard, Editor. *Aaron Copland: a reader; selected writings 1923–1972.* New York; London: Routledge, 2003.

Kostelanetz, Richard. *Conversing with Cage.* New York; London: Routledge, 2003.

Kostelanetz, Richard. *On innovative musicians.* New York: Limelight Editions, 1989.

Kostelanetz, Richard, Editor. *Virgil Thomson: a reader ; selected writings, 1924–1984.* New York; London: Routledge, 2002.

Kowalke, Kim H. *Kurt Weill in Europe.* Ann Arbor, Michigan: UMI Research Press, 1979.

Krehbiel, Henry Edward. *The pianoforte and its music.* New York: Cooper Square Publishers, 1971.

Kruseman, Philip, Editor. *Beethoven's own words.* London: Hinrichsen Edition, 1948.

Kurtz, Michael. *Stockhausen: a biography.* London: Faber and Faber, 1992.

Lam, Basil. *Beethoven string quartets.* Seattle: University of Washington Press, 1975.

Lambert, Constant. *Music ho!: a study of music in decline.* London: Faber and Faber, Ltd. 1934.

Landon, H. C. Robbins. *Beethoven: a documentary study.* London: Thames and Hudson, 1970.

Landon, H. C. Robbins. *Beethoven:*

his life, work and world. London: Thames and Hudson, 1992.

Landon, H. C. Robbins. *Essays on the Viennese classical style: Gluck, Haydn, Mozart, Beethoven.* London: Barrie & Rockliff The Cresset Press, 1970.

Landon, H. C. Robbins. *Haydn: chronicle and works/Haydn, the late years, 1801–1809.* Bloomington: Indiana University Press, 1977.

Landon, H. C. Robbins. *Haydn: his life and music.* London: Thames and Hudson, 1988.

Landon, H. C. Robbins. *Haydn in England, 1791–1795.* London: Thames and Hudson, 1976.

Landon, H. C. Robbins. *Haydn: the years of 'The creation', 1796–800.* London: Thames and Hudson, 1977.

Landon, H. C. Robbins. *Mozart: the golden years, 1781–1791.* New York: Schirmer Books, 1989.

Landon, H. C. Robbins. *1791, Mozart's last year.* London: Thames and Hudson, 1988.

Landon, H. C. Robbins *The collected correspondence and London notebooks of Joseph Haydn.* London: Barrie and Rockliff, 1959.

Landon, H. C. Robbins: Editor. *The Mozart companion. London: Faber, 1956.*

Landowska, Wanda. *Music of the past.* London: Geoffrey Bles, 1926.

Lang, Paul Henry. *Musicology and performance.* New Haven: Yale University Press, 1997.

Lang, Paul Henry. *The creative world of Beethoven.* New York: W. W. Norton 1971.

Laurence, Dan H., Editor. *Shaw's music: the complete musical criticism in three volumes.* London: Max Reinhardt, the Bodley Head, 1981.

Lawford-Hinrichsen, Irene. *Music publishing and patronage: C. F. Peters, 1800 to the Holocaust.* Kenton: Edition Press, 2000.

Layton, Robert, Editor. *A guide to the concerto.* Oxford: Oxford University Press, 1996.

Layton, Robert, Editor. *A guide to the symphony.* Oxford: Oxford University Press, 1995.

Lebrecht, Norman. *The maestro myth: great conductors in pursuit of power.* London: Simon & Schuster, 1991.

Lee, Ernest Markham. *The story of the symphony.* London: Scott Publishing Co., 1916.

Leibowitz, Herbert A., Editor. *Musical impressions: selections from Paul Rosenfeld's criticism.* London: G. Allen & Unwin, 1970.

Lenrow, Elbert, Editor and Translator. *The letters of Richard Wagner to Anton Pusinelli.* New York: Vienna House, 1972.

Leonard, Maurice. *Kathleen: the life of Kathleen Ferrier: 1912–1953.* London: Hutchinson, 1988.

Lesure, François and Roger Nichols, Editors. *Debussy, letters.* London: Faber and Faber, 1987.

Letellier, Robert Ignatius, Editor and Translator. *The diaries of Giacomo Meyerbeer.* Madison: Fairleigh Dickinson University Press; London: Associated University Presses, 4 Vols., 1999–2004.

Levas, Santeri. *Sibelius: a personal portrait.* London: J. M. Dent,

1972.

Levy, Alan Howard. *Edward Mac-Dowell, an American master.* Lanham, Md. & London: Scarecrow Press, 1998.

Levy, David Benjamin. *Beethoven: the Ninth Symphony.* New Haven, Connecticut; London: Yale University Press, 2003.

Leyda, Jay and Sergi Bertensson. *The Musorgsky reader: a life of Modeste Petrovich Musorgsky in letters and documents.* New York: W.W. Norton, 1947.

Lewis, Thomas P., Editor. *Raymond Leppard on music: an anthology of critical and personal writings.* White Plains, N.Y.: Pro/Am Music Resources, 1993.

Liébert, Georges. *Nietzsche and music.* Chicago: University of Chicago Press, 2004.

Liszt, Franz. *An artist's journey: lettres d'un bachelier ès musique, 1835–1841.* Chicago: University of Chicago Press, 1989.

Litzmann, Berthold, Editor. *Clara Schumann: an artist's life, based on material found in diaries and letters.* London: Macmillan; Leipzig: Breitkopf & Härtel, 2 Vols. 1913.

Litzmann, Berthold, Editor. *Letters of Clara Schumann and Johannes Brahms, 1853–1896.* New York, Vienna House. 2 Vols. 1971.

Lloyd, Stephen. *William Walton: muse of fire.* Woodbridge, Suffolk: The Boydell Press, 2001.

Locke, Ralph P. and Cyrilla Barr, Editors. *Cultivating music in America: women patrons and activists since 1860.* Berkeley: University of California Press,

1997.

Lockspeiser, Edward. *Debussy: his life and mind.* London: Cassell. 2 Vols. 1962–1965.

Lockspeiser, Edward. *The literary clef: an anthology of letters and writings by French composers.* London: J. Calder. 1958.

Lockwood, Lewis, Editor. *Beethoven essays: studies in honor of Elliot Forbes.* Cambridge, Massachusetts: Harvard University Department of Music: Distributed by Harvard University Press, 1984.

Lockwood, Lewis and Mark Kroll, Editors. *The Beethoven violin sonatas: history, criticism, performance.* Urbana: University of Illinois Press, 2004.

Loft, Abram. *Violin and keyboard: the duo repertoire.* New York: Grossman Publishers. 2 Vols. 1973.

Longyear, Rey Morgan. *Nineteenth-century romanticism in music.* Englewood Cliffs: Prentice-Hall, 1969.

Lowe, C. Egerton. *Beethoven's pianoforte sonatas: hints on their rendering, form, etc., with appendices on definition of sonata, music forms, ornaments, pianoforte pedals, and how to discover keys.* London: Novello, 1929.

Macdonald, Hugh, Editor. *Berlioz: Selected letters.* London: Faber and Faber, 1995.

Macdonald, Malcolm, Editor. *Havergal Brian on music: selections from his journalism: Volume One, British music.* London: Toccata Press, 1986.

MacDonald, Malcolm. *Varèse: astronomer in sound.* London: Kahn & Averill, 2003.

MacDowell, Edward. *Critical and historical essays: lectures delivered at Columbia University.* Edited by W. J. Baltzell. London: Elkin; Boston: A.P. Schmidt, 1912.

MacFarren, Walter. Memories: an autobiography. London: Walter Scott Publishing Co.,1905.

Mackenzie, Alexander Campbell. *A musician's narrative.* London: Cassell and company, Ltd, 1927.

McCarthy, Margaret William, Editor. *More letters of Amy Fay: the American years, 1879–1916.* Detroit: Information Coordinators, 1986.

McClary, Susan. *Feminine endings: music, gender, and sexuality.* Minneapolis: University of Minnesota Press, 1991.

McClatchie, Stephen, Editor and Translator. *The Mahler family letters.* Oxford: Oxford University Press, 2006.

McVeigh, Simon. *Concert life in London from Mozart to Haydn.* Cambridge: Cambridge University Press, 1993.

Mahler, Alma. *Gustav Mahler: memories and letters.* Enlarged edition revised and edited and with and introduction by Donald Mitchell. London: John Murray, 1968.

Mai, François Martin. *Diagnosing genius: the life and death of Beethoven.* Montreal; London: McGill-Queen's University Press, 2007.

Del Mar, Norman. *Orchestral variations: confusion and error in the orchestral repertoire.* London: Eulenburg, 1981.

Del Mar, Norman. *Richard Strauss: a critical commentary on his life and works.* London: Barrie & Jenkins. 3 Vols. 1978.

(La) Mara [pseudonym]. *Letters of Franz Liszt.* London: H. Grevel & Co., 2 Vols. 1894.

Marek, George Richard. *Puccini.* London: Cassell & Co., 1952.

Marek, George Richard. *Toscanini.* London: Vision, 1976.

(De) Marliave, Joseph. *Beethoven's quartets.* New York: Dover Publications (reprint), 1961.

Martin, George Whitney. *Verdi: his music, life and times.* London: Macmillan, 1965.

Martner, Knud, Editor. *Selected letters of Gustav Mahler.* London; Boston: Faber and Faber, 1979.

Martyn, Barrie. *Nicolas Medtner: his life and music.* Aldershot: Scolar Press, 1995.

Martyn, Barrie. *Rachmaninoff: composer, pianist, conductor.* Aldershot: Scolar, 1990.

Massenet, Jules. *My recollections.* Westport, Connecticut: Greenwood Press.1970.

Matheopoulos, Helena. *Maestro: encounters with conductors of today.* London: Hutchinson, 1982.

Matthews, Denis. *Beethoven.* London: J. M. Dent, 1985.

Matthews, Denis. *Beethoven piano sonatas.* London: British Broadcasting Corporation, 1967.

Matthews, Dennis. *In pursuit of music.* London: Victor Gollancz Ltd., 1968.

Matthews, Denis. *Keyboard music.* Newton Abbot: London David & Charles, 1972.

Mellers, Wilfrid Howard. *Caliban reborn: renewal in twentieth-century music.* London: Victor Gol-

309

lancz, 1967.

Mellers, Wilfrid Howard. *The sonata principle (from c. 1750).* London: Rockliff, 1957.

Mendelssohn Bartholdy. *Letters from Italy and Switzerland.* London: Longman, Green, Longman, and Roberts, 1862.

Mendelssohn Bartholdy, Paul. *Letters of Felix Mendelssohn Bartholdy, from 1833 to 1847.* London: Longman, Green, Longman, Roberts, & Green, 1864.

Menuhin, Yehudi and Curtis W. Davis. *The music of man.* London: Macdonald and Jane's, 1979.

Menuhin, Yehudi. *Theme and variations.* London: Heinemann Educational Books Ltd., 1972.

Menuhin, Yehudi. *Unfinished journey.* London: Macdonald and Jane's, 1977.

Messian, Olivier. *Music and color: conversations with Claude Samuel.* Portland, Oregon: Amadeus, 1994.

Miall, Antony. *Musical bumps.* London: J.M. Dent & Sons Ltd, 1981.

Michotte, Edmond. *Richard Wagner's visit to Rossini (Paris 1860): and, An evening at Rossini's in Beau-Sejour (Passy), 1858.* Chicago; London: University of Chicago Press, 1982.

Mies, Paul. *Beethoven's sketches: an analysis of his style based on a study of his sketchbooks.* New York: Johnson Reprint, 1969.

Milhaud, Darius. *My happy life.* London: Boyars, 1995.

Miller, Mina. *The Nielsen companion.* London: Faber and Faber, 1994.

Milsom, David. *Theory and practice in late nineteenth-century violin performance: an examination of style in performance, 1850–1900.* Aldershot: Ashgate, 2003.

Mitchell, Donald, Editor. *Letters from a life: the selected letters and diaries of Benjamin Britten 1913–1976.* London: Faber and Faber. 3 Vols., 1991.

Mitchell, Donald and Hans Keller, Editors. *Music survey: new series 1949–1952.* London: Faber Music in association with Faber & Faber, 1981.

Mitchell, Jon C. *A comprehensive biography of composer Gustav Holst, with correspondence and diary excerpts: including his American years.* Lewiston, New York: Edwin Mellen Press, 2001.

Moldenhauer, Hans. *Anton von Webern: a chronicle of his life and work.* London: Victor Gollancz, 1978.

Monrad-Johansen. Edvard Grieg. New York: Tudor Publishing Co., 1945.

Moore, Gerald. *Am I too loud?: memoirs of an accompanist.* London: Hamish Hamilton, 1962.

Moore, Gerald. *Farewell recital: further memoirs.* Harmondsworth: Penguin Books, 1979.

Moore, Gerald. *Furthermoore: interludes in an accompanist's life.* London: Hamish Hamilton, 1983.

Moore, Jerrold Northrop. *Edward Elgar: a creative life.* Oxford: Oxford University Press, 1984.

Moore, Jerrold Northrop. *Elgar, Edward. The windflower letters: correspondence with Alice Caroline Stuart Wortley and her family.* Oxford: Clarendon Press; New York: Oxford University Press, 1989.

Moore, Jerrold Northrop. *Elgar, Edward. Edward Elgar: letters of a lifetime.* Oxford: Clarendon Press; New York: Oxford University Press, 1990.

Moore, Jerrold Northrop. *Elgar, Edward. Elgar and his publishers: letters of a creative life.* Oxford: Clarendon, 1987.

Moreux, Serge. *Béla Bartók.* London: Harvill Press, 1953.

Morgan, Kenneth. *Fritz Reiner, maestro and martinet.* Urbana: University of Illinois Press, 2005.

Cone, Edward T., Editor. *Music, a view from Delft: selected essays.* Chicago: University of Chicago Press, 1989.

Morgan, Robert P. *Twentieth-century music: a history of musical style in modern Europe and America.* New York: Norton, 1991.

Morgenstern, Sam., Editor. *Composers on music: an anthology of composers' writings.* London: Faber & Faber, 1956.

Morrow, Mary Sue. *Concert life in Haydn's Vienna: aspects of a developing musical and social institution.* Stuyvesant, New York: Pendragon Press, 1989.

Moscheles, Felix, Editor and Translator. *Letters from Felix Mendelssohn-Bartholdy to Ignaz and Charlotte Moscheles.* London: Trübner and Co., 1888.

Mudge, Richard B., Translator. *Glinka, Mikhail Ivanovich: Memoirs.* Norman: University of Oklahoma Press, 1963.

Munch, Charles. *I am a conductor.* New York: Oxford University Press, 1955.

Mundy, Simon. *Bernard Haitink: a working life.* London: Robson Books, 1987.

Musgrave, Michael. *The musical life of the Crystal Palace.* Cambridge: Cambridge University Press, 1995.

Music & Letters. *Beethoven: special number.* London: Music & Letters, 1927.

Musical Times. *Special Issue.* John A. Fuller-Maitland London: Vol. VIII, No. 2, 1927.

Myers, Rollo H., Editor. *Twentieth-century music.* London: Calder and Boyars, 1960.

National Gallery (Great Britain). *Music performed at the National Gallery concerts, 10th October 1939 to 10th April 1946.* London: Privately printed, 1948.

Nattiez, Jean-Jacques, Editor. *Orientations: collected writings – Pierre Boulez.* London: Faber and Faber, 1986.

Nauhaus, Gerd, Editor. *The marriage diaries of Robert & Clara Schumann.* London: Robson Books, 1994.

Nectoux, Jean Michel. *Gabriel Fauré: a musical life.* Translated by Roger Nichols. Cambridge: Cambridge University Press, 1991.

Nettl, Paul. *Beethoven handbook.* Westport, Connecticut: Greenwood Press, 1975.

Neumayr, Anton. *Music and medicine.* Bloomington, Illinois: Medi-Ed Press, 1994–1997

Newbould, Brian. *Schubert and the symphony: a new perspective.* Surbiton: Toccata Press, 1992.

Newlin, Dika. *Schoenberg remembered: diaries and recollections (1938–76).* New York: Pendragon Press, 1980.

Newman, Ernest. *From the world of music: essays from 'The Sunday Times'.* London: J. Calder, 1956.

Newman, Ernest. Hugo Wolf. New York: Dover Publications, 1966.

Newman, Ernest, Annotated and Translated. *Memoirs of Hector Berlioz from 1803 to 1865, comprising his travels in Germany, Italy, Russia, and England.* New York: Knopf, 1932.

Newman, Ernest. *More essays from the world of music: essays from the 'Sunday Times'.* London: John Calder, 1958.

Newman, Ernest. *Musical studies.* London; New York: John Lane, 1910.

Newman, Ernest. *Testament of music: essays and papers.* London: Putnam, 1962.

Newman, Richard. *Alma Rosé: Vienna to Auschwitz.* Portland, Oregon: Amadeus Press, 2000.

Newman, William S. *The sonata in the classic era.* Chapel Hill: University of North Carolina Press 1963.

Newman, William S. *The sonata in the Classic era.* New York; London: W.W. Norton, 1983.

Newmarch, Rosa Harriet. *Henry J. Wood.* London & New York: John Lane, 1904.

Nicholas, Jeremy. *Godowsky: the pianists' pianist; a biography of Leopold Godowsky.* Hexham: Appian Publications & Recordings, 1989.

Nichols, Roger. *Debussy remembered.* London: Faber and Faber, 1992.

Nichols, Roger. *Mendelssohn remembered.* London: Faber and Faber, 1997.

Nichols, Roger. *Ravel remembered.* London: Faber and Faber, 1987.

Niecks, Frederick. *Robert Schumann.* London: J. M. Dent, 1925.

Nielsen, Carl. *Living music.* Copenhagen, Wilhelm Hansen, 1968.

Nielsen, Carl. *My childhood.* Copenhagen, Wilhelm Hansen, 1972.

Nikolska, Irina. *Conversations with Witold Lutoslawski, (1987–92).* Stockholm: Melos, 1994.

Nohl, Ludwig. *Beethoven depicted by his contemporaries.* London: Reeves, 1880.

De Nora, Tia. *Beethoven and the construction of genius: musical politics in Vienna, 1792–1803.* Berkeley: University of California Press, 1997.

Norton, Spencer, Editor and Translator. *Music in my time: the memoirs of Alfredo Casella.* Norman: University of Oklahoma Press, 1955.

Nottebohm, Gustav. *Two Beethoven sketchbooks: a description with musical extracts.* London: Gollancz, 1979.

Oakeley, Edward Murray. *The life of Sir Herbert Stanley Oakeley.* London: George Allen, 1904.

Lucas, Brenda and Michael Kerr. *Virtuoso: the story of John Ogdon.* London: H. Hamilton, 1981.

Oliver, Michael, Editor. *Settling the score: a journey through the music of the twentieth century.* London: Faber and Faber, 1999.

Olleson, Philip. *Samuel Wesley: the man and his music.* Woodbridge: Boydell Press, 2003.

Olleson, Philip, Editor. *The letters of Samuel Wesley: professional and social correspondence,*

1797–1837. Oxford; New York: Oxford University Press, 2001.

Olmstead, Andrea. *Conversations with Roger Sessions.* Boston: Northeastern University Press, 1987.

Orenstein, Arbie, Editor. *A Ravel reader: correspondence, articles, interviews.* New York: Columbia University Press, 1990.

Orenstein, Arbie. *Ravel: man and musician.* New York: Columbia University Press, 1975.

Orledge, Robert. *Charles Koechlin (1867–1950): his life and works.* New York: Harwood Academic Publishers, 1989.

Orledge, Robert. *Gabriel Fauré.* London: Eulenburg Books, 1979.

Orledge, Robert. *Satie remembered.* London: Faber and Faber, 1995.

Orledge, Robert. *Satie the composer.* Cambridge: Cambridge University Press, 1990.

Orlova, Alexandra. *Glinka's life in music: a chronicle.* Ann Arbor: UMI Research Press, 1988.

Orlova, Alexandra. *Musorgsky's days and works: a biography in documents.* Ann Arbor: UMI Research Press, 1983.

Orlova, Alexandra. *Tchaikovsky: a self-portrait.* Oxford: Oxford University Press, 1990.

Osborne, Charles, Editor and Translator. *Letters of Giuseppe Verdi.* London: Victor Gollancz, 1971.

Osmond-Smith David, Editor and Translator. *Luciano Berio: Two interviews with Rossana Dalmonte and Bálint András Varga.* New York; London: Boyars, 1985.

Ouellette, Fernand. *Edgard Varèse.* London: Calder & Boyars, 1973.

Paderewski, Ignacy Jan and Mary Lawton. *The Paderewski memoirs.* London: Collins, 1939.

Page, Tim: Editor. *The Glenn Gould reader.* London: Faber and Faber, 1987.

Page, Tim. *Music from the road: views and reviews, 1978–1992.* New York; Oxford: Oxford University Press, 1992.

Page, Tim and Vanessa Weeks, Editors. *Selected letters of Virgil Thomson.* New York: Summit Books, 1988.

Page, Tim. *Tim Page on music: views and reviews.* Portland, Oregon: Amadeus Press, 2002.

Palmer, Christopher. *Herbert Howells, (1892–1983): a celebration.* London: Thames, 1996.

Palmer, Christopher, Editor. *Sergei Prokofiev: Soviet diary 1927 and other writings.* London: Faber and Faber, 1991.

Palmer, Fiona M. *Domenico Dragonetti in England (1794–1846): the career of a double bass virtuoso.* Oxford: Clarendon, 1997.

Palmieri, Robert, Editor. *Encyclopedia of the piano.* New York: Garland, 1996.

Panufnik, Andrzej. *Composing myself.* London: Methuen, 1987.

Parsons, James, Editor. *The Cambridge companion to the Lied.* Cambridge: Cambridge University Press, 2004.

Paynter, John, Editor. *Between old worlds and new: occasional writings on music by Wilfrid Mellers.* London: Cygnus Arts, 1997.

Pestelli, Giorgio. *The age of Mozart and Beethoven.* Cambridge: Cambridge University Press, 1984.

Peyser, Joan. *Bernstein: a biography:*

revised & updated. New York: Billboard Books, 1998.

Phillips-Matz, Mary Jane. *Verdi: a biography.* Oxford: Oxford University Press, 1993.

Piggott, Patrick. *The life and music of John Field, 1782–1837: creator of the nocturne.* London: Faber and Faber, 1973.

Plantinga, Leon. *Beethoven's concertos: history, style, performance.* New York: Norton, 1999.

Plantinga, Leon. *Clementi: his life and music.* London: Oxford University Press, 1977.

Plantinga, Leon. *Romantic music: a history of musical style in nineteenth-century Europe.* New York; London: Norton, 1984.

Plaskin, Glenn. *Horowitz: a biography of Vladimir Horowitz.* London: Macdonald, 1983.

Pleasants, Henry, Editor and Translator. *Hanslick, Eduard: Music criticisms, 1846–99.* Baltimore: Penguin Books, 1963.

Pleasants, Henry, Editor and Translator. *Hanslick's music criticisms.* New York: Dover Publications, 1988.

Pleasants, Henry, Editor and Translator. *The music criticism of Hugo Wolf.* New York: Holmes & Meier Publishers, 1978.

Pleasants, Henry, Editor and Translator. *The musical journeys of Louis Spohr.* Norman: University of Oklahoma Press, 1961.

Pollack, Howard. *Aaron Copland: the life and work of an uncommon man.* New York: Henry Holt, 1999.

Poulenc, Francis. *My friends and myself.* London: Dennis Dobson, 1978.

Powell, Richard, Mrs. *Edward Elgar: memories of a variation.* Aldershot, Hants, England: Scolar Press; Brookfield, Vermont, USA: Ashgate Publishing. Co., 1994.

Poznansky, Alexander, Editor. *Tchaikovsky through others' eyes.* Bloomington: Indiana University Press, 1999.

Praeger, Ferdinand. *Wagner as I knew him.* London; New York: Longmans, Green, 1892.

Previn, Andre. *Antony Hopkins. Music face to face.* London, Hamish Hamilton, 1971.

Prieberg, Fred K. *Trial of strength: Wilhelm Furtwängler and the Third Reich.* London: Quartet, 1991.

Procter-Gregg, Humphrey. *Beecham remembered.* London: Duckworth, 1976.

Prokofiev, Sergey. *Prokofiev by Prokofiev: a composer's memoir.* London: Macdonald and Jane's, 1979.

Rachmaninoff, Sergei. *Rachmaninoff's recollections told to Oskar von Riesemann.* London: George Allen & Unwin, 1934.

Radcliffe, Philip. *Beethoven's string quartets.* Cambridge: Cambridge University Press, 1978.

Radcliffe, Philip. *Piano Music in: The Age of Beethoven, The New Oxford History of Music, Vol. VIII.* Gerald Abraham, (Editor), 1988, p. 340.

Ratner, Leonard G. *Romantic music: sound and syntax.* New York: Schirmer Books, 1992.

Raynor, Henry. *A social history of music: from the middle ages to Beethoven.* London: Barrie & Jenkins, 1972.

Rees, Brian. *Camille Saint-Saëns: a*

life. London: Chatto & Windus, 1999.

Reich, Willi, Editor. *Anton Webern: The path to the new music.* London; Bryn Mawr: Theodore Presser in association with Universal Edition, 1963.

Reid, Charles. *John Barbirolli: a biography.* London, Hamish Hamilton, 1971.

Reid, Charles. *Malcolm Sargent: a biography.* London: Hamilton, 1968.

Rennert, Jonathan. *William Crotch (1775–1847): composer, artist, teacher.* Lavenham: Terence Dalton, 1975.

Rice, John A. *Antonio Salieri and Viennese Opera.* Chicago, Illinois: University of Chicago Press, 1998.

Rice, John A. *Empress Marie Therese and music at the Viennese court, 1792–1807.* Cambridge: Cambridge University Press, 2003.

Richards, Fiona. *The Music of John Ireland.* Aldershot: Ashgate, 2000.

Rigby, Charles. *Sir Charles Hallé: a portrait for today.* Manchester: Dolphin Press, 1952.

Ringer, Alexander, Editor. *The early Romantic era: between Revolutions; 1789 and 1848.* Basingstoke: Macmillan, 1990.

Roberts, John P.L. and Ghyslaine Guertin, Editors. *Glenn Gould: Selected letters.* Toronto; Oxford: Oxford University Press, 1992.

Robertson, Alec. *More than music.* London: Collins, 1961.

Robinson, Harlow, Editor and Translator. *Selected letters of Sergei Prokofiev.* Boston: Northeastern University Press, 1998.

Robinson, Harlow. *Sergei Prokofiev: a biography.* London: Hale, 1987.

Robinson, Paul A. *Ludwig van Beethoven, Fidelio.* Cambridge: Cambridge University Press, 1996.

Robinson, Suzanne, Editor. *Michael Tippett: music and literature.* Aldershot: Ashgate, 2002.

Rochberg, George. *The aesthetics of survival: a composer's view of twentieth-century music.* Ann Arbor, Michigan: University of Michigan Press, 2004.

Rodmell, Paul. *Charles Villiers Stanford.* Aldershot: Ashgate, 2002.

Roeder, Michael Thomas. *A history of the concerto.* Portland, Oregon: Amadeus Press, 1994.

Rohr, Deborah Adams. *The careers of British musicians, 1750–1850: a profession of artisans.* Cambridge: Cambridge University Press, 2001.

Rolland, Romain. *Goethe and Beethoven.* New York; London: Blom, 1968.

Rolland, Romain. *Beethoven and Handel.* London: Waverley Book Co., 1917.

Rolland, Romain. *Beethoven the creator.* Garden City, New York: Garden City Pub., 1937.

Roscow, Gregory, Editor. *Bliss on music: selected writings of Arthur Bliss, 1920–1975.* Oxford: Oxford University Press, 1991.

Rosen, Charles. *Beethoven's piano sonatas: a short companion.* New Haven, Connecticut: London: Yale University Press, 2002.

Rosen, Charles. *Critical entertainments: music old and new.* Cambridge, Massachusetts; London: Harvard University Press, 2000.

Rosen, Charles. *The classical style: Haydn, Mozart, Beethoven.* London: Faber and Faber, 1976.

Rosen, Charles. *The romantic generation.* Cambridge, Massachusetts: Harvard University Press, 1995.

Rosenthal, Albi. *Obiter scripta: essays, lectures, articles, interviews and reviews on music, and other subjects.* Oxford: Offox Press; Lanham: Scarecrow Press, 2000.

Rostal, Max. *Beethoven: the sonatas for piano and violin; thoughts on their interpretation.* London: Toccata Press, 1985.

Rostropovich, Mstislav and Galina Vishnevskaya. *Russia, music, and liberty.* Portland, Oregan: Amadeus Press, 1995.

Rubinstein, Arthur. *My many years.* London: Jonathan Cape, 1980.

Rubinstein, Arthur. *My young years.* London: Jonathan Cape, 1973.

Rumph, Stephen C. *Beethoven after Napoleon: political romanticism in the late works.* Berkeley; London: University of California Press, 2004.

Rye, Matthew Rye. *Notes to the BBC Radio Three Beethoven Experience, Friday 10 June 2005,* www.bbc.co.uk/radio3/Beethoven.

Sachs, Harvey. *Toscanini.* London: Weidenfeld and Nicholson, 1978.

Sachs, Joel. *Kapellmeister Hummel in England and France.* Detroit: Information Coordinators, 1977.

Saffle, Michael, Editor. *Liszt and his world: proceedings of the International Liszt Conference held at Virginia Polytechnic Institute and State University, 20–23 May 1993.* Stuyvesant, New York: Pendragon Press, 1998.

Safránek, Milos. *Bohuslav Martinu, his life and works.* London: Allan Wingate, 1962.

Saint-Saëns, Camille. *Outspoken essays on music.* Westport, Connecticut: Greenwood Press, 1970.

Saussine, Renée de. *Paganini.* Westport, Connecticut: Greenwood Press, 1976.

Sayers, W. C. Berwick. *Samuel Coleridge-Taylor, musician: his life and letters.* London; New York: Cassell and Co., 1915.

Schaarwächter, Jürgen. *HB: aspects of Havergal Brian.* Aldershot: Ashgate, 1997.

Schafer, R. Murray. *E.T.A. Hoffmann and music.* Toronto: University of Toronto Press, 1975.

Schafer, R. Murray, Editor. *Ezra Pound and music: the complete criticism.* London: Faber and Faber, 1978.

Schat, Peter. *The tone clock.* Chur, Switzerland; Langhorne, Pa.: Harwood Academic Publishers, 1993.

Schenk, Erich. *Mozart and his times.* Edited and Translated by Richard and Clara Winstin. London: Secker & Warburg, 1960.

Schindler, Anton Felix. *Beethoven as I knew him.* Edited by Donald W. MacArdle and Translated by Constance S. Jolly from the German edition of 1860 London: Faber and Faber, 1966.

Schlosser, Johann. *Beethoven: the first biography, 1827.* Edited by Barry Cooper. Portland,

Oregon: Amadeus Press, 1996.

Schnabel, Artur. *My life and music.* London: Longmans, 1961.

Schnittke, Alfred. *A Schnittke reader.* Bloomington: Indiana University Press, 2002.

Scholes, Percy Alfred. *Crotchets: a few short musical notes.* London: John Lane, 1924.

Schonberg, Harold C. *The great pianists.* London: Victor Gollancz, 1964.

Schrade, Leo. *Beethoven in France: the growth of an idea.* New Haven; London: Yale University Press, H. Milford, Oxford University Press, 1942.

Schrade, Leo. *Tragedy in the art of music.* Cambridge, Massachusetts: Harvard University Press, 1964.

Schuh, Willi. *Richard Strauss: a chronicle of the early years 1864–1898.* Cambridge: Cambridge University Press, 1982.

Schuh, Willi, Editor. *Richard Strauss: Recollections and reflections.* London; New York: Boosey & Hawkes, 1953.

Schuller, Gunther. *Musings: the musical worlds of Gunther Schuller.* New York: Oxford University Press, 1986.

Schumann, Robert. *Music and musicians: essays and criticisms.* London: William Reeves, 1877.

Schuttenhelm, Editor. *Selected letters of Michael Tippett.* London: Faber and Faber, 2005.

Schwartz, Elliott. *Music since 1945: issues, materials, and literature.* New York: Schirmer Books, 1993.

Scott, Marion M. *Beethoven: (The master musicians).* London: Dent, 1940.

Scott-Sutherland, Colin. *Arnold Bax.* London: J. M. Dent, 1973.

Searle, Muriel V. *John Ireland: the man and his music.* Tunbridge Wells: Midas Books, 1979.

Secrest, Meryle. *Leonard Bernstein: a life.* London: Bloomsbury, 1995.

Seeger, Charles. *Studies in musicology II, 1929–1979.* Edited by Anne M. Pescatello. Berkeley; London: University of California Press, 1994.

Selden-Goth, Gisela, Editor. *Felix Mendelssohn: letters.* London: Paul Elek Publishers Ltd, 1946.

Senner, Wayne M., Robin Wallace and William Meredith, Editors. *The critical reception of Beethoven's compositions by his German contemporaries.* Lincoln: University of Nebraska Press, in association with the American Beethoven Society and the Ira F. Brilliant Center for Beethoven Studies, San José State University, 1999.

Seroff, Victor I. *Rachmaninoff.* London: Cassell & Company, 1951.

Sessions, Roger. *Questions about music.* Cambridge, Massachusetts: Harvard University Press, 1970.

Sessions, Roger. *The musical experience of composer, performer, listener.* New York: Atheneum, 1966, 1950.

Seyfried, Ignaz von. *Louis van Beethoven's Studies in thorough-bass, counterpoint and the art of scientific composition.* Leipzig; New-York: Schuberth and Company, 1853.

Sharma, Bhesham R. *Music and culture in the age of mechanical reproduction.* New York: Peter Lang, 2000.

Shaw, Bernard. *How to become a musical critic.* London: R. Hart Davis, 1960.

Shaw, Bernard. *London music in 1888–89 as heard by Corno di Bassetto (later known as Bernard Shaw): with some further autobiographical particulars.* London: Constable and Company, 1937.

Shaw, Bernard. *Music in London, 1890–1894.* London: Constable and Company Limited, 3 Vols., 1932.

Shedlock, John South. *Beethoven's pianoforte sonatas: the origin and respective values of various readings.* London: Augener Ltd., 1918.

Shedlock, John South. *The pianoforte sonata: its origin and development.* London: Methuen, 1895.

Shepherd, Arthur. *The string quartets of Ludwig van Beethoven.* Cleveland: H. Carr, The Printing Press, 1935.

Sheppard, Leslie and Herbert R. Axelrod. *Paganini: containing a portfolio of drawings by Vido Polikarpus.* Neptune City, New Jersey: Paganiniana Publications, 1979.

Short, Michael. *Gustav Holst: the man and his music.* Oxford: Oxford University Press, 1990.

Shostakovich, Dmitry. *Dmitry Shostakovich: about himself and his times.* Moscow: Progress Publishers, 1981.

Simpson, John Palgrave. *Carl Maria von Weber: the life of an artist, from the German of his son Baron, Max Maria von Weber.* London: Chapman and Hall, 1865.

Simpson, Robert. *Beethoven symphonies.* London: British Broadcasting Corporation, 1970.

Sipe, Thomas. *Beethoven: Eroica symphony.* Cambridge: Cambridge University Press, 1998.

Sitwell, Sacheverell. *Mozart.* Edinburgh: Peter Davies Limited, 1932.

Skelton, Geoffrey. *Paul Hindemith: the man behind the music; a biography.* London: Victor Gollancz, 1975.

Smallman, Basil. *The piano trio: its history, technique, and repertoire.* Oxford: Clarendon Press; Oxford; New York: Oxford University Press, 1990.

Smidak, Emil. *Isaak-Ignaz Moscheles: the life of the composer and his encounters with Beethoven, Liszt, Chopin, and Mendelssohn.* Aldershot, Hampshire, England: Scolar Press; Brookfield, Vermont, USA: Gower Publishing Co., 1989.

Smith, Barry. *Peter Warlock: the life of Philip Heseltine.* Oxford: Oxford University Press, 1994.

Smith, Joan Allen. *Schoenberg and his circle: a Viennese portrait.* New York: Schirmer Books, London: Collier Macmillan, 1986.

Smith, Richard Langham, Editor. *Debussy on music: the critical writings of the great French composer Claude Debussy.* London: Secker & Warburg, 1977.

Smith, Ronald. *Alkan.* London: Kahn and Averill, 1976.

Snowman, Daniel. *The Amadeus Quartet: the men and the music.* London: Robson Books, 1981.

Solomon, Maynard. *Beethoven.* New

York: Schirmer, 1977.

Solomon, Maynard. *Beethoven essays.* Cambridge, Massachusetts; London: Harvard University Press, 1988.

Solomon, Maynard. *Late Beethoven: music, thought, imagination.* Berkeley; London: University of California Press, 2003.

Solomon, Maynard. *Mozart: a life.* London: Hutchinson, 1995.

Sonneck, Oscar George Theodore. *Beethoven: impressions of contemporaries.* London: Oxford University Press, 1927.

Spalding, Albert. *Rise to follow: an autobiography.* London: Frederick Muller Ltd., 1946.

Spohr, Louis. *Louis Spohr's autobiography.* London: Longman, Green, Longman, Roberts, & Green, 1865.

Stafford, William. *Mozart myths: a critical reassessment.* Stanford, California: Stanford University Press, 1991.

Stanford, Charles Villiers. *Interludes: records and reflections.* London: John Murray, 1922.

Stanley, Glenn, Editor. *The Cambridge companion to Beethoven.* Cambridge; New York: Cambridge University Press, 2000

Stedman, Preston. *The symphony.* Englewood Cliffs, New Jersey; London: Prentice-Hall, 1979.

Stedron, Bohumír, Editor and Translator. *Leos Janácek: letters and reminiscences.* Prague: Artia, 1955.

Stein, Erwin, Editor. *Arnold Schoenberg: letters.* London: Faber and Faber, 1964.

Stein, Erwin. *Orpheus in new guises.* London: Rockliff, 1953.

Stein, Jack Madison. *Poem and music in the German lied from Gluck to Hugo Wolf.* Cambridge, Massachusetts: Harvard University Press, 1971.

Stein, Leonard, Editor. *Style and idea: selected writings of Arnold Schoenberg.* London: Faber and Faber, 1975.

Steinberg, Michael P. *Listening to reason: culture, subjectivity, and nineteenth-century music.* Princeton, New Jersey: Princeton University Press, 2004.

Steinberg, Michael. *The concerto: a listener's guide.* New York: Oxford University Press, 1998.

Steinberg, Michael. *The symphony: a listener's guide.* Oxford; New York: Oxford University Press, 1995.

Sternfeld, Frederick William. *Goethe and music: a list of parodies and Goethe's relationship to music; a list of references.* New York: Da Capo Press, 1979.

Stivender, David. *Mascagni: an autobiography compiled, edited and translated from original sources.* New York: Pro/Am Music Resources; London: Kahn & Averill, 1988.

Stone, Else and Kurt Stone, Editors. *The writings of Elliott Carter: an American composer looks at modern music.* Bloomington: Indiana University Press, 1977.

Stowell, Robin. *Beethoven: violin concerto.* Cambridge: Cambridge University Press, 1998.

Stowell, Robin: Editor. *The Cambridge companion to the cello.* Cambridge: Cambridge University Press, 1999.

Stowell, Robin: Editor. *The Cambridge companion to the string quartet.* Cambridge: Cambridge

University Press, 2003.

Stratton, Stephen Samuel. *Mendelssohn.* London: J.M. Dent & Co.; New York: E.P. Dutton & Co., 1901.

Straus, Joseph N. *Remaking the past: musical modernism and the influence of the tonal tradition.* Cambridge, Massachusetts: Harvard University Press, 1990.

Stravinsky, Igor. *An autobiography.* London: Calder and Boyars, 1975.

Stravinsky, Igor. *Themes and conclusions.* London: Faber and Faber, 1972.

Stravinsky, Igor and Robert Craft. *Conversations with Igor Stravinsky.* London: Faber and Faber, 1959.

Stravinsky, Igor and Robert Craft. *Dialogues and a diary.* London: Faber and Faber 1968.

Stravinsky, Igor and Robert Craft. *Memories and commentaries.* London: Faber and Faber, 2002.

Strunk, Oliver. *Source readings in music history, 4: The Classic era.* London: Faber and Faber 1981.

Sullivan, Blair, Editor. *The echo of music: essays in honor of Marie Louise Göllner.* Warren, Michigan: Harmonie Park Press, 2004.

Sullivan, Jack, Editor. *Words on music: from Addison to Barzun.* Athens: Ohio University Press, 1990.

Symonette, Lys and Kim H. Kowalke, Editors and Translators. *Speak low (when you speak love): the letters of Kurt Weill and Lotte Lenya.* London: Hamish Hamilton, 1996.

Swalin, Benjamin F. *The violin concerto: a study in German romanticism.* New York, Da Capo

Press, 1973.

Szigeti, Joseph. *With strings attached: reminiscences and reflections.* London: Cassell & Co. Ltd, 1949.

Tanner, Michael, Editor. *Notebooks, 1924–1954: Wilhelm Furtwängler.* London: Quartet Books, 1989.

Taylor, Robert, Editor. *Furtwängler on music: essays and addresses.* Aldershot: Scolar, 1991.

Taylor, Ronald. *Kurt Weill: composer in a divided world.* London: Simon & Schuster, 1991.

Tchaikovsky, Peter Ilich. *Letters to his family: an autobiography.* Translated by Galina von Meck. London: Dennis Dobson, 1981.

Tertis, Lionel. *My viola and I: a complete autobiography; with, 'Beauty of tone in string playing', and other essays.* London: Paul Elek, 1974.

Thayer, Alexander Wheelock. *Salieri: rival of Mozart.* Edited by Theodore Albrecht. Kansas City, Missouri: Philharmonia of Greater Kansas City, 1989.

Thomas, Michael Tilson. *Viva voce: conversations with Edward Seckerson.* London: Faber and Faber 1994.

Thomson, Andrew. *Vincent d'Indy and his world.* Oxford: Clarendon Press, 1996.

Thomson, Virgil. *The musical scene.* New York: Greenwood Press, 1968.

Thomson, Virgil. *Virgil Thomson.* London: Weidenfeld & Nicolson, 1967.

Tillard, Françoise. *Fanny Mendelssohn.* Amadeus Press: Portland, 1996.

Tilmouth, Michael, Editor. *Donald Francis Tovey: The classics of music: talks, essays, and other writings previously uncollected.* Oxford: Oxford University Press, 2001

Tippett, Michael. *Moving into Aquarius.* London: Routledge and Kegan Paul, 1959.

Tippett, Michael. *Those twentieth century blues: an autobiography.* London: Hutchinson, 1991.

Todd, R. Larry, Editor. *Nineteenth-century piano music.* New York; London: Routledge, 2004.

Todd, R. Larry, Editor. *Schumann and his world.* Princeton: Princeton University Press, 1994.

Tommasini, Anthony. *Virgil Thomson: composer on the aisle.* New York: W.W. Norton, 1997.

Tortelier, Paul. *A self-portrait: in conversation with David Blum.* London: Heinemann, 1984.

Tovey, Donald Francis. *A Companion to Beethoven's Pianoforte Sonatas.* Revised by Barry Cooper. London: The Associated Board, [1931], 1998.

Tovey, Donald Francis. *Beethoven.* London: Oxford University Press, 1944.

Tovey, Donald Francis. *Essays and lectures on music.* London: Oxford University Press, 1949.

Tovey, Donald Francis. *Essays in musical analysis.* London: Oxford University Press, H. Milford, 7 Vols., 1935–41.

Tovey, Donald Francis. *The forms of music: musical articles from The Encyclopaedia Britannica.* London: Oxford University Press, 1944.

Toye, Francis. *Giuseppe Verdi: his life and works.* London: William Heinemann Ltd., 1931.

Truscott, Harold. *Beethoven's late string quartets.* London: Dobson, 1968.

Tyler, William R. *The letters of Franz Liszt to Olga von Meyendorff, 1871–1886, in the Mildred Bliss Collection at Dumbarton Oaks.* Translated by William R. Tyler. Washington: Dumbarton Oaks, Trustees for Harvard University; Cambridge, Massachusetts: distributed by Harvard University Press, 1979.

Tyrrell, John. *Janácek: years of a life. Vol. 1, (1854–1914) The lonely blackbird.* London: Faber and Faber, 2006.

Tyrrell, John, Editor and Translator. *My life with Janácek: the memoirs of Zdenka Janácková.* London: Faber and Faber, 1998.

Tyson, Alan, Editor. *Beethoven studies 2.* Cambridge: Cambridge University Press, 1977.

Tyson, Alan, Editor. *Beethoven studies 3.* Cambridge: Cambridge University Press, 1982.

Tyson, Alan. *Mozart: studies of the autograph scores.* Cambridge, Massachusetts; London: Harvard University Press, 1987.

Tyson, Alan. *The authentic English editions of Beethoven.* London: Faber and Faber, 1963.

Underwood, J. A., Editor. *Gabriel Fauré: his life through his letters.* London: Marion Boyars, 1984.

Vechten, Carl van, Editor. *Nikolay, Rimsky-Korsakov: My musical life.* London: Martin Secker & Warburg Ltd., 1942.

Vinton, John. *Essays after a dictionary: music and culture at the close of Western civilization.* Lewisburg: Bucknell University

Press, 1977.

Volkov, Solomon, Editor. *Testimony: the memoirs of Dmitri Shostakovich.* London: Faber and Faber, 1981.

Volta, Ornella, Editor. *A mammal's notebook: collected writings of Erik Satie.* London: Atlas Press, 1996.

Wagner, Richard. Beethoven: *With [a] supplement from the philosophical works of A. Schopenhauer.* Translated by E. Dannreuther. London: Reeves, 1893.

Wagner, Richard. *My life.* London: Constable and Company Ltd., 1911.

Walden, Valerie. *One hundred years of violoncello: a history of technique and performance practice, 1740–1840.* Cambridge: Cambridge University Press, 1998.

Walker, Alan. *Franz Liszt. Volume 1, The virtuoso years: 1811–1847.* New York: Alfred A. Knopf, 1983.

Walker, Alan. *Franz Liszt. Volume 2, The Weimar years: 1848–1861.* London: Faber and Faber, 1989.

Walker, Alan. *Franz Liszt. Volume 3, The final years, 1861–1886.* London: Faber and Faber, 1997.

Walker, Bettina. *My musical experiences.* London: Richard Bentley and Son, 1890.

Walker, Ernest. *Free thought and the musician, and other essays.* London; New York: Oxford University Press, 1946.

Walker, Frank. *Hugo Wolf: a biography.* London: J. M. Dent, 1951.

Walker, Frank. *The man Verdi.* London: Dent, 1962.

Wallace, Grace, *[Lady Wallace].*

Beethoven's letters (1790–1826): from the collection of Dr. Ludwig Nohl. Also his letters to the Archduke Rudolph, Cardinal-Archbishop of Olmutz, K.W., from the collection of Dr. Ludwig Ritter Von Kòlchel. London: Longmans, Green, 2 Vols., 1866.

Wallace, Robin. *Beethoven's critics: aesthetic dilemmas and resolutions during the composer's lifetime.* Cambridge; New York: Cambridge University Press, 1986.

Walter, Bruno. *Theme and variations: an autobiography.* London: H. Hamilton, 1948.

Warrack, John Hamilton. *Writings on music.* Cambridge: Cambridge University Press, 1981.

Wasielewski, Wilhelm Joseph von. *Life of Robert Schumann: with letters, 1833–1852.* London: William Reeves, 1878.

Watkins, Glenn. *Proof through the night: music and the Great War.* Berkeley: University of California Press, 2003.

Watkins, Glenn. *Pyramids at the Louvre: music, culture, and collage from Stravinsky to the postmodernists.* Cambridge, Massachusetts; London: Belknap Press of Harvard University Press, 1994.

Watkins, Glenn. *Soundings: music in the twentieth century.* New York: Schirmer Books London: Collier Macmillan, 1988.

Watson, Derek. *Liszt.* London: J. M. Dent, 1989.

Weaver, William, Editor. *The Verdi-Boito correspondence.* Chicago; London: University of Chicago Press, 1994.

Wegeler, Franz. *Remembering Beethoven: the biographical notes of Franz Wegeler and Ferdinand Ries.* London: Andre Deutsch, 1988.

Weingartner, Felix. *Buffets and rewards: a musician's reminiscences.* London: Hutchinson & Co., 1937.

Weinstock, Herbert. *Rossini: a biography.* New York: Limelight, 1987.

Weiss, Piero and Richard Taruskin. *Music in the Western World: a history in documents.* New York: Schirmer; London: Collier Macmillan, 1984.

Weissweiler, Eva *The complete correspondence of Clara and Robert Schumann.* New York: Peter Lang, 2 Vols., 1994.

Whittaker, William Gillies. *Collected essays.* London: Oxford University Press, 1940.

Whittall, Arnold. *Exploring twentieth-century music: tradition and innovation.* Cambridge; New York: Cambridge University Press, 2003.

Whittall, Arnold. *Music since the First World War.* London: J. M. Dent, 1977.

Whitton, Kenneth S. *Lieder: an introduction to German song.* London: Julia MacRae, 1984.

Wightman, Alistair, Editor. *Szymanowski on music: selected writings of Karol Szymanowski.* London: Toccata Press, 1999.

Wilhelm, Kurt. *Richard Strauss: an intimate portrait.* London: Thames and Hudson, 1999.

Will, Richard James. *The characteristic symphony in the age of Haydn and Beethoven.* Cambridge: Cambridge University Press, 2002.

Willetts, Pamela J. *Beethoven and England: an account of sources in the British Museum.* London: British Museum, 1970.

Williams, Adrian, Editor and Translator. *Liszt, Franz: Selected letters.* Oxford: Clarendon Press, 1998.

Williams, Adrian. *Portrait of Liszt: by himself and his contemporaries.* Oxford: Clarendon Press, 1990.

Williams, Ralph Vaughan. *Heirs and rebels: letters written to each other and occasional writings on music.* London; New York: Oxford University Press, 1959.

Williams, Ralph Vaughan. *Some thoughts on Beethoven's Choral symphony: with writings on other musical subjects.* London; Oxford University Press, 1953.

Williams, Ralph Vaughan. *The making of music.* Ithaca, New York: Cornell University Press, 1955.

Williams, Ursula Vaughan. *R.V.W.: a biography of Ralph Vaughan Williams.* London: Oxford University Press, 1964.

Wilson, Conrad. *Notes on Beethoven: 20 crucial works.* Edinburgh: Saint Andrew Press, 2003.

Wilson, Elizabeth. *Shostakovich: a life remembered.* Princeton, New Jersey: Princeton University Press, 1994.

Winter, Robert, Editor. *Beethoven, performers, and critics: the International Beethoven Congress, Detroit, 1977.* Detroit: Wayne State University Press, 1980.

Winter, Robert. *Compositional origins of Beethoven's opus 131.* Ann Arbor, Michigan: UMI

INDEX

Index to the Piano Sonatas Op. 90 to Op. 111 and a Beethoven timeline of significant musical and related events.

The order adopted for the listing of the individual entries in this index, for each of the piano sonatas under consideration, is chronological — according to the sequential unfolding of events under discussion. Thereby, the reader is provided with both a guide to the contents discussed in the main text and a timeline of the principal events bearing on Beethoven's life and work.

ance on the harpsichord
Donald Tovey, power of opening
Anton Schindler, Beethoven's interest in mystical poet and musician Christian Schubart
Ernst von Elterlein, harmonious expression of feeling
Barry Cooper, character of opening
Donald Tovey, on repeat passages
Charles Rosen, pianistic challenges
Use of material from youthful Piano Quartet No. 3, WoO 36
Carl Czerny, religious character
William Kinderman, choral-like main theme
Vaughan Williams, personal study of Op. 2, No. 2
Playful character, influence of Haydn's String Quartets Op. 33 of 1782
Rondo Grazioso, debt to Mozart
Edwin Fischer, on performance
Egerton Lowe, recollections of Theoder Leschetizky
Donald Tovey, estimation of Op. 2, No. 2
Performance on a fortepiano by William Stodart of 1808

OP. 2, NO. 3 PP. 49-54
Johann Albrechtsberger, debt to for contrapuntal writing
Carl Czerny, bravura piano writing
Alfred Brendel, symphonic character
Reworking of youthful Piano Quartet No. 3, WoO 36
Parallels with Clementi's Piano Sonata Op. 36
Donald Tovey, newness of long series of free modulations
Beethoven's innovatory use of sforzandi
Adoption of free-form fantasia
Limitations of five-octave pianoforte keyboard
Role of cadenza and display of virtu-

osity
Feelings of inward happiness and religious solemnity
Romanticism approaching poetry and painting
Frolicsome joy and jocular character
Allegro assai, a showcase for virtuosity
Thoroughly Beethovenish Finale with a coda
Bernard Shaw, London concert review (1877)
Rimsky-Korsakov, St. Petersburg Conservatory recollections
Claudio Arrau, youthful orientation to Beethoven and Op. 2, No. 3
Donald Tovey, high regard of Sonata in C Major — worthy of Mozart or Haydn
Performance on a fortepiano by Mattäus Hellman of the period 1770–5

OP. 7 PP. 56-66
Beethoven's expansion of form
Donald Tovey, vast new developments
London Musical Times (1927), regret at relative neglect
Wiener Zeitung (Vienna Journal), announcement of publication by Ataria
Babette de Keglevics, dedicatee
Babette anecdote — when Beethoven's pupil and affection for
Die Verliebte, contemporary nickname for Op. 7
Beethoven's growing standing in Viennese society
Beethoven's first masterpiece
Sound-worlds of Dussek and Clementi
Anton Schindler, prosaic estimation
Further editions of Op. 7
Onset of deafness, disclosure to Franz Gerhard Wegeler

328

333

336

ABOUT THE
AUTHOR

Terence M. Russell graduated with first class honours in architecture and was a nominee for the coveted Silver Medal of the Royal Institute of British Architects. He is a Fellow of the Royal Incorporation of Architects in Scotland (retired), was formerly Reader in the School of Arts, Culture and Environment at the University of Edinburgh, a Fellow of the British Higher Education Academy, and Senior Assessor to the Scottish Higher Education Funding Council. Alongside his professional work in the field of architecture — embracing practice, teaching and research — he has maintained a lifetime's interest in the music and musicology of Beethoven. He has an equal admiration for the work of Franz Schubert and was for many years an active member of the Schubert Institute, UK. His book writings in the field of architecture include the following:

The Built Environment: A Subject Index, Gregg Publishing (1989):
- Vol. 1: Town planning and urbanism, architecture, gardens and landscape design
- Vol. 2: Environmental technology, constructional engineering, building and materials
- Vol. 3: Decorative art and industrial design, international exhibitions and collections, recreational and performing arts
- Vol. 4: Public health, municipal services, community welfare

Architecture in the Encyclopédie of Diderot and D'Alemebert: The Letterpress Articles and Selected Engravings, Scolar Press (1993)

The Encyclopaedic Dictionary in the Eighteenth Century: Architecture, Arts and Crafts, Scolar Press (1997):
- Vol. 1: John Harris, Lexicon Technicum
- Vol. 2: Ephraim Chambers, Cyclopaedia
- Vol. 3: The Builder's Dictionary
- Vol. 4: Samuel Johnson, A Dictionary of the English Language
- Vol. 5: A Society of Gentlemen, Encyclopaedia Britannica

Gardens and Landscapes in the Encyclopédie of Diderot and D'Alemebert: The Letterpress Articles and Selected Engravings, 2 Vols., Ashgate (1999)

The Napoleonic Survey of Egypt: The Monuments and Customs of Egypt, 2 Vols., Ashgate (2001)

The Discovery of Egypt: Vivant Denon's Travels with Napoleon's Army, History Press (2005)